UNKNOWN MEXICO

Explorations in the Sierra Madre
and Other Regions
1890–1898

CARL LUMHOLTZ

In Two Volumes
VOLUME II

Dover Publications, Inc., New York

Published in Canada by General Publishing Company, Ltd., 20 Lesmill Road, Don Mills, Toronto, Ontario.

Published in the United Kingdom by Constable and Company, Ltd., 10 Orange Street, London WC2H 7EG.

This Dover edition, first published in 1987, is an unabridged republication of *Unknown Mexico: A Record of Five Years' Exploration Among the Tribes of the Western Sierra Madre; in the Tierra Caliente of Tepic and Jalisco; and Among the Tarascos of Michoacan*, originally published by Charles Scribner's Sons, New York, in 1902. The foldouts of the original have been printed over consecutive pages for this Dover edition, except for the color maps, which are now attached to the back cover of the second volume. The color plates of the original have been reprinted in black and white for this edition, and some have been relocated closer to their text references.

Manufactured in the United States of America
Dover Publications, Inc., 31 East 2nd Street, Mineola, N.Y. 11501

Library of Congress Cataloging-in-Publication Data

Lumholtz, Carl, 1851–1922.
  Unknown Mexico.

  Reprint. Originally published: New York : C. Scribner's, 1902.
  Includes index.
  1. Indians of Mexico. 2. Mexico—Description and travel. I. Title.
F1220.L85 1987   972'.00497   86-29335
ISBN 0-486-25364-3 (v. 1)
ISBN 0-486-25413-5 (v. 2)

CONTENTS

CHAPTER VI

CHAPTER VII

CHAPTER VIII

CHAPTER IX

CHAPTER X

CHAPTER XI

CHAPTER XII

CONTENTS vii

CONTENTS

LIST OF ILLUSTRATIONS

PLATES

Two maps are attached to the inside back cover. Others follow pages 16 and 176.

El distinguido naturalista y muy afec-
cable caballero Dr. Lumholtz, portador de
esta carta-circular a los Sres Jefes Políticos,
recorre la República para hacer importantes
estudios, sobre todo de Anthropología; y reco-

de las ilustradas Autoridades á quienes ésta presente, á fin de que el mejor éxito corone sus nobles afanes.

México Junio 8 de 1894.

[firma]

UNKNOWN MEXICO

CHAPTER I

A FEW houses could be discerned, scattered here and there near the edge of a llano about three miles long and one mile broad, rather an unusual size for this part of the Sierra Madre, and bordered with dense pine forests. The church and La Comunidad constituted, as usual, the main part of the village; but, as we passed, we noticed a peculiar, large, circular structure, with an extensive straw-thatched roof. This was the pagan temple of the place.

Quite a number of Indians had come to the village to attend a rain-making feast. As they saw us coming, several of them were so put out at the unusual sight of the expedition that they threw down

A Huichol.

their hats and fled into the forest. But the great majority received us in stolid silence, evidently accepting my baneful presence as something they were powerless to avert. In view of the rumours that had preceded me, I could hardly expect another welcome. As an instance, I will mention that one stupid and superstitious Mexi-

Huichol Women.

can trader had told them I was fattening people in order to kill and eat them, and that I used the blood for dyeing cotton cloth. It is to the credit of the Indians that they placed less faith in this absurd story than did their informant.

As it was raining, I placed my baggage alongside of the wall in La Comunidad, a large, rickety shelter of adobe, with a wide, open entrance. Don Zeferino sent me a door, the only one in the country, to serve me as a bedstead, which I could use by placing it over two boxes. The Indians, while waiting for the sun to set and the feast to begin, walked inquisitively in and out of what I considered my camp, behaving as unconcernedly as you please, and I was as much surprised at their personal appearance as they were at mine.

The women wear short skirts and tunics of cotton cloth, sometimes nicely embroidered. The clothing of the men is more elaborate, though the legs are left bare. It consists mainly of a shirt made from coarse cotton cloth or woven from wool, and often decorated with embroidery. Over the shoulders is worn a small shawl or neckerchief of cotton cloth, richly embroidered with red and blue thread, and finished at the lower edge with a wide band of red flannel. The tribe does not manufacture blankets nowadays, the small demand for such garments being supplied by Mexican dealers. The shirt is held tight around the waist by a long girdle artistically woven in wool or cotton. Both men and women are very fond of such girdles, and the richer ones may wear two, or even more, one over the other. The same fashion is followed by other Indian tribes.

Very striking in the costume of the men are the pouches woven of either wool or cotton in as great a variety of designs as the girdles. Two or three such bags generally hang from the shoulder, and one, which is never missing, is suspended in front of and below the girdle. In this the Huichol carries his tobacco, flint and steel for striking fire, etc., all of which give the pouch the necessary weight to hold the shirt in place. The other pouches are largely ornamental, and rows of small ones, measuring only three inches by six, but of exquisite workmanship, are fastened to each other sideways at the upper corners and worn in front below the girdle. On festive occasions, such as the present, a man may be adorned with as many as twelve pouches, hanging on both sides of his body from the shoulders.

Generally only the men wear straw hats of native make, but both men and women may tie around their

Huichol Men.

heads narrow hair-ribbons of home manufacture. There are three styles of wearing the hair. One way is in a single queue with a coloured hair-ribbon wound around its lower part; underneath this ribbon two others are placed lengthwise, each doubled over and with the ends extending beyond the braid. This is the most elaborate coiffure, and is used mostly by men. Another way is to gather the hair at the neck with a ribbon, the ends of which are passed around the head to the forehead, and there tied in a bow-knot. A third way of wearing the hair, and the simplest, is to let it hang loose; this is adopted mostly by women. Sandals of the usual cowhide pattern are now worn by both sexes.

Front View.   Side View.

Huichol Woman, showing a common way of wearing the hair.

The women often wear in their ears large, round ornaments, made of a network of strings of variously coloured beads, and both men and women have necklaces composed of pounds of beads, especially the small milky-white and the blue ones. Bracelets and anklets are made by threading or interweaving strings of the same kinds of beads into broad bands. At a gathering like this, when all are clothed in their best, the beautiful and striking designs and the rich combination of colours, especially red, white, and blue, produce quite a theatrical

effect, not unlike that of Romans on the stage.   In San
Andres most of the people wear the hair long and flowing, and their quick, easy movements add to the picturesqueness of a crowd.

My arrival did not prevent the feast from coming
off, as the Indians never postpone a ceremony.   The
principal feature of the rain-making feasts nowadays is
the killing of an ox, which was to be attended to next
morning.

It is peculiar that, while the other feasts of the Huichols are not influenced by the advent of the whites,
the feasts by which rain is to be obtained have been
much enriched and modified in consequence.   Slaugh-
tering an ox or two is now considered quite as efficient
a sacrifice to the gods as the killing of deer, squirrels,
turkeys, or whatever the tribe used before.   Candles,
employed in the same way as by the Catholics, have
been adopted, and invariably before a rain-making feast
a man goes to Mezquitic to procure this new requisite,
and also a small quantity of bread-rolls (*pan*) and chocolate, which are thrown upward at night as a food-offer-
ing to some of the rain-mothers, who are abroad only at
that time.   Other gods receive their sacrifices in daylight.

In addition to these foreign requisites, a new dance
has been adopted.   The early missionaries, seeing the
indomitable inclination of the Indians toward feasts and
show, cleverly met it by teaching them, as a means of
attracting them to the Christian feasts, dances and means
of display, which, however, had no significance to the
aboriginal mind.   This is the origin of what is called
the dance of the matachines, the purpose of which
soon became diverted.   To obtain rain, the Indians
want the co-operation of the saints, and to gain it they
execute this dance inside of the old churches.   This peculiar worship is performed by men especially appointed

for it, who are most gaily dressed with ribbons attached to the waist, pouches, and feathers.

The dance of the matachines began a little before sunset, and I went over to the dilapidated old church to look at it. They all danced nimbly around, and their graceful movements and the rhythmical pattering of their feet were in perfect time to the music of the home-made violin. I could not but admire their skill, but after a while I went over to witness a far more interesting performance which began after sunset on the verandah of the prison-house, only about fifteen yards from my camping-place. Here the Indians had made a fire, around which they grouped themselves. The stage-setting was the white man's, but the acting was aboriginal. The singing shaman, who was the leader, sat in a peculiar arm-chair used by the tribe. There was

A Singing Shaman Holding his Plumes.

nothing in his dress to distinguish him from the rest of the people, but a bunch of shaman's plumes lay in front of him.

These plumes consist of a couple of eagle or hawk feathers attached to a stick which serves as a handle. The movement of birds, especially of those that soar highest, is incomprehensible to the Indian, and such birds are thought to see and hear everything, and to possess mystic powers, which are inherent in their wing- and tail-feathers. Hence plumes of the eagle and hawk

are coveted by all American tribes for the wisdom, courage, and protection against evil which they impart.
The so-called shaman's plumes enable the shaman to see
and hear everything both above and below the earth ;
and with their help he performs his magic feats, such
as curing the sick, transforming the dead, calling down
the sun, etc.   When he wishes to bring the supernatural forces of his plumes into action, he holds the
handle in his right hand, generally giving it a slight
trembling motion.   The power of the hanging feathers
is supposed to emanate from the tips.   No shaman is
ever seen without one or more such plumes in his hand,
and on festive occasions they are tied to the heads of
the principal performers.

Every stanza as he sang it was repeated by the
people facing him, the chorus-leader being an assistant
shaman who was seated in a chair similar to that of his
superior opposite to him.   I was astonished at the fertility of the Huichols in what we should call legendary
lore, but what to them is gospel truth and history.   As
a rule, the singing lasts only for two nights ; but a good
shaman, if he have the physical endurance, can sing new
verses night after night for at least a fortnight.   In
their songs they relate how the gods, in the beginning,
composed the world out of chaos and darkness; how
they instituted the customs of the Huichols, and taught
the people all they had to do to please them ; to build
temples, hunt deer, and go for the hikuli plant ; to raise
corn ; and to make bows and arrows and ceremonial
objects.   There are no written records kept of these
traditions.   They live on the lips of the people, as
national heirlooms, passing from one generation to the
next, as originally did the sagas and folk-songs of the
ancient Northmen.

The gods are supposed to be standing all around the

horizon, seeing and hearing everything, and the snaman, in his prayers, turns toward the four quarters, or the four winds of the world, because, if one god does not respond, another one may. Rarely does he address a long prayer to any one direction. The gods are angry with man and begrudge him everything, particularly the rain, which is of paramount importance to the very existence of the tribe. But when the deities hear the shaman sing of their deeds, they are pleased and relent, and they liberate the clouds which they have been keeping back for themselves, and rain results. Thus the shamans—and indirectly the people themselves—are able to make it rain.

Torrents of rain were already falling before the performers started their ceremonies, but this in no wise abated their fervour in singing; their object now being to prevent the rain from stopping. My wishes were just as eager to the contrary, as the rickety shed which had been assigned to me, though the best available, was by no means water-proof. It is trying, in any case, to have to make one's self at home against the wishes of one's host, and the inclemency of the weather much intensified the discomforts of the situation. I became reconciled to my fate, however, by the really beautiful singing of the leader. As a matter of fact, I have never in any primitive tribe heard such good singing as among the Huichols. The steady downpour of the rain, punctuated by fitful flashes of lightning, formed a weird and fantastic accompaniment to the sympathetic singing, which came to me through the pitchy darkness of the night like a voice from fairyland. It sounded different from anything I had ever heard among Mexican Indians or elsewhere, and it was as novel as it was enchanting. I give, on the next page, one stanza of this song.

The Huichols, indeed, need a great deal of rain to

enable them to carry out their primitive agricultural methods. They cut down the brush from the steep hillsides, burn it, and sow the corn into holes dug with a stick. The rain, of course, does not penetrate far into the unploughed ground, but runs off the steep declivity; and it is only by continuous soaking during weeks of rain that the plants are saved from being dried up by the intense heat of the sun. During the dry season and a

HUICHOL RAIN-SONG

O'-to Tá-wi me-ma-nó-ti Wa-wat-sá-li me-ma-nó-ti
Deer god of the Northland sprang forth! Deer god of the Southland sprang forth!

Sa-kai-mó-ka me-ma-nó-ti   Ko-yo-(yo-)ni me-ma-nó-ti
God of the Setting-sun then sprang forth! God of the north, the north god
sprang forth!

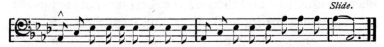

To-la-hú-li-pa me-ma-nó-ti Sa-kai-mó-ka me-ma-nó-ti a—a
Gods began to chase the deer forth! God of the Setting-sun sprang forth!

LITERAL TRANSLATION

O'to Táwi sprang forth.   Wawatsáli sprang forth.
Sakaimóka sprang forth.   Koyóni sprang forth.
To run deer sprang forth. Sakaimóka sprang forth.

part of the wet—that is to say, from the beginning of April to the end of August—the Huichols are constantly making feasts to produce rain.

Whenever it stops raining for two or three days, the principal men gather in the temple to consult the shaman as to what the gods can be angry about, and it is decided to make another feast and kill more oxen to satisfy them. The people in the ranches all over the country follow suit. There is always somebody ready to

give an ox, for it is supposed that the donor, besides gaining rain and good luck for the whole district, obtains
also a special blessing for his fields and his house.   He
also provides the corn and beans necessary for the feast ;
and meat and broth, tortillas, tamales, and beans are gratuitously offered to the people.   The host generally keeps
a large part of the animal for himself, and may even sell
some of it afterward.   Very often two or three households join in giving a feast.

Frequently during the night processions were made
from where the shaman was singing to the church, and
around the ox, which was tied up close by.   Two children,
a boy and a girl, led ; the first represents the Sun as he was
before he appeared as we see him to-day ; the other represents the Moon's daughter.   They are in full ceremonial
dress, with shaman's plumes tied to their heads with pretty
hair-ribbons.   Each of them carries a lighted candle and a
votive bowl containing chocolate and bread.   They are
followed by the shamans, and then comes the music, one
or two men playing on the violin a march of Huichol
composition.   The people who follow walk two and two.

At daybreak they begin to make preparations for the
sacrifice, the procession now going directly to the ox,
approaching him from the right.   One of the children
carries on the bowl the knife with which he is to be
killed.   The legs of the ox are tied and he is thrown in
such a way that, as he lies on the ground, his legs turn
toward the east.   Flowers are then fastened to his horns,
violins are played, and the people pray abundantly round
the fallen animal, while the two shamans with their
right hands lift their plumes toward the east.

Just as the rays of the sun shoot above the horizon,
the priests move their plumes slowly down toward the ox,
all the time fixing their eyes curiously on them, as if beholding something really coming down.   They pass the

plumes over the ox, and over the knife with which he is to be killed. Presently a man thrusts the steel into the throat of the ox, and the blood is received in bowls by the women, to be later on filled into the intestines,

The Priests Holding their Plumes toward the Sun.

boiled and eaten. The first blood that spurts forth from the dying animal is smeared on the often beautiful ceremonial objects made for the occasion. These are expressions of prayers and adoration, and are afterward hung up in the caves of the respective gods that have been invoked.

The women then boil the meat and make the food, which, after another night's singing, is distributed among the people present, the first portions having, of course, been duly sacrificed to the gods. There is no singing during the day, but much playing of the violin, and dancing goes on in an informal way, anyone, man or woman, performing the so-called danza whenever the spirit moves him.

The feast I saw was concluded in front of the church and the adjoining cemetery, where the people gathered to eat and drink. The women had brought tamales, corn-cakes, the sweet stalk of mescal, zapote, etc., and also, not the least important, jars with native brandy (toach). One man carried in a sheep's hide a large quantity of this liquor, which he offered for sale. It was pleasing to ob-serve that no family ate their provisions by themselves, but all shared with one another, exactly as civilised peo-ple are wont to do at picnics. The men went around offering toach from small jars to all their friends, male and female. The women in the same way divided the eatables. All was harmony and gaiety. Gradually the effect of the liquor began to be felt, with the women less than the men, as they drank less. Toach is weak enough, but the strength of the people had been sapped by two sleepless nights ; besides, the Huichols become intoxi-cated more easily than white men.

The men indulge in harmless railleries, push one an-other, wrestle, and perform many ludicrous antics, such as sitting on the face of an adversary, who has been thrown to the ground. By and by, some grow really angry and begin to quarrel. Like the fighters of Ho-meric days, they first abuse each other violently with words. To the uninitiated this disparagement seems wholly unprovoked, but there is always some domestic difficulty or a small theft at the bottom of it. These people never fight about anything else. But unlike their forerunners of old, the Huichols, when entering a bout, throw away whatever weapons they may have about their person. Generally a man carries a machete or big knife in his girdle, but when he is about to fight,

he very sensibly hands the weapon to his wife, or throws
it on the ground.

Soon many combatants are wriggling about in the
mud, pulling hair and pommelling the faces of one
another, while the women add to the confusion by
trying to separate the men. The prison is close at hand,
and the "soldiers," who exercise the functions of po-
licemen, and who are as drunk as the rest, may attempt
to carry off some disturber. As many of these would-
be maintainers of the peace as can possibly get hold of
the prisoner seize him, like so many ants carrying off a
worm, but not infrequently they have to drop their cap-
tive, falling against and over one another. Sometimes
when the wife of the arrested man is a resolute woman,
she will induce some of her husband's friends to liberate him. Consequently, the close of the day finds
but few offenders in the little adobe jail.

The Cora Indian and two of my Mexicans returned
to their homes the day after my arrival, but the cook
and the chief packer remained a few days longer, until
I could establish myself in more satisfactory quarters,
as the Casa Real was getting to be exceedingly uncomfortable. I was nearly swamped and had to make ditches
in front of my " hotel " to save it from being flooded.
Don Zeferino had shown me a dry but otherwise rather
repulsive place in the old Curato, in which he was living. Entrance to it had to be effected through the only
window the room boasted of, and the light being obstructed by the overhanging verandah, the lodging was
as dark as a prison cell. But as my belongings would be
safer there, and as I at the same time should be able to
discharge the rest of my men, I made up my mind to
accept it. I was determined to make the Huichols like
me, and the first move in that direction was to sever all
associations with Mexicans.

Don Zeferino was not married, but his sister kept house for him. Each of them had a grown son. As the family was poor and could not furnish my board, I had either to cook for myself or apply for Indian board. I detest doing my own cooking as much as wielding the tailor's needle, and under pressure have generally contented myself with the two dishes most easily prepared : boiled rice and hot water sweetened with honey. I still had some California honey, a last remnant of civilisation, and some rice, obtained in Mexico. However, I could now—that is, during the wet season—procure some milk, and also hens and eggs. But that my housekeeping was light is proved by one day's expense account, which I find among my notes :

Rice (estimated), *pro rata*.....................	3 cents
Milk..	6 "
Total for entire expedition, one day......	9 cents

This calculation is in Mexican money, so that the whole was not quite five cents American money.

Though this was satisfactory from an economical point of view, I gladly accepted a change which soon offered itself when I became acquainted with one of the few Indian families who lived permanently in the village. The father, Carillo, was almost six feet tall, and thin, with long flowing hair. His strongly marked features gave his face the appearance of being made of stone. His wife was under-sized, but very intelligent. With the old couple lived their orphaned granddaughter, whose name was " Flower Skirt " (Rūtúli Jbí). This name refers to the robe of the principal water-goddess, who brings the rain from the east and produces the spring flowers, poetically considered her garment. Another orphan girl, whose name was " Northern Cloud," frequently came to the house.

Carillo knew very little Spanish, and the women still less, and the conversation in the beginning was carried on with much difficulty. But gradually we became familiar with each other's mode of expression. It amused and pleased the girls that I called them by their poetic native names, which the Huichols always use among themselves, although the custom of taking Spanish names besides has become quite general. This is due partly to the influence of the Church, and partly to the idea the Indians have that it will facilitate their business dealings with the Mexicans.

Twice a day I took my pots over to their house, about two hundred yards away, where the girls were induced to help me in preparing my meals. They soon learned to attend to it unaided. It was two or three weeks, however, before they had sufficient confidence in me to bring the food to my window. Afterward for many an evening they followed me to my house, carrying the food, and lighting the way with torches of resinous pinewood. I shall always remember with pleasure the morning and evening hours I spent by their hospitable fire, watching the girls as they made tortillas and cooked my food. Though not exactly " feasts of reason," such occasions might well be called " flows of soul"; and I do not know how I should have gotten on in those dreary weeks and weeks of rain, had it not been for this family, who showed me so much consideration.

The rest of the people, from the authorities down, treated me, for a couple of months, with utter indifference, and it was very evident that they would have preferred never to have seen me. The gobernador was a true Indian, conservative in his customs and religious beliefs, and extremely reserved. In spite of being quite well-to-do, he was very close-fisted, though honourable in his dealings. He was entirely unsophisticated, which

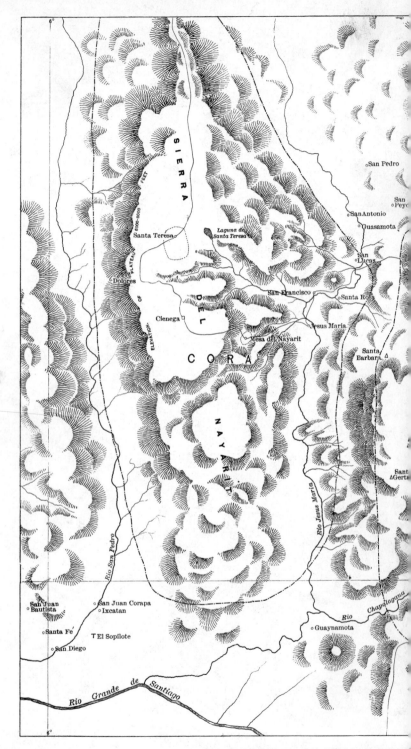

Map Showing Country of the Huichol and Cora Ind

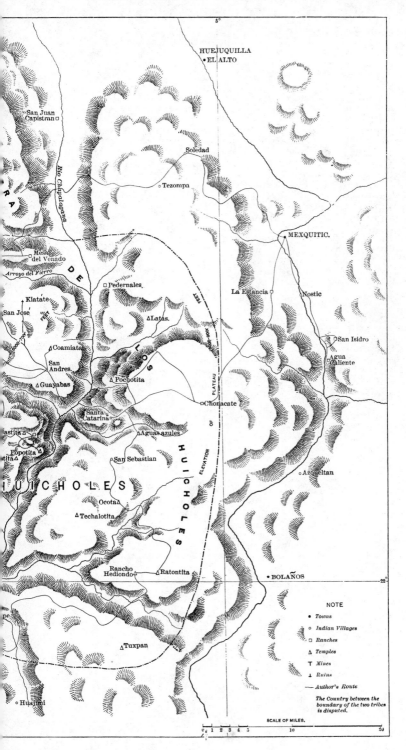

5°

HUEJUQUILLA
• EL ALTO

• San Juan
Capistran □

Soledad

• Tezompa

MEXQUITIC.

Mesa
del Venado

Arroyo del Fierro

□ Pedernales.

La Estancia □   • Nostic

Kiatate

San José   △ Latas.

San Isidro

△ Coamiata

San
Andres.   △ Pochotita   Agua
Caliente

△ Guayabas

astita △   Santa
Catarina □   □ Chonacate

Popotita △   △ Aguas azules

tita △   San Sebastian   Azqueltan

H U I C H O L E S   Ocota △

△ Techalotita

Rancho
Hediondo   △ Ratontita   • BOLAÑOS   22°

NOTE

• Towns

○ Indian Villages

□ Ranches

△ Temples

T Mines

⊥ Ruins

— Author's Route

The Country between the
boundary of the two tribes
is disputed.

△ Tuxpan

SCALE OF MILES.

○ Huajimi

0 ½ 1 2 3 4 5   10   20

Adjacent Territory.   (From Author's Notes.)

was not the case with the alcalde, who knew something
of the ways of the wily Mexicans, and was one of the
rich men in the tribe—that is, he owned about two hundred head of cattle, and raised a considerable quantity
of corn and beans. There was at first not much help to
be obtained from these men. The only thing they did for
me was to order a boy to watch my mules, which I
turned loose, as there was nothing else to do but to remain here and make the best of what opportunities I
had to study the people.

Whoever passed my window was encouraged to stop
by little presents of beads, food, etc., and I began to
make a few friends, although the Indians who are most
forward are never of the best kind. Still no one's
friendship should be slighted, I believed, for it might
lead to other relations.

Among the first who visited me were the married
daughters of Carillo, one of them the wife of a Huichol
who spoke Spanish. Though I had little confidence in
any Spanish-speaking Huichol, I did my best to entertain
them, giving them plenty to eat, and amusing them with
sleight-of-hand tricks. A day or two later the husband
came, telling me that the women wanted to know
what kind of people there were in the country I came
from, and if there were Indians there. I welcomed the
opportunity of closer association, and urged him to
bring the women again to my camp, so that I could tell
them all they wanted to hear.

I showed them the illustrations to my articles on the
Tarahumare Indians in *Scribner's Magazine*, explaining
them as one would to small children. They took great
interest in the caves, houses, and cooking-utensils of
their distant cousins, and agreed with one another that
these people looked very much as they did themselves.
They manifested still more interest in society at Bar

Harbor, the American sea-side resort, in the costumes of the ladies there, in the men and women rowing about in canoes, etc. I did not notice, however, that the American type of womanly and manly beauty made any special impression on them. The simple illustrations on the advertising pages, especially those with pictures of animals, seemed to appeal to them most.

HUICHOL RAIN-SONG

This song implores Væ′lika (royal eagle) uimáli (young girl), who, in the Huichol conception, holds the world in its talons. The stars are her dress, and she guards everything from above.

Væ - li-ka u-i-má-li   Væ   -   li-ka u-i-má-li
Royal eagle! Young mother eagle!   Royal eagle!   Young mother eagle!

(Va - væ-) me-má-na kaui (Va - væ-)   me-má-na - kaui (Va-
Is float-ing, floating a-bove! Is   float-ing, floating a-bove!   Is

væ-) me-má-na kaui (Va-) ta-hæ-ma-me (me-) má - na - kaui (Va-)
floating, floating above!   Above us floating, floating above!   A -

ta - hæ-má-me (me-)   má - na kaui (Va-væ-) me-má-na kaui (Va-
bove us floating, floating above!   Is floating, floating above, Is

væ-) me   má - na kaui   (Va - væ-) me - má-na kaui
float-ing, float-ing above!   Is   float-ing, floating above!

Even if I had wanted to, I should not have been able to get away, on account of the rains, which had begun in earnest. Generally during the wet season, the brightness of the forenoons offset the dulness of the rainy remainder of the twenty-four hours; but in San Andres, on account of the elevation, at one time a heavy mist lay every day over the country until two o'clock in the afternoon. Then it would clear, but two hours later the rain would again begin to fall and continue all night. Sometimes I was awakened by fear-

HUICHOL RAIN-SONG

ful thunder-storms, which seemed to come from the northeast. At a distance they were magnificent to behold, on account of the incessant lightning, that changed night to day. Portentous thunder-claps, multiplied by the echoes, rolled like a continuous cannonade of artillery over the highlands. In less than a quarter of an hour the storm would be upon us. All its demons seemed to be let loose, threatening to lift the roof from the house. The blinding lightning and deafening thunder made one feel as if his last hour had struck. But the awe-inspiring tempest moved on, and in a few minutes all the danger was over.

There were occasionally fine days; even for a week or longer the rain would cease and the sky clear up. Such times I utilised for making excursions to the ranches north and south. To my delight I found the Huichols outside of San Andres more approachable, so much so that I even thought of establishing my camp among them. But after all, the Curato was the best place for me to stay for any length of time; first, because my things were fairly safe there, and second, because San Andres is the centre of the country west of the river. Many feasts are held here, and there is much coming and going of the Indians. But it certainly was

not a cheerful place for me, least of all at that season
of the year.

HUICHOL RAIN-SONG

Transcribed from graphophone.

Section A is an introduction, Section B is repeated from three to five times,
subject to slight interpolations, evidently connected with the changes in the words
of the song, and which do not alter the character of the music.

Toward the end of July the gods responded so liberally to the prayers of the people that there was no more
need of rain-making feasts. The Indians, accordingly,
remained at their ranches, and my existence grew so
dull that I almost began to hate the place. But though
white people feel more or less depressed in heavy
weather, the thicker the fog and the wetter the world
the brighter and happier are the Huichols.

The soil finally became so soaked with the continued
rain that I could not undertake even short excursions, for
the mules would sink into the ground up to their bellies.
I really felt myself "a stranger in a strange land"; but
all things come to him who waits.

CHAPTER II

THESE Indians are named by the Mexicans *los Huícholes*, a corruption of Vīshálika, or Vīrárika, as they call themselves, the word signifying "doctors" or "healers," which name they fully deserve, as about one-fourth of the men are shamans. Many of these do not confine themselves to their own tribe, but make professional tours among the Coras and Tepehuanes, and even

Woman Spinning.

21

among illiterate "neighbours," going as far as Milpillas Chico, in Durango.

The Huichols (pronounced Veetchol), although related to the Aztecs, belong to the tribes which remained in barbarism while the main stock of the family developed and reached a state of culture culminating in the establishment of the Aztec Empire. Montezuma's reign came to a tragic end nearly four hundred years ago, while the humble Huichols have maintained themselves to the present day in their almost inaccessible mountain fastnesses. True, they, too, were conquered by the Spaniards in 1722, and Franciscan missionaries followed the victorious soldiers, and built five churches. Nominally the tribe then became converted to Christianity, and the introduction of

Making Twine.

cattle, sheep, mules, and certain iron implements modified to some extent their mode of living, though not as much as one would expect. To-day, however, the churches are in ruins, and there is no priest living among the Huichols. The most civilised of them know how to make the sign of the cross, and are familiar with the names of Maria Santissima, Dios, and Diabolo. Many are clever enough to put on an external show of Christianity toward people from whom they expect some favour. All of them observe the leading Christian feasts, which offer occasions for prolonged enjoyment of eating and drinking, and they worship the saints as so many gods.   The ancient beliefs, customs, and ceremonies still have a firm hold on the minds of the people, and the Hui-

chols jealously guard their country against the encroachments of the whites. The impress the victors made was superficial, and to-day the natives are practically in the same state of barbarism as that which they enjoyed the day when Cortes first set foot on American soil.

The mountainous region, difficult of access, which is still left to the tribe, is about forty miles long by twenty-five miles wide. There are four pueblos, which, with the exception of San Andres, lie on the

Huichol Basket, made from split bamboo, for keeping wool, clothing, etc. Height, 67 ctm.

eastern side of the Chapalagana River, which traverses the country from north to south. According to their own traditions, the Huichols originated in the south; as they wandered northward, they got lost under the earth, but reappeared in the country of the hikuli; that is, the central mesa of Mexico, to the east of their present home. The sun when rising speaks to the people in five languages, their own and four others, which they know.

The colour of the skin of the Huichols is similar to that of the Tarahumares and the other tribes hitherto met with. They are very healthy, and rarely die from anything but old age. Their women are often good-looking, and the children are generally pretty. The principal food, all the year round, is corn and beans. At the lower elevations one may come on small orchards of bananas and sugar-cane, the latter crop being consumed by chewing the cane. In the wet season, one or two kinds of fungi are eaten. The hunting of deer and the killing of cattle are always connected with religious ceremonies, the meat being eaten at feasts, which abound from one end of the year to the other. Cotton, as well as the añil or indigo plant, is raised on a small scale.

As to their mental status, they are very bright, and have better memories than the Mexicans, but their morals are somewhat affected by their cunning; they are quicker to invent a lie than any Indians I have met. A Huichol knows how to look out for himself, and he is not over-scrupulous about mine and thine; but he is kind-hearted and hospitable. Although he does not ask a visitor to sleep in his house, he always gives him food; and if he has only one tortilla, he will share it with him. Their self-esteem is equal to anyone's. Never for a moment will a Huichol allow that any other race may be superior to his. Even when far away from home, among the whites, the Huichols bear themselves as if they had never known masters. Yet they have no personal courage, and prefer assassination of a stranger to meeting him in open fight. Murder is rare. They are somewhat lascivious, though the women are modest. Taking it all in all, their great gift of music, combined with their ready response to emotional influences, the immense wealth and depth of their religious thought, and their ingenuity in expressing it pictorially, cannot help but fascinate the observer.

Huichol Ranch near Pochotita. The private god-house is seen in the rear in the middle,

Most of the dwellings are circular, built of stone, and covered with thatched roofs. The entrance is right-angled and so low that one has to stoop when going in. There is never more than one room in such a house, and this serves for parlour, bedroom, and kitchen; but the cooking for feasts is done outside, on the patio, which in most cases is large. When the weather permits, the people may also sleep outside of the house.

The temples (tokípa), of which there are about twenty in the country, are built on the same plan as the houses, only much larger. Their doorways face east, and are never closed with doors. Sometimes, however, a pole or a log may be laid across the opening to prevent cattle from desecrating the shrine. In the centre of the temple floor is a place for the fire, which is lighted only at festivals. The idols are kept in sacred caves in the mountains.

Adjoining the temples there are always a number of god-houses, the interiors of which present a striking appearance on account of the numerous symbolical objects deposited there to please the gods. These god-houses are generally rectangular in shape, made of stone and mud, and covered with thatched gable roofs. There is a hole in the front wall over the door, and a corresponding one in the rear wall. Through these holes the house is supposed to breathe, and the parts of the wall next to them are sometimes decorated on the outside. Every ranch, too, has its own private god-house, dedicated to its patron deity, but these structures are rarely of the same size or as substantial as those belonging to the temples.

The first excursion I made from San Andres was to San José, ten miles to the north. The native name of San Andres is Tāté Íkia, " House of Our Mother" (tāté), alluding to a mythical serpent which was born and lived there, and then went down to the coast. The native name of San José is Háiokalita, " Where there are Springs," and is the term applied to a number of ranches belonging to the native jurisdiction of San Andres ; but only two of them are in the immediate neighbourhood of the temple of the locality, which was my objective point. Here the greatest feast of the year was about to be celebrated, that of eating cakes of unhulled corn. This feast is made for the people of the underworld, whom the shamans, when singing in the temple, can see underneath the fireplace, with their eating-bowls raised, waiting to get them filled. If the Indians should not give them anything, the wind would lift up the fire in the volcanoes, which would stand in the way of the clouds.

Chief among the people of the under-world are the God of Fire and the Mother of the Gods. They also exist above ground, but are more important in their nether-world functions, because the volcanic fire is older than the fire above ground ; and all vegetation, of which this goddess is creator, springs forth from the darkness beneath the surface.

At the time of my arrival at San Andres, Don Zeferino had staying with him temporarily a Mexican who a number of years before taught school in San Andres. Although I doubted whether this man's relations with the Indians were of the right kind, at the solicitation of Don Zeferino I took him along, because he was acquainted with one of the principal men of San José, and had also some knowledge of the Huichol language.

The track leads through pine forests and slightly hilly country, and on the level, San Andres and San José being at about the same elevation. We took along only one pack-mule to carry my camera and

our blankets.   We were well received by the owner
of the little ranch, a stately Indian, who gave us for
quarters his private god-house.

The house was merely a gable roof placed on four
poles, and was so low that it was only by stooping very
much that I could enter.   Ceremonial arrows and deer-
tails were stuck into the roof from within, and symbolical ornaments, bundles of snares for catching deer, as
well as wreaths of yellow flowers, were hanging from it,
the latter having been left over from the last feast of
green squashes.   The house was exactly 5 feet 8 inches
long, and 4 feet 10 inches broad, hardly roomy enough,
therefore, to allow both of us to sit down at the same
time.   However, the novel sensation of sleeping in a
man's private chapel made, or ought to have made, us
forget the absence of commodiousness.   Besides, a heavy
rain had begun.   I hobbled the three mules and let them
loose to graze, and then with the aid of our saddles and
saddle-cloths we made ourselves quite comfortable for
the night.

At dusk I went up to the temple, about one hundred and fifty yards distant, and dedicated to the sun
(Ta-yáu, "Our Father").   Like most of the Huichol
temples it is situated on a point that affords a fine view
of the surrounding country.   It is the largest temple on
the western side of the river, about twenty-eight feet in
diameter and twenty-two feet high.   Contrary to rule,
its walls are constructed of adobe.   There is a famous
god-house of the Sun near San José.   Therefore the
whole western side of the river is thought to be under
Father Sun's dominion and the people here are called
" Sun people."

I found the interior warm and dry.   Although
smoky and filled with a great number of people, it gave
me a feeling of comfort.   The large crackling fire threw

The Temple of San José.

a strong light on the faces of those nearest to it, and fairly lit the temple, except in the smoky recesses under the high truncated roof. The principal men sat in a large half-circle around the fire ; the shaman in the middle, facing east. They had spent all of the previous night in singing, and were evidently tired ; in fact, most of them were sleeping in their chairs. The expression on the faces of those who were awake was happy and meditative. They were enjoying the pleasures of *dolce far niente* in the benign influence of their greatest god, the fire, while they waited for the shaman to recommence his singing.

None of them rose when I entered, nor was anyone in the least disturbed by my presence, all being too deeply absorbed in the contemplation of what was about to come. I was told to take a seat in one of the chairs— quite a compliment to me. These chairs, which at first sight suggest civilised influence, are decidedly of aboriginal invention, and, furthermore, of considerable religious importance. They are stools to which backs and arms have been attached. The stool, according to the myth, is the flower of the sotol, the century plant, which is prominent in the tradition of the Huichols, and from which the native brandy is made. To carry out the flower idea, the seat is edged with a roll made from sotol leaves torn into strips. The rest of the stool, as well as the back and arms, is mostly of bamboo, the various parts being securely held together by means of twine, and glue from a certain plant, which is put on in big daubs, like cartilage around the joints of bones. On all festive occasions, the shaman and the principal men use such chairs, and after the feast is over everybody takes his chair home with him.

The gods, too, have their chairs, and are supposed to rest in them ; but gods' chairs are small and look much like children's toys; their principal purpose is to express adoration of the deities. At this feast there were several specimens of these curious contrivances which bring the gods into the presence of the people. Often small symbolic objects expressive of various prayers are hung on the little chairs or placed on the seat. On

A God's Chair.

beholding such a chair, one instinctively calls to mind the easy-chair of a grandfather whom little children wish to ask for presents, and, as they cannot read or write, hang objects indicative of their desires on or around his chair. He will understand their meaning when he comes to rest in it. In the accompanying illustration is seen such a chair dedicated to the God of Fire. Two diminutive tobacco-gourds are attached to it, one praying for luck in raising the kind of squashes from which tobacco-gourds are made, the other one for luck in killing deer.

After a while, deer meat in its broth was offered to all present, and when it had been served the shaman took his seat behind the drum west of the fire. On each side of him sat an assistant shaman, and the officers of the temple grouped themselves on either side of the trio. In front of the principal shaman were a number of ceremonial arrows stuck into the ground, and his plumes were also lying there.

While singing, the shaman accompanied himself on a drum. This instrument is nothing but a log cut from

a big-leaved oak-tree, hollowed out, and covered at one end with a deerskin, while the other end has been cut to form three rude legs. It is placed upright on a disk of solidified volcanic ash embedded in the floor, an arrangement which increases the resonance of the sound. The statues of the gods rest on similar disks, which represent their shields; and as the drum, like every-

The Shaman Singing and Beating the Drum.

thing in the Huichol conception, is alive, it stands like a man or a god. The shaman beats this drum with the palms of his hands, lifting the right one high up and bringing it down once, while the left hand makes two quick beats. The corresponding beats of right and left are not perfectly synchronous, though very nearly so, and the effect at a distance is that of equal beats. The tempo is the same as that produced on the musical bow of the Cora

The Festival Dress of the Huichol Used by those that Offer Food as well as by the Matachines.

with the two sticks, and the sound of the two instruments is somewhat similar, especially at a distance, though the bow is by far the more musical.

Several times during the night the skin has to be tightened. This is done by holding a piece of burning resinous pinewood inside of the drum, to contract the skin by the heat. The inside of the log is thus smoky and charred, which gives the casual observer the idea that it has been hollowed out by fire.

Both men and women participated in the dance, which was practically identical with the mitote of the Tepehuanes and the Coras. The jumping was less pronounced, yet, on the other hand, the column would more often make backward steps, and the leader on such occasions distinguish himself by executing a good deal of lively backward kicking.

In the morning, after midday, and finally before sunset of the next day, food was distributed by half a dozen men dressed in their best clothes, the most conspicuous feature about them being, as usual, the great quantity of beautiful ribbons and pouches. A few individuals had short breeches of cotton cloth, to the outer seams of which were fastened small bells, bought in Mexican shops. One man sported a handsome pair of buckskin breeches, bound with a border of red flannel and adorned with small white buttons, and with small bells along the seams. All of them had a great many plumes, wings, and tails of hawks stuck in their straw hats.

The offering of food is done in the following way: Two of the distributers, carrying it in small bowls, or rather sections of gourds, step inside of the temple and make a ceremonial round, while others, similarly laden, stand outside waiting to join the pair when they come out again. Then all of them run toward one of the principal men to whom they are going to offer the food

—tamales, nopal, beans, sweet mescal, in fact, all the best dishes the Indians have. As soon as he is spied they pounce upon him, yelling fearfully, and stretching out their bowls. He accepts the vessels smiling and in silence, handing them quickly to his wife, who empties them into jars which she has brought with her for the occasion. The shouting then subsides, and all retire in order to refill their bowls and go through the same performance with the next man. The noise is like that of a pack of dogs in pursuit of a deer, and no doubt this ancient custom has some reference to the hunting of the deer, the killing of a certain number of which must precede the feast.

The event toward which all the ceremonies thus far have been tending, namely, the distribution of cakes of unhulled corn, took place a little before sunset on the second day of the feast. As a great quantity of cakes is needed, the people are busy making them for several days before the feast. The unhulled ground corn is mixed with water and formed into oval rolls or cakes, which are baked. For this purpose an oven (Spanish, *horno*) is built, of stone and mud. It is about four feet high and shaped like a bee-hive. The inside, including the floor, is well plastered with mud. Two openings are left near the ground, each about a foot square, and through them the wood is put in, the draught being obtained through an additional hole at the top.

As soon as the oven is sufficiently heated, in about an hour, it is well cleaned out, and the cakes are placed in it, each enveloped in one or two leaves from the big-leaved oak-tree, and then the three openings are covered with flat stones. In Santa Catarina these rolls are baked on a comal, the earthenware tray on which tortillas are made. The leaves are afterward carefully gathered and burnt at the end of the feast.

These rolls are very palatable ; they are hard and have a sweet taste that is entirely wanting in the tortillas. For camp use they make a very superior bread, and can be kept a week or two without losing their flavour. I have often tried to induce the Indians to make this bread for my constant diet; but they were unwilling to prepare it except for this one feast of the year. Among the Mexicans, however, similar cakes are in use.

Straw is meanwhile being carefully spread before the entrance to the temple, so as to form a circular space on which the rolls, which the men are bringing in sacks, are to be deposited. Women, who have been sitting in a circle around this space, take charge of the bags as they come in, each taking her stand directly behind her own bag.

When the bags, numbering ten, have been received, four of the principal men appear upon the scene. They have made the required ceremonial circuits within the temple, and now take their places opposite one another at the four cardinal points of the prepared space. In their outstretched right hands they hold plumes, and as the women empty the sacks upon the bedding of straw the shamans wave their plumes over the food to invite the gods to come. Two of them standing opposite each other carry in the same hand with the plumes a stick of red brazil-wood, the symbol of authority. They next make circular rounds, then stop, and the two with staffs in their hands lower them until they touch the rolls, while all four exclaim, "Yam-te yam-te yam!" ("To all, to all!"), thereby offering the food to the gods. They continue making circuits around the heap and repeating the dedicatory words. At last they burn dried bunches of the anise-plant as incense, and then return to the temple from which they came.

At this point, the rolls were distributed among the people present, and shortly afterward I noticed that two of the principal men put on their quivers full of arrows, took their bows in their hands, and filled their pouches with rolls. Each took besides a small jar of native brandy. They were making ready to meet delegates from the temple of San Andres and from another one near by. Information had just been received that they had arrived in the neighbourhood, and were waiting to be escorted in. The two delegates made several rounds in the temple and then started off quickly to meet the guests. The Indians are always formal and correct in their ceremonies. This never struck me so much as at this time. Everything moved with precision, as if they had watches. The scenes were shifting all the time, yet there were no slips. Many take part in the performance, and everyone knows exactly what to do and when to do it, because they have been rehearsing it all their lives.

After long and loud prayers by the shaman, the second night's dance was commenced, shortly after sunset. It varied slightly from that of the night before, inasmuch as the procession, consisting only of the officers of the temple, moved in single file. The most characteristic feature of the dance was the yelling, shouting, and even whistling of the performers. Each man carried a sort of sceptre made from a coarse grass, the seed of which is the favourite food of the wild turkey. The solemn men involuntarily reminded me of old-fashioned pictures of saintly bodies with palms in their hands.

As all the officers were now dancing, the shaman and his two assistants remained alone at the drum. He was a man of great reputation, and of course some suspected him of sorcery and were afraid of him. He sang with

Ribbon. Main Design: Squash Vine Yielding Tobacco-Gourds. The Leaves and the Gourds with Their Excrescences are Shown.

tremendous enthusiasm, and his voice and the drum acted like magic on the audience. Being, like so many of his class, fond of strong drink, he refreshed himself in the short pauses he made with copious draughts, and became very much intoxicated. Deeper and deeper he sank into his chair, until only his two hands could be seen above the drum, working with undiminished vigour and in perfect time like an automaton. His voice, a powerful bass, sounded as strong as ever, and the tinge of hoarseness blended admirably with the haze of antiquity that pervaded the atmosphere. His assistants

Song at the Feast of Eating Cakes of Unhulled Corn

The gods went out deer-hunting, but they could not get anything until one of them brought beautiful blue plumes.

(Va-) mo - yé - li   yo - a - wí-me   kye-poi me-no   ho - liœ'-ne— hay!
Plumes   blue!   Who   will bring them ?—hay!

attended to the stretching of the skin, and at times relieved him in the beating of the drum.

I had brought no provisions along, chiefly because I had none to take, and thought that tortillas and beans could always be obtained at a feast like this. The authorities had duly deputed a woman to cook beans and make tortillas for me and my companion ; but the feast was of much more importance to her than our comfort, and in spite of the orders given her she did not waste any time on us. Even to buy something from the natives was very difficult, as they always consider it a favour to

sell food. The Indians apparently did not care much
for my companion, and, as I was a perfect stranger to
them, I could hardly expect much from them myself.
Our share in the general distribution was altogether in-
adequate for our wants.   A man cannot help feeling depressed when he has only unsavoury food,—tamales filled
with beans,—and insufficient at that, while others are
feasting. For the first time the thought flashed through
my mind: Am I not wasting my time in this wilderness,
and shall I ever get at the inner meaning of what I see ?
Will these natives ever reveal to me their thoughts, and
throw any light on the early stages of human culture ?

An important part of the feast is a deer-hunt, which
insures luck for the coming year. While birds and most
of the animals are killed with arrows, the Huichols, in
hunting deer, use snares.   Sometimes as many as twenty
are put up in places where the game is likely to pass, and
then the quarry is driven into them, even with dogs.
The end of a snare is tied to the trunk of a tree ; while
the loop, filled in with meshes that are drawn up by it,
is placed upright in the shape of an approximate square,
between two bushes or two poles on either side of the
track.   The upper edge of the snare is about half a
yard long.

Soon after dark the hunters begin to prepare for
the event that is to come off next day.   They gather
around the fire and pray aloud.   It was almost impossible to distinguish any words in the general buzz of the
worshippers' voices, but I frequently caught the word
Tévali (Grandfathei), as they call the God of Fire, the
greatest of all shamans.   Only those pure of mind can
take part in the deer-hunting, as the deer would never
enter a snare put up by a man who is in love ; it would
just look at it, snort " pooh, pooh," and then turn and go
back the way it came. Good luck in love means bad luck

in deer-hunting. But even those who have been abstinent have to invoke the aid of the fire to take out whatever blemish there may still be in them. Therefore they all try to get as close as possible to the flaming god, and turn every side of their bodies to him. They also hold out their open hands, warming the palms, then spit into them and rub them with quick strokes over their joints,

Snare for Catching Deer.

legs, and shoulders, as the shamans do in curing, in order that their limbs and muscles may become as strong as their hearts are pure for the task they have to perform.

Everybody was in readiness before sunrise. The last rite consisted in the burning of thorns from a certain tree, and the sprinkling of the ashes on the symbolic objects that were to be used in the hunt. Chief among these were curious ceremonial arrows, the emblems of the chase and capture of the deer. They were stuck through rings of twisted grass, and carried in a horizontal position suspended by means of a string, across the backs of the bearers. The men thus honoured are further distinguished by shamans' plumes,

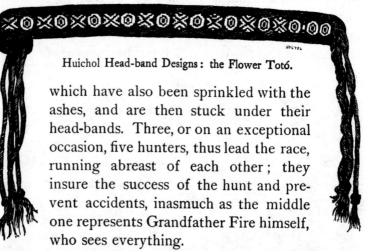

Huichol Head-band Designs: the Flower Totó.

which have also been sprinkled with the ashes, and are then stuck under their head-bands. Three, or on an exceptional occasion, five hunters, thus lead the race, running abreast of each other; they insure the success of the hunt and prevent accidents, inasmuch as the middle one represents Grandfather Fire himself, who sees everything.

Presently the hunters started off on a brisk walk, no less than forty-five of them, with bows and arrows, man behind man. All were dressed in their best, newly washed clothes. Innumerable ribbons, pouches, and feathers were fluttering from all parts of their figures, and bells tinkling from their clothes made music too enticing for the deer to resist.

Only a few men remained behind, among them certain officers of the temple, and several young fellows who on account of love-affairs were disqualified for the hunt. The principals seated themselves on easy-chairs, under a bower that had been erected near the temple entrance. Behind them, squatting on a cowhide, I noticed our runaway cook with a shaman's plume standing up from the back of her head, under the head-band. She had prepared to fulfil the duties of the office given her, and was waiting for her turn to come.

Not all the people about the temple observed the rule

of fasting and praying that is supposed to contribute toward the getting of the deer. The important thing is that the principal men and the woman do not infringe on the law of fasting. They follow the hunters in their thoughts all the time and pray to the fire and the sun and all the other gods to give success, and thus happiness, to all. The deer is the emblem of sustenance and fertility, and his blood is sprinkled over the seed corn, that it may become equally sustaining. He is the sacrifice most valued by the gods, and without him rain and good crops, health and life, cannot be obtained.

Now and then some of the fasters would rise and pray aloud, and with so much fervour that they and all the rest were moved to tears. Frequently, too, they would make circuits inside of the temple, stopping in front of the little chairs, and talking to them as if the gods were sitting in them. Much of the result depends on these prayers to the chairs. Once on a similar occasion two deers were caught, and this luck was ascribed chiefly to the good work of the principal men, who had risen every moment to visit the little chairs and invoke their deities.

I was looking around, observing the people and things in general, but did not think it advisable to attempt a photograph, because any failure of the hunt might eventually be attributed to me. It struck me, however, that this was an opportunity to gain influence by repeating some sleight-of-hand tricks, which I had shown to a few the day before, and which had been much talked about. My offer to entertain the fasters was well received, and I was assured that it would do no harm to either them or the hunters. When I stepped in and quietly commenced to show my " powers," two old men were crying like children while telling the sun how the crops would swell if they could only get the deer, but even they turned slowly in their chairs to watch me. One of my tricks consisted in making a red ball disappear and come back at will. As luck would have it, the image of the sun, which the Indians keep in the god-house here, resembles this ball very much in size and colour. The natives began to wonder whether their Father Sun was not really at my disposal, and I felt that I was gaining in their estimation.

Hardly had I finished my performance when I observed a sudden excitement among the people; their expressionless faces lit up, and they began to chatter quickly. What they in hope and fear had been waiting for was appearing at the edge of the forest—a messenger was coming. He was one of the five young men who carried the peculiar arrows. The excitement of the people became intense. The day was won! The prayers of the fasters had been answered. The gods had granted the deer! As he approached, he was seen to hold a deer snare in his hand, but the principal thing he brought was contained in his pouch.

The woman with the plume, as the boy arrived, rose and filled her mouth from a large drinking-gourd containing water from several sacred springs. This she sprayed several times from her lips over the messenger, while all the people stood and said prayers. After receiving this shower-bath with evident pleasure, the young man handed his pouch to the shaman, who took it into the temple, and opened it in front of a niche in the wall opposite the entrance, where offerings are made to the main god of the temple. It contained a small piece of intestine from the deer, tied up at each end and filled with blood. With his finger the shaman smeared the blood, first on the drum, then on all the diminutive chairs of the gods, and finally on the chairs of the principal men.

Food had at once been offered to the boy, and the fast was now broken by all present. After half an hour the rest of the party came in, headed by a man carrying the deer, which is always brought to the temple entire with the exception of the small intestines, which are taken out and burned on the spot. The line of picturesquely clad men made a fine sight as they wound their way triumphantly through the tall grass back to the temple.

A layer of straw had been spread outside of the temple at the right side of the entrance, and on this the deer was carefully deposited. It was thus received in the same way as the corn-rolls, because, in the Indian conception, corn is deer. According to the Huichol myth, corn was once a deer, an idea due to the fact that, in earliest time, deer, no doubt, was the main subsistence of the tribe.

The animal was laid so that its legs were turned toward the east, and all sorts of food and bowls of tesvino were placed in front of it. Everyone in turn stepped up to the deer, stroking him with the right hand from the snout to the tail, and thanking him because he had allowed himself to be caught.

"Rest thyself!" they said, addressing him as "Elder Brother." If it be a doe, they call her "Elder Sister." A shaman may talk to the dead animal for a long time: "Now they let thee loose, Grandfather Fire, Grandfather Deer-Tail, Father Sun, and all the other gods. Now thou hast arrived in our house. Many thanks that thou camest. Thou art not in love. How couldst thou come here to us, so much in love as we are, all of us? Rest thyself, Elder Brother. Thou hast brought us plumes, and we are profoundly thankful."

The deer's antlers are looked upon as shaman's plumes, and the deer itself is of such fundamental importance in the religious life of the tribe that if by any

chance it should become extinct, the religion of the
Huichols would have to be modified. The philosophy
of their entire life may be summed up in the sentence
to which one of their shamans once gave utterance : To
pray to Grandfather Fire, and to put up snares for catching deer, that is to lead a perfect life.

The deer was quickly skinned and the hide carefully
preserved for future use, perhaps to be carried by the
dancers at a hikuli feast, or to be made into quivers or
into buckskin. The Huichols never sleep on deer-skins,
believing that they would be troubled with pains in their
backs if they did so.

A hole was dug in the ground in which the carcass
was cooked between hot stones ; leaves were placed
next to the meat to protect it from contact with the
earth, and the whole was covered with an earthen
mound. This is the way in which deer is always cooked.
The blood is boiled in a jar.

Meanwhile, the hunters made pinole of five grains
of corn and sacrificed it to the temple fire, which was
then put out and covered with ashes. Then every person contributed five grains of corn, which were ground,
mixed with water, and made into a cake baked in the
hot ashes of the fire. This cake is a payment to those
of the nether-world, and is the first food the hunters eat.

I was told that in the southeastern part of the
country a tamal is made in the shape of a deer-head,
which the shaman afterward eats. The tamal is laid at
the foot of a pole, which is placed upright on the patio,
and ropes are tied to it. Men dressed like women hold
on to the ropes and dance around it like men. The
dance consists in turns from one side to the other, and
is performed in adoration of the sun.

Shortly after dusk the ceremonial arrows of the hunt
were burned, as well as the straw sceptres, and all the

leaves in which the corn-rolls had been wrapped. Then dancing was resumed in the same way as on the night before. The people had already been dancing for two nights, so one could hardly expect much of the third. The dancing soon stopped, and the rest of the night was spent in eating and drinking. All the families had brought large quantities of food of different kinds, and native brandy was offered, both for sale and gratuitously. During the general rejoicing, it was discovered that the dogs had scented the deer and had dug it out and devoured it; this fact, however, did not seem to have any ill-effect on the minds of the people, as all demands had been complied with, and the gods had given the deer.

After a while many grew very drunk, and by and by most of them were lying on the temple floor, sleeping off their intoxication. It was raining, so all the people remained here until next day. Before sunrise, the principal shaman sprinkled sacred water over the heads of all present with a bunch of red orchids, to give health and life. Water was also sprinkled outside of the temple, over the floor, upward, and to all sides, to ward off evil.

The feast culminated in a ceremonial race for life, which took place next morning among the young people. This is yet another form of prayer to the underworld people, and the name harari, which in the northwestern part of the country is given to the whole feast, alludes to this race.

A goal had already been prepared in the forest. Two shaman's plumes, one for the boys, the other for the girls, had been fastened to trees with appropriate incantations, and a man danced before the plumes until the goal was reached by the racers.

Most of the elderly men were so overcome with native liquor and want of sleep that they could hardly

walk from the temple to assist at the race, but, strange
to say, no detail of the ceremony was lost.   The performing shaman looked only half alive, but he managed
to take his seat behind the drum, which had been
brought outside.   He beat it mechanically and still
made himself heard, while the others staggered through
their parts.

Conspicuous in the crowd were two shamans, each
of whom carried a curious banner, a diminutive reed
mat tied to the top of a long bamboo stick.   The mats
differed slightly from each other in construction, as one
was for the boys and the other for the girls.

All were eager for the race to begin, and at the first
signal the men started off at full speed, the women following in their wake.   Fortunately for the banner-
bearers, they were not expected to run in front of their
teams, but behind them, the easier rôle after the days
and nights of fasting and feasting,   The intemperance
of the older people in no wise affected the behaviour
of the young set.   The latter did not see anything in-
decorous in the condition of the principal men, who had
fully complied with their duties to the gods ; but they
themselves were perfectly sober.   The privilege of imi-
tating the gods and getting intoxicated extended apparently only to the elders.

The old men made up for the untrustworthiness of
their legs by frantically waving their banners and vo-
ciferously shouting to urge the runners onward.   One
person ran after another, as the custom is.   Should one
happen to fall, he must remain lying on the spot until
the whole party comes back, when he follows behind the
others.   Otherwise he will not gain life.

In front of the drum was spread a blanket, and on
this a great number of cakes were deposited, shaped to
represent animals, such as the deer, turkey, rabbit, etc.

They are made from a certain seed, which is ground and mixed with water. The seed, and the plant from which it is obtained, are called wā-vë. The herb (*Amarantus leucocarpus*, Spanish, *chia* or *choal*) grows wild, although it is also, to a small extent, cultivated by the Huichols. Being yellow, it belongs to the god of fire. The tribe probably made use of this grain before they had corn. At present it is used chiefly for ceremonial purposes, except when the corn runs short. No one is permitted to eat it until this race is over.

About fifteen minutes after the start, two men came running back. They feigned to pierce one of the cakes on the ground with a piece of straw, then returned again to the woods. After another lapse of fifteen minutes, a young girl arrived at full speed, carrying in her hand a black and white plume. She was immediately treated to a spray of water from the mouth of the woman with the plumes, who spouted it out over her neck and chest. The victorious maiden pierced one of the cakes with the pointed handle of the plume, and passed it over to the shaman. The other girls, who now came in quickly, one after another, were also sprayed with water, just as the first one had been, and then each of them with a straw pierced one of the cake animals and handed it to one of the principal men. As the boys came in, they, too, were sprayed and gave their cakes to their elders, who in eating them secured, in return, health and life for all. Thus ended this very ancient ceremony, the race for life. No man gets sustenance from the gods without effort, without ceremonies and fasting, personal sacrifice and labour. These are the price the gods of the netherworld demand for letting the corn, the beans, and the squashes grow.

In the southeastern part of the country this race is connected with the hikuli feast, by which people inaugurate the eating of toasted corn for the year. Here the cake animals are kept in the ashes of the temple fire for five days, whereupon each principal eats a piece. On the ashes being removed, the cakes are frequently found to be completely burnt, and whenever this is the case it is ascribed to the greediness of the people of the under world. Another variation in the manner of observance is, that balls made of pinole are pierced by the racers, further that the goal is marked by two shamans' plumes for each sex, and the piercing is not done until all are in. In addition the pinole balls are pierced with deer-tails drawn over sticks like a glove over a finger, which were presented to every racer by the man dancing at the goal in the forest. When the boy winner hands his plumes over to the shaman, he in turn receives from him a plume and a small girdle; while the girl, who gives her plumes to the wife of the shaman, receives in return a bowl and a bracelet of glass beads.

People now began to leave for their homes, yet many lingered until the next day, amusing themselves with la danza and the music of the violin. In the afternoon, when they were trying to arrange some business matter inside the temple, I saw an exhibition of Huichol temper. A man had refused to pay his debts, and the discussion suddenly became violent. Several persons jumped up from their chairs and talked at close range into one another's faces, gesticulating wildly, and pouring forth torrents of words in shrill tones, as the French peasants are apt to do. One expected them every moment to come to blows, but in a few seconds the storm had passed and quiet was restored. The Huichols are emotional, and easily moved to laughter, tears, or anger. Suicide occurs sometimes among both sexes, instigated by jealousy and domestic troubles. They are far more excitable than any other tribe I have ever met. Still, scenes such as that just described occur only when the participants are under the influence of brandy.

At length, I had a chance to photograph the temple and some of the people. As I placed my camera on the tripod, two Indians, each carrying a lighted candle, came and knelt down on either side of the apparatus, as if it were a saint whom they worshipped. After much deliberation, they finally let me have the five diminutive chairs that had been used at the feast. My companion and I were the last to depart, out of the number of one hundred and seventy persons all told who had assembled. I was well satisfied with the result of my trip, and arrived at my lodging in San Andres just in time to escape a drenching.

CHAPTER III

ENCOURAGED by my success in San José, I immediately planned another excursion, this time to the temple of Guayabas (in Huichol: Temolikíta, "where trees and flowers are budding"). It is situated only a short distance to the south of San Andres, and at a lower elevation. On this trip I depended mainly on the good-will of a Huichol shaman, Maximino, who, having been much among the Mexicans, spoke Spanish and was less distrustful of strangers and more sociable than the average Indian.

The sun had dried the slippery, crooked trail leading down the steep descent to Guayabas. We succeeded without accident in reaching our destination, and rode our animals directly into the temple to take off the saddles and unload the pack. The shaman in charge, a friend of Maximino, was sent for and showed himself inclined to meet our wishes. He also brought us plenty of wood and something to eat. As usual, rain began at dusk, but we made a fire, and seated in the arm-chair which the shaman Josecito had lent me, I concluded that I had as comfortable a camping-place as any traveller at that moment—dry and warm, and with good ventilation.

In San Andres, Josecito was reputed to be a sorcerer, and therefore he never dared to leave his ranch, which was close to the temple. In his own district, however, he had the reputation of being a powerful rain-maker. Beside his ranch and one other, there were several small houses in the immediate neighbourhood of the temple which during feasts served as dwellings for the officers. Now these houses, which were circular or rectangular, were abandoned, and the door-openings were filled with stones. When I once had to sleep in the smallest of these structures, I found it barely long enough to admit of my stretching out at full length. Throughout the Huichol country you will generally find some ranches near the temple, but, as a rule, people do not live close to their place of worship. It is only at the time of feasts that the population assembles there. Then the temple officials with their families camp in the god-houses that usually stand near by. At Guayabas, the only god-house near the temple was too small to serve for sleeping-quarters, and, as the others were too far off, special accommodations had been provided.

The shaman went to call the people from the ranches, and during my short stay they came in every day, the women bringing me tortillas and the palatable, thin gruel atole. I showed my appreciation by presents of glass beads, of which the Huichols are inordinately fond.

A pleasant incident occurred one day, when unexpectedly an Indian messenger arrived, with news from the outer world. The Commandant-General of the Territory of Tepic had the courtesy to send me letters in spite of the great distance, and the official in the cañon of Jesus Maria below forwarded them to me. This served me in more ways than one ; first, it gave me favour in the eyes of the Indians to see that the highest authorities showed me so much consideration ; second, one of my letters contained an invitation to take part in the Ninth Congress of Americanists, which was to be held in the City of Mexico in November of that year (1895). Although I could not accept, it was pleasant in such barbaric surroundings to find one's self remembered by those in civilisation.

In the evening a few of the officers of the temple came to hear what I wanted, among them a young shaman, who, on entering the temple, went straight to the fire, and threw a piece of wood upon it, and then remained standing in prayer before it. " I arrived here," he addressed the fire, " without meeting with any accident on the road. Here you have me at your orders ! Help me again, when I go home, that nothing may happen to me." Having finished his devotions, he placed a few glowing coals in a small clay vessel, put some copal on them, and made a ceremonial circuit so that the incense smoke went up along the walls.

Accompanied by the principal men, I went to visit a god-house on top of the mountain northwest of the temple. After an hour's climbing, we found ourselves at the summit, in a forest of big-leaved oak-trees and shortly afterward came upon a rather insignificant rectangular structure, built of stone and mud, and covered with a gabled thatched roof. It stood on a small open plain, only twenty feet from the precipice that falls away to the arroyo of Guayabas. As we approached, I noticed numerous arrow-points sticking through the roof. The entrance, as usual without a door, was at the short side of the building, but toward the north.

After the Indians had made a ceremonial circuit around the house, I crept inside with two of them. We found the floor strewn with ceremonial arrows and shields, deer-horns, etc., that had been discarded, because all ceremonial things cease to be of value after a lapse of five years. There was an altar in the rear of the little building, made solidly from stone and mud. It was full of ceremonial arrows, stuck upright into small god-chairs, and many other symbolic objects, such as " eyes," " beds," etc. The ceiling was one mass of ceremonial arrows, to which feathers and other attachments had been fastened.

I commenced to pick up various things from the floor, but the well-meaning Indians told me to select some of the newer things, as according to their ideas these sacrifices decrease in value with age, and, of course, they assumed that what was of little value to them could not be of much worth to me, either. I took the hint, and in a few minutes made a valuable ethnological collection. At last I drew my companions' attention to a basket which I had discovered on the altar among the multitude of arrows. It was one of the kind in which the Indians carry their paraphernalia for making arrows, some twelve inches long, low and narrow. It had been placed on one of the little chairs, and in front of it was a drinking-gourd with tesvino. From all this I inferred that there was something important inside, and, therefore, did not hesitate to take it up. In doing this I upset the liquor, which evidently was an offering, but the Indians did not seem to mind it.

" This, perhaps, you cannot get permission to open," Maximino said; "because inside is the Inhabitant of the House." The Inhabitant! Why, nothing could stop me from making his acquaintance. I earnestly expressed my desire to see him, promising that I would not carry him off, but merely look at him. The Indians consented, and two of them opened the case, and reverently unfolded a bundle of rags which it contained.

The first thing brought to light was the winged part of an arrow ; it was without feathers, but prettily decorated with symbolic designs. This portion of the arrow is considered its vital part, or heart, and, therefore, represents the entire weapon. Then several small, soft back-shields with woven designs were found, and with them the rattle of a rattle-snake. The serpent belongs to the god and is a warrior, who always carries his rattling "bell" with him. Unpacking still further we came upon a small but heavy greenish stone with a few yellow veins, and I was allowed to take it in my hands. The mineral, about one inch long, was in its natural state. This was the god, and the Indians explained to me that he was very fierce. " He comes from the blue sea," they said, "and is Elder Brother." His colour and origin had made him a powerful water-god, and to the Huichols he was not only alive, but a warrior with his full ceremonial outfit. As I reluctantly handed him back, he was again swaddled in his trappings, placed in his basket, and seated on his chair, as on a throne.

Huichol Reed Flute, with scratch-ing, repre-senting rattles of rattle-snakes. Length, 24.5 ctm.

Ever since my arrival here, I had heard a distant thundering as of a cataract, and as soon as I had satisfactorily finished my examination of the god-house I walked over to the edge of the mountain, where a surprisingly fine view opened out. I found myself on one side of a gap, the head of the valley of Guayabas. To the right a beautiful cascade fell perpendicularly into the narrow gorge, and thence the water rushed eastward and down to the cañon to join the main river of the valley, scarcely seven miles away, but at least three thousand feet below the height on which I was standing. On the highland above the fall, I could trace the course of the stream, swollen as it now was, for some distance in the pine and oak forest. During the greater part of the year, it can hardly be much more than a brook; per. haps no water remains except in some of the deeper pools. On the ridge forming the opposite side of the cañon, I could see another god-house, but no dwellings were in sight. It was really surprising to note how uninhabited the country looked.

On my way back to the temple, I stopped to visit a kutsála, or holy spring, which lies close to the track and is considered especially beneficial to children. The water forms a small still pool, crystal clear, which never dries up. Numberless arrows, each representing a prayer or an expression of adoration of the spring's deity, were stuck into and around the basin.

The Huichols adore water. Every one of them, big and little, washes face, head, and hands every morning in order to gain the blessings with which, to them, all water, and especially that from springs, is replete. The springs are sacred, and the gods in them are mothers, or serpents, that rise with the clouds and descend as fructifying rain. Health and strength are assured to all who lave with or drink from the water that comes direct from the well-spring of all life, Mother Earth. Of the four elements, water is the most generally revered. At every feast the people sprinkle water on their heads from some spring. As there is a special water for the various occasions, there is a constant carrying about of gourds from one place to another full of it. Every child born in the tribe must be washed with the water from several springs. If it is impracticable to take the babe to them, the water has to be carried to the child. No water is more highly valued for external and internal use than that which the hikuli-seekers bring from the distant country where they find this plant.

Having obtained from the Indians all available information and explanations regarding the ethnological specimens gathered here, I packed up my collections and started back to San Andres. It was one of those unlucky days in which, spite of one's best endeavours, everything tends to go wrong. My mule stumbled over a slippery stone in a river, so that I barely escaped a ducking, but it struggled up again, and we continued the ascent, Maximino leading the pack-mule. The air was sultry almost beyond endurance. As it had been raining for many days, big stones and rocks were all the time loosening and rolling down. The night before I had heard several of them tumbling to the bottom of the valley with tremendous noise. About half way up the steep hillside, I came upon a stretch of ground where an avalanche had swept bare the rocks, cracking and bending young trees and bushes like reeds, and marking its path for a breadth of about twenty yards with demolition and ruin. To add to my discomfort, I was exceedingly anxious lest something should happen to the pack-mule, for an Indian never cares well for animals on the road ; and, looking back, I just caught sight of my big white mule, El Chino, the same that had had so many mishaps, bumping his aparejo against a rock that stood out prominently on the track. He fell on his knees, and for a few moments it looked as if he would roll over, taking with him to the bottom of the hillside the most valuable and irreplaceable part of my outfit, the photographic apparatus. It was enough to take one's breath away. But the plucky beast recovered his foothold, and a vital part of a successful expedition was saved.

My second trip, too, had been fruitful of good results, and this made it the more disheartening to find, on
my return to San Andres, that the people there were as
repellent and disobliging as ever. The Huichols are
very clannish. Maximino, who had been of so much
help to me in Guayabas, had no influence in San Andres, where the people still clung to their prejudice
against me, actuated by the absurd rumours they had
heard in the beginning.

Three small children were one day buried in the
cemetery of San Andres while I was there. It seemed
a wonder that not more people, both young and old, died
from exposure during the wet season. The children
may have succumbed to influenza, for some such ailment was epidemic just then, especially among the
children. With adults, it took the form of a rather
severe catarrh. The Indians, who can never trace illness and death to natural causes, attributed the prevalence of disease to the action of the Devil. At a
recent rain-making feast the candles that had been lit in
the church had been blown out in the course of the
night. This disturbing occurrence was ascribed to the
jealousy of the Devil, because no feast had been given
for him. His anger had caused all the illness, and
the principal men resolved that a god-house should be
erected and a feast made in his honour, so that he should
be satisfied.

During the wet season, when little or no outdoor
work can be done, many a Huichol may be seen busily
engaged in the manufacture of straw hats. Long, fine
strips of palm-leaves are plaited into bands, which afterward are sewn together so as to form a hat. The bands
while being plaited are rolled up in coils, which the makers fasten to their girdles and carry with them wherever
they go, as a German housewife carries her needlework.

Their fingers never seem to tire. Even at the sessions of the native court the judges are all busily braiding while they conduct the trial and pass sentence. The idea of straw hats has been adopted from their "neighbours," but the Indians modify the style according to their own taste. They make the rim immensely wide and out of all proportion to the crown, which is so small and low that the hat would never remain on the head if it were not for the narrow home-made ribbon which is sewed to the under sides of the crown and passes under the chin.

The trimming of the hats is not subject to changes of fashion, but is sometimes elaborate, varied, and original. Small crosses formed from short strips of red flannel, and woollen tassels, adorn the upper surface of the brim or the crown, which is always encircled with a pretty native-woven ribbon. The upper side of the rim may be decorated with bits of skin from the red plum, or pieces of white cocoons found on the madroña trees.

Former Head-dress of the Huichol. Length of network, 16 ctm.

I secured during my stay among the Huichols a head-dress, called wīpí (net), which carries one back to pre-Columbian times. It is an oval network of fibre, adorned at each end with a modern attachment, a rectangular piece of red flannel. It was put on the head lengthwise, a head-band passing over the two ends to keep it in place.

The monotony of the wet season was one day interrupted by the capture of two "neighbours," who in laying out their ranches had encroached on Huichol territory. The native authorities commanded them to give up the land they had usurped, but the captives refused to do so, and were promptly put into prison. Here they lingered several days without receiving, officially, any food. In the Indian conception, captivity is no punishment unless it is coupled with hunger. Indians can stand a good deal of privation, but instances have been recorded where even they have become so reduced in strength that on being released they barely crawled out on all-fours. The two Mexicans were saved from actual starvation by the kindness of Don Zeferino, who sent them food; but the strain on their stomachs was severe enough to bring them into submission, and they promised to remove the ranch, leaving their mule, valued at eighteen pesos, as security. It is gratifying to see the Indians get the best of their "neighbours" once in a while.

About this time a messenger arrived bringing me a personal letter from the Bishop of Tepic, who expressed his regret for the trouble I had had in the valley of Jesus Maria, and advised me that he had taken steps to rectify matters by giving special orders to the priests to help me. This was gratifying, though by this time I had already overcome those obstacles that at one time had threatened serious delay to the progress of the expedition. Afterward the padre in Guaynamota, to carry out the bishop's orders, sent more than once messengers to inquire when he could come to see me. I thanked him for his good-will, but saved the poor man the inconvenience of swollen rivers and precipitous ascents.

After considerable searching I found a man willing to accompany Maximino to Tepic, to fetch my mail and some parcels of photographic films that had been waiting there for some time. By sending Maximino on this errand I was left without an attendant for my contemplated excursion to the southern part of the Huichol country, when suddenly my old landlord, Carillo, took it into his head to go with me. It seemed rather hazardous to accept him on account of his meagre knowledge of Spanish; but there was no prospect of finding a more suitable companion, and I preferred the risk of encountering considerable hardships, with a slight chance of good results, to remaining longer inactive.

CHAPTER IV

EARLY on one of those hot, bright mornings in the wet season, when the grass and the trees sparkle in the brilliant sunshine as if studded with diamonds, and one feels happy in spite of tortillas and beans and the unsympathetic people about one, we started. Carillo dragged the pack-mule along, and my two dogs did their best to show their joy at being on the road again.

Carillo.

There are but few ranches immediately to the south of San Andres. The trail we followed passed only one inhabited place, and this belonged to the gobernador. Although Bastita, the district I was bound for, cannot be, as the crow flies, more than fifteen miles away, the distance I had to cover was more than twice that, on account of the circuitous route we had to take to avoid the deep valley of Guayabas. Suddenly the old horse I had brought along, as a companion to the mules, bolted and showed generally a strong desire to turn back. The flowing hair and barbaric pict-

63

uresqueness of Carillo's attire was not suited to his
fancy, but after half an hour of gentle tactics we managed to catch him and continue our journey.

Carillo was not at all a bad companion, but he did
not speak more than a dozen Spanish words, and these
he employed awkwardly. He had learned *Quien sabe ?*
("Who knows?"), the common, emphatic expression
for "No," and he had a few other sentences at his
disposal, such as *No, esta bueno* ("No, it is all right"),
Mas arriba ("Higher up"). If I asked him what road
to take, he always answered with the latter sentence.
To my other questions he would reply *Quien sabe ?* or
Si, puede ("Yes, it is possible"), not knowing exactly
what the words meant. His answers finally became so
exasperating that I gave up conversation altogether.

After three hours' riding, we passed the river which
forms the waterfall above Guayabas. The only indications of human life we now came upon were one lonely
cornfield and a deserted ranch. Quietly we journeyed
on through the pine forest, up and down all the time,
over the little gulches running down from one main
ridge, which extended in an easterly and westerly direction. At the eastern end of this was our destination.
After ascending a seemingly endless arroyo, we finally,
at dusk, reached the summit. It had been a most
fatiguing journey for the poor animals, and they were
beginning to give out. The distant roar of thunder
warned us that rain was not far off, in fact a few drops
were falling already. We had made twenty-three miles,
which was a good day's journey. So I decided to camp
then and there, as we could not possibly reach an Indian
ranch that evening.

Close to a young manzanillo lay a tree trunk to
which we set fire, knowing that it would burn all night.
Carillo found water, and after he had filled my pots we

sat down to a sumptuous supper of tamales. Out of some boughs, a piece of canvas, and a couple of saddlecloths made of palm fibre, I managed to construct a covering for my head and the camera. The cannonade of thunder, which was constantly heard in the distance, became louder and louder. A tremendous wall of black clouds approached rapidly from the southwest. The oak and pine forests creaked and groaned under the advancing tempest. In a few minutes, and before we had finished our meal, the rain was upon us. I covered myself in my bedding, while Carillo stoically turned his back to the gale, as the mules were doing. A little pine that reached only to his neck, and his Indian straw hat, were his sole shelter as he sat facing the fire.

Next morning, after having as far as possible dried my blankets, we pushed on, trying to reach Bastita in time for a feast which we heard was to be concluded that day. About six miles farther on, after descending a sharp point on the mountain-side, we arrived at the ranch of a rich Indian, but found only his household here, watching his cattle. I was told that this nabob had at least two other ranches beside this one, and that he was the owner of some two or three hundred head of cattle.

We learned that the feast had been finished the day before, and Carillo, therefore, wisely resolved to go on to the ranch of the principal shaman. I followed him almost blindly, because his lack of Spanish made it impossible to plan with him for our journeying. The shaman, when we entered his ranch, had just returned from the feast. He was a thick-set man, with a good-tempered expression, and wore a very much embroidered shirt. The Mexicans, who, not without reason, saw something Mongolian in his make-up, had given him the name Chino, by which he was now generally known. Judging from his name and his fair Spanish, he must have had in his day considerable intercourse with the neighbours, going, no doubt, as some of the Huichols do at certain seasons, to work on the cotton plantations of the coast. Chino's ranch commanded a splendid view, and many other ranches could be seen on the fertile slopes. I remarked with admiration how clean and neat all the little buildings on his ranch looked, as well as the patio between them.

He received us very politely. It was quite a treat to speak a few words to him, though he seemed very tired after singing for two nights at the feast. He promised, however, to call the people to meet me next day at the temple, and we accordingly started for this rendezvous to be on hand for possible callers. We passed two ranches, the occupants of which seemed much astonished at the sight of a white man here. Nearly all the houses were round and constructed of stone and mud ; a few were almost large enough to be taken for temples.

The temple was situated on the northern slope of the ridge we had followed, about two miles beyond the point at which the track crossed the divide. From the summit of the ridge a fine view opened out to the northeast, overlooking the river and the main valley, in fact, all the central part of the Huichol country.

Before us to the right, high up among the mountain valleys, but hidden from view, lay Santa Catarina, the main village and religious centre of the tribe. Directly opposite to it, on the left bank, rose the high plateau of San Andres, drawn against the sky as with a ferule. The Huichol country is well watered by the Chapalagana and its tributaries. The main valley is steep, and narrow at the bottom, but gradually broadens out, and the sides rise to a height of from 6,000 to 8,000 feet. The country thus consists of two parallel ridges

The Central Part of the Huichol Country, Viewed from the South.

with the valley between, the heights being covered with pine forests, the abode of numerous deer (the Sonoran deer, *Dorcelaphus couesi*).

At the lowest elevation, the climate is very warm, and, as the banks are steep, scarcely anyone lives there permanently, although the Indians frequently come down to the river to catch fish and crayfish. The pine-clad highlands are only the hunting-ground of the tribe, most of the ranches being situated at a moderate elevation.

Except from the north, where the view is open, the temple of northern Bastita, which is thickly surrounded with trees, cannot be seen until one comes close up to it. I found the space in front of the edifice strewn with offal from an ox that had been killed at the feast, and the smell was far from pleasing to my olfactory nerves after they had been revelling in the delicious exhalations of the pine forests. The temple was old; and the roof overhung the wall in such a way as to leave an open space all round between it and the wall, though protruding sufficiently on all sides to prevent the rain from entering. It was by no means as snug a camping-place as the other temples I had visited. Besides, it had for religious reasons been erected on ground so moist that the water stood in pools in several places. I told Carillo that I would not sleep here, but he replied, "*No, esta bueno*," and lay down on the narrow bench of stone and mud which, as usual, ran along part of the inner wall. He tried to make me believe that the ranches of the neighbourhood just then had no people in them, everybody being away in the fields; in short, he was not to be moved one inch further. His reluctance to trespass on the hospitality of his compatriots was no doubt due to the Huichol custom of visiting one another only on business. Their idea is that if anything should be missed in the house the visitor would be suspected of having taken it.

While I was looking for a tree under which I could sleep, I perceived three men at a distance coming toward the temple. When they reached me, I found that one of them could speak a little Spanish, and I managed to draw out the information that there was a ranch not far from here, but hidden by the forest. I immediately said, " *Vamos!* " and Carillo, seeing there was no help for it, consented to go with us. Led by the newly arrived Indians, we went on another mile to a small house, where an elderly woman and her young granddaughter hospitably allowed us to stop.

Of course I thought that the women would go to sleep somewhere else, for it was one of the smallest dwellings I had ever seen. The house consisted mainly of a thatched gable roof which came within eighteen or twenty inches of the ground. Side-walls had been dispensed with, but there was a stone-and-mud wall in the rear. The front would have been entirely open had it not been for a large corn-crib that stood in the middle of the house, almost blocking the entrance and leaving scant room for the occupants. In one corner was their bed, a matting of split bamboo, stretched over four upright forked poles like a low altar. This was quite unusual; the customary way is to sleep on such mattings spread on the floor.

On the opposite side of the room were the indispensable metate, the requisite jars and cooking-utensils, and a heap of firewood. When we were all inside and the girl was grinding corn, it was difficult to avoid stepping on or falling over one another. We could not all eat our tortillas at one time. But the greatest trouble was to get out of the house; you had either to crawl along the little space left between the sloping roof and the corn-crib, or else make a short-cut by delving under the eaves of the roof. However, the women were kind and good-natured, and we managed to get on nicely. Glad to have a dry place to sleep in, I stretched myself along one side of the corn-

Huichols from Bastita.

crib under the edge of the slanting roof, and, in spite of rain, storm, and lightning, slept soundly.

In the morning I went to the temple, accompanied by Carillo and the two Indians, who carried my camera. To my surprise, there were already about twenty men congregated there. They not only readily submitted to being photographed, but at my request sent two men to a god-house at a distance from the temple, to bring various symbolic objects, which I bought at a reasonable price.

After spending another profitable day on the ranches hereabouts, I recrossed the ridge, but in a more easterly direction. From the summit, after travelling about two miles, I had a fine view of the valley, which in a gentle curve slopes downward on the south side of the ridge. The river is still farther down and cannot be seen from here. Many ranches were visible, and the southern and larger temple of Bastita was within easy reach; but I continued my journey at the same altitude without descending. The track led along the rather steep side of a high mesa, called the Red Mesa, easily seen from San Andres or Santa Catarina. As we wended our way, Carillo sang out to the people on the ranches we were passing to meet me the following morning at the temple of Popotita, our next resting-place. It was about twelve miles to the southeast of the northern temple of Bastita.

Toward the end of the ridge we were, I should say, 7,000 feet above sea-level, and steep gorges ran down from the hilly, narrow plateau, clad in luxuriant green, toward the river and the deep valleys on both sides. Three miles farther on we arrived at the temple of Popotita, "where there is *popote* (a stiff straw)." The native name, Epithápa, means a kind of stiff grass. Its neighbourhood commands a grand view of the main river. On the slopes to the right and left of the temple are scattered many ranches.

About fifty people assembled here, some of them sleeping in the temple, where I, too, was quartered. I visited all the ranches, which lay so close to the temple as almost to form a village. The owners complaisantly showed me the contents of their houses, and sold me whatever I wanted to buy. I think Carillo spoke well of me, and the Indians were evidently much impressed with my ability to sing a verse or two of one of their principal rain-songs. The people here were pleasant to deal with. It seemed a novelty to them to receive a visit from a white man.

From a god-house near the temple I secured some things of interest ; and having accomplished all that

Huichol Sitting in the Shade of his House ; Store-house in Background.

I could reasonably expect, I returned to San Andres. This time we passed straight across the Red Mesa, and I was surprised to find a family living there in a natural cave. Aside from this I found only one other instance of cave-dwellers among the Huichols. We stopped for the night at the ranch of the gobernador, but, his Honour being in the village, the people in charge would not allow us to sleep in the house. We found some shelter under the projecting eaves of a store-house. The corn when shelled is kept in round store-houses made of stone and mud. It is put in from above, and taken out through an opening near the ground, a stone serving as a door for this aperture, which is kept tightly closed. The store-houses are very small, as the Huichols harvest only from four to five fanegas of corn a year. Some content themselves even with two, while a few rich men may lay up as many as twenty fanegas.

In the morning I saw something unusual in that country—women engaged in dairy work. During the wet season, the only time of the year when the cows give milk, a few of the ranches make cheese to be sold to the "neighbours," who are quite fond of this *queso*. Butter is unknown. We enjoyed very much the clabber liberally offered by the women from a big jar in which the curding of the milk is done. As there are yet very few pigs in that country, the whey is given to the packs of hungry dogs that always infest the ranches. The Huichols are very fond of dogs, and if you kill one, its owner grows angry; but they do not give them much to eat. The dogs fortunate enough to belong to a dairy farm, however, have a regular feasting time at this season.

My belongings which I had left behind in San Andres were all found intact. But my animals became more and more a source of annoyance. They seemed to grow wild in their uncivilised surroundings, and to contract the bad manners of the Indian mules. One of my horses was lost for seven weeks, but was finally recovered with the aid of the natives.

I was agreeably surprised to find that the Indians of San Andres had markedly changed their attitude toward me. They had ceased to look upon me as a nuisance, and were ready to treat me with esteem. Probably they had become convinced that I would not take advantage of them, as so many other white men had done. Then, too, they had good reports about me from their countrymen, as well as from the Coras, and they had been impressed not a little by the messengers that came to me from the civil and ecclesiastical authorities in Tepic, a circumstance which more than anything else made me in their simple minds a man of importance. What won their affection especially, however, was my ability to sing some of their songs. This they esteemed highly meritorious on my part. Besides, the mere mention of the names of their gods in this way protected me to a certain extent against any evil designs they might have had. How could they kill a man who knew all about the gods? The gods themselves might get angry and not send rain if any harm were done to him. I have even had occasion to utilise this knowledge among other tribes, who did not understand the words, yet comprehended that the melody was of their own race, not the white man's, so that any utterance of it struck a responsive chord in their hearts. All this had conspired to bring about a change of heart, and now they began to think I might be of benefit to them.

During the preceding weeks I had again and again tried to arrange interviews with shamans, in order to learn something of their religious beliefs and ancient history, but they had always found an excuse for delay; now they were willing to tell me all I wanted to know, to show me all I wanted to see, and to have their photographs taken. They even confided their troubles to me. One of these, bred by their clannishness, was a boundary dispute with Santa Catarina.   Another and more important source of worry was the intrusion of the whites on their lands.   All these overtures I heeded with appreciation, and messengers were sent out to bring the people together to have a meeting with me.

CHAPTER V

VOTIVE BOWLS—MY FAITHFUL DOG APACHE DIES, IN SPITE OF A
SHAMAN'S PRAYERS—THE HUICHOLS GATHER FROM FAR AND
NEAR TO MEET ME—CHARACTERISTICS OF THE HUICHOLS—
CARRYING CAPACITY — SLEEP — MOVEMENTS — DISEASES — HOW
INFANTS LEARN TO WALK—FILIAL AFFECTION—WILL-POWER
—MAN AND WOMAN—MARRIAGE CUSTOMS, OLD AND NEW.

A MONG the things I brought back from my excursions were some votive bowls. These are
simply the ordinary drinking-
gourds of the Huichols, that
is to say, sections of gourds
painted inside red or green.
When intended for a sacrifice
to the gods they are adorned
with beads of various colours,
attached by means of beeswax,
generally only to the inside of
the bowl, either singly or in
strings, so as to form coils,
rolls, human figures, and other
designs expressive of the do-
nor's thoughts and prayers. In ancient times shell
beads were no doubt used for the purpose. Grains of
corn, artificial flowers, wads of cotton-wool, and sometimes even feathers may be used in the decoration of
the bowl. In the accompanying illustration is seen one
which expresses a prayer for plenty of corn. The spots
inside of the bowl are daubs of beeswax on which have

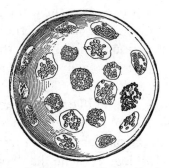

The Inside of a Votive Bowl
Dedicated to the Goddess of
Eastern Clouds. Diam., 9 ctm.

been placed white and blue beads symbolic of grains of corn. The idea actuating the Huichols in such sacrifices is that the gods, when they come to use their bowls, will drink in the prayers of the people. Bowls are, therefore, considered effective conveyers of prayers, and every family has its votive bowl, which is taken out into the fields whenever the men hunt deer, plant corn, etc.

In San Andres lived a man who was remarkably clever in making votive bowls. He had been a good deal among Mexicans, which may have influenced his taste, and he bestowed great pains on his work, so that his productions were much more elaborate than is usual with the tribe. Although at heart he remained a true Huichol, the beautiful beadwork on the three bowls he made for me somewhat betrayed the white man's influence. He would cover the entire surface of the bowl with beeswax, then, picking up bead by bead, with the point of a maguey thorn, form his figures, without any previous design, until the whole bowl was covered, the work on each bowl consuming the better part of several days.

While decorating the last of the bowls I had ordered of him he became an actor in a sorrowful event that took place soon after my return from Bastita. My faithful dog, Apache, had contracted an illness on this excursion, and suffered from a violent cough which nearly choked him every time he tried to eat. He was growing worse every day, and I missed him much on my daily tour for a bath in the arroyo, where he had always kept the obnoxious dogs of the Indians at bay. Without him, too, I had no one to advise me of strange Indians, who sometimes noiselessly approached from behind the bushes while I was in the water. Apache hailed from San Francisco. He was presented to me by a young friend, and while yet in his infancy had ventured out alone, in an express box, to join my expedition at Bisbee, six summers ago. On his mother's side he came from one of the best canine families in the United States, and throughout my travels in Mexico had been my constant and efficient aide-de-camp. While the pack-train was moving, he would run tirelessly forward and back, as if to see that no one stayed behind.

Apache with the Mules on my First Expedition.

Whenever we entered a Mexican village, he would clear the way for the expedition, by fighting the packs of ill-tempered curs that infested the streets, rolling with half a dozen of them into the open stores. His greatest merit was that he never bit people, yet had a mien and deep bass voice so forbidding that no one dared approach my tent while he lay under the curtain.

With my thoughts on the poor dog, I one day visited the bowl-maker, who was sitting outside of his house.

working away. A mutual friend, a shaman, coming along, I told him that my dog was ill, and asked him if he could not cure him. "But suppose he should die?" he diplomatically interposed. I assured him that in that case he would not be held responsible, but that if he effected a cure I would reward him well. The bead-worker also thought that the shaman had better try, and added: "I will make a picture of the dog on the bowl and present him to Father Sun; then we will see whether he will let him live or not." Encouraged by this unexpected assistance in the treatment of the dog, the shaman consented to undertake the cure. I led him over to the shed where poor Apache was lying, already half blind, though he could still recognise me, and he rose as we entered.

We took off his bandages of mustard and lard; then the shaman, pointing, with his plumes in his right hand, successively to the different quarters of the world, made prayers to the gods to cure him. He declared that something was the matter with the dog's heart. Passing his hands carefully over the right side of the animal, he put his lips to a spot behind the right foreleg, and sucked vigorously, then rose and produced from his mouth a grain of corn, the visible form of the disease, which he promptly gave to me, requesting me to be sure to have it burned.

With his plumes he now made passes along the dog's back. Scooping water with his hand into his mouth from the dog's drinking-tray, he sprayed it all over the animal. "If he lives five days longer, he will not die," he said. "Otherwise he will die on the fourth day from to-day." Later he came back, and, with tears rolling down his cheeks, implored all the gods to make his cure effective.

But the noble beast succumbed to his fate, dying on

PLATE VIII.

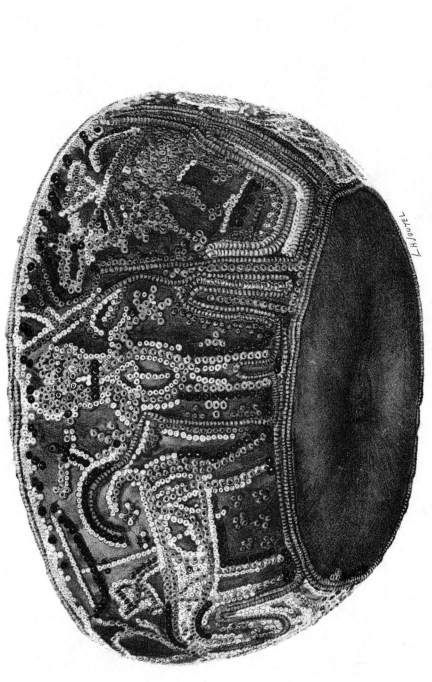

the fourth day, as the shaman had prophesied. I at once got Carillo, another Indian, and my little friend "Flower Skirt," to make a grave on a pretty spot near by, and here we laid him to rest with his head to the south, the region toward which he was always anxious to push on. We buried him, like an Indian brave, with his belongings, his collar and chain, his trays and bedding. The Indians wanted to keep these things for their own use, but I objected, as the dog might have had some contagious disease. I should not wonder, however, if they dug them up later.

It may be that the Frenchman expressed a pessimistic view of mankind when he said, "What is best in man is the dog." But anyone who loves those faithful, disinterested creatures will sympathise in my loss, which in those surroundings I felt as keenly as if Apache had been my best friend. Thank you, my loyal companion, for the hundreds and hundreds of miles you followed me these years, over the plains of Sonora and Chihuahua, in the snow of the Sierra and the heat of the barrancas, swimming rivers and climbing rocks ! Wherever I was, there were you, always happy, compelling respect, loved by all, Mexicans and Indians alike.

The bowl on which the dog was pictured was a splendid specimen, and I was so much pleased with it that I wanted the maker to duplicate it, which he agreed to do. But with the usual inability of Indians to make two things alike, he turned out a very different vessel. The illustration shows the dog with his drinking-bowl over him, as there was no space for it in front. At one side is seen the Sun, to which the bowl was dedicated. In front of the dog is a deer god, holding in his right hand his bow and plumes. In the next section the arrow is seen piercing the deer, and the bow from which it was sped may be observed above it.

The day on which the people were to meet me arrived, and I was glad to see that about forty men and a few women and children had come from different parts of the country this side of the river. Some of them were induced to remain here two or three days.

The oldest shaman present allowed himself to be interviewed for two days. The Huichols respect age and believe that the longer a man lives, the more he knows.

Front View.   Side View.
Huichol Man.

This man was called Æaká (Wind). Those who journey to the east to get the sacred hikuli plants are given new names on each journey. This name seemed particularly appropriate, because his wild hair always looked as if blown by the wind. Shrivelled and thin, with the dreamy eyes of the seer, he lived in a supernatural world, which was to him reality. He told us in a low voice, as if confiding a great secret, how once, in the hikuli country, he had seen with his own eyes grains of corn actually mixed in with the plant. The fact is that the hikuli plant, which is thought to be so necessary to secure good crops, is in itself regarded as corn, just as the deer is corn ; or, in other words, sustenance.

The Indians at the meeting despatched two men to the god-house of the Sun near San José, to fetch a number of interesting ceremonial objects.   It was curious to observe that only two of the Indians present carried arms, that is to say, bows and quivers full of arrows.

Front View.   Side View.
Huichol Woman.

The Huichols are not warriors, and in that respect differ from the Coras, who seem to be born for fighting. When the Huichols arm themselves, as on all their hunting expeditions or when travelling outside of their country, they carry bows in their right hands, and a few arrows stuck into their girdles, for they rarely use quivers. The arrows are very light, and have points of brazilwood.

The marksmanship of the Huichols is tolerably good and they shoot with considerable force.   I once saw a

young man shooting at a distance of 106 feet. He hit
the trunk of a zapote tree fairly well twice, the first
arrow entering 1¼ inch, the second 1⅝ inch. The bark,
which is, of course, softer than the wood, was nearly ⅞
of an inch thick. Considering that this man was not as
good a shot as many others, and that the arrow-point was
only of wood, though of hard wood, the result surprised
me. The Indians assured me that an arrow shot from
the same distance at a deer would penetrate over 5
inches. A fourteen-year-old boy with a bow 33½ inches
long shot his arrow 400 feet.

I took this opportunity of ascertaining the average
height of those present, with the following result : Out of
forty-three men measured, 40 per cent. were below 5 feet
4⅙ inches (1.63 metres), 30 per cent. above 5 feet 6⅐
inches (1.68 metres), and 30 per cent. between these
two figures, giving an average height of 5 feet 5 inches
(1.65 metres).

The Huichols are a remarkably pure-bred people. I
know one Mexican who is married to a Huichol woman
and has children by her ; but outside of that family I
have, in all my travels through their country, seen only
two half-caste children. One of these was a boy about
three years old. His pure-bred half-sister, some three
years older, took care of him. The boy seemed to be
cross and ill-tempered all the time, probably inheriting
this from his Mexican father, as the Huichol children
are good-natured. It took all the little girl's time to
attend to him. She played with him, danced before him,
and sung to him the temple songs she had caught from
the singing shaman. The boy was fat and robust, and
looked as if some day, when old enough, he might turn
his brothers and sister out of the nest.

The two middle teeth of the Huichols are placed
obliquely against each other, turning inward, making a

symmetrical and not unpleasant break in the row of teeth.

These natives take their chief meals in the morning and at night. They eat more toasted corn than tortillas and they also toast squash-seeds. Pinole, too, is used, though rarely. Meat is eaten fresh or even when partly decomposed, but rats, mice, pork, dogs, vultures, crows, snakes, or lizards are not used for food. Most of their meat is boiled or broiled, always without salt. The people also boil beans without salt, and eat them with the water in which they are cooked. Here, as with other tribes, salt is used as a relish, with chile. Officers of the temple are never allowed to help themselves to salt; others must serve them with it.

We may conquer climatic conditions, but we cannot overcome that instinctive but inexplicable feeling of attraction or repulsion toward all persons we encounter. I, for one, am more dependent on human associations than on weather or beauty of surroundings. As a traveller I can put up with any kind of inconvenience and discomfort, if my hosts are kind-hearted and well-meaning. What most affects our personal relations is that other potent quality which we call personal magnetism, inherent in every individual in varying degrees, for good or for bad. Morals have nothing to do with this unconscious law of give and take. More than once have I felt the influence of the Indian's strong animal magnetism. Never did I leave one of their assemblages without experiencing a feeling of restfulness and a quieting of my nerves. Their effect on me was, perhaps, comparable to that which horses and cattle exert on persons who have much to do with such animals. Butchers, according to statistics, are the healthiest men in any community, and the good health of stable-boys is almost proverbial. Indeed, the custom obtains in some European countries of having the attendants of the cattle sleep in the stables; and cases are known where persons with weak vitality, even consumptives, have been benefited by spending their time mostly in cow stables.

There is a distinct, though not strong, odour about

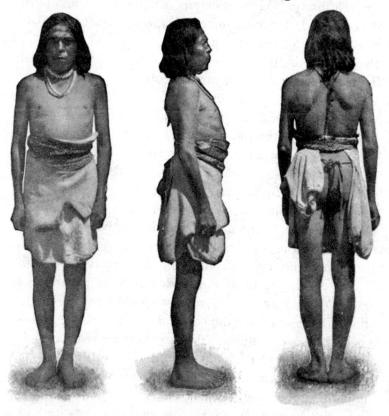

Front View. Side View. Back View.
Huichol Man.

the Huichols, especially with women and young persons. It reminds one of that of a wet dog, with a smell of smoke intermixed. I could perceive no difference between this and the odour of the Australians.

Women, when fetching water, may carry as many as four gourds (Spanish, *bule*), a total weight of no less than

100 pounds. Three gourds are hung from the head down on her back, and one is suspended from her neck over her chest. A man easily carries a fanega of corn, weighing 120 pounds, in three days from Mezquitic to Santa Catarina, a distance of fifty miles and including an ascent

Pack Net, for Carrying Burdens. Width, 50 ctm.

of the Sierra. Mexicans cannot do this. The Huichols also carry similar weights from the deep valleys up to their houses. A favourite mode of carrying a burden is to place it in a net, or blanket, suspended from the body by a strip of hide (*mecapal*). This strip is tied to the bundle at two places, and passes over the upper part of the chest and arms. With smaller burden the weight is thrown on the head. The women sometimes carry jars, gourds filled with water, etc., in pack-nets of bark fibre, provided with hoops. Such a utensil hangs on the back from the head. While the thighs of both men and women are unusually large, their arms are thin and they cannot lift weights as well as the Mexicans.

I saw one woman who was squint-eyed, and one man who played the violin with his left hand.

The Huichols cannot stand loss of sleep as we do. To do any brain-work after having passed a sleepness night is impossible for them. I became acquainted with a Huichol who gave me much intelligent information; but one morning, after he had spent the night in the temple singing and indulging in toach, their weak native brandy, I found him a different man altogether. Although he was not intoxicated, I could get no information out of him, and finally he fell asleep. A young friend of mine, Pablo, when on a journey to the hikuli country, watched the mules for two consecutive nights. On the third night he fell asleep standing, although it was raining heavily; but as he dropped to the ground the pain he suffered in falling woke him up.

The people generally sleep on their backs, but also on either side. If they put anything at all under their heads, it is usually a piece of firewood, or their girdles folded up. When at ease they stand on both legs, one stretched, the other slightly bent. They micturate as white men do (the Coras sit down). To answer calls of nature, they go, like other Mexican Indians known to me, quite a distance from their dwellings.

The body is well balanced in walking, even with old men. Out of fifteen persons I observed—two of them women—twelve turned their toes in. They place the heel down first and walk with quick steps in an easy way, and with some energy. The head is well set and carried slightly backward. The knees are somewhat bent, and the arms swing, hanging with the palms to the thigh. Their attitudes are easy. In moving a heavy object they push it.

They have three ways of swimming : (1) As the Mexicans, *a brazo partido*, one arm at a time thrown upward and forward; or (2) both arms simultaneously downward, the hands pushing down and backward, without coming together ; or (3) like the dog; this mode is used when they have burdens. They dive head first. They are experts at climbing trees, cutting footholds with the machete held in the right hand, and carrying bow and arrows with them. In this way they hunt squirrels.

Huichol Climbing a Tree.

They have no power to move the ears or scalp, and they have difficulty in keeping one eye open while shutting the other, though they generally succeed. Their feet are made but slight use of for holding objects; for instance, in weaving the ceremonial back-shields, the man, sitting down, holds the little weaving-frame in place with his big toes. In winter-time the Huichols suffer from colds, so much so that they are sometimes confined to the house, lying down most of the time. An inflammation of the eyes, with suppuration, is quite common, and swellings of various parts of the body also occur. Malarial fever is not frequently met with, yet occasionally some die from it. Pneumonia, too, is rare, and cases of small-pox are hardly ever severe. Insanity is unknown.

I was told that in case a husband is not a shaman, or has not the proper understanding, a shaman must be called in to " compose the stomach " of a pregnant woman, that her child may be born right. It is easy for

him to do this, since he sees everything, as if she were
"transparent, like a bottle," to use a shaman's expression in telling me about this custom. Few fathers, unless
they are shamans, are present when their children come
into the world. The woman ties a girdle tightly around
her waist, but does not squat down until labour commences, when she holds on to a pole or stick. Another
woman is always present to take up the baby, and the
umbilical cord is cut with a stone. The mother immediately bathes herself without taking off her clothes,
which she allows to dry on her body. She follows no
diet, but eats whatever fruit may be in season, and goes
about her work as usual. The child is nursed until the
next one comes, and gets besides any food the mother
may take. Many little ones die from diarrhœa caused
by unripe fruit, and the mortality among children is
greater than among adults.

Infants, in going on all-fours, do not put their knees
to the ground as white babies mostly do. It is a curious
sight to see these youngsters before they can stand up,
moving in this way almost like monkeys and very fast,
but, of course, for no great distance at a time, as they
like to keep near their mothers. I took instantaneous
photographs of some of them, persuading the mother to
make her child creep by stepping aside and calling it.
At Galup railroad station, in New Mexico, I noticed a
Zuñi baby going on all-fours in this same way.

There are from eight to ten children in every family.
Up to the age of five or six, boys and girls run about
naked, the boys playing with bows and arrows, the girls
with balls of cotton-wool; but there are no games of
any kind among the adults in the Huichol tribe.

The children have not much love for their parents,
though the mothers are much devoted to their little
ones, and never ill-treat them. Occasionally older ones

PLATE IX.

Sidney Starr

PLATE X.

may be punished, if, for example, they carelessly break some earthenware. Though apt to be spoiled by their mothers, the children are never rough; in fact, at ages varying from five to ten years they are charming, handsome, and attractive, and never rude or forward.

Mothers always object to waking a child. When I once sent for a little one to photograph it, the mother, although she knew that she would be well paid for it, replied that she could not bring the baby, because it was sleeping. Another time, while I was photographing a little boy, the mother took him away as soon as he fell asleep, without even allowing me to finish my exposures.

The Huichols occasionally made comments that betrayed very fair reasoning powers. One of them once said : " If Christians pray to the saints that are made by the carpenters, why should not the Huichols pray to the Sun, which is so much better made?—"Why is it necessary to have a priest in order to get married?" they wanted to know on another occasion. " It is a matter between the two, who can meet at the house of their parents and establish the union."

Though lazy, they have a certain will-power. When they make up their minds to do a thing, opposing circumstances never deter them from doing it. No amount of money could bribe them into neglecting any of their many duties toward the gods, such as the preparations for a feast, the making of arrows, the putting up of snares, the clearing of the fields, etc. Anyone who approached even with an urgent business proposition an Indian thus employed, would get for answer, " I am engaged, and cannot listen to you."

That jealousy is highly developed among them is shown by their strenuous resentment of matrimonial indiscretions. Of course there are some couples who

live peacefully together all their lives; but as a rule
hearts are easily won and easily lost. A husband in
his rage may even beat his wife, or she, on discovering
that her spouse has been led astray, may be so offended
as to leave him. On the whole, the women are more
faithful than the men. The sexes are dependent upon
each other in more ways than one; for one provides,
the other prepares
the food. Nowhere
as much as here
do hunger and love
keep the world a-
going. When a sep-
aration occurs, if the
angry wife remains
obdurate for weeks
and months, and can-
not be induced to
come back to the old
home and grind the
corn, the deserted
one has to look out
for another partner.

Huichol Young Couple.

An independent girl may put several lovers on probation before she decides with which of them she is willing
to share her life. Under such liberal conditions the fair
sex is much more appreciated; and this being so, the
women as a rule are able to decide their own fates.
Their position in the family is high. If someone comes
to the house to buy something and the woman objects,
there is no sale. On the other hand, being so rigorously
sought after, the women in this tribe are less well preserved than among the other tribes I visited.

Young people show affection in public, kissing and
petting each other; but the women do not like white

men even to touch them. Courting or wooing is exceedingly brief, and there are no love-songs for either sex. If a boy takes a fancy to a girl whom he sees in her home or at a feast, he goes to her with some

Huichol Ribbon. Main Pattern : Two Banana Leaves with a Flower between Them.

present, a grey squirrel, a fish, a crayfish, or something of similar value. If she likes him, she may make a ribbon for him, and they get the consent of their parents and are married. The girl goes to fetch water in the night, and the man goes for wood. On the second day they fast and run deer. The parents of the girl give to the boy clothes, an axe, a machete, and a deerskin in which to bring wood.

Among the young people, the man seeks the woman ; but among persons of more mature age the woman seeks the man. Formerly the young people were strictly separated, but at present, so an old man told me, no one watches his daughters. In many cases neither the boy nor the girl asks the parents' consent. They make their agreement at a feast where the violin is played, and, though the parents when they hear of it are very angry, the affair is easily settled by the native courts.

According to the ancient marriage customs, still in vogue in some parts, only the old people can arrange marriages properly, as a well-brought-up girl never says "yes" at once. It devolves upon the father of the boy to secure the girl. Having first consulted his son as to whether he likes her, he goes to her house, and after sunset begins to talk of his errand in a speech which continues for five nights. If a man does not know how to do this he has to hire a shaman to talk for him at a price of a dollar a night. He commences his oration with the beginning of the world, and narrates many mythological events, in order, as he expresses it, "to reach the birth" of the Goddess of the Western Clouds, the Aphrodite of the Huichols, in behalf of the girl, and that of the Sun, in behalf of the boy. Matters will not be right with the gods if the account does not start with the beginning of things; the offspring of the match, for instance, may be malformed. Therefore, the birth of all the gods has to be explained. The narrative is especially sad when, on the fifth day, he reaches the birth of the mother of the girl, and his own birth, and he weeps, and apologises for touching the painful subject. At last he comes to the point. " Pardon me, if my words have offended you, but I now want to know the naked truth : Is there a woman here suitable for a young husband ? " The parents then go to ask the consent of the girl, to whom nothing has yet been said about the matter. If she refuses the suitor, her father has to make his reply in a speech of five nights, also beginning in chaos, because, as he expresses it, he does not want to die in the birth of the Mother of the Western Clouds. If she accepts he is spared the effort, and, therefore, the girl is strongly urged to smile upon the proposal.

In the case of a happy solution, the boy, on the fifth day, accompanied by his mother, joins the father in the house of the bride-elect. All the uncles and aunts gather to give good advice to the girl, and to tell her not to have any fear. The mother of the bride hands the young couple a reed mat on which they are to sleep, and the father covers them with a blanket.

Her parents take off her skirt and tunic, which they withhold from her until morning. Often the bridegroom has to use all his strength to overcome her natural modesty, as she is capable of making violent resistance, sometimes even striking him heavy blows. She may have to be taken to bed by force, or the mother may have to stay with them all night. There is always the further risk that in the morning, when her clothes are returned to her, she may run away. The parents therefore watch her night and day. Every morning when they bring the couple food they make them sit together, and try to induce her to eat with him, saying : " You cannot always remain alone. Give in to this boy," etc. Some of the guests go, but many still remain in order to see the end, because, if she persistently objects, the marriage will come to nothing. At last, when the bride receives food from the groom, it is a sign that she positively accepts him.

Next the shaman is sent for to make "medicine" for the wedding-cake, which consists in tortillas and beans, and the eating of it by the couple constitutes the marriage ceremony. The shaman makes his incantations over the food early in the morning, praying to Father Sun to help him properly to unite the two people. He breaks a tortilla in two and talks a little to each piece, beginning with the crackling of the fire, that is, the speech of Grandfather Fire. Then he gives one piece to the boy and one to the girl, who are to exchange them. She may even now throw her piece to the ground, but the father picks it up, and she is made to eat it. Sometimes the parents bring in a stick to give weight to their arguments, and if she still remains obstinate they may carry their threats into execution. As soon as she eats her piece, all is considered arranged, even if she does not take any other food that day. The shaman now tells them to be faithful to each other, holding up to them, as an example, the matrimonial loyalty of the macao, the bird of the God of Fire, and the raven, the bird of the Huichol Goddess of Love. He also prays to these birds, who to this day go in pairs. They were people in ancient times and married in the right way ; therefore they are asked to bless the marriage, that the young couple may never separate.

Nowadays the native judges more than the shamans arrange matrimonial affairs, and with such "modern improvements" to aid and abet connubial vagaries the strictness of olden times is becoming more and more obsolete with the growing generation. The ties of marriage were probably never very strong among the Huichols ; yet while guarded by religious beliefs they were far more secure than now, when nothing but the fear of corporal punishment, lashes and the stocks in prison, restrains the people from indulging their fancy too freely. In marrying a couple the judges never invoke the help of the gods ; they simply tell the con-tracting parties that from now on they must live to-gether, under penalty, if one should run away from the other, of being punished. Fear of punishment has never and nowhere brought about moral reforms.

I may state here that among the Indians I know, there is no feast-making connected with the marriage ceremony ; at least, nothing to compare with the day and night celebrations attached to the feasts for the gods. With the "neighbours" it is all the other way. Their weddings are the greatest feasts of their lives. A young Mexican, who for a long time was in my employ, told me that a man has to work for three years in order to earn enough to pay his wedding expenses, to which his father generally has to add his share. As a rule, the latter contributes the most important item, the bridal outfit, which has to be provided by the groom's family. The expenses at this man's wedding ran as follows :

The bride's clothes, including a fortnight's trip to town to obtain them..............................	$120 00
The padre's fee..........................	15 00
The judge's fee for the civil ceremony................	5 00
An ox, other food, brandy, etc., sufficient for eighty guests.	90 00
Total......................................	$230 00

The men are well content to pay for the trousseau and the wedding, according to custom, for they say it pays well to get a wife : she watches the property !

Vol. II.—7

CHAPTER VI

SCARCELY had the Indians dispersed when a Mexican on horseback appeared, an unusual sight in these mountains. He came from the Director Politico in Mezquitic to take a census of the western side of the Huichol country, in accordance with the order of the Mexican Government that it should be taken that year (1895) for the whole Republic. The Huichols belong, politically, to Jalisco, and the Governor of that State is, aside from the Federal Government, their highest authority. Under him is the Director Politico in Mezquitic, with whom the tribe mainly has to deal.

The census man had been much impressed by the terrific thunder-storms of the sierra, and asked me how I could endure them. Never before had he experienced such violent storms as on this journey, nor had he ever come upon so many trees split by lightning. He was accompanied by his brother, who had permission to dwell in the Huichol country, and who kept on good terms with the Indians by treating them fairly. As he had a Huichol wife, he was regarded by the tribe as one of them. Moreover, his business contributed toward

his popularity, because he manufactured mescal and employed only Indians in his distillery. This man knew
most of the important Indians, and was a great help to
his brother in bringing the people together and explaining to them the object of the visit. Many of the Indians received Spanish names for the occasion, as it was
impracticable to take down their aboriginal appellations.
In running through the list afterward I noticed that
nearly half of them had adopted the name "Cross" (*de
la Cruz*), the word being of special significance to them
on account of the embodiment of their cosmic views in
that emblem.

This changing of names was confusing to some of
the natives, who could not always remember the Spanish
names of their wives and children, or even in some instances their own. One of them, when asked for the
name of his son, answered, "He is entire," meaning that
his native name had not yet been taken away from
him.

The native names of the people are derived from
mythological incidents, or from the names or attributes
of the deities, or from natural phenomena. Every man
among the Huichols is the son of some special god,
every woman the daughter of some goddess, and their
names often indicate this. Women are also frequently
called after the maize plant in the various stages of its
growth. The grandfather, or, in case he has not sufficient knowledge, the shaman, dreams the baby's name
and gives it to the little one when it is five days old.
The ceremony of naming is performed about eleven
o'clock at night, when the child is bathed with water
from some spring near its birthplace mixed with water
from various other springs. Five days later the child is
taken to Santa Catarina itself and bathed in the springs
there. I was assured that some people had no names

because their parents were too poor to pay the shaman his fee of twenty-five centavos.

After about ten days' work at counting, the Mexicans went away, and the commotion they had brought about among the Indians, which had been very interesting to me, subsided. The officials averred that a record had been made of all the inhabitants of the western side of the river, with the exception of about 200, whom neither persuasion nor threat could induce to report at San Andres. This census, which was taken simultaneously in Santa Catarina for the eastern side of the river, gives the tribe a total of about 4,000 Indians, some 1,500 of them belonging to the western side.

In the meantime the two messengers I had sent to Tepic returned after an absence of about three weeks. They brought me some photographic films, a few tins of preserved meat, and $75 in silver, the latter just in time, as I was almost entirely without money. Asked about the unusual delay, they told a " hard-luck " story about lightning that had struck them twice, and caused their feet to swell up so they could scarcely walk. They had also come near being stopped and searched, because the Government, advised that a revolution was brewing in the Sierra, had ordered a sharp look-out, and only on being shown a letter which the commanding general of the Territory sent me would the officials desist from opening my films. Besides all this, with the Indian's characteristic lack of appreciation of time, Maximino had lost two days before starting out, in singing to cure a little child of his companion, and two days more had been spent in his house on his return to rest after the fatigues and excitements of the journey.

It had ceased to rain for a space of ten or twelve days, as it always does in August, but had started again, and travel was still impossible. I was now ready to explore the eastern side of the country, if only it would stop raining for two or three weeks, so that the river I had to cross might subside sufficiently to allow me to ford it. The chances otherwise were that I could not get away until October or November. I told the Indians jokingly that I was going to pay a shaman to sing in order to stop the rain because they had had enough, and I wanted to get away ; but they declared that the rain could not be stopped, no doubt because, with so many shamans all over the country singing for its continuance, my shaman's voice would be drowned.

I had not yet visited Santa Catarina, the Mecca of the Huichols, where are the main sacred places and the principal temple of the tribe. It may be seen from the extreme limit of the mesa of San Andres, high up on the other side of the river, and from that point may be reached on foot in about half a day ; but the track is too dangerous for pack animals. I was compelled to make a rather long circuit, going first about fifty miles to the north, crossing the river Chapalagana at a ford called Las Puentitas, and then turning southeast as far as Mezquitic, just outside of the Huichol country. This town was my immediate aim. Once there, I knew that with the help of the Mexican authorities I should be able to get men to take me to Santa Catarina. It is true that the brother of the census-taker had warned me that the alcalde of Santa Catarina was not in favour of my coming. The alcalde had declared, he said, that if I, a *protestante*, and therefore a very bad man, should enter his village, the people would surely kill me ; but having gained good standing among the people on this side of the river, I felt confident that I should be able to overcome the opposition of those on the other side also.

The difficulty of getting men hampered me as much as did the rain. Sometimes I had secured three or four

and was only seeking the others, when the first grew tired
waiting and deserted by the time I won new recruits.
Many refused my offers because the feast of squashes
was coming on, after which they had to start on their
long journey to fetch hikuli. Most of them had no
desire at all to go, being averse to departing from their
everyday routine. Carillo's son-in-law, through whose
influence I had hoped to get men to accompany me,

Huichol Woman Grinding Corn on the Metate.

had for some time promised to come to the village from
his ranch ; but days came and days went without bringing him. Every time I asked Carillo about him, he
said, " He will be here *mañana y otro mañana* " (the
day after to-morrow and another to-morrow). The day
of my departure seemed further off than ever when the
Indians, in addition to the feast, began to busy themselves with clearing their fields from weeds, a work undertaken three times before the corn is ripe.

Meanwhile with the help of the native authorities

I engaged three women to come to my camp to make tortillas and toast, and dry them so that they could be carried along as provisions whenever I got ready to start. Mexicans on their travels always take a man cook along, but men among the Huichols do not grind on the metate or boil beans; and hence I felt the need of laying in as large a supply of these staples as was practicable. Making tortillas, however, is very slow work, and, as my women had to be fed on the product of their labours as part of their payment, the net result was discouraging. After a number of days there was only enough on hand to carry the expedition for twenty-four hours. It was only upon my at last succeeding in engaging two women to cook on the road that my difficulties seemed to lighten.

This happy result was brought about mainly through the arrival of a handsome young Indian, Pablo, who one day, *sans façon*, entered my window and told me in good Spanish that he wanted to go with me. At first I thought him rather too much Mexicanised for my purpose, but I soon discovered that he was the very man I needed. We quickly became friends and remained so for months to come. One of the kitchen fairies fell in love with him, and, when he decided to go with me, quickly made up her mind to accompany us. A young man and his wife soon followed suit.

My sweet little Indian girl Flower-Skirt also expressed a desire to continue cooking for me when I should go away, though her family objected. She had gradually, from being wild as a roe, become quite tame. I had taught her some Spanish, and was often amused by her quick wit and merry, natural ways. She confided to me that her aunt was very angry with her. One day I missed her, and on inquiry learned that she had been taken away by that relative to be married to

the latter's lazy son, her cousin.   Of course, it was of
advantage to the woman to have the hard-working girl
in her family ; and the poor child, an orphan, with no
one to protect her, had to submit to her fate.

Through Pablo's and Maximino's efforts I soon secured the men I needed.   Besides these, as few of the
Huichols, if any, know how properly to manage mules,
of which I still had eight, I engaged as chief packers
the two Mexican boys in Don Zeferino's family.   At
last, after having spent nearly all day in packing the
mules and getting things ready, I was able, on August
27th, to make a start from San Andres.   A good many
people were present in the afternoon to see the white
man depart.   Having mounted my mule I rode over to
bid the women good-bye, when Carillo's wife stepped forward and offered me her hand, as she had learned to do
from the Mexicans ; at the same time, to my utter surprise, turning her face aside and weeping.   I was still
more astonished to see that the other women, too, were
visibly affected, most of them weeping silently.   This
flattering tribute might have turned my head, if it had
not occurred to me that this sadness was, perhaps, as
much due to parting from all the things that so often
had gladdened their hearts—beads and red flannel, not
to mention raisins and the small bells they were so fond
of sewing to their dresses—as from me.

As we passed the house of my friend Carillo, he unexpectedly joined us, stepping out with his blanket
folded in the manner of the Huichol traveller, that is,
hanging over the pouch at his side.   I had altogether a
party of twelve men, Indians except for the two Mexicans, most of whom were required to carry my ethnological collections.   Boxes being unheard of in the
Huichol country, I had packed the articles in parcels
suitable for each man to carry, wrapping them, as far as

possible, in coarse cotton cloth. As my belongings were
of every conceivable size, form, shape, and colour, the
procession looked fantastic and picturesque enough.

Until one can secure boxes, there is
no better way to transport such
wares over rough country than on
the backs of the Indians, the most
careful carriers under the sun. The
only damage could come from the
rains; but in the afternoons, if the
clouds were ominous we hurried on
as fast as possible to a place to put
up my tent, under which they could
be safely stored for the night. I
always slept by the side of my treasures.

Pattern of a Huichol
Pouch.

The alcalde and Don Zeferino, according to the
time-honoured custom of the country, accompanied me
on their mules to our first camping-place, where we
arrived at dusk, after a ride of six miles. The Indians
at once disposed themselves, half sitting, half lying, on a
very big sloping stone, on which cold, hard bed, most of
them without any covering, they slept all night. We
supped on the provisions we had brought with us;
everybody was very tired, and soon all were fast asleep.

As was to be expected with so many inexperienced
hands, things did not move very smoothly the first
days. The mules, after nearly three months of idleness,
were unmanageable, and gave us no end of trouble.
Almost every ten minutes the packs had to be rear-
ranged. Although the two Mexicans were taken along
expressly for the mule service, it was necessary for the
others to help them—after their own leisurely fashion.
Every time Maximino lent a hand in straightening out
the packs, he had to put down his two bundles—one

containing the precious votive bowls, the other the ceremonial shields. The bowls had to be handled with the

Designs of the Grey Squirrel in Textile.

utmost care, because if they rubbed against each other,
or if the sun melted the wax, the beautiful bead pictures

Pouch with Squirrel Designs. Width, 13 ctm.

on them would be destroyed. One young Indian frightened the mules with a big black cylinder, part of a Cora
distillery, which he carried on his back; and the many
jars, quivers, arrows, and carved dancing-sticks did not
tend to quiet them. Yet we managed to get along
without accident, though still with much apprehension
on my part. The track, which follows the high ridge
northward, was bad, and the road heavy. Sometimes
the trail disappeared altogether.

Before long great excitement sprang up over the discovery of a grey squirrel (*Sciurus nayaritensis*). The men left their bundles, and, yelling lustily, started with their dogs to give chase. The squirrel ran swiftly up a pine tree, but was cornered and killed. Part of the excitement was due, no doubt, to the fact that squirrels are not only valued as a great delicacy among the Huichols, but are also of much importance in their religious life. The squirrel, indeed, is one of their great hero-gods, and played an important part at the time when the

Pouch with Row of Squirrels. There Are also Two Rows of Doves with a Deer inside the Design of each Dove. Width, 27.5 ctm.

Sun was born. The Huichols, like the Aztecs, believe that they themselves made the Sun.

In the beginning, the Huichols will tell you, there was only the light of the moon in the world, and the people were much inconvenienced. The principal men came together to see what could be done to give the world a better light. They asked the moon to lend them her only son, a limp and one-eyed boy. She first

objected, but at last consented.   They gave the boy a
full ceremonial dress, with sandals, plumes, and tobacco-
gourds, and his bow and arrows, and they painted his
face.   They then threw him into an oven, where he was
consumed ; but the boy revived, ran under the earth,
and five days later arose as the Sun.

When the Sun radiated his light and heat over the
world, all the nocturnal animals—the jaguars and the
mountain lions, the wolves, the coyotes, the grey foxes,
and the serpents—became very angry, and shot arrows
at him.   His heat was great, and his glaring rays blinded
the nocturnal animals ; and with eyes closed they retired
into caves, water-pools, and trees.   Still, if it had not
been for the grey squirrel and the gigantic woodpecker,
the Sun would not have been able to complete his first
journey across the sky.   These two were the only ones
who defended him ; they would rather die than allow the
Sun to be shot, and in the west they placed tesvino for
him, so that he could pass.   The jaguar and the wolf
killed the grey squirrel and the gigantic woodpecker,
but to this day the Huichols offer sacrifices to these
hero-gods and call the squirrel father.

From their diurnal habits it is believed that these animals are the Sun's companions and delight in his company.   The woodpecker carries the colour of the sun
on his magnificent scarlet crest, and that the squirrel
knows more than other animals is shown from his hiding
nuts and finding them again.

At our second camping-place I was rather surprised
to find that the Indians, Carillo taking the lead, had
stolen a lot of new squashes from a lonely field we
passed on the road.   Of course, I knew that the Huichols have no very clearly defined ideas in regard to
property rights ; nevertheless, the incident astonished
me, as the eating of this vegetable is forbidden until

the feast of squashes has been celebrated.   Perhaps the
restrictions are binding only upon the owners of fields,
so that these fellows, not owning the land, need not ap-
prehend any misfortune for themselves or their own
crops.   Pablo was an honourable exception.   He told
me that though he passed close to a big squash he let
it alone.   But he was a shaman, and knew the consequences better.

The following day we arrived at Mesa del Venado,
an insignificant plain some 500 feet long and 300 feet
broad.   Here lived the brother of the man who had
taken the census in San Andres, and he showed me some
ancient remains near by.

These included some small ridges of earth showing
the ruined site of a small pueblo, which could not have
belonged to the Huichol tribe.   This was significant,
inasmuch as the Huichol country, until very recently, extended at least fifty miles farther north.   Thence we descended about 300 feet into a gorge where two caves
lay close together.   They were quite shallow, and the
interior walls were entirely covered with the pickings
of figures representing mostly snakes, suns, and female
genitalia.   These carvings undoubtedly owe their origin
to the Huichols.

I should have liked to look for skulls in some caves
a little farther down and near to the river, in one of
which a shaman had told me the ground was covered
with skeletons, with a stone image standing among them.
However, access to them from where I was would have
been difficult, and an excursion would have cost me at
least two days.   The weather being exceedingly unset-
tled, and clouds gathering again, I felt that I must give
up the idea, lest the river should rise and cause me the
loss of another month.

The men I had sent ahead to clear the track from

brushes in the most difficult passages had done their work well ; so we descended without mishap into warmer regions, and arrived at a level spot in the Arroyo de Tapexte. It was not a particularly attractive camping-place, with little or no grass for the mules in the dense tropical shrub surrounding it, water nearly an hour away in the arroyo below, and, worst of all, the ground on which we had to sleep covered with small stones, the abode of numerous scorpions. As soon as camp was made, Pablo, who in spite of his rather youthful looks was quite an experienced shaman, took the necessary precautions against these obnoxious creatures. He mixed a little ground corn with water which he put into a shallow gourd bowl, and from this made an offering to the god in our camp-fire, throwing a little of the meal with his forefinger to the four sides of the fire and into the middle of it. He then made a circuit of our camping-place, making a like sacrifice three times to the scorpions. What Pablo secured by these offerings was : from the Fire, health and luck ; and from Elder Brother Scorpion, consent not to sting us. The dreaded creatures were apparently satisfied with the payment they had received, for in spite of the great number of them nobody was stung.

That night it rained copiously, and the next day the road was heavy. At last, however, we caught sight of the river, which at a distance looked brown and muddy. To me it seemed very large, but my heart was gladdened by the Indians, who with one voice declared that it was " dry," that is to say, passable. We hurried on, following the zigzag track down the hillside, reached the river, and lost no time in crossing it. Although the water was high, the passage was effected without accident, and I felt easier when I had all my men, mules, and collections safe on the other side. Beyond this was no other

Part of Huichol Ribbon.   Double Flower Design.

water-course to detain me. One hour after we passed, the water, which had been rising all the morning on account of rains higher up its course, commenced to swell with great rapidity, and the crossing became dangerous. In the evening it would have been impossible to reach the other side, and no one knows how long I might have been detained if I had reached the stream an hour or two more tardily than I actually did.

One of the pack animals in ascending the river embankment lost his foothold and was nearly killed. When Pablo brought the poor old beast in he remarked to me : " How can you expect an animal that carries a dead one to get on well ?   It is sure to give out before long." This revealed to me that the Huichols, too, have the same superstition regarding the dead that is common throughout Mexico. It also showed that the Indians not only knew that I had taken a skull away from Guayabas, but also which of the animals was carrying it. The Indians know everything that happens in their country, although a traveller may think they do not. To an astonishing degree they also get information of what may happen of interest to them outside of their country—almost as if they had newspapers or telegraphs.

We cleared the brush from an ancient village site about one hundred feet above the river, and made our camp. The Huichols could give no clew as to the origin of these rude low stone walls, at present barely recognisable. I slept within one small circular enclosure of stones put on edge, in diameter just as long as my bed.

No doubt these ruins belong to the same period as the remains of ancient habitations just mentioned.

The next morning we worked our way laboriously up through the rich grass lands to the top of the slope which forms the east side of the valley. The hacienda of San Juan Capistran could plainly be seen to the north, but, though there is a crossing of the river at that place, I was told that at this time of the year it could seldom be forded with pack-mules. There was a sort of raft ferry built by the hacienda, but it was not reassuring to know that this was liable to frequent upsets on account of faulty construction and the inexperience of the men handling it.

Gradually as we advanced, the view toward the north became more and more extended. The western ridge of the Huichol country appeared to grow steadily lower, and to the east and northeast of the river quite extensive lowlands spread themselves, slowly rising again toward Huejuquilla el Alto. In an easterly direction lay the broad, fertile valley within which the villages of Soledad and Tezompa are situated. They formerly belonged to the Huichols, who still remember that they had temples in both places; but in recent years this part of the country has drifted entirely into the possession of the "neighbours."

As we arrived among Mexican settlements I was in constant anxiety lest some inquisitive stranger should interfere with my unsophisticated carriers, and pilfer some of my best things, though inappreciative of their value. The procession of Indian men and women, gaudily dressed and carrying so many curious, brightly coloured objects, presented an extraordinary appearance and was sure to attract attention. I tried to keep the train together, but, tempted by the ripe fruit of the nopal, the men would stroll ahead, or linger behind

with their strange burdens, assuring me that they knew
the way of the Mexicans and how to get on. About
one league east of Soledad, a rich man from the village
called at my camp. He examined my belongings with
great curiosity, and was anxious to learn the object of
my visit. " Can it be to ascertain about the lands ? " he
suspiciously asked one of his companions. He owned
more than the others, and perhaps felt some twinge of
conscience for having driven the Huichols from their
property. On hearing that he had rice from Tepic for
sale, I sent Pablo over to buy some, and once more enjoyed this food, which for a long time I had not been
able to obtain.

The eastern ridge of the Huichol country consists, in
the north, where we were travelling, largely of ranges of
hills that run in a southerly and northerly direction, some
7,000 feet high, growing lower northward. South of the
two villages the plateau rises slowly, and is less fertile.
The valley of Mezquitic, east of this ridge, is much
broader and of a higher elevation than the valley of the
Huichol country. East of Mezquitic, toward Zacatecas,
the ridges still have a tendency to run north and south,
but these are outside of the Sierra Madre ; and where the
long, broad, fertile valleys of Jerez and Villa Nueva are
encountered the country gradually merges into the central plateau of Mexico.

When making ready for the start next morning we
missed one of the mules, and lost a whole day searching
for it. It was extremely difficult to get the Indians to
look for the animal. I sent them out in different directions, but most of them returned in half an hour saying
that they could not see it anywhere. Some of them
remained away longer, probably lying down to sleep in
a cool place. Altogether it takes almost superhuman
patience to manage Huichol " help." They are unwill-

Part of Huichol Ribbon.   Pattern: the Toto Flower.

ing to depart from their own slow way of doing things, and have no idea of what one might reasonably expect from them.   Exasperating almost beyond endurance is one's inability to move them when something is urgently needed, the difficulty of mastering their language aggravating the situation.   Some will not even answer when one addresses them.   If I gave one an order, the reply might be : " I am taking breakfast," or, " Julian will go, I am engaged," etc.   And if I wanted to make the cook hurry dinner I was sure to find her occupied hunting vermin in her lover's hair.

What could I do ?   They were easily offended, and if I allowed myself to get into a rage, they would quit on the spot, without even stopping to ask for their wages. It is hard enough to starve among Indians in order to study them, though certainly the information gained compensates one for all privations—but it is a different matter to depend upon them for progress on a journey.   I had to endure it all, and to give my orders very clearly, as if talking to children, counting on the possibility of repeating my words three or four times, and then philosophically console myself with the thought that even a snail once climbed a mountain.

There was, however, one advantage about this enforced waiting—the women got time to make tortillas. There is more work than one might imagine in preparing this national dish of Mexico ; and the two women cooks had, during the journey, to work late in the even-

ing and early in the morning to provide even a scanty
supply for the large party. The metate was loaded on
one of the mules, and the women had to carry the rest
of the cooking utensils, the jars of clay, the gourds, etc. ;
no great weight, but tiresome on a hot day, and I had
constantly to make concessions to them.

The Mexicans have a saying that as long as you give
something to a Huichol he will work for you ; but as
soon as you stop giving he will leave you. Still, one
has to use discretion, for the more one gives to the Indians the more they want, and a liberal traveller is apt to
be imposed upon. Nor do they consider themselves
under any obligation to you for your presents or kindness, but in spite of such favours will ask prices just as
high as before for anything you want to buy from them.
However, if you suggest to them that you have given
them much, and they, too, should give you something,
they will see the fairness of your propositions and comply.

One of the cooks could only be brought to work by
her husband. She was a docile young woman of a nice
disposition, but dependent entirely on the whims of her
lord and master, whose jealousy she feared. He was
something of a scamp. His first wife had run away
from him, and the present one on a recent occasion,
after a flogging, threatened to follow her predecessor's
example ; but, luckily, before my start from San Andres
the couple had become reconciled and decided to go
with me. Her devotion to him did not seem much
diminished by occasional thrashings. She continued
very meek and careful in her behaviour, hardly daring
to look up for fear someone might speak to her and
provoke his anger. He appreciated her submission,
and at present all seemed sunshine. Like true Indian
lovers they showed their affection in the way common

to all primitive people. She had lost all her hair in a recent illness and, though the new crop was quite short, he went through the motions in the conventional way.

Altogether love played a considerable part in my progress. I should not have gotten on at all had it not

Pablo.

been for the other cook's infatuation for Pablo. Anxious to retain his affection, the lazy woman would grind all day at a word from him. He had also taught her to answer at once when I spoke to her, and not, as the other women were wont to do, show her modesty by silently turning her back to me.

Fortunately I have never, in my travels among aborigines, been without a friend to alleviate the annoyances unavoidably connected with such experiences. Now it was Pablo who showed valuable qualities and true sincerity of friendship for me. While the others were frittering away their time in useless and silly pretences of tracing the lost mule he suddenly came forward and offered to look for it. " I assure you," he said, " I will not return without having seen it." He told me that once when on a journey to the hikuli country he had lost a mule at this very place, and had found it again by taking a zigzag path through the forest. Accordingly he provided himself with food in order to sleep out if necessary, hoping, however, to return next morning in time for our start. Sure enough he came back in the evening : he had discovered the mule grazing with some wild mares. As it would have been useless for us to attempt to "cut her out," having no corral to run them into, I decided to leave the mule, and send for her later from Mezquitic.

Pablo was a rather short but powerfully built fellow, with a face that was winning by its gentle, kindly expression. I judged him to be about thirty-two years old, though he looked much younger. He came from the northwestern part of the country, and his people, whose district formerly had a temple of its own, now worshipped at the temple of San José. His manner was very affable, and he was a great favourite with the women, although as yet he had not decided to take one for good and all. Being free and independent of family cares, he had had no trouble in making up his mind to go with me, and the longer he remained with me the more serviceable I found him. Strangely enough he was free from the two particular defects of the Huichol character, stealing and lying. Like all his countrymen, he was slow to move, but when I called he was pretty certain to come sooner or later, though sometimes not until my patience was almost exhausted. One annoying peculiarity was that, like Mr. Pickwick's Joe, he could go to sleep at any time—after breakfast, in the middle of the day, or in the afternoon. He was always found sleeping ; it seemed to be his main occupation. I could not put him to watch anything, for he was sure to fall asleep before long. Once I sent him to fetch water for me, and, as I did not particularly impress upon him the need of returning quickly, he took a bath, and returned in two hours instead of fifteen minutes. Yet his mild temper always disarmed my provocation. I could not help sometimes giving him a sharp reprimand,

which would have caused others to leave me, but not
Pablo, who was as patient with me as I was with him;
and, as I say, he never deceived me, so I came to like
him sufficiently to put up with his failings.

Although he dressed as a Huichol Indian, he spoke
Spanish fairly well, having occasionally worked in the
cotton and maize fields of the Tierra Caliente. He
therefore at least understood me when I spoke to him,
and could communicate to the others what I wanted.
Last, but not least, this young shaman gave me much
valuable information in regard to his tribe. He knew
everything about the religious observances, customs, and
habits of his compatriots, who unanimously declared
that one day he would be a very great shaman indeed.
As I learned to look at things from his point of view,
he always spoke to me with the sincerity and convic-
tion any good shaman displays when one has gained his
confidence.

CHAPTER VII

OUR PROCESSION EXCITES THE WONDERMENT OF THE MEXICANS—
ARRIVAL AT MEZQUITIC—ANCIENT REMAINS—A HOT SULPHUR
SPRING—THE TEPECANO INDIANS—AN INDIAN LOVER—HIKULI-
SEEKERS—THEIR PILGRIMAGE—CONFESSIONS—THE SACRED
YAKWAI—WHAT THE PILGRIMS HAVE TO ENDURE.

FROM the summit of the ridge we saw Mezquitic
on the eastern bank of the river, which at that
point is quite insignificant. The place, with its pretentious church-towers, looks at a distance quite a town,
although in reality its inhabitants, mostly poor, do not
exceed 1,500. Its name, which is of Aztec origin,
means "Among *mezquite* trees" (mizquitl); and the
Huichol designation has the same meaning.

At a small ranch in its outskirts, we met two women
greatly excited at our procession, who ran after us exclaiming : "Pray, sir, what is all this ? And what do
the boxes on the mules contain ?" I had already passed
as they came out, and, as I could see no objection to
gratifying their natural and quite excusable curiosity, I
left my two Mexicans to answer them and rode on.
But these wiseacres evidently entertained other views
on the subject, and the poor women, who would have
welcomed any break in their monotonous life, got very
little satisfaction. It is an inviolable rule with Mexican muleteers never to tell outsiders what they are carrying, or whence they come or whither they go, and
to give evasive answers to all questions of that sort—a
habit originating in the state of insecurity that for cen-

turies prevailed throughout the land, and has only recently been abated.

We passed by many thriving cornfields, and on September 9th, having pulled down part of a gateway to
allow my mules with their bulky burdens to pass, entered Mezquitic. I installed myself in the meson, and
after having, in accordance with my custom, washed and
cured the backs of my animals, had a square meal in the
kitchen. It was a great relief to be at rest, and to have
no longer to depend on my fickle Huichols. Although
my living here was of the most frugal kind, there being
no fresh vegetables, my stay was an agreeable change
from the rude life of the past year. The climate is unhealthful, and in the summer before the wet season the
heat between the glaring white adobe walls is as fierce
as that from a furnace; but I found the people excep-
tionally nice and kind. It is said that there are no
thieves among them.

The burning question with me was always how to
get a check cashed. Having succeeded in that matter with the *director politico*, I paid off my men and
discharged them, with the exception of Pablo and one
cook, and Carillo and his son-in-law. These I thought
would be of assistance to me in making some excavations
in the neighbourhood, or doing any work that might
turn up.

My collections, which I laid out in my room, made
quite a museum, a standing wonder to the Mexicans, who had never thought that the Huichols had so
many and such pretty things. Not even the Bishop of
Zacatecas, they said, when, sixteen years ago, he made
his missionary journey to the Huichols, had been able
to secure a single ceremonial shield, of which I had so
many.

One day some men from Santa Catarina came to

Mezquitic to buy candles, bread, and chocolate for a rain-making feast. They paid me a visit, and on catching sight of my votive bowls they were moved to tears by their beauty, and at once began praying aloud to the gods to whom the bowls were dedicated. No doubt they would have liked to keep them for themselves, but this being out of the question they endeavoured to get as much good out of them as possible, and each of them on departing left an offering of one centavo in the bowl of the Goddess of the Eastern Clouds. They had not had enough rain yet !

There are ancient remains in the valley of Mezquitic, as well as in the neighbouring country, especially to the east and southeast, consisting in traces of houses and villages, mounds, etc. At Monte Escobedo I later on bought some large obsidian lance-points and arrowheads, which had been found with skeletons in a cave at a depth of ten yards. Near Valparaiso, to the north, I heard that large jars with comparatively small openings had been found in the bank of the river, with human bones inside. There is also a large cave near Colotlan, where many small earthenware objects had been taken out, some tiny jars being of especial interest. A Mexican here carried about, attached to his girdle, an ancient pair of sandals, believing that as long as he had them he would never lack for anything to eat.

On account of a difficulty in procuring boxes, it was some time before I could get my collections packed for transportation to the United States. This work at last finished, I left town with my four Indian followers for an excursion down the river, arriving first at the village of Nostic. This name is a Spanish corruption of the Aztec Nochtic, " Where there are nochtli " (the tuna, or fruit of the nopal cactus). The Tepecano name for the village, Návtam, has the same significance. Most of the

people here are Aztecs who have long since forgotten
their native language, and are lazy and indolent.

Rumours about me and my intention to make excavations soon attracted many people. Of course they all
thought I was looking for silver and gold, and brought
me proposals accordingly. Some told me that fires
were frequently seen at night on the slopes of the
mountains and in some of the old village sites, a sure
indication of minerals and buried treasures, according to
the common Mexican belief. One widow sent me
word that there might be a chance of finding money
in the courtyard of her house, where sometimes moan-
ings and the clanking of chains were heard. It was
thought that her husband came to see his money. He
had been rich, but had buried his hoard and died without
telling anyone where it was. Everybody thought it
must be in that courtyard, and wanted to make an agreement with me to excavate and share the profits.

The valley of Mezquitic is at the bottom seven or
eight miles broad and very fertile. Some fifteen miles
south of Mezquitic it narrows, and the mountains form
at last a narrow cañon which forces the track to follow
the river in innumerable crossings. Farther down on
the same river is the well-known mining town, Bolaños.
I made my camp scarcely a quarter of a mile from Agua
Caliente, a name given to some copious hot sulphur
springs found close together on the east bank of the arroyo at the foot of an almost perpendicular rock about
1,000 feet high. These springs have for the last fifty years
enjoyed great fame for their curative properties. They
have been dammed in, and a few rough houses erected
close to them, for patients who in the dry season, from
January to April, come to bathe here. Now and then
large stones become detached from the rock above and
fall down, making the bathing establishment somewhat

unsafe for use, at least during the wet season. Some cases of syphilitic and other cutaneous affections are alleged to have been cured here in nine days. If half the cures credited to the water are true, it must have high medicinal properties. Baths are taken twice a day. The water is very clear, but leaves a yellow sediment, and is so hot that you can barely hold your hand in it. The perspiration which it induces, and which is still further increased by drinking a glass or two of the water, is almost appalling, as I can testify from personal experience. I heard that some people faint in the bath before becoming accustomed to the heat, and I can readily believe it.

While in this vicinity I made excavations in various burial-caves in the neighbourhood, and the objects found seemed to belong to the Tepecano Indians. It had been my intention to go farther down the river to see the Tepecanos at a village called Alquestan, a name which should be correctly pronounced Asqueltan, meaning "Where there are *asqueles*" (small ants). The native name of the place, Totonaltám, has the same significance. But I had to give up this trip, as I was not feeling at all well at the time. I succeeded, however, in having three members of the tribe come to see me. They were dressed in the ordinary garb of the working classes of Mexico, and were altogether civilised Indians, and seemed talkative and impulsive. I photographed them, took down some of their language, which is a branch or dialect of the great Nahuatl family of languages, and got some notes on this tribe, which calls itself "the people" (Xumátcam). The Huichols refer to them and to the Tepehuanes as Wáculi, a name which they also give to a mountain near the mining town of Catorze, their name in full for the eminence being, of course, "Elder Brother Wáculi."

According to my informants the Tepecanos have at present only two villages, of which Alquestan is the more important. While the adults there still speak their mother tongue as well as Spanish, the children are rapidly losing their native language, because many Mexicans live in the village. When my visitors were children, they said, they had seen men and women wearing their hair in one braid, and the men used breech-cloths (*zapeta*). But the "neighbours" are now growing all-powerful and often destroy the sacred emblems and arrows which the Indians place in the mountain caves.

The Tepecanos pray much to the mountains, and sacrifice to them votive bowls, ceremonial arrows, and glass beads. Anyone who wants a favour from a mountain must do a great deal of fasting, and visit it on five consecutive days. The tribe also do reverence to a human head carved out of solidified volcanic ash, such as I had been excavating. Another practice is to keep large serpents to watch their gardens. They believe that when the serpent strikes the earth with its tail it shows its watchfulness and drives away evil and robbers. Every shaman has a tame rattlesnake in his house, and, when he wants to know something, he takes it up, holds its head toward the east, and talks to it, the reptile responding from the five regions of the world.

The Tepecanos still keep up their feasts, but celebrate them privately, as the "neighbours" ridicule their customs. The feasts, all of which must be preceded by a great deal of fasting, are the following: The Feast of Green Corn, in September; of Pinole, on January 5th; and the Feast connected with the Planting of the Corn, in April. The ceremonies attending the latter festival are repeated until it rains. On the altar (tapexte) is placed a large votive bowl adorned with glass beads and filled with wads of cotton; underneath the cotton are some precious stones, which my informants significantly called *chalchihuite*, in Tepecano kapaksósum. The sacred cactus hikuli is used by them and called by this name. As recently as three years ago the Tepecanos themselves went for the plants, but now they buy them from the Huichols. A form of common hemp called *mariguana* or *rosa maria* (*Cannabis sativa*) sometimes takes the place of hikuli. The leaves of this injurious narcotic are smoked throughout Mexico, but mostly by criminals and the depraved.

Formerly there was an exchange of hospitalities between Alquestan and Nostic on the occasions of the feasts. The religion of the tribe is evidently very similar to that of the Huichols. They, too, use gods' eyes and other symbolic objects, and they still had many things to show me if I would go to see them.

In recent times many families of the Tepecano tribe have emigrated farther down the river on account of scarcity of rain and consequent bad harvests. I was informed that these colonists lived in caves in an utterly demoralised and miserable condition.

On my return to Mezquitic, toward the end of October, I let Carillo and his son-in-law go back to their own country, as for some time they had been anxious to do. I suggested that they should take my cook along, because one of the Christian feasts was approaching, and, as she was a tenancha (a kind of church charwoman), she would be needed there. But she positively refused to be separated from her lover, and Pablo had to escort her home. He declared, however, that he would come back. The Mexicans laughed at my belief in him, and cited their proverb: "The Indian, the bird, and the deer are gone when they are gone." But after five days this extraordinary Huichol returned, having faithfully performed his mission. He saw his would-be sweetheart well over the river, gave her provisions, and then came quickly back again. "She wept very much," he said, but he himself seemed to have no regrets. Perhaps I felt more pity for her than he did, but maybe he was justified. Two months later, on his return from an errand for me to San Andres, he told me that he had seen her with a new beau.

Twice during my stay at Mezquitic I was visited by parties of home-bound Huichol hikuli-seekers, October and November be-ing the season for their journeys in search of the sacred plant. They all were disgustingly dirty, the hikuli cult forbidding them to wash them-selves. They were also much emaci-ated and exceed-ingly hungry, and they highly appre-ciated the food I gave them.

Huichol Hikuli-seekers.

When the rainy season is over and the celebrations at-tending the harvesting of squashes and green corn have been duly observed, the thoughts of the tribe turn toward the far-away protecting genius of their country, the little cactus called hikuli (Vol. I, page 356). The locality in which the sacred plant is gathered is not far from the mining town of Real Catorze, in the State of San Luis Potosi. The journey consumes forty-three days. Delegations are sent from each of the main temples. Sometimes it is difficult for a district to get up an expedition because of the severe fasting and the restrictions imposed, especially on the leader; but patriotism, with the certainty of substantial benefits in the shape of rain, good crops, health, and life, is generally sufficient incentive to an Indian to subject himself to the requisite privations.

The parties consist of from eight to twelve persons. Before starting on their pilgrimage they take a bath, and then go to the temple, where they and their wives sleep that night. In the morning the men pray much, standing around the fire with their bundles, bows, and arrows. Some of them have tails of the grey squirrel attached to the crowns of their hats, and all carry tobacco-gourds, an essential part of the outfit of the hikuli-seeker, who thereby assumes a priestly function. These small, round gourds are raised for the purpose; those with many natural excrescences being the most highly valued. Each gourd is provided with a string and

Tobacco-gourd, a Necessary Adjunct of the Priest. Width, 10.7 ctm.

a stopper, and is worn hanging from the shoulder. A man may have as many as five tobacco-gourds rattling against each other as he walks; some of which contain a little tobacco, but most of which are empty. The hikuli-seekers sacrifice five tortillas to the fire, and with a deer-tail sprinkle over their heads water in which certain herbs have been steeped. Everyone now bids farewell to his wife, placing his right hand on her left shoulder, and saying: "Good-bye! We shall meet here again." All weep, both men and women.

The mules are packed with trays of split bamboo, one hanging from each side of the animal. In these trays plants will be brought home, but at the start they contain tortillas, the provisions for the journey. Four captains are selected, two of whom walk at the head of the party and two in the rear. The principal leader represents Grandfather Fire and is called by that name.

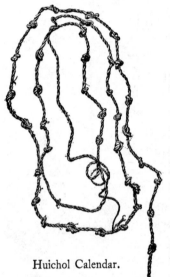

He carries in his pouch the fire-making implements, and is the only one allowed to strike fire while on the road.

The pilgrims now start on their journey, one behind another, while one of the principal men remains in the temple, constantly following them in his thoughts day by day. For this purpose he has a string of bark fibre with as many knots as there are days in the journey. The principal leader of the hikuli-seekers is provided with a similar tally. Every day one knot on each string is untied. As the travellers always camp at the same places they are kept in touch with the people at home and thereby protected from accidents. When the hikuli-seekers return, each of them puts the string calendar twice across his back, once around each foot, once around the body, then down to each knee. This is done inside of the temple, and the watchman does the same with his calendar; thereupon both tallies are burnt.

Huichol Calendar.

The women contribute toward the safety of their husbands by never walking fast, much less running, while the men are on the road. They also do their share toward securing the benefits expected from the journey by subjecting themselves to restrictions similar to those imposed upon their husbands. From this time until the feast of hikuli is given, which may be four months, neither party washes except on certain occasions, and then only with water from the hikuli country. They also fast much, eat no salt, and are bound to observe strict continence.

Anyone who infringes on this law is punished with illness, and, moreover, jeopardises the result all are striving for. Health, luck, and life are to be gained by gathering hikuli, the drinking-gourd of the God of Fire; but inasmuch as the pure fire cannot benefit those who are impure, the men and the women must not only commit no transgressions for the time being, but must also purge themselves from any past sin. In the afternoon of the fourth day, therefore, all the women gather to confess to Grandfather Fire with what men they have been in love from the beginning of their lives until now. They must not omit even one ; if they should, the men would not find a single hikuli. In order to help their memories each one prepares a string made out of strips of palm-leaves, on which she has tied as many knots as she has had lovers. This twine she brings to the temple, and standing before the fire she mentions aloud all the men she has scored on the string, name after name. Having finished, she throws her list into the fire, and, when the god has accepted and consumed it in his flame, all is forgotten and she becomes clean. No hard feelings result from these confessions, for the important thing is to become clean and to get the hikuli, and if the god of fire has righted the wrong it must be forgotten. From now on, the women are averse even to having men pass close by them.

The men make a similar confession a little before

arriving at a place called La Puerta de Cerda, on the other side of Zacatecas. They have recalled all their frailties and made knots in their strings as they walked along. In the afternoon of that day, when they go to camp, they first "talk to all the five winds," and then deliver their "roll-call" to the leader to dispose of,

Country West of Zacatecas, Traversed by the Hikuli-seekers.

that is to say, to burn. Pablo told me that when he went on the hikuli journey he made twelve knots, besides seven for instances where women had caught him by the hand or the arm or the shoulder. Now the hikuli-seekers are gods, and henceforth the four captains fast until the party arrives in the hikuli country, still five days distant; that is, they do not eat anything except stray hikuli which perchance they may find on the road.

The leader also carries the yákwai, a ball of native-grown tobacco, called in Mexico *macuchi*. After having passed the Puerta de Cerda the solemn ceremony of distributing this tobacco is performed. In the afternoon ceremonial arrows are placed toward the four quarters of the world; and in the middle of the night the men are still seated around the fire, to whom the tobacco belongs. The leader, having prayed much, places the ball of tobacco on the ground, touches it with his plumes, and prays aloud. Then he wraps very small portions of it in pieces of corn-husks, so that they look like diminutive tamales, and hands one such little bundle to each member of the party, who places it in a special tobacco-gourd tied to the quiver, apart from the other ones. To the Huichols this act symbolises the birth of the tobacco, and those who have the sacred little parcel have to watch it very carefully and are separated from the rest of the world. From this time on, the men must preserve strict order on the march, and no one is allowed to pass another or to go by himself. If one should have to respond to a call from nature, he advises the one walking next behind him and hands him his tobacco-gourd to hold until he comes back. Meanwhile the whole file stops, and the journey is not continued until the man returns, receives his gourd, and resumes his place in the line. The order in which they follow each other is strictly adhered to, as well on the return as on the journey out, and also during the time of the preparation for the hikuli feast. When making camp at night, they take off their tobacco-gourds, and, having rested them on a bed of grass spread on the ground, place them in the crates of the mules. Not until this duty is performed are they allowed to walk about at their ease. If anyone should pass in front of a hikuli-seeker, he would be regarded as having offered an insult, and would be sure to fall ill very soon. Should a Mexican on horseback happen to get ahead of a party of hikuli-seekers, he would not ride very far before he and his horse would drop to the ground, because the wrath of the sacred tobacco and the arrow of the God of Fire would be aroused.

On account of the yákwai, the men on their return home generally remain in the temple, while their wives

sleep in the houses.   Women must never touch the tobacco, nor even the gourds in which it is carried, for if
they did they would fall ill.   All households are afraid
of the hikuli-seekers, none of whom ever enters a
house, but takes a seat outside if he has to make a business call.   Finally, at the hikuli feast, the sacred little
bundles are given back to Grandfather Fire—in other
words, they are burned—and then the men cease to be
" his prisoners."   Considering the sanctified character
of the tobacco, it was very flattering to me to have a
shaman in San Andres give to me the name of Yakwai.
In accordance with the custom of the tribe he had
thought the matter over until he dreamed a name, and
after several days he announced his decision, for which
he charged the regular fee of twenty-five centavos.

The route the hikuli-seekers take is from beginning
to end full of religious associations.   Once upon a time,
long, long ago, the gods went out to seek hikuli, but
they grew tired and remained out there ; and as the
Huichols now travel, they meet their deities all along
the road, in the shape of mountains, stones, and springs.

The dreams of the men on the road are of great importance in deciding the religious arrangements for the
coming year—who is to make the fires at the hikuli
feasts, and who is to sacrifice cattle during the dry season in order to get rain.   If one party of hikuli-seekers
meets another on the road, they stop for half a day to exchange salutations.   Even when two Huichols encountered each other in ordinary life I used to hear the names
of the gods pronounced by both as part of the greeting,
each calling down divine blessings upon the other.

On arriving at the ground, as soon as the mules
have been unloaded and taken care of, the Indians fall
into line, and each man places an arrow on his bow and
stretches the string, as if ready to shoot, pointing the

arrow toward the six regions of the world, first toward
the sun (east), then to the right and the left side, then
backward, then upward, and at last downward, without letting it fly. They are presently to shoot the
plants as if they were deer, because in ancient times

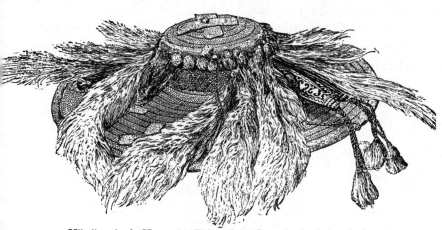

Hikuli-seeker's Hat, with Tails of the Grey Squirrel Attached.
Diameter, 49.5 ctm.

hikuli first appeared as a deer. Therefore, the captain, indicating a high mesa, which is considered the
principal altar, says, "Yonder is the deer, standing at
the first altar." But only he sees it. Then they march
forward, still with their bows drawn, aiming ahead, the
advance being directed by the four captains. If any of
them sees a hikuli, he shoots toward it, but takes care
not to hit it, as the plants have to be taken up alive.
One arrow lodges to its right, and another to its left,
the two crossing each other over the plant. In this way
everyone shoots at five hikuli on the march, without
stopping to pick up either the plants or the arrows.
Thus they proceed to ascend the first mesa, where the
captain saw the deer. Having reached the top, they all
make a ceremonial circuit, and the deer assumes the
shape of a whirlwind, but only to disappear again, leav-

ing in its track two hikuli, one toward the north, the
other toward the south.

At this place the pilgrims leave their best offerings
—beautiful votive bowls, arrows, back-shields, paper
flowers, coins, and glass beads—as prayers for health,
addressing as usual the five winds of the world. They
also ask the hikuli, which in former times were people,
not to make them crazy. This ceremony completed,
the signal is given to return, in order to pull up the

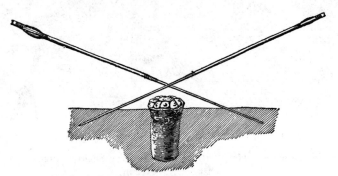

Diagram Showing Manner of Shooting a Hikuli.

hikuli and the arrows left with them. They find the
latter covered with dew. Each man carefully takes up
his five plants, and again they ascend to the first altar,
where the offerings were left. They eat some hikuli
with great delight, as a kind of fruit. The deer, which
before had been seen only by the captain, now appears to all of them, because they are under the influence of hikuli. Offerings similar to those left on the
mesa are also deposited in the various sacred springs of
the locality.

The men now gather plants for three days, taking
them up with the help of knives, but without injuring
them. The proceedings are in reality an imitation of
the deer-hunt, the first day being, as they express it, the
running of the arrow of Grandfather Fire, the second

day the running of the arrow of Great Grandfather
Deer-Tail, and the third for all the gods.

On the fifth day they start homeward. First, each
man places a hikuli in front of him, and asks it for luck
on the road. The camp-fire is always built so that the
logs lie from east to west, the direction in which the
men travel. Just before they start, they reverse the
logs. In the same way from now on they sleep with
their faces toward the west, while on the journey out
they slept looking east. The whole train makes a ceremonial circuit around the fire-place, and the journey
westward is begun. Most of the hikuli are packed in
the trays brought along for the purpose; but a good
many are threaded on strings, and festooned around the
mules or carried by the men, the latter mode of trans-
porting the plants being evidently the ancient and original one.

As the women are not allowed to accompany the
men on this journey, the female portion of the population at the outset prepare tortillas for the travellers to
take along. The hikuli-seekers are supposed to fast
mostly, and the supply is, therefore, by no means made
abundant, so that on the return trip it generally gives
out. The pilgrims may buy food from the "neighbouri,"
but it may happen that for days they will have to sub-
sist on fresh hikuli. In El Valle, five days' journey from
home, the returning travellers are always met by people
from their district bringing them a fresh stock of tortillas, though not a sufficiently large one to remove the
traces of starvation and privation impressed upon the
pilgrims during all these weeks of want and exertion.
Consequently, they return to their homes much emaci-
ated and reduced in weight, but highly elated at having
accomplished their task and fulfilled their duty toward
the gods. However, the pleasure of marching to their

temple is still deferred. Upon reaching the big pine forests that border their country, they must hunt deer for two or three days before they can make their triumphal entry into the temple, where for some time to come they will make their headquarters, engaged in running deer and preparing for the feast of hikuli.

CHAPTER VIII

BEFORE starting out again into the mountains, I had to send to the town of Colotlan (Aztec, "Where there are scorpions"), a distance of seventy-five miles, to have a check cashed. As the messenger had been despatched for me by the Mexican authority, no trouble was spared by the merchant in filling my order, and, beside the cash, my courier brought back some fresh though rather miserable vegetables, and, still better, a dozen tins of condensed milk. The dealer, in his letter accompanying the goods, expressed his gratification at being able to procure these tins for me, as condensed milk is seldom seen in Colotlan. Visions of future treats rose before my mental eye from this product of civilisation, of which I am very fond. But on opening the first tin, what was my disappointment to find it spoiled! I opened another, and another, and another—they might have dated back to the time when preserved milk was invented. The *fata morgana* of luxury disappeared. My aspirations had soared too far beyond the safe level of tortillas and beans.

At last, in the middle of November, having been detained for a week with malarial fever, I started toward the Huichol village of Santa Catarina, travelling in a southeasterly direction. The first day we advanced far enough to make camp a little way up the sierra,

where we found the air refreshingly cool after the heat
of the valley of Mezquitic.

The high elevation of the eastern part of the present
Huichol country makes it generally undesirable for settlement. The Indians have allowed one "neighbour"
to reside here at a place called Chinacate (Wild Onion),
in consideration of a small annual sum; but he finds it
difficult to eke out a living by agriculture, because the
maize does not thrive well and is frequently nipped by
frosts.

I was desirous of visiting the temple of Pochotita,
half a day's journey north of Santa Catarina, and not
much out of my way. Pochotita means "where there
are *pochotes*," silk-cotton trees. The native name Ra-
wéyapa has the same significance. We experienced
considerable difficulty in finding the track from the
sierra down to the temple, because Pablo, though he
had been here before, could not at first find the path,
and there were no Indians living here to direct us. By
and by, however, he got his bearings.

Even in this lonely forest the Huichols have their
sacred places. Pablo pointed out to me, on a beautiful
little meadow, the remains of an ancient temple, some
insignificant hillocks, not half a foot high. Later, as
we looked down into one of the precipitous gorges that
yawn from the edge of the sierra, our eyes fell on a row
of gigantic rocks along one side of the cleft. These,
Pablo said, were ancient people who had tumbled
down there; hence the name of the place, Taimarita,
"They fell down."

Ancient people are, of course, gods, and the whole
country is full of what we might call natural fetiches.
Offerings of food and water, as well as ceremonial
arrows, must be made to many of them, because they
are alive and their help is needed to protect the cattle

and to bring rain and good-luck. They are stones of peculiar shape or colour, generally chalcedony, and they are particularly plentiful around San Andres.

Some years ago a couple of priests visited that locality and were shown a heap of such fetiches. In their zeal to abolish idolatry they broke two of the stones, the curious shape of which suggested long, stretched necks, limbs, etc. But their action in no way influenced the Indians' opinion. A change in that direction could only be brought about by carrying away, not only every piece of chalcedony in the land, but every stone the shape of which suggested a figure, human or animal.

We attempted a descent, but the track proved too dangerous for the mules. One of them rolled down a small precipice and flew at least seven yards through the air before she landed on her back. Luckily she was carrying the sacks of corn, which broke the fall and saved her from hurting herself. There was nothing to be done under the circumstances but to turn the mules and retire to the plateau above. Here we made camp for the night, and I sent Pablo with one of the Mexicans down to Pochotita to clear the road and to get men to help us down. They returned next day with a lot of bashful Indians, and we immediately began the descent, each man taking a mule by the halter and carefully guiding it along the dangerous places.

Pablo reported that the hikuli-seekers had arrived some time ago at the temple and were preparing the feast of welcome to the plants, which was to commence that afternoon. During the last part of the descent along the steep but fertile slopes, I could discern people moving between the temple and two or three ranches scattered over the little hillside valley.

Pablo, no doubt, had impressed upon the people the importance of my visit, because when I approached the temple I found that the brushwood had been cleared so as to form a broad path, about a hundred yards long, leading down to the edifice. It was a kind of triumphal road, such as might have been prepared for a bishop or

The Hikuli-seekers Painting Their Faces.

other great dignitary, though no such personage had ever found his way into this lonely hamlet.

There were some big aguacate (alligator-pear) trees growing close to the temple, and the ground about them had been made ready for my camp. I felt pleased at the good-will of the Indians, but, remembering the constant noise to which I should be exposed night and day, I selected a camping-place a little farther off from the place of worship.

Inside of the temple, in the rear, hung on the wall heavy strings of hikuli, like gigantic necklaces. These were to be used in the coming year. Many were to be ground and mixed with water at the hikuli feast, which was to be celebrated as soon as the necessary number of deer were killed. As the Huichols always want a goodly number of them, the feast rarely comes off before January.

All the time the preparations are in progress, as well as during the feast itself, the hikuli-seekers and their wives paint their faces with various designs in yellow, the colour of the God of Fire. The colouring matter is obtained from a root which, as well as the stone on which it is rubbed and the water with which it is mixed, is brought from the hikuli country. When the hikuli-seekers arrive at the temple on their return from the journey, not only their faces and wristlets, but also the heads and legs of the mules that carry the loads, are decorated with symbolic designs. The tobacco-gourds, too, are almost always adorned in a similar way.

White men are inclined to consider the painting of the face, which is met with in savage and barbaric people, as a childish extravagance. But primitive man does nothing that is meaningless, as we find out, if we take the trouble to look into the matter. The face-painting with the Huichol always represents the faces, or masks, of certain gods, and expresses prayers for material benefits, such as rain, luck in hunting deer, good crops, etc. I reproduce here two paintings of hikuli-seekers' faces.

In the one to the left the barbed lines on top, sides, and chin are clouds. On the cheeks and nose is a picture of cornfields, the barbed longitudinal lines on the sides showing the boundaries of the fields. Between the boundaries are ears of corn, indicated by spots.

The illustration seen to the right shows four hikuli. On the nose are clouds. On the middle of the forehead are two coiled serpents, symbols of rain, and three rows of clouds. From the clouds fall rain, depicted in the

Facial Painting of Great-Grandfather Deer-Tail.

Facial Painting of the Goddess of Western Clouds.

vertical lines on each side of the face. The effect of rain is pictured by the grains of corn painted as spots below, as well as a squash vine with fruit and leaves painted over the chin.

Shortly before sunset the hikuli-seekers seated them-selves in a group on the ground outside of the temple, most of them holding small mirrors before them. The paint was applied with a straw. A few who did not know the art well were painted by others, and the women are as expert at it as the men.

The ceremonies commenced with prayers for luck, all the hikuli-seekers standing around the big fire in the temple. Then the wives entered, with their faces well painted, and some of them wearing wreaths of flowers in their hair. They seated themselves in the background, apart from the men. As on this occasion no one but a hikuli-seeker may take a light from the temple fire, another fire had been built farther back in the temple for the women and the people at large. Most of the women had their children with them, and busied themselves with ministrations peculiar to all primitive people. The fitful light from splinters of fat pinewood that flared up brightly under the curling smoke revealed a scene which, with its striking shadow and light effects in the smoky, shifting atmosphere, might have made a fitting picture for a Rembrandt. To my mind, the light and the fire conjured up views of ancient Norway, when the torches blazed in the log-walled hall of the vikings, in which the faithful wives sat awaiting the return of their seafaring heroes.

Presently the pilgrims seated themselves in their chairs and began to sing about Great-grandfather Deer-Tail, the Morning Star, and all the other gods, who, long, long ago, had gone out to fetch hikuli. The singing continued throughout the night, but there was no dancing. The women all the time kept strictly to themselves, and at sunrise each one of them was in exactly the same spot on which she had seated herself the evening before.

In the morning the men, and afterward the women, washed their faces, heads, and hands in water which had been brought from the hikuli country. At this I was rather dismayed, because they had agreed to be photographed with their paintings on. But they assured me that after a while they would paint themselves again. Until the great feast comes off, these people frequently decorate their faces in this way. With clean faces, men and women next came out from the temple to salute the rising sun. The procession was headed by two men, one of whom carried incense in an earthenware vessel, the other a small bowl, containing water from the hikuli country, with a few flowers in it. They made reverence to Father Sun, waved incense toward him, and with the flowers sprinkled water to the four quarters of the world, while praying for life and for luck in hunting deer. This ceremony was so short that I had barely time to get my camera ready before they returned to the temple. I wanted them to let me photograph the scene, but there was one shaman in the assembly who objected. He had brought for sale at the feast a muleload of sugar-cane, the poor man's candy in Mexico, and—though I had observed that shamans were as a rule more modestly dressed than ordinary Indians—was gotten up very showily in embroidered clothes. He was very excitable, though a good-looking man, and now stepped forward and declared, "Our Lord the Sun does not like this to be repeated." Nevertheless, I placed my camera on the tripod, and invited the people to look into the focussing-glass. Usually it amused them greatly to see the figures upside down, and they would gradually consent to pose; but on this occasion everybody hesitated, as if afraid to approach the strange thing. My fanatical antagonist, among others, took a hasty peep into the glass, and immediately turned back with a very serious expression on his face.

Now, among those present was an Indian who, as a boy, had been one of the nine taken up by the Bishop of Zacatecas. He spoke Spanish very well and took my part. Stepping into the temple, he made a speech, explaining to the people that photographing had not harmed anyone in San Andres; why should it here? "This man comes recommended by the Government," he continued, "so you had better give in." But the opposing shaman re-entered the temple and made an eloquent appeal, turning first to the fire. "Who is the father of the fire?" he asked. "Does the foreign man know that? He comes here to take pictures. It is no good, and when the people submit to it they will die.

That is what Grandfather Fire tells me. If this man uses his machine here, against the will of Grandfather, I am going to sing, and call the Goddess of the Eastern Clouds and her of the Western Clouds to hunt him off."

As was natural, the shaman's speech made a deep impression, and the people hung back. But I did not

A God-house in Pochotita.

give up, nor did my zealous friend. He threw himself into the fight again, yet without much effect. To end the controversy, I said to the people : " If you do not want to be photographed, it is by no means necessary ; you may have your way." This set them thinking, and I felt confident that by and by they would yield. The indignant shaman loaded his mule and departed for his ranch near Santa Catarina, where I was later to feel his revenge.

After he had gone, some of the men came and told me that they could see no harm in being photographed; all the hikuli-seekers, they said, and their wives, would have their faces painted and allow me to take their pictures. The difficulty, to my surprise, thus ended in a complete victory for me. The same afternoon I photographed the men, and next day the women. Two years later, when I revisited the tribe, I learned that my adversary had died while singing in the temple. His demise added to my prestige, as it proved to the Indians that I had the greater influence with the gods. " He was a fool to oppose you," they said, and in this I could not but agree with them.

In order to reach Santa Catarina from here we had to climb up the track on which we had come down, and, after going a few miles farther along the edge of the ridge, descend to our destination. Though none too easy, the track here was passable, and we arrived in the village early in the afternoon, but only to find it deserted. My adversary from Pochotita had told terrible stories of my killing people by hanging them head downward. This he had seen himself, as he had looked into the murderous machine. Accordingly, the population, with the exception of two women, had left, fearing they might be strung up by the feet. The alcalde, too, was away on his ranch, though he was expected back the next day. La Comunidad looked dark and uninviting, so I pitched my tent on a little slope just above the temple. I hardly know how I should have been able to procure the necessary food for the day had it not been for a friend I had gained in Pochotita, and who had followed me here. He helped me to buy a sheep on one of the adjoining ranches. As the people of Santa Catarina are poor, it was difficult to obtain among them such a luxury as mutton.

Santa Catarina is, perhaps, the smallest Indian pueblo I have seen. It consists of eleven little huts scattered here and there between zapote-trees. If it were not for the usual adobe buildings of Spanish missionary times— the church, the curato, the court-house, etc.—the casual observer might think himself on an Indian ranch.

The pueblo lies on comparatively level ground, on the top of a little spur, from which in all directions, ex- cept toward the east, deep gorges and valleys run down to the Chapalagana River. There is fine mountain scenery all around. From the main valley immediately below us to the west rises the Tiger Mountain, famous in Huichol mythology and sheltering the principal sa- cred caves of the tribe. But the most characteristic feature is the high range, the western part of the Huichol country, that looms up in front of one across the river. Toward the south is a deep gorge which contains the sacred cave of the Goddess of the Eastern Clouds; and on the plateau beyond, but hidden from view, lies the pueblo of San Sebastian. Prominent toward the east are two hills, one above the other. They are considered ancient men, companions of the God of Fire, and they are called Tōapúli ("where there is amole"), a name also applied to the pueblo of Santa Catarina.

Only a stone's throw from the Christian church stands the heathen temple, which, with a number of god- houses surrounding its spacious patio, forms an interest- ing group of buildings. This is the principal place of pagan worship in the country, and it bears itself boldly alongside of the old church, expressing in silent but eloquent language the state of culture of the Indians.

There is no striking difference in the sizes of the various temples. The largest, that of Santa Catarina, dedicated to the God of Fire, measures thirty-six and a half feet from north to south, and thirty-four feet three inches from east to west, and is thus as nearly circular as one could expect. The wall is about seven feet high and two feet thick, and is made of stone and clay, plastered over with clay inside. The doorway reaches all the way up to the roof, and is five feet wide. A bench of stone and mud runs along the inner side of the wall in

The Temple of Santa Catarina and Adjoining God-houses, Seen from Northwest.

the eastern half of the temple for the comfort of the participants of feasts. At the door-opening, however, a threshold takes the place of the bench, with two steps on the outside.

The roof is supported by two upright pine poles forked at the top, and a third pole resting horizontally between them. The uprights stand between north and south, at some distance from the wall, and a little farther in than the fireplace. Around each of them, at the height of a man's head, is tied a ring of deer-antlers on which the men may hang their pouches, tobacco-gourds, and the like, while engaged at their work in the temple. All the woodwork in the building is from "the male pine," the poles being stripped of the bark. A special kind of coarse grass is used for thatching the roof.

There are peculiar arrangements in every temple, the utility of which is not at first sight obvious. High up under the rafters and next to the beam are fastened several long, thin bunches of grass. These represent opossums, who in ancient times stole the fire from the gods to bring it to the Huichols, and who are still watching it from the ceiling. Threads of bark fibre run underneath the roof toward the four cardinal points, crossing each other in the centre. These make the house secure against wind and lightning. Any other evil that threatens the building is warded off by two bunches of big leaves which rustle with the slightest stir of air. The floor is of earth, and before a feast it is always sprinkled with water. Through the action of the dancers' feet it has become quite level and hard, so that no dust rises from it.

The main feature in the interior of the temple is the fireplace (áro) in the centre, a circular basin of clay with the rim slightly raised above the floor. While a feast is in progress, the fire is kept burning; at other times the hearth is brimful of ashes and two pokers of wood are lying on either side, each on a kind of shelf in the brim. In the illustration one shelf may be noticed. The object lying across the ashes is the poker of the God of Fire, also called his arrow. The point is placed toward the west.

As the fire is always in the middle of the temple or the house, so the temple of the God of Fire is in the middle of the Huichol country or, from the

Huichol point of view, in the middle of the world. At
other than feast times the temples present a sombre
appearance, and the gloominess inside is heightened by
the murky roof, which contains no outlet for the smoke.

The Fireplace in the Temple of Santa Catarina. Diameter, 4 ft. 5 in.

Soot hangs from every vantage-point and covers everything with a coating of shining black.

Inside of the temple, in the wall toward the west, is
a row of small niches or recesses, like large pigeon-holes.
One or two similar cavities may also be seen in the wall
toward the north and south. Each of them is devoted
to a god, and an officer of the temple has charge of
each of them and its god. Here are kept the ceremonial
objects, from their first inception until they are taken to
the sacred places for which they are intended. Flowers
may also be offered in these niches, with loud praying.

In front of each temple is a square open space with
a few god-houses on the sides. In Santa Catarina this
plaza measures eighty-four feet from east to west, and
sixty-four feet from north to south. Three of the god-
houses are made of adobe, but the others, five in number, are of the usual stone and mud construction. In
this temple are twenty-two officers, each called after
the god whose custodian he is, and of whose sacred

places he has charge. The most important of these officials, as may be expected, is the one who represents the
God of Fire, and he is the general superintendent of all
the sacred places belonging to the temple. The duties
of the officers are mainly the making of ceremonial
objects, arranging the feasts, and providing the wood for
the temple fire. Their wives bring water, sweep the
floor, and cook the food at the feasts.

Apart from these officials, a man is selected to serve
as the singing shaman of the temple. He ranks higher
than any other shaman, and his dignity is even greater
than that of the guardian of Grandfather Fire. In fact,
he is the spiritual head of the community, and sets the
dates for all the feasts and observances in accordance
with communications he is supposed to receive direct
from the gods themselves. This singing shaman, or
maleákami, is the actual chief and even superior to the
tatowán, or gobernador.

An officer is always watching the temple on behalf
of maleákami, and, therefore, with his family, lives close
by the sacred building, in a god-house, or under some
boughs. All the officers, as well as their wives, are
pledged to strict faithfulness toward each other during
their term of office. They are chosen every five years,
when the temple, too, is renovated, freshly thatched, etc.
A great feast, lasting a week, inaugurates each cycle of
five years, and the day of Guadalupe, the patron saint of
Mexico, always falls within that week.

CHAPTER IX

AS soon as the alcalde arrived, I went to see him. I found him a very bright man, who had been considerably among the "neighbours," and who spoke Spanish quite well. He had, of course, for a long time been hearing much of my doings, but was now convinced that no harm could ensue from my presence here. He was the very alcalde against whom I had been warned; but he was a shaman, and somehow or other, I always get on with that class of men, the only exception that I can recollect being the eccentric member of the profession who had opposed me at Pochotita.

I had a satisfactory meeting with the principal men, all of whom agreed to meet my wishes; but first they had to take a trip into the sierra, where the "neighbours" were encroaching upon their forests. I secured two Indians to go to Tepic for my mail, and a man named Felipe, who had a ranch near by, rented me three cows, which I had one of my men milk. That settled the question of provisions as far as I was concerned, so much so that one of the Indians said to me: "You do not eat tortillas or beans, only milk, milk. How is

that? Perhaps you are a god?" Yet the people of
Santa Catarina are the least accommodating of all the
Huichols. Being great travellers and coming much in
contact with the whites, they have become spoiled.
They are in a sense the men of the world among the
tribe, in the good and in the bad signification of the
term. Because they possess the main temple and most
of the main sacred localities they consider themselves
superior to their compatriots.

No sooner had the men gone to settle their difficulties with the "neighbours" than a party of hikuli-seekers arrived. To my great delight, such trivial matters
as boundary disputes could not divert these men from
their religious devotion. All they wanted was to procure the necessary number of deer for the feast that was
to come off by and by. Until then they lived mostly in
the temple, the starting-point for their hunting expeditions. The custom is to run deer for five days in
succession, after the seekers have duly prepared themselves by fasting. They pray and sing throughout the
night, and at the first flush of dawn come out of the
temple, perform the rites incidental to the start, and are
off with their dogs before the sun is clear of the horizon.

On returning in the afternoon, none of the hunters
go far from the temple. They generally sit about in
their chairs resting and meditating, and wait for the
evening to come in order to renew their singing and
prayers. The longer the time before the requisite number of deer is brought in, the more excited the men
grow, and the more strenuous are their efforts to induce
the gods to grant their prayers. The pauses between
the singing, generally two or three in the course of the
night, are by and by reduced to one short stop. The
supplications become more and more fervent, and when
in my tent, some hundred yards off, I heard the great

Huichol Deer-Hunting Song

Transcribed from graphophone.

It is part of a long song, which tells of the adventures of the Red-headed Vulture, who is a great magician, and with his beak revived the deer, which the gods had killed. The gods caught the vulture and took his arrows from him, at a sacred mountain called Airulíta, which is red in color, and another locality credited with the birth of the fire. Since then the vulture cannot kill his prey, but has to eat corpses.

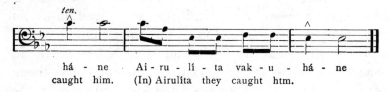

Víleke Víleke vak-u - há - ne   Víleke Víleke vak-u - há - ne
Vulture, Vulture, they caught him.   Vulture, Vulture, they caught him.

Yu-tchu-kjá - te   vak-u - há - ne   Ai - ru - lí - ta   vak-u -
They smoothed his feathers, (when) they caught him. (In) Airulíta they

há - ne   Ai - ru - lí - ta   vak - u - há - ne
caught him.   (In) Airulíta   they   caught   htm.

Huichol Deer-Hunting Song

Transcribed from graphophone.

It is accompanied by the rubbing of two notched deer bones.

hubbub of voices ring through the quiet night, I won-
dered whether the roof of the temple could resist the
force of their devotional exertions.

If the results of the five-days' hunting are unsatis-
factory, another cycle is decided upon, and, should the
vicinity of the temple prove inauspicious, the men may
take their sacred things up in the sierra, where they are
sure to find all the deer they
want. The rubbing of two
notched deer-bones is considered an efficacious accompaniment to the hunting song, and
is often used, the noise being
thought to decoy the deer into
the snare. The shoulder blade
is held with the right hand by
the spine and rubbed against
the notched bone held in the
left hand. Another accompaniment is the beating of the
musical bow (Vol. I., page

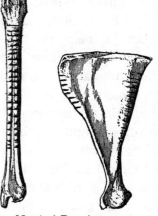

Notched Deer-bones.

475). In mind and body the hikuli-seekers live for the
time being only for one object—to kill deer and bring
the feast to an end, so as to free themselves from the
many restrictions. They always get the deer, because,
as they say, the shaman prays to the fire until the fire
says, "Yes." Whenever a deer is brought in, the meat
is cooked and cut into small squares, which are then
threaded on strings and hung up to dry and harden, in
which condition it keeps until the feast comes off.

In this way they may go on hunting for weeks and
weeks until they are satisfied that they have killed deer
enough to please the gods. It may well be asked how
they can endure the physical strain, in which lack of
food and sleep is combined with the strenuous exer-

tions of the chase. And the answer is that their endurance and spirit are kept up by means of hikuli. Each of the hunters carries in his pouch from three to six hikuli, all of which he eats in the course of the day. Every now and then a man will take a plant from his pouch, cut off a longitudinal slice, and eat it, as we would eat a piece of an apple. In this way from a quarter to half a plant is consumed at a time.

Wherever met, the hikuli-seekers are easily recognised by the happy smile on their faces and the peculiar glare in their eyes. They are always merry, and they sing much. Their walk and movements are quicker than ordinarily, yet always steady, and their ecstasies are in no wise comparable to the effects of alcoholic drinks. Sometimes after large quantities of hikuli—perhaps as many as twenty have been eaten—the effect of the drug is more intense, and a man may have a sudden outburst of violent excitement. In the afternoon, when resting in the temple after the hunt, a man may suddenly jump up from his chair, throw his arms wildly around, and rush about with his face turned upward, as if wanting to fly away, talking all the time at the top of his voice and making a fool of himself generally. It looks as if he had gone mad, and everybody laughs. Suddenly he stops, returns to his chair and sits down, then jumps up again, and seats himself once more with a quiet and happy expression on his face. The attack lasts only a few minutes, and subsides as suddenly as it came on, though a person may become very violent, tear off his clothes, and run against the others with threatening gestures and wild, loud talking. In that case he is seized, and tied hand and foot until he regains his senses. Such paroxysms are ascribed to infringements on the law of abstinence imposed by the cult, and no assurance of innocence would ever receive credence.

I never discovered that the hikuli-seekers sustained any lasting ill-effects from the use of the plant. The Huichols seldom partake of hikuli outside of the season devoted to its worship. While using it they feel no baneful symptoms; but after they stop taking it, they suffer from severe headache that lasts for a day or even longer. There is no doubt that the plant has valuable medicinal properties. It is, for instance, an absolute cure against the painful stings of scorpions, and as such deserves to be widely known.

My chief packer, a Mexican, had once an exciting experience with a furious scorpion that hit him four times in the small of the back. The man seemed to be on the bad books of the scorpions, as he had already been attacked a number of times, and occasionally had been laid up for days from the stings. If there were any of these pests about, he knew it, to his sorrow. On the occasion alluded to, he had taken the precaution to sleep between two of his companions, but had been found out, and one of the mozos came running to my tent at two o'clock in the morning, asking for help. Having perfect confidence myself in the remedy, I did not even rise, but sent the sick man one fresh hikuli with the advice not to drink brandy, the medicine usually resorted to in such cases. When I saw him next morning, he felt stiff all over, but was able to walk about, and the effect of the stings was much less severe than it had been on previous occasions. He did not feel any fear, nor was his throat swollen, and early in the afternoon all pain was gone. About three weeks later he was again stung, in the hand; but he sucked the wound, tied a string around the wrist, ate one hikuli, and escaped without pain.

I arranged with the custodian of the God of Fire that he, with some of the hikuli-seekers, should conduct me

through the sacred caves in the deep gorge three or four
miles west and below the village. Accordingly, on a
bright Sunday morning in late autumn the old man
with four of his companions called for me at my tent,

The Custodian of the God of Fire.

and we were on the point of starting, when an unexpected sight presented itself. A travelling party,
consisting of a padre and his attendants, appeared and
rode straight to the old curato, where they made camp.
At first I thought that out of courtesy to the priest I
ought to postpone my excursion; but as all had been

arranged for the trip, and as the Indians would suit their own convenience about appointing another day, I realised that delay would jeopardise my chances of seeing the caves. I therefore quickly made up my mind in the matter, and on we went to the sacred valley.

Its entrance can clearly be seen from Santa Catarina, at which point riding-animals must be given over, because the valley can be explored only on foot. It had been agreed that I should ride as far as that place, and that the Indians, preferring a short cut, should meet me there. A few minutes after my arrival the old priest of the God of Fire appeared on the scene, followed, to my amazement, by the whole long file of hikuli-seekers. The native authorities and a few women were the only persons who had remained in the village with the padre. I was sorry that the majority of the inhabitants had deserted the distinguished visitor; but then they were hardly in a receptive mood for Christian teachings, being completely under the influence of their magic plant. They showed great excitement, and were eager to " visit the gods," as they expressed it.

Leaving my mule in charge of one of my men until my return in the evening, I followed the lead of the Indians into the sacred precinct. I was the first white man to visit it with the consent of the Indians. Some forty years ago, I was told, a renegade Huichol had shown to a priest the first of the caves, but had gone no farther. Lately, also, a Mexican peon had been taken through the valley by a civilised Indian, but being an ignorant man he was unable to appreciate what he saw.

We climbed up to the pass that leads into the valley. It is a deep crack in a rock, of nearly uniform height throughout, about fifty yards long, and four yards broad. Even this passage contains holy spots. At the left is the entrance to the cave of Great-grandmother

Nākawé, the Mother of the Gods and of Vegetation, and right in the midst of the path is an outcropping stone, around which the Indians, with their machetes, commenced to clear away grass and bushes, that I might see it distinctly. " This is no stone," they said ; "it is one of the ancient people, or gods." Near the end of the passage, toward the right, water oozes from the rock wall, barely enough, however, to keep the spot moist. This rock, the Indians told me, is a blind god. No doubt its continued moisture and dark colour, together with its location in a dark, gloomy place, suggested to the vivid imagination of the Indians the idea of running sore eyes and blindness.

Ceremonial arrows were deposited at the foot of this rock, and numerous wads of cotton were stuck on the moist places, sacrifices made in order that the eyesight of the children, bathed in the principal holy pool near by, might be preserved. Cotton wads are symbols of rain, because they look like fleecy clouds ; and as the rain brings good crops and hence health, they are also symbolic of health.

As we emerged from the pass, we found ourselves descending to a little plain, with shady trees inviting to rest. Here, at night, camp the people who come to bathe themselves, or their children, in the holy springs. Close by, to the left, a brook rushes wildly downward between the high, narrow sides of the valley. Its course is constantly obstructed by rocks, and here and there small waterfalls may be seen, as well as pools, with refreshingly cool, clear water. On each side of this stream are numerous caves, particularly in the upper part of the valley, and most of them near the banks. Hence all the caves are damp ; in one of them water drips from the roof ; in others there are little pools or springs in the ground. All this seems wonderful to primitive man, who reverently believes each cave to be the abode of some particular deity. From all the caves along the river the Huichols carry water to their homes or temples for use at feasts, when the people may

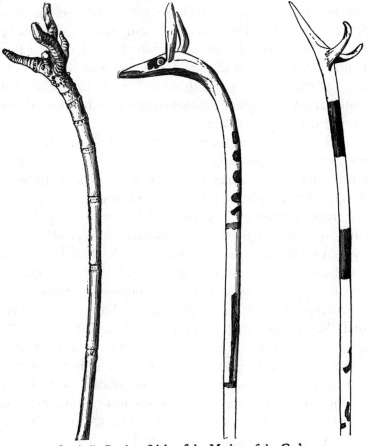

Symbolic Bamboo Sticks of the Mother of the Gods.

sprinkle it over their heads. When they take the water they of course leave at the cave a payment in the shape of arrows, votive bowls, food, and chairs.

The holiest cave of all, because it contains the spring of the Mother of the Gods and of Vegetation, is not

far from where the passage-way opens into the valley.
It is a spacious cavern, about forty yards wide and fifteen deep, through which the stream passes. The right
side and the rear wall of the cave rise in an acute
angle, and if one ascends· here some ten yards the holy
spring of the cave, a small body of water, is encountered. All adult Huichols, men and women, must once
a year, during the dry season, wash themselves with this
magic water. Even though a Huichol should be working far away with a "neighbour," he must wash with
water from this place ; either coming here himself, or
having it brought to him.

My companions informed me that formerly there
was an oddly shaped, hollow rock over the spring,
which the people considered the jar in which the goddess presented the water to the Huichols. Now only
the base remains. The priest who once visited this
cave—the easiest of access—destroyed the jar, thinking
by that means to upset the belief of the idolaters. He
also broke some stone idols that stood above the spring.
But the people replaced them by new ones, which they
now keep in a more secluded spot. Through his over-
zeal that priest made himself so hated that he had to
flee for his life. "Surely," the Indians said to me,
"some misfortune must have befallen him for perpe-
trating such a sacrilege." Later on another priest came
to the tribe, who, according to my informants, did not
interfere with their old customs, realising that one can
never make a Christian of a pagan by violent measures.

Near the upper edge of the holy spring was strewn
hair from the heads of many children. More striking
was a heap of bamboo sticks, which had been deposited
still higher up by people who prayed for long life.
The prongs of the root had been left on the sticks, and
with a slight stretch of imagination they assume the

shape of the snout and the ears of an animal, the cane being the body. It was easy to understand that these sticks are viewed as serpents. The suggestive appearance of the sticks is often improved upon by cutting, painting, and adorning. Great-grandmother Nakawe who is the oldest woman in the world, has to lean on

The Mother of the Gods. Height nearly 38 ctm.

such staffs. The bamboo is chosen because it is considered the oldest plant on earth. In every way there is an association of old age with these sticks, which ultimately represent the serpent goddess herself.

Climbing still higher, I noticed a sort of recess near the roof of the cave, from which two roughly carved wooden figures of the inhabitant of the cave were brought down to me. The Huichols would not part with these, but later on a shaman agreed to make for me a similar representation of the goddess with all her

paraphernalia, including her serpent sticks, each of which
bears the name of a serpent, with appropriate markings,
the two on her sides being conceived of also as her
northern and southern arrows, the other two her eastern
and western bows.   She wears two tunics, in accordance
with the Huichol women's custom of wearing all the tunics they can afford—which is sometimes even more than
two—one on top of the other. Her neth-
er tunic, a lower corner of which is visible to the right, shows the most ancient

Armadillo, the Husband of the Mother of the Gods,
Carried by the Clown at Certain Feasts.

pattern known to the Huichol, that of the
honeycombed tripe of the deer. Her head
is covered with white hair, made from the
fine wool of the pithaya.

In front of the goddess is her drinking bowl, adorned
inside with many symbolic designs expressing various
prayers to her. A wad of cotton covers the inside,
symbolic of clouds, which bring rains, and thus life and
health. At her sides are her beds, the northern on her
left side and the southern on her right. The first bed
represents the bamboo and expresses a prayer for luck
in making chairs of bamboo. The second represents
moisture, clouds, etc., and is a prayer for rain.

Her favourite habitation is deep down in the earth,
and from her lap spring forth trees, bushes, and plants,

which the Huichols use as foodstuffs. Therefore the body of the figure, as well as the face, is painted with black, red, and yellow spots, symbolic of black, red, and yellow maize. On her face is a bean plant, represented by an irregular curved line with short side lines.

The husband of this old goddess of the earth is the armadillo, an animal which has the well-known ability of burrowing in the ground, sinking out of sight, as it were, before an enemy. The peccary with its wrinkled face and the bear also belong to her.

The hikuli-seekers, excited by the spirit of the plant, moved quickly onward, but always in single file, and each man in his place. It was all I could do to keep up with their feverishly quick gait, as they hurried forward to the tune of the rattling tobacco-gourds dangling in profusion from their shoulders.

After nearly an hour's march along the right side of the steep valley we arrived at the birthplace and first home of the God of Fire, a large, shallow cavern, called Hainótega, which means "the place of haino," a small bird from the coast, which Grandfather Fire used to keep while residing here. In the middle of the cave lies a huge block of tuff, supposed to be the god himself when he was an infant. Near the wall of the cave, at a little distance from the block, I was shown his actual birthplace, where he sprang forth as a spark. Some volcanic force has evidently been at work, manifested by some deep, murky-looking cracks in the rock. On the east of the god, and close to him, were ruins of ancient stone houses.

The most conspicuous object here was a diminutive temple. It looked very new, and I was told that when, a few years ago, drought was threatening the country, the Huichols averted the calamity by building this little temple and setting up inside of it a new image of the

god himself.   The structure is a miniature reproduction
of the ordinary temple, except that the entrance is toward
the west instead of the east.   The clumsy little statue
stands on a disk of tuff as a warrior might stand on his
shield.   This disk is about a foot in diameter and on a
level with the floor.   Upon my request to see what was
underneath, they willingly lifted the figure into one of
the three chairs that stood behind it, removed the disk,
and disclosed a circular aperture about two feet deep and
widening toward the bottom.   Here another image of
the same god stood on a little chair.   It was only eight
inches high, and, like the one above, made of solidified
volcanic ash.   In front of it had been placed a few ceremonial arrows with symbolic attachments, a votive bowl,
and a small tuff disk, on which the god's food is offered,
such as grains of corn, bread, chocolate, tesvino, etc.
This figure is ancient, and is more sacred to the Huichols
than the larger one, because volcanic fire represents the
god more directly and forcibly.   The god above ground
talks to the sun in the daytime, while the one underneath
talks to him at night, when the sun is travelling underground.   We rested a while in the cool quarters of the
deity, and then the Indians consented to take out the
idol and its chairs, so that I could photograph them.

In order to reach the next sacred place, we had to go
back a good part of the way we had come, and then descend some thousand feet into the narrow valley.   After
three-quarters of an hour's quick marching we found ourselves on a piece of level ground at the foot of an ar-
gillitic rock about fifty yards high and inclined slightly
forward.   The level spot was scarcely ten yards square,
and about thirty yards above the river.   Here a small
temple and seven god-houses had been erected, having
the effect of a little village.   The temple, which in the
illustration can be seen in the background, makes up in

Te-akata, the Most Sacred Locality in the Huichol Country.

importance what it lacks in size, because it is dedicated to the God of Fire, who, after his extensive journeys and after founding the temple of Santa Catarina, finally came here to settle down.

The locality, the most sacred in the entire Huichol country, derives its name, Te-akata, from the cavity (te-aka) underneath this little temple. The word "te-aka" designates the hole in the ground in which deer-meat and mescal-hearts are cooked between hot stones under cover of an earth mound. The name, therefore, means "the place where there is the te-aka *par excellence*," and gives one an insight into the original conception of the principal god of the Huichols as the one who cooks the food dearest to the tribe, on which in ancient times they no doubt mainly subsisted.

Passing by the god-houses, I made directly for the little temple toward the east and nearest to the rock, the dark red colour of which, as well as the intense heat reflected from it, forcibly suggested the presence of His Fiery Majesty. Although the temple is, perhaps, a little larger than the other houses, it is so low that one has to stoop to enter it. The cool, thatch-covered home of the old god offered a grateful relief from the burning heat outside.

The idol, of solidified volcanic ash and more than twelve inches high, stood facing the door in the middle of the room, perhaps a little nearer to the entrance than to the rear wall. Arms and legs were only rudimentally indicated; but the head was somewhat better in execution, though, through lack of skill on the part of the artist, it was slightly turned upward—a pose which gave the little figure a rather curious expression. On his right side two tobacco-gourds were suspended from strings passing over his left shoulder, indicating that he, too, was a priest; and a few fresh hikuli had been placed in front of him, on the tuff disk on which he stood. The workmanship was no better than that in an image of the same god which a Huichol of some renown as a sculptor made for me with his machete. The idol was very dirty and smeared with blood, but in his right side was a hole showing the natural white colour of the material, contrasting strangely with the dusky appearance of the rest of the figure. This hole owes its existence to the belief that the power of healing and the knowledge of mysterious things are acquired by eating a little of the god's holy body, which the people thus threaten to absorb ultimately into themselves. Curing shamans come to visit the place, and, having deposited different kinds of food or hikuli, or, better still, a votive bowl, scrape off with their finger-nails particles of the god's body and eat them. Afterward they must not partake of salt, and must keep apart from their wives for five months. Women even have been known to imbibe wisdom and healing power in this way; but every visitor must come alone.

"What do you think of this one?" the Indians proudly asked me. "He, surely, long, long ago, came here of his own accord." Such is always the case! All know that the idols are made by one of their tribe, by order of some shaman or officer of the temple. Before the image becomes a god it must be inaugurated, so to speak, much in the same way as the Catholic saints' pictures mean nothing until they are blessed by the church. But when, after generations, the record of "his birth" is lost, the mysterious "long ago" makes the people believe that "he" was never made, but created himself.

Noting that the disk on which the god stood sounded hollow, I wished to see the underground idol; but the objections of my companions were so strong that I did not insist. They told me that the cavity here was larger than in the other temple, and that the same votive offerings were placed in it, the only addition being a baton of red brazil-wood, the emblem of the god's dignity and power. At certain times food is given to both idols with appropriate incantations.

On my second visit to the valley, in 1898, the statue was no longer in its place. One day the Indians had found it gone, and its disk covered with earth. They would not, or could not, give any explanation of its whereabouts, but I learned from outsiders that a distinguished trav-eller had obtained it.

I once asked an intelligent Hui-chol: "Why are there so many idols of the God of Fire in the country? Is there more than one God of Fire?" "It is just as with the saints," he replied; "there are many images of Guadalupe, but there is only one Guadalupe. Ta-tevali, our grandfather, the God of Fire, is far away from here; you cannot see him; a man would get dizzy if he tried to. It is for this reason that we pray to his images.

Wooden Figure of a Macao.

Every five years we make a new god of fire, because the old ones are of no further use; and, besides, they often disappear by themselves, if we do not comply with their wishes."

The entire rear portion of the temple was filled with the symbolic objects which faithful worshippers had de-posited as expressive of prayers and adoration. Arrows with all their various appendages stood there by the hun-dreds. Most of them were stuck in the seats of little chairs, three and three of which were joined side by side with one back. I was told that this was a special ar-

rangement for this god. The interior of the house presented a curious exhibition of every sort of ceremonial
object ever devised by the shamans, the colours red and
blue prevailing. To an ethnologist it was a veritable
treasure-house, and the Indians permitted me to take
almost anything I wanted, as the Huichols do not object
to parting with anything if it was sacrificed long enough
ago. The main point in their conception is that the sacrifice has been made and accepted by the god. Even if
a collector should take away something but recently deposited, the Indians, though of course annoyed, would
fear no evil consequences for themselves, since they had

A Disk Used as a Seat for
Children. Diameter, 8.5 ctm.

performed their duty. The
matter would have to be settled
between the god offended and
the offender, who would be
punished with illness or accident.

Among the objects I se-
cured was a small disk of solidified volcanic ash that had
been placed on the main disk
in front of the idol. It had

been used for children to stand or sit on while being
bathed in the temple. I also obtained a clay figure of
the Mother of the Gods, which I found on the floor just
behind that of her son, the God of Fire. This image
was made a few years ago in Santa Catarina as a prayer
for rain. Blood from an ox sacrificed in honour of the
goddess at a feast had been smeared over the figure.
Both arms had already been broken off and carried away
as amulets to secure luck in agricultural pursuits. Lying
on the floor was also a wooden figure of a macao, the
bird which, on account of its brilliant red plumes, belongs to the God of Fire. It was represented in an

upright position and painted red, so that it looked more like a clumsy figure of a soldier than that of a bird.

At my request the Indians brought the statue of the God of Fire outside to be photographed. Some of his chairs and ceremonial objects were also brought along, and the principal men seated themselves behind. The

Ancient Statue of the God of Fire.

tall, narrow-brimmed straw hat, which in the illustration is seen to grace the head of the custodian of the god, was the only specimen of its kind I met with. It is nearly fifteen inches tall, and I was told that in former days the principal men wore hats still higher and with tops carried to very fine points.

My companions, longing for their bath in the kutsalas, or holy springs, were impatient to descend to the caves along the river, the murmur of which was an ever-present delight to us, and, the position of the sun just then being unfavourable for photographing the place, I postponed this task until my return in the afternoon from the upper portion of the valley. As we started downward we passed a heap of discarded ceremonial

objects that had been thrown out of the god-houses.
Noticeable among them were numerous deer-antlers,
often still attached to the
bleached skulls. All had
at one time or other been
sacrificed as by way of
adoration of the gods or
as prayers for luck in
hunting deer. Sometimes
deer-heads, skinned and
stuffed, are also offered.

**Deer-head Entangled in a Snare, Used
as a Prayer.**

The natives ran ahead
and soon disappeared, but
I reached the cool, shady trees by the river alone without difficulty. How freshly green those trees were,
and how delightfully cool were the narrow gorges! I
worked my way up stream, jumping from stone to
stone, or climbing between the huge roots of cotton-
trees laid bare by floods, and after a few minutes overtook the Indians. They were already busily washing
their heads, arms, and chests with the water that dripped
from the roof of a large cave. It never occurred to
them to refresh themselves by bathing in the river. It
was the religious rite, not the physical refreshment, they
desired, and they had therefore hurried to the first cave,
where sacred water dripped into four small hills of rock
with natural depressions at the summits. Each of these
" drinking bowls " belongs to a principal god, and near
one of them flowers had been sacrificed, kept fresh by
the constant spray of water.

The Indians were enthusiastic about the properties
of the water, and professed to be greatly benefitted by
the very small quantities they administered to themselves
internally and externally. It seemed supernatural to
them that the dripping should never cease, not even in

the dry season, as they proudly assured me was the case. They also strongly advised me to hold my head for a little while underneath one of the drippings, as it would prolong life and keep me in health. I did so, but felt it more refreshing afterward to dip my face in the crystal-clear waters of the river. In the wet season the stream

In the Cave of Sacred Dripping Water.

here rises about ten yards above its normal level, and the gods are evidently not able to hold their own against the might of the water, as I found many sacrificial offerings scattered farther down its course.

The next cave we visited, dedicated to the Goddess of the Western Clouds, is situated some two hundred yards farther up the river, in a very picturesque locality. The gorge here closes in, and the mountain streams fall in cascades over the rocks. To go farther up the valley is possible only by circuitous climbing. The cave was high and spacious, but dark, as the light had to creep in

at the sides of a big boulder that blocked the entrance. I
followed the Indians through the gloom into the farthest
corner, where two small pools of water, each less than a
foot across, were pointed out to me.   That these pools or
springs never dry up is the miraculous feature of the
locality.   They are the abode of two water goddesses
who were once seen here in the shape of serpents.   My
friends scooped up a few drops of water with their
hands, smacking their lips as if it were the most delicious wine.   Their prayers were uttered in a loud voice
and with much enthusiasm, but in a spirit of jollity and
with laughter, all solemnity and seriousness being conspicuously absent.

I struck a match to see the objects that had been
dedicated to these deities, and found them to consist of
a few ceremonial arrows and votive bowls.   Nearly exhausted with the heat, fatigue, and hunger, I was pro-
voked at finding nothing but a couple of insignificant
pools in a dark cavern.   The heavy gloom and the atmosphere of superstition depressed me, and made me
impatient to return to the outer world, a charming
glimpse of which could be obtained through one of the
openings alongside of the boulder.   There the stream
formed a beautiful cascade, which fell into a deep rock
basin whence it rushed smoothly onward in the intense
sunlight.   There was neither grass nor trees, neither
bird nor beast to gladden the eye ; yet the scene outside
of the dark confines of cave and boulder was truly enchanting, the mirror-like surface of the rapidly flowing
water enticing me with its murmur to follow its lead
into a brighter and happier world.

When on a later occasion I revisited this valley I
witnessed the bathing of a child in this very cave.   No
sooner had I entered the sacred precinct than I was
startled by the cry of a child resounding from the cave

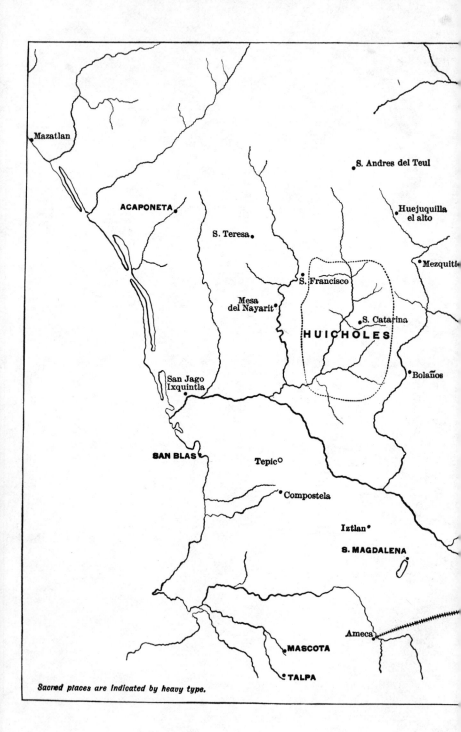

Sacred places are indicated by heavy type.

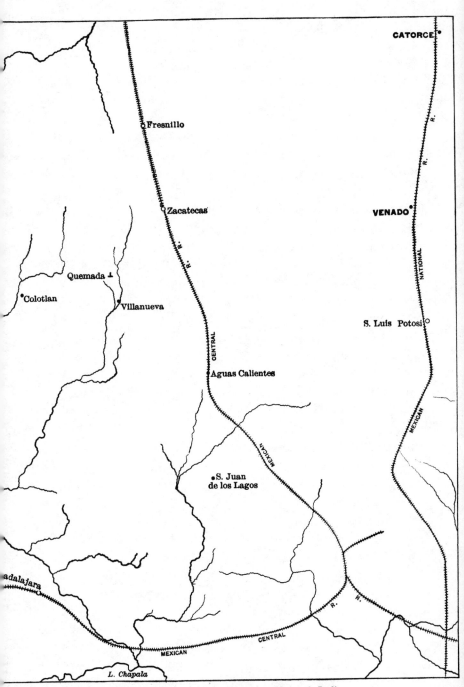

Map Showing Sacred Places Visited by the Huichol Indians.

of the Mother of the Gods. The parents, I was informed, were making the customary pilgrimage to the sacred places, to bathe their little daughter in the holy springs, and to present her to all the gods. They must always go first to the cave of the Mother of the Gods, and then to Te-akata, where the child is shown to Grandfather Fire, Father Sun, and the Goddess of Corn. Outside of the sacred buildings belonging to each of these deities the little one was washed with water taken along for this purpose from the main holy spring. To finish their devotional round, they came to the cave where we now found ourselves, and, proceeding at once to the dark recess, uttered a short prayer. Then the mother held up the little girl, who was barely two years old, and naked, as all Huichol children are at that age. The father, clutching a couple of arrows of the Goddess of the Western Clouds in one hand, with the other poured the water over the child. She screamed with all her might, " Ali ! ali ! ali ! " (Enough ! enough ! enough !) But she had yet to receive the final baptism of the principal spring of the cave. The man, filling with cold water a votive bowl deposited there, poured liberal quantities of it over the struggling child in spite of her vociferous protestations. This must be done, for not until then would all the blessings of the springs in the valley be bestowed on her.

My excursion proved rather fatiguing, but it gave me an opportunity to put hikuli to a practical test. Under ordinary circumstances the plant was nauseating to me ; but now, when I was thirsty and tired, I could, rather to my surprise, swallow the cool, slightly acid cuts without difficulty. I found them not only refreshing, quenching thirst and allaying hunger, but also capable, at least for the moment, of taking away any sense of fatigue, and I felt stimulated, as if I had had some strong drink.

I had taken my breakfast of rice and milk at sunrise on that day, and afterward I had eaten only about an ounce of chocolate and three very small wafers. But when I had gradually consumed two hikuli of medium size I did not feel any weariness to speak of, although I had been active all day, and was just convalescing from a recent attack of malaria. Now, in Te-akata, as I packed up my large camera for the fifth or sixth time, after having made some thirty exposures, there had come over me such a feeling of exhaustion that I had to sit down, completely played out. The sun was nearing the horizon, and the shadows in the narrow gorge were getting very long. How could I ever climb up again? It seemed to me utterly impossible to ascend to the place where I had left my mule, less than two miles away, nor could the Indians carry me up the steep rocks.

"Here I must sleep," I said. But they would not give ear to this. It was incomprehensible to them that I was unable to walk farther. They volunteered to bring me water and to give me hikuli, after which they were sure I should be strong again. I consented to take their medicine, hoping that the plant might help me to recuperate again. They quickly brought me a gourd of water from the river below, which, however, as the Indians use their gourds in common, and as a strong epidemic of whooping-cough prevailed just then (particularly among the children), did not present a very tempting draught. However, in defiance of whooping-cough and anything else the gourd might contain, I drained it, and ate one hikuli. The effect was almost instantaneous, and I ascended the hill quite easily, resting now and then to draw a full breath of air. Yet I must confess, that when at dusk I reached my mule after an hour's walk, I felt as if I should not have been able to take another step.

I washed my face in the cool stream near by, and mounted my intelligent *mula parda*. Eager to get home, she hurried up the hills at a pace which soon left my companions behind. Anyone unaccustomed to Mexican riding might have thought it too hazardous to ascend the steep hillside on a pitch-dark night at so quick a tempo. I, too, if less tired than I was, should probably have thought it safer to get off at certain places and walk. As it was, I confided in my clever and spirited animal. Mules see much better than men at night; besides, she did not give me much time for reflection, but pushed on, as if she, too, had had hikuli, along the narrow track that with many sharp turns zigzagged upward. At the last of these dangerous places she actually jumped with me up a bank two feet high, the chances for the moment being that man and beast would roll down into the yawning abyss. But she landed me safely, and half an hour later I was in my camp.

During the night I suffered from the after effects of the drug, which, when my eyes were closed, showed themselves in colour visions consisting of beautiful purple and green flashes and zigzags. I was also nauseated, and had no appetite until noon next day, by which time I had entirely recovered.

CHAPTER X

BEFORE long the padre came to see me. He was a young and agreeable man from the hacienda San Antonio, and the only priest who visited the Huichols. Every year, he told me, he made a trip to Santa Catarina and to San Andres, in order to baptise and marry. This time, however, he could not do anything, for the Indians were too busy with their land disputes, and he had therefore decided to go away again the next day.

The Huichols make no objection to being baptised, for they themselves have sacred water, and think that they might as well not miss any virtue that the white man may add to it. They will also consent to be married; but they do not regard the ceremony as any more binding than their own custom. The Bishop of Zacatecas, about sixteen years previous to my visit, married several couples in the village of San Andres; but to-day not one man is living with the wife then united to him.

One day, after a particularly cold bath in a grotto, I had another attack of malaria, and during my prolonged stay at Santa Catarina I was to some extent hampered by the weakness that always follows this malady. How-ever, I managed to visit the places in the neighbourhood which I had planned to take in, and while I was confined to my tent the Indians would come to see me. From such interviews I gained considerable information, though great shamans were scarce.

The pleasure of having won the confidence of the Indians was not wholly unmixed with annoyances. It was rather trying to my patience, especially while I was not feeling well, to have people smelling of smoke and old clothes unexpectedly enter my tent early in the morning, when perhaps I had just dozed off after a restless night. Many a time the temptation was strong to speak my mind under such provocation; but afterward I was always glad that I had controlled my tongue, for they would certainly have been offended. They never noticed my irritation because apparently they were unable to read my thoughts in the expression of my face. Some of these *soi-disant* ill-mannered Indians turned out to be of great service to me, while others brought me presents of eggs, young dried corn (*huachales*), the sweet root of mescal, and similar dainties.

The natives would, of course, at times go back to their ranches, but others were sure to arrive in a day or two. There was a constant going and coming, as Huichol life is mostly made up of feasts to appease the gods. Sometimes there were criminal matters, such as stealing, or an elopement with someone else's wife, coming up before the native court. So altogether I could not complain of lack of opportunity to study the people.

Felipe, the same from whom I rented my invaluable three cows, was one of those who rendered me good service. He was honest (a rare quality among the Huichols), of an amiable disposition and gentlemanly manners, and one of the most influential men in the district. He was also the principal maker of idols, perhaps the best then living in the country, and he made for me the image of Grandfather Fire. Though he told me that he had carved it with his machete, the

work was in all probability started with the proper ancient tool. The material was that ordinarily used, solidified volcanic ash. There was
a curious likeness between the
artist and his work, traceable
perhaps even in the illustration.

Felipe, the Maker of Idols.

Among Felipe's possessions
was a native distillery for the
production of the weak brandy
called toach. Like most alcoholic drinks in Mexico, this
liquor is produced from an
agave, the variety employed
being in this case the sotol.
Various kinds of agaves yield
different kinds of liquor, the
most famous of all being mescal, obtained from the maguey.
The manufacture of alcoholic
beverages from century plants
is an industry widely spread
over Mexico. The methods
remain crude, although such
modern accessories as metal
boilers and tubing have now generally been substituted
for the original implements. Of late years thoroughly
up-to-date factories have reared their tall chimneys,
especially in the town of Tequila, State of Jalisco, which
gives its name to the best brand of mescal.

The preliminary treatment of the plant is in all cases
the same, whether the Huichol wants to make his rather
harmless toach, or the Mexican his strong mescal. The
hearts of the plants are baked between hot stones in an
earth mound ; then they are crushed, mixed with water,

and left to ferment in cowhides, each of which is
suspended between four
poles. After the mass has
stood in this way in the
open air for about a week
it is ready for distilling.

A primitive method of
distillation, which I am inclined to consider pre-
Columbian, may yet be
found in practical opera-

Suspended Cowhides for Fermentation.

tion among the Huichols in their remote mountain fastnesses. Their distillery consists of a mound of stone and

Discarding the Refuse.

mud, built around a large earthen jar or boiler, with two additional vessels which complete the apparatus. The lower part of the mound forms an oven with two openings on opposite sides, for the draught, and here the fire is built around a stone, on which rests the big vessel that contains the fermented mass. The upper part of this jar fits tightly into the mound, which forms a kind of funnel above it. Three thick rings of grass are laid, one on top of the other, over the rim of the boiler to make the funnel more solid.

A Huichol Distillery; Sectional View.

The condensation is effected by means of a copper vessel placed on top of the funnel and kept cool by being constantly refilled with cold water. A receiver, in shape of a small earthen jar, is suspended above the large pot by two strings of yucca fibre, which, in turn, are kept in place by the pressure of the cooling-vessel against the inner wall of the mound. It is thus in the proper place to intercept the drops of condensed vapours as they fall from the bottom of the cooler. The man in attendance every now and then removes the condenser, to see how the distilling progresses. When he finds the receiver filled, he lifts it up and pours the liquor into a jar standing close at hand. He then carefully replaces the vessels to continue the operation, plastering mud thickly around the cooler to make sure that none of the steam escapes.

The copper vessel is, of course, bought in Mexican stores, but in former times its place was taken by a thick wooden disk with a knob in the middle to facilitate handling.

The liquor produced is very rarely distilled a second time, and is therefore rather watery, but not unpleasant to the taste. Taken in large quantities it is intoxicating, though it does not seem to affect the constitution of the Huichols. The drink is never kept long, and must be made fresh for every feast.

The process of distilling among the Huichols is, to my knowledge, the most primitive on the American continent. Only a step higher is the method employed by their neighbours

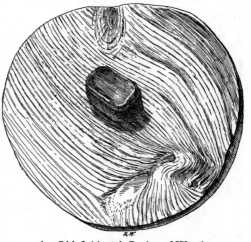

An Old-fashioned Cooler of Wood.
Diameter, about 33 ctm.; thickness, about 4 ctm.

and relatives, the Cora Indians, where the funnel is a cylinder, over a yard high, and formed of a piece of bark from the mountain cedar by joining the long sides firmly together with native glue.

As a receiver the Coras use a trough, consisting of a maguey-leaf cut in the shape of a spoon—hence its name *cuchara*. The bowl of this spoon is fitted obliquely inside of the funnel, to catch the condensed vapours, while the stem passes through a square hole in the lower half of the cylinder. The liquid is in this way carried outside of the funnel, and falls directly into a jar placed under the end of the trough.

The Coras distil their liquor twice, except when it is to be used at the feast of puberty, when it is drunk in its first stage, and appropriately called *agua vino* (water wine).

The distilling by the Tarasco Indians is practically identical with this.

The Huichols also make "wine" from cornstalks, in the same way as the Tarahumares, and they know how to produce an intoxicating drink from guayabas, by mashing the fruit and putting it into jars after mixing it with water. On the fourth day this fermented mass is distilled. According to such information as I had it tastes well, but leaves a headache.

A more important beverage of Huichol manufacture is the tesvino (nāwá). It is thicker and much sweeter than the tesvino of the Tarahumares, to which it is inferior in every way. It is also used more sparingly than in the north, but, here as there, exclusively for religious purposes. The Huichol method of making tesvino is as follows :

Part of a Cora Distillery.

On the patio, which is first carefully swept, clean, fresh sand is placed in a low heap about a yard in diameter. This is moistened, and then a single layer of corn, varying in quantity from two almudes to one fanega, is spread over it, and covered with grass and sticks as a protection against the wind, birds, and obnoxious animals. Every morning and evening the corn is watered, and after six days it begins to sprout. Then it is carefully gathered up, ground on the metate, and put into jars, in which it is boiled for about thirty-six hours, care being taken to add water from time to time to replenish evaporation. At last the thick decoction is mixed with water and strained into gourds, where it is left for twelve hours. No ferment of any kind is added, yet in that short time it is ready for use.

On the 17th of December the Indians commenced their Christmas feast, with which is connected the election of authorities, according to the custom introduced by the Spaniards. Every night there was dancing of the matachines in the church, and both day and night small Mexican-made rockets were constantly fired off. The men walked about drunk and shouting. It furnishes food for reflection that, while at their own feasts religious restrictions keep the Indians in order, the Christian feasts (called also " feasts of the violin," because this instrument furnishes the music to the dancing) are considered proper occasions for licentiousness, and are far more disorderly than the pagan feasts.

During the celebration the images of the saints were taken from the church and exhibited on the verandah of the court-house. There were two large and badly executed crucifixes, and four horrible paintings, leaning against the wall, representing " Señor San José (St. Joseph) and Nuestra Señora Guadalupe, as the Virgin Mary is called throughout Mexico. In addition there were two images representing, respectively, Santa Catarina, the patron saint of the place, and San Antonio. All the saints were adorned with plumes, pouches, ribbons, bells, and bead necklaces ; in other words, the festive outfit of the matachines, who, to emphasise their devotion, put their adornments on the images during the day, while at night they used the things again in dancing.

I was astonished to find a great number of old and new silver coins decorating the pictures. Two red ribbons were drawn across each painting, and coins, one by one, were strung their entire length. When rain is wanted, or when somebody is ill or wishes to increase his herd of cattle, he pays money to whichever saint the shaman may designate. The image may even be taken out on a ranch, where the proprietor, in honour of the occasion, sacrifices a cow and makes a feast, at which la danza and the singing of the shaman are conspicuous features. The image is never returned without getting its payment, which is placed on the ribbon. I counted the money, and calculated that the strings on the four pictures represented the value of two hundred Mexican dollars—a very considerable sum for the Indians.

The two "Christs," the Indians said, were even richer than the other saints. They receive their payments in ordinary Huichol pouches, which each of them carries slung over the shoulders; but their money was not displayed. All the wealth, when not exhibited on occasions like this, is kept in some secret place by the custodians of the respective images. Indeed, the most important duty of the ecclesiastical authorities is to take care of this money; and defalcations are unknown.

The Christmas feast was said to be over on December 23d, having lasted six days; but in reality the merrymaking continued some time longer, because the election of the native authorities was now to be duly celebrated. This function is called *cambiar la vara*, literally "changing the staff," which refers to the staff that every official carries as an emblem of his dignity.

Both the newly elected and the retiring judges had to appear before the Mexican authorities in Mezquitic. Meanwhile, the rest of the people indulged in la danza every night in their honour, and a "neighbour" came to sell some vile kind of brandy (sotol), which raised the hilarity to an unbounded height.

When returning from the district capital, after an absence of eight days, the newly accredited district judges

stopped at a place two hours' journey from Santa Catarina, and from there sent a messenger to notify the people of their return, whereupon a delegation started out
to welcome them and to escort them in. The dancing
and singing went on until the 5th of January, when the
people at last scattered to their ranches, the festivities
having lasted, all told, twenty days.

As for myself, I never in my life spent a more miserable Christmas Eve, the only "surprise" I received being
renewed symptoms of malarial fever.

The very day after the people had dispersed, the hikuli-seekers arranged for a special rain-making feast,
which, including the preparations, lasted the better part
of a week. By that time they had obtained five deer,
and were amply provided for the main hikuli feast to
come. But, for some reason or other, they were not entirely satisfied with the outlook for next year's crops, and
therefore made special efforts to appease the gods. They
even pressed the saints into service by taking them from
the church over to the pagan temple. But their strongest appeal was through a variety of ceremonial objects,
the making of which occupied the principal men and
officers for a number of days in the temple.

The fire in the temple was extinguished and the
hearth covered with ashes. Two oxen were killed in the
middle of the night to the Goddesses of the Eastern and
the Western Clouds, and shortly afterward these mothers received their sacrifices—a mixture of blood from the
oxen, chocolate, tesvino, tortillas, bread from the "neighbours," and bananas, all the solids being broken into
small bits and the whole slightly stirred. At sunrise two
more oxen were slain, for Grandfather Fire and Father
Sun, and in the afternoon the ugly heap of ashes, as well
as the space around for a couple of feet, was covered with
baskets full of all sorts of food. On top of the heap had

been placed the ceremonial arrow of Grandfather Fire.
This is always made thicker than the ordinary arrow. It
was much smeared with blood, and a number of plumes
were attached to it.

Everything looked neat and in holiday attire. The
hikuli-seekers, under the influence of their magic plant,
were saying funny things and making fools of themselves,
moving about all the time, chattering and laughing im-
moderately. The people were very hospitable, and gave
me liberal shares of their provisions. In the autumn the
Huichols use a dainty dish—squash-flowers boiled and
served with boiled squashes. This does not require any
great skill in its preparation, and Huichol cooking is altogether less palatable than that of other tribes; still, I
always complied with the dictum of Indian etiquette,
never to refuse food proffered. A guest must eat a little, at least, of what is given him. If he declines, the
host will never again offer him anything. The acme of
politeness is to eat every bit and crumb given you, then
to wipe the bowl with your finger, before you return it
to your host; drink every drop of liquor, wipe the gourd,
and then hand it back. If you cannot eat all the food,
pour the contents of the dishes into a jar, which good
manners require you to bring along, then hand back the
empty vessels. Social form is complied with if one only
put the victuals to one's lips and take a mouthful; the
rest is sent home, where there is always somebody ready
to enjoy it.

As soon as the feast was over, messengers started out
in the four directions, to deposit in the abodes of the
various deities the numerous ceremonial objects that had
been prepared. Votive bowls were sent everywhere.
Arrows and shields were carried to the Pacific Ocean
and stuck into the water at the shore near San Blas.
In each direction one man only is sent; when he reaches

the border of the Huichol country he invites one or two Huichols living there to accompany him on his trip through the foreign land.

Among the objects thus sent away was what we might call an ark, an imitation of the log-boat in which the first Huichol rescued himself, when, according to tradition, a great flood drowned everything alive on earth. Such arks are deposited in the Laguna de Magdalena, nearly a week's journey south of the Huichol country. The lake is considered the Goddess of the Southern Rains, and the ark is set afloat on its waves with the idea that what was once associated with water may again bring about the same effect.

The Huichols, like many other races, have a tradition of a deluge, and their version runs as follows :

A Huichol was felling trees to clear a field for planting. Every morning he found that the trees he had cut down on the previous day had grown up again. He worried over this and grew tired of working. On the fifth day he came to try once more, determined to find the cause of the disturbance. Soon there rose from the ground in the middle of the clearing an old woman with a staff in her hand. She was Great grandmother Nakawe, the goddess of earth, who causes vegetation to spring forth from the nether world. But the man did not know her. With her staff she pointed toward the south, north, west, and east, above and below ; and all the trees which the young man had cut down immediately stood up again. Then he understood how it happened that his clearing was always covered with trees.

Annoyed, he exclaimed : " Is it you who are undoing my work all the time ? " " Yes," she said, " because I want to talk to you." Then she told him that he was working in vain. " A great flood is coming," she said. " It is not more than five days off. There will come a wind, very bitter, and as sharp as chile, which will make you cough. Make a box from the salate (fig) tree, as long as your body, and fit it with a good cover. Take with you five grains of corn of each colour, and five beans of each colour; also take the fire and five squash-stems to feed it, and take with you a black bitch."

The man did as the woman told him. On the fifth day he had the box ready and placed in it the things she had told him to take. Then he entered, with the black bitch; and the old woman put the cover on, and caulked every crack with glue, asking the man to indicate wher-ever there was an opening. Then she seated herself on the top of the box with a macao perched on her shoul-der. The box rode on the waters for one year toward the south, for another year toward the north, during the third year toward the west, and in the fourth year toward the east. In the fifth year it rose upward, and all the world was filled with water. The next year the flood began to subside, and the box settled on a mountain near Santa Catarina, where it may still be seen. The man took off the cover and saw that all the world was still covered with water. But the macaos and the par-rots made valleys with their beaks, and as the waters began to run off the birds separated them into five seas. Then the land began to dry, and trees and grass sprang forth.

The old woman became wind, but the man went on clearing his field. He lived with the bitch in a cave, and in the daytime, while he was in the field, she re-mained at home. Every afternoon on coming home, he found tortillas ready for him, and he was curious to know who made them. After five days had passed, he hid himself behind the bushes near the cave to watch. He saw the bitch take off her skin and hang it up. Then he noticed that she was a woman, who knelt down

by the metate to grind corn.   He stealthily approached
her from behind, and quickly caught the skin and threw
it into the fire.   " Now you have burned my tunic ! "
she cried, and began to whine like a dog.   He bathed
her head with water mixed with ground corn that she
had prepared, and she felt refreshed, and from that time
on she remained a woman.   They had a large family,
and their sons and daughters married.   So the world
was peopled, and the inhabitants lived in caves.

The illustration shows the Huichol ark and the ances-
tor, with his bitch and squash-stems for keeping the fire

The Huichol Noah and his Ark.   Length, 23.5 ctm.

going.   The boat is a small log of salate-wood, hollowed
out and closed at both ends with disk-shaped covers.
On top are horn-like protuberances, in imitation of deer-
antlers, which, on the original ark, had been put there
for the purpose of entangling the craft in the bushes,
when the water subsided.   The ark is painted blue with
yellow designs of butterflies, toto flowers, and the waves
of the sea.

The same myth survives among the Cora Indians,
only that in their version the man is ordered to take
along also the woodpecker, the sandpiper, and the
parrot.   He embarked in the middle of the night, when

the flood began. As soon as the water had subsided he waited five days and then sent out the sandpiper, in order to see if it was possible to walk on the ground. " Ee-wee-wee ! " said the bird when he came back, from which the man understood that the earth was still too wet. He waited five days longer, and then sent out the woodpecker to see if the trees were hard and dry. The woodpecker thrust his beak deep into the tree and moved his head from side to side to observe the effect. Only with difficulty could he draw out his beak again, as the wood was still very soft, and he had to use so much force that he lost his balance and fell to the ground. "Chu-ee, chu-ee!" he exclaimed when he returned. The man waited again five days, and once more sent out the spotted sandpiper. This time his legs did not sink deep into the mud, but he could jump around as he was wont to do, and he reported that now the earth was right again. Then the man came out of the ark, stepping very carefully, and saw that the land was dry and all on a level.

In spite of the apparent similarity of this legend to the biblical story of the deluge, it is original with the Indians, and not "edited" by the whites.

In extreme cases, when rain is urgently needed, the Huichols may resort to the following ingenious way of attracting the clouds : Water from a sacred spring in the hikuli country, two hundred miles to the east, is taken west to the Pacific Ocean, and the spring is replenished by an equal quantity of water from the western sea. The water, according to Huichol conception, will feel strange in its new surroundings and will want to go back to its original home. It has no other way of travelling than by rising in the shape of clouds, and it has to pass over the Huichol country, where the two clouds meet, and, from their impact, fall down as rain.

When a temple is to be built, six stones, supposed to be male and female, are brought from the sea. Of these, one pair is buried under the fireplace, the second under the altar, and the third under the doorway. The Indians believe that, as these stones have been in the water, they will draw water after them.

CHAPTER XI

THE gods of the Huichol are obviously natural
phenomena personified, and the principal gods
represent the four elements: fire and air (male), earth
and water (female). The male gods are called Great-
grandfathers, Grandfathers and Elder Brothers. The
greatest of the gods, the Fire, is called Grandfather, because he existed before the Sun, who is called Father.
The female gods are called Mothers, and are the source
of vegetation and fructifying rains. There is one
Mother at each cardinal point and there is one above
who keeps the world from falling down. These five
Mothers and the Great-grandmother Nakawe underneath the earth constitute the six world regions of the
Huichol. The moon is Grandmother, but is not considered important.

In the beginning of time people were mostly animals, serpents, jaguars, and mountain lions, the Huichols
say—gods, animals, and ancient people being one in the
Huichol conception.

The shamans think themselves able to catch a certain
class of deities in votive bowls, and when thus caught
the gods, they believe, assume the shape of small stones.
Nowadays it is seldom that anyone can accomplish this

feat, but in former times it was a common performance of the shamans.   About thirty years ago, so an Indian told me, a shaman near Santa Catarina informed the people that the Sun wished to visit the place.   A great many people gathered, and the women brought many ceremonial "beds" for the use of the distinguished visitor.   My informant averred that he would not have thought it possible for such a thing to happen as he saw on that occasion.   Three boys and two girls, holding votive bowls, stood outside of the temple beside the shaman.   He had been singing all night with the people, and

held his plumes in one hand and a votive bowl in the other, ready to receive the Sun when he came down.   After a while

Rock - crystals Representing Respectively a Grandfather and a Grandmother.

the man began to reel, put his plumes into the bowl, and fell to the ground.   The principal men rushed toward him and began to bathe his head and his heart with water, for he was perspiring like a horse on a steep hill.   As soon as he regained his senses, he asked for his bowl.   "Let me see it," he exclaimed, and to the astonishment of the multitude he produced from it a small stone, very hard and red (probably a rose quartz).   This stone, which was more intensely red on the inside than on the outside, was afterward very carefully kept in one of the god-houses of the temple at Santa Catarina, but after five years it disappeared, nobody knew how.   Only the cotton wadding in which it had been wrapped still remains.

A Rockcrystal in its Wrapping, Attached to an Arrow.

Rock-crystals are said to be mysterious people, dead or alive, who at the shaman's bidding come flying through the air as tiny white birds, which afterward crystallise. They are called grandfathers, and are thought to bring special luck in hunting deer. A Huichol's ambition is to have a number of such fetishes, and some keep as many as ten carefully wrapped and stored away in a secluded part of the house, generally cradled in a basket. The condition necessary for living people's becoming rock-crystals is that they must be true husbands and wives, therefore such crystals are rare.

Sometimes, when a man is ill, the shaman will tell him: "Your dead father wants to come back. You will have to hunt deer. Make your arrows for the different gods!" The welcome information received, the man remains in the house, apparently indifferent to everything going on; while his sons, in compliance with the order of the shaman, immediately put out snares to catch deer. The wife makes a good deal of tesvino, and the couple remain drunk while the hunt continues for many days. When a deer is brought in, one of the sons takes a little deer-blood in his hand, dips a stick into it, and paints five lines (rain symbols) down the right cheek of his father. These marks must not be washed off, but allowed to disappear gradually of themselves. The painting is repeated every time a deer is killed, until the number five has been reached. Then the shaman is called to the house, and, holding his plumes over the antlers, make the "astral body" appear. The man for whom it is produced feels very badly in his stomach for a day or two.

Deer-hunters after death become crystals and accompany the sun on its travels. They live where the sun rises, which place is called Hai Tonólipa ("clouds liberating themselves"). In that region are believed to be many clouds, which spread themselves out like plumes. Indeed, clouds are sometimes conceived of as plumes.

Since the coming of the whites an interesting prac-
tice, supposed to increase the herds of domestic animals,
has sprung up: A Huichol and his wife go to the cave
of the Goddess of the Western Clouds, in Te-akata, or to
that of the Goddess of the Eastern Clouds, near Santa
Catarina. They take with them several candles, enough
to last them through the night, and sit down in the cave,
burning one of the candles in front of them. They also
take a votive bowl, a flower, and a small female figure.
The latter, which looks as if it were stone, is really made
from a mixture of wax and an earth containing salts,
which the cattle like to eat. The figure is adorned with
beads, and has tied to it, with a ribbon, hair from the tail
of a cow or a mule. Every time the Huichol kills an ox
or a cow, he offers some of the blood to the figure, who
is the master of all the cattle, and represents the young
female eagle that holds the world in her claws. While
the man and the woman are sitting at night in the cave
the mountain lions, jaguars, and serpents come to frighten
them ; the serpents crawl even up to their necks. If the
couple get frightened, they lose their chance of gaining
their purpose with the gods ; but, if they keep up their
courage, the lions and other animals will soon assume the
shape of cows. A voice says : " Here is what you are
looking for," and a cow is heard to moo once. When
the morning dawns the man puts his votive bowl into
his pouch, and he and his wife go home. Not until
five years later do they return, and during this time it is
necessary for them to be strictly faithful to each other.
On their second visit to the cave, they sacrifice the figures
of an ox and a cow made of cheese and many small
cheeses. Then they have won their case and do not return any more. When the man dies the waxen fetish is
buried with him.

The Indians, of course, are much concerned for the

preservation of the cattle, and have many superstitions relating to them. For instance, if the milk boils over into the fire they throw salt into the flame that the udder of the cow may not burst. Mexicans have the same custom.

These people live only in the present. When getting up, at sunrise, the Huichol prays: " I rise feeling well; I am now going to work, and I hope it will turn out well." And when he goes to rest at night, he says: " I hope to have a good night. I wish that the scorpion may not sting me, and that I may remain well, and rise well." The future concerns him only so far as the securing of the next crops. The trend of his thoughts is toward obtaining something to eat, and his only hope of success is in the fulfilling of his duties toward the gods. The main food supply of the Huichols—corn, beans, and squashes—depends upon plenty of rain; therefore all their prayers call first and especially for rain, and next, for health, luck, and long life. The shaman's singing, the dancing, the sacrificing of animals, all aim at the same result. But the intense religious feeling of the people, and their desire to remain on good terms with the gods, are not satisfied yet. It urges them on to make a number of remarkable ceremonial objects, as evidence of adoration and embodiments of prayers.

As might be expected from beings whose lives move in such a narrow horizon, the symbolic articles in which their pious thoughts find expression are those of everyday life, including paraphernalia that have now gone out of use, as the front- and back-shields of the warrior. The wishes of the supplicant are itemised in many ways, by colouring or carving or representation in or on textile fabrics, or else by attachment. In the manufacture of these articles the people often use only fibre of the agaves, pochote (silk cotton), and other indigenous material that they had before the arrival of the whites ; and such objects can therefore give us an idea of the stage of culture which the Huichols had then reached.

The topic is a very wide one, but having treated it exhaustively in a previous publication, I shall here confine myself to the merest sketch of the principal ceremonial objects—namely, the arrow, the front-shield, the back-shield, and the god's eye. The votive bowl, which also belongs in this category, has already been spoken of (page 77).

Huichol Arrow Release.

There is no problem in ethnology so difficult to solve as the meaning of the arrow in its different applications. It has a personal significance, and one of relation to the clans into which the tribe is divided ; and, obliging though the Huichols were to me, they always shrank from revealing so personal a matter. I have, however, succeeded in lifting a little of the veil of mystery that overhangs the arrow, and can give some brief explanations.

It is conceded, I suppose, by most ethnologists, that the arrow is a bird with outstretched neck ; and the mystic power of the bird to see and hear everything is also attributed to it. As the heart of the bird is between the wings, so the vital part, or heart, of the arrow is

thought to be that portion to which invariably feathers
are attached, the so-called "winged part." On this are
painted the symbolic decorations, generally longitudinal
lines, indicating the path of the arrow, and zigzag lines,
suggesting its lightning-like speed and strength.

Even primitive man seems to have some idea of evolution and the struggle of mankind toward perfection, for
we find in the Huichols'
myths that originally the
arrows of the gods were
made of a kind of stiff,
coarse grass resembling
bamboo, but lacking its
strength. Those arrows
were too frail and fragile
for hunting deer, and the

Huichol Making Arrows.

gods could only kill rabbits with them. They smeared the
blood of these animals on their arrows; but this was not
very effective, the arrows still remaining weak and ugly.
However, by-and-by the gods succeeded in killing a doe,
and after they had smeared the blood of this game on
the arrows, the weapons became at once strong and powerful, so that the gods could now kill deer. The arrow
is a synonym for power, especially the power of the god;
thus the rattlesnake, the scorpion, and even the meteors,
are the arrows of certain deities.

Aside from the arrows of the chase, there is the equally important ceremonial arrow, which is used solely for sacrificial purposes. In appearance the latter is much like the bow arrow, but as a rule the rear shaft is more extensively decorated. What these designs and bands mean in each case is still largely problematic; but this is certain: in a sense, they are symbolic of the god to whom the arrow is dedicated; his coat-of-arms or monogram, so to speak. In some arrows these markings are rather complicated and divided into several fields, each having its own meaning. One may represent the face of the god; another, his wristlet; a red one may stand for the blood of the deer; a green one, for hikuli, etc. Plumes, which are invariably attached to the arrow to speed its flight and to accentuate its mysterious power, are always selected from a bird belonging to the god to whom the arrow is addressed; for instance, the arrows of Grandfather Fire are adorned with feathers from the royal eagle and the macao, the latter on account of its splendid, fiery plumage.

Ceremonial Arrow Expressing Prayers for Luck in Killing Deer. Attachments: A Snare as Placed in the Field, Two Bows and a Snare Folded Up. Length, 58 ctm.

Ceremonial Arrow with a Netted Shield Attached, Symbolic of the Death of the Deer. Length, 49 ctm.

The most common way to sacrifice an arrow is to stick it upright into the ground. Thus they may be found in all sacred localities, in springs and lagoons, in deep crevices between rocks, on the mountains, on the shore of the Pacific Ocean, in fact, wherever a god may dwell whom the imaginative Huichol desires to implore or appease. The arrow stands for him personally, or for the tribe, saying its silent prayers. "I want to speak to the gods," the devout Huichol asserts; "and the feathers I put on the arrow, and the cotton and the sinew and the paint express my thoughts. The arrow talks alone," says he, meaning that it does not need the aid of the shaman.

Life is a constant object of prayer with the Huichols; it is, in their conception, hanging somewhere above them, and must be reached out for. Symbolically, it is expressed by a spiral painted around an arrow, or by the colour red. "We make ceremonial arrows in order to gain life," said an Indian once to me by way of explaining their meaning, and then he naïvely queried: "What do you use in your country? Surely you, too, have something for that purpose?" The arrow is the form in which the Huichol most generally embodies his prayer, and it is inseparably connected with his life. When preparing for any event of importance, he makes an arrow, thereby asking favour or protection from the gods. When a child is to be born into the family the father's first duty is to make an arrow, and he continues to make arrows every five years for each of his offspring, until the boys are old enough to make their own, or until the girls marry, when the husband assumes this responsibility. When the Huichol wants to hunt deer, or till the soil, or build a house, or marry, he has to make an arrow to insure success. In case of illness, arrows must be made to restore the patient to health; and when he dies, an arrow is stuck in the house that the dead may not come back to disturb the survivors. Thus, from the cradle to the grave, in all conditions of his existence, arrows are made to smooth man's road as he journeys through life. Besides, in making arrows a man gains knowledge of all sacred things.

Not only are the arrows sacrificed by themselves, but they are also often used as carriers of special prayers. The Huichol ties to them small front-shields, back-shields,

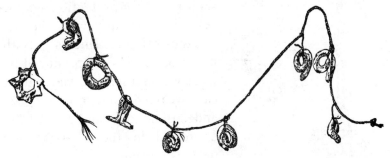

A Cake String.   Length, 95 ctm.

or mats, diminutive tobacco-gourds, sandals, bows, and many other objects expressive of certain desires. The idea is, no doubt, that the prayer is thus shot to the god, whose address is painted in coloured designs on the rear shaft.

A peculiar sacrifice to the gods at the rain-making feasts is that of small, hard cakes of maize baked in the shape of serpents, snail-shells, flowers, etc., tied to a string, which becomes a necklace of a god. They are then slung round arrows of the respective gods, as seen in the illustration.

Other symbolic objects frequently offered to the gods are shields made in imitation of those of the ancient warrior. He carried two shields : a round one, with which he protected the front of his body ; and a rectangular one, which covered his back against the fierce rays of the sun, as well as against the arrows of the enemy, and which at night served him as a mat or bed on which to sleep. It is the Sun's shield the Huichols see every time he rises in the east. As the gods themselves used such shields, the modern reproductions are expressions of adoration. In addition to this, there are often distinct prayers connected with them, such as one for protection against evil, in conformity with the use of the original shields. Both kinds of shields are produced by what we, in a general way, might call weaving, and mythological and cosmic ideas and prayers are expressed in the characteristic designs woven in.

Cake Strings Slung Round Arrows.

The front shield (ne-alika) is made from split bamboo reeds interwoven with variously coloured crewel, so as to form a flat disk. Sometimes the traditional hole, through which the warrior could see his foe, is left in the centre ; but often the opening is only indicated in the weaving. Such a shield may be only three inches in diameter, but there are many that measure twenty and even twenty-five inches across. What these symbolic objects lack in substantiality, they generally make up in artistic merit, and the effect produced is often astonishing, considering the material at the command of the makers.

In Plates XI. and XII. may be seen representations

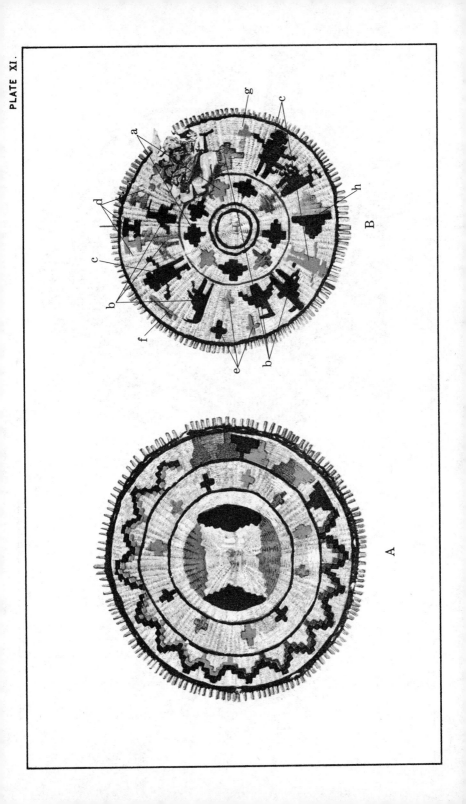

PLATE XI.

A

B

PLATE XII.

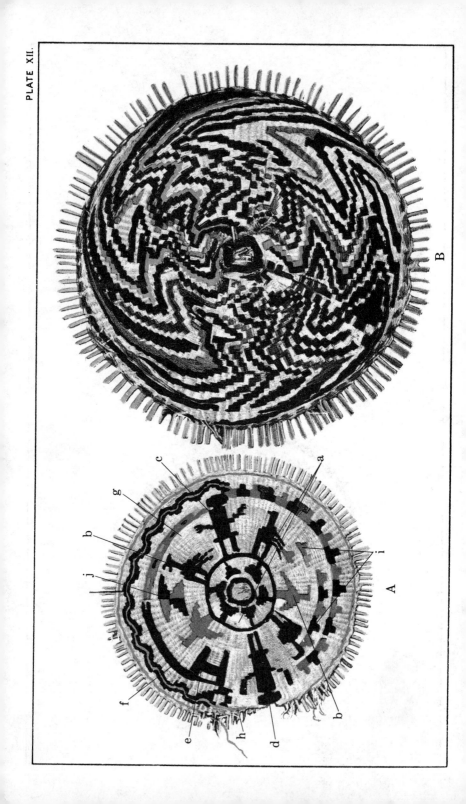

of such front-shields; XIa, and XIb, and XIIa, which were dedicated to the Goddess of the Eastern Clouds, were brought me from the famous cave of this Mother near Santa Catarina.

The central figure in white in XIa represents four rising clouds; and the four figures surrounding these, four swifts soaring above the clouds. The cross-shaped figures in the succeeding section symbolise corn of various colours. The goddess herself is represented by the large zigzag band, a river, or, what is the same thing, a serpent. The nine triangular-shaped figures between the head and tail of the serpent represent as many hikuli. The prayer embodied in this shield is for rain and for health.

In Plate XIb are shown (*a*) hikuli; (*b*) seven humming-birds; (*c*) four hikuli-seekers, one at each quarter of the world; (*d*) three double drinking-gourds; (*e*) symbols of corn; (*f*) the original cereal of the Huichols and the gods, wa-vë; (*g*) a certain small, red insect of the wet season, symbolic of corn; (*h*) a swift. A paper flower from the Mexican shops has been attached to the front part of the shield. The shield expresses a prayer that the hikuli-seekers may be free from illness.

Plate XIIa shows the following designs: (*a*) butterflies; (*b*) five humming-birds; (*c, d*) the two children who lead the sacrificial procession at the feast; (*e*) the ox that is sacrificed; (*f, g, h*) various serpent manifestations of the goddess; (*i*) certain red insects of the wet season, symbolic of corn; (*j*) a double water-gourd. This shield expresses a prayer for rain, referring to the sacrifice of an ox at the feast.

In Plate XIIb is reproduced a front-shield of the Goddess of the Western Clouds, taken from the cave of this goddess near San Francisco, in the Cora country. The designs represent the ripples of the water—in other words, serpents of various colours—in accordance with the Indian conception. The object of the prayers of the shield is plainly indicated to be rain.

It was the contemplation of such votive shields hung up in a row which caused my deceased friend Cushing to suggest that the symbolism depicted on them makes it highly probable that they are related to the dance-shields which the Zuñi and other northern tribes use in their sacred dances. He thought that if these shields were hung up in the temples in some orderly array, they would soon come to be considered as "speaking shields," or an attempt to record events or deeds in visible form, and the next step would be to carve or paint them on the walls of the temples themselves precisely as are the shield-shaped writings or so-called glyphs of the ancient Maya ruins.

Stiff Back-shield, Expressing Prayers to the Eagle Above. Length, 2.7 ctm.

Soft Back-shield of Woollen Textile with Embroidered Figures Expressing Prayer that the Scorpion May Not Sting the Fowls. Width, 19.5 ctm.

The back-shields (náma) or beds may be either stiff or soft. The former style is made in the same way as the front-shields; but the latter consist of textile fabric of fibre or wool, woven on a special little loom which the weaver holds in position between his big toes and his girdle. The ceremonial back-shields are very popular media of prayers, because the idea connected with them is that the gods and goddesses are sleeping on them. Hence, the prayers embodied in the designs are thought to be brought most efficaciously to the notice of the deities, who must perceive them when they come to rest on their beds.

On the back-shield to the left is seen a picture of the royal eagle, which is supposed to hold the world in its talons. As usual the eagle is depicted with two heads like the double-headed European eagle. But the Indian, unable to make a perspective drawing of a front view of the bird, shows both sides by splitting the head and neck.

The back-shield on the next page is a piece of loosely woven textile of fibre in which three transverse rows of black woollen wads are wrought. It expresses a prayer that many lambs may be born in the herd and that they all may be black.

No Huichol woman

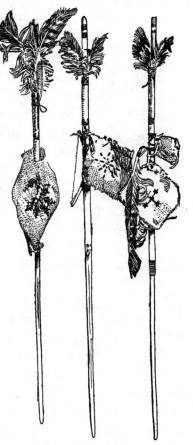

Soft Back-shields Hung on to Arrows, Expressing Women's Prayers for Luck in Embroidery.

ever undertakes any handiwork without first asking the gods for help in her undertaking. A common way of expressing luck in embroidery is to embroider a small figure, often but half finished, on a scrap of wool or cotton—a back-shield—and hang it to an arrow.

A symbolic object of deep interest is the god's eye

(síkuli). It is made by interweaving a small cross of bamboo sticks with variously coloured crewel or twine in the form of a square set diagonally, like an ace of diamonds. The idea is that the eye of the god may rest on the supplicant, and keep him in health and life. It may also express other prayers. He who wants to pray for something by a síkuli should sit next to the man who makes it. At the feast of new squashes, which is a children's feast, each child carries an "eye" under his hair-band, symbolising the male squash - flower.

Soft Back-shield of Fibre Attached to an Arrow, Expressing a Desire for Many Black Lambs. Length, 25 ctm.

A Huichol God's Eye Used by a Child. Length, 18 ctm.

On page 211, at the left, is shown a god's eye piercing a piece of textile fabric. This offering was presented to a god by a woman as a sample of the work she intended to do, with the prayer that he might keep his eye on her, and help her in carrying out her purpose. On the same page, on the right, the god's eye pierces a piece of cotton cloth on which a bit of embroidery has been worked. This expresses in a similar way a woman's prayers for luck in some embroidery she is about to undertake. I have already alluded to the existence of the god's eye among the Tepehuanes. The Tarahumares have also this device and call it wishíma or teyíke. I came across only one specimen, which was made of black and yellow wool; the colours red and white may also be employed. It is with the Tarahumares suspended to the cross on the patio or attached to a long bamboo stick, which the shaman waves to and fro to ward off disease.

The god's eye has a wide distribution along the west-ern coast of North America, and in Peru these symbolic objects are found abundantly in the ancient burial places; in some cases they have been placed on the false heads of the mummies, serving actually as eyes; these are always diamond-shaped, and are applied in such a manner that the acute angles corre-spond to the corners of the eyes of the mummy head. The symbolic eye is a striking illustration of the homogeneity of the American races. A thorough study of one tribe may thus shed light upon the problems presented by other tribes, though far removed in time and space.

Huichol God's Eye, with Appendage Expressing a Woman's Prayer for Luck in Embroidery. Length, 15 ctm.

Huichol God's Eye with Ap-pendage Expres-sing a Woman's Prayer for Luck in Textile Work. Length, 16 ctm.

The people are kept busy making these curious ob-jects, of which I here have given a short exposition, and before a feast the principal men may be seen in the temple thus engaged. To the uninitiated the scene suggests a factory for children's toys rather than the sol-emn and prayerful preparations of a pious and devout people for a great religious ceremony. With their primi-tive implements and crude methods the products of this devotional industry are, of course, perishable. Consider-ing the primitiveness of the tribe, it is but natural that there should be much diversity of meaning in their symbols. Thus a pair of sandals of ancient pattern, worn nowadays only by the shamans at the greatest feast of the Huichols, become, in diminutive reproduction, a synonym for a prayer that the feast may pass off well and no harm befall him; and, inasmuch as the feast cannot be celebrated until a number of deer have been killed, such a pair of sandals also expresses a prayer for luck in killing deer; finally, as in olden times sandals were worn only by men, they may be offered

Tarahumare God's Eye Attached to a Bamboo Stick.

as a woman's prayer for a husband. But despite all diversity of meanings, we can always trace a connection between the symbol and the thought it stands for.

A Pair of Diminutive Sandals Made of Strips of Palm Leaf, Attached to an Arrow. Length of Sandal, 13 ctm.

To primitive man religion is a personal matter, not merely an institution, as with most Christians, and therefore his life is one continuous devotion to his deities. His moral code is not always in accordance with ours; but we must bear in mind that he is most devoutly sincere in his beliefs, no matter how absurd they may appear to the white man's reasoning. Religious feeling pervades the thoughts of the Huichol so completely that every bit of decoration he puts on the most trivial of his everyday garments or utensils is a request for some benefit, a prayer for protection against evil, or an expression of adoration of some

Huichol Women; the Middle One Wearing a Very Elaborately Embroidered Tunic.

deity. In other words, the people always carry their prayers and devotional sentiments with them in visible form.

There are to-day few, if any, investigators who doubt that the decorations of primitive man are the results of his contemplation of nature and natural objects. No savage ever sat down to decorate an article from mere fancy with meaningless designs. With the Huichols all designs are derived from the animal and plant world,

from objects important in the domestic economy and religious life of the tribe, and from natural phenomena familiar to the people. The designs are found almost entirely in the wearing apparel of the people and may be woven, embroidered, or formed in beadwork. Those which I have illustrated here are all woollen textile work, with the exception of one, which is embroidered.

Textile Design: Humming-birds on a Flower of the Hápani Vine.

Girdles and ribbons, inasmuch as they are considered as rain-serpents, are in themselves prayers for rain and for the results of rain, namely, good crops, health, and life; and the designs on these objects are made in imitation of the markings on the backs of the real reptiles, as they appear to the eye of the Indian, and are meant to set forth the desires of the maker or wearer of the band. The double water-gourd, even in its most conventionalised form, means a prayer for water, the source of all life and health. Animals, like the lion, the jaguar, the eagle, etc., express prayers for protection, as well as adoration of the deity to which the creatures belong.

The assertion has been made that plant or flower designs in aboriginal America are due only to foreign influence, to the early missionaries, who desired to divert the mind of the natives from decorations of deep symbolic and religious significance to the innocent motives of the plant world. This is true only to a certain extent. It applies, for instance, to the Tarasco Indians in Michoacan, who in their beautiful lacquer work generally copy flowers from nature. But the statement certainly does not hold good with the Huichols, because,

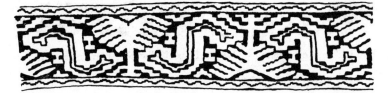

Part of Ribbon, with Alternate Designs of the Double-headed Serpent and a Palm-tree.   Small Water-gourds May be Observed.

in the first place, the missionaries have made, comparatively speaking, only small and transient changes in the mental status of the tribe.   Secondly, flowers play, and always have played, an important part in the religion of these Indians.   With them flowers, like the plumes of birds, are prayers for rain and life.   They are sacrificed to the God of Fire and to other deities, being deposited in the niches of the temples, at springs and pools, in caves and other sacred localities.   No flower is ever plucked unless with some pious intention.   At certain feasts the women wear wreaths of flowers on their heads, or place single blossoms behind the ear, while the men fasten flowers to their hats.   It is, therefore, but natural that flower-designs should have become as prominent as animal-designs in the decorative art of the Huichols.

I use this expression, although there is no such thing as ornamentation for decorative purposes, *per se*, with the Huichols, nor, probably, with any primitive people. Neither does the theory of chance suffice to explain primitive designs ; nor can an ornament be explained by guessing its meaning according to white man's reasoning, for it should always be remembered that in interpreting primitive symbols and designs it is never the first and most obvious explanation which is true.

A design may in time become so conventionalised that a white man will fail to recognise the object the artist intended to represent, unless the Indians them-

Embroidery Representing a Creeper Hápani, Showing Flowers and Leaves.

selves interpret it for him. Nevertheless, the results obtained are highly pleasing, and thus eloquent of the sense of beauty innate in the race. Even should the original meaning of any one design be forgotten, the belief in its efficacy still survives, and on this account the figure is perpetuated.

In looking over Huichol patterns we cannot help being struck with the fact that hardly any two are exactly alike. This variety is characteristically Indian. This varies, of course, with the skill and imagination of the artist. It may happen that a woman, always alert to find a pattern more pleasing to her than the one she has, may copy one from a friend. Another deciding circumstance is the size or shape of the article to be decorated. In very narrow ribbons or girdles, for instance, the patterns have to be compressed, and consequently assume changed aspects.

The articles which the Huichols buy from the Mexicans, and which are of more or less consequence to the art industries of the tribe, are mainly : coarse cotton cloth (manta), thread and needles, red flannel, beads, printed handkerchiefs, crewel, and steels for striking fire. Along with the foreign material a slight foreign influence has come into the designs, though in the main they have remained intact. Some new forms have been added, such as that of the steel for striking fire, the jew's-harp, the horse, ox-horns, etc. The shape of the steel, quite handsome in itself, has been developed by the Huichol into interesting conventional designs for his girdles and pouches. In fact, these Indians, who revere the steel on account of its connection with the

God of Fire, have worked it into designs even more
beautiful than the original.   Glass beads with their various colours have facilitated the rendering of symbolic
designs, and enhanced their beauty; thus their influence, too, has been rather advantageous to the development of Huichol art.

The coloured handkerchiefs cannot be considered
equally beneficial.   Fortunately, the gorgeously painted

Huichol Woman Weaving a Girdle.

animals and flowers, although they appeal to the Indian strongly, are mostly too difficult for him to copy.
Only the purely ornamental designs are within easy
reach of his capabilities.   Although he puts into them
his own meaning, it can quite readily be seen that foreign influence is finding a way to infect his primitive
art.   The detriment so far wrought, however, is not
great, as the possession of such handkerchiefs is rare,

and there is seldom a pattern on them that appeals to him sufficiently to induce him to copy it.

The loom on which the often really artistic work is executed is of the most primitive construction. One end is tied to a tree or stick, while the weaver fastens the other to her girdle. The " beating stick " is made of Brazil-wood. Woollen shirts, of which at present not

half a dozen specimens exist in the tribe, are made in one long strip, which is folded over and sewn up at the sides, short sleeves being put in separately. The loom on which such large pieces are woven lies on the ground.

If a woman were constantly at work on her loom, it would take her about six days to finish a girdle; but as she has many other duties to attend to it often requires three weeks and more to make one. The pattern at the ends of the girdles is always somewhat different from that used in the main part. There are generally some transverse zigzag lines, symbols of lightning, seen here. The portion of the warp left open at both ends is plaited into one braid, sometimes into two, and fastened with a knot.

A Pouch Before Being Sewn Together. Design: the Flower *Corpus*, and Combs Placed Lengthwise. Length, 12.5 ctm.

Ribbons are mostly like small girdles, and, owing to their narrowness, the designs are generally more delicate and also more finely executed. Pouches are woven in one piece, which is then folded in the middle and sewn up at the sides.   Embroidery, sometimes done by men as well as women, is executed in cross-stitch with mar-

vellous accuracy.   It is always made on cheap cotton cloth, the thread being obtained by unravelling red flannel.   In the possession of the American Museum of Natural History, New York, is a skirt with a beautifully embroidered border four feet eight inches long and four and a quarter inches wide, in ever-varying patterns.

In my purchases of decorated articles, as well as of other symbolic objects, I always made a point also of getting the interpretation of the decoration.   Often the men knew nothing definite about the meaning of the designs on their girdles, ribbons, and pouches ; and it was difficult to find a woman able to interpret the designs worked by another.   As a rule the people are willing to part with their beautiful work, but

The End of a Girdle.   Main Design: a Double Representation of the Flower Piríki.

The End of a Girdle.   Probably Ancient Flint Tips of the Arrow Are Shown in the Design.

there are also instances in which no influence, not even that of the gobernador, will induce a woman to sell any of her handiwork.

The double water-gourd furnishes the motives most commonly met with.   The gourd itself is simply an abnormal growth of the ordinary gourd, resembling two gourds connected with a slender neck. It is provided with a stopper, sometimes consisting simply of a corn-cob, and

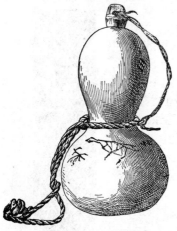

it is carried by a string tied around the middle. Such gourds are used by the hikuli-seekers for bringing water from the home of the holy plant. Such a gourd as the one depicted here is of the size the Huichol carries about with him for everyday use. The double water-gourd is considered magical, and has become the strongest symbol of water. It is also, with the exception of the cross, the most extensively used design in America. It was commonly used among the Aztecs as well as among the ancient Peruvians.

The Double Water-gourd of the Hikuli-seeker. Height, 22.5 ctm.

In the full-page picture, page 221, in the two upper rows, I have given a table of the evolution of the double water-gourd designs, the result of a study of a very large number of Huichol pouches, girdles, ribbons, etc. The first figure to the left in the upper row is a fair representation of a double water-gourd, and the reader will easily be able to follow the successive stages of the design until it finally becomes simply a triangle: half and at last a quarter of the gourd.

In the second row the string around the middle of the gourd has been added in the shape of a transverse line. Here the stopper, too, has been incorporated in the pattern, and for the sake of symmetry it has also been applied to the bottom of the gourd. The second design is simply half of the first cut lengthwise. In the third the stoppers have been left out. The fourth is the upper part of the first with the stopper left out, and

R. Weber, del.

The Double Water-gourd Designs and Their Application.

Ribbon, with Double Water-gourd Designs.

the fifth is simply half of the fourth. The sixth is a more symmetrical rendering of the first, two pairs of angular points being added; a god's eye has been made in the middle. The seventh is half of the sixth. In the eighth and ninth the number of points is increased and even more rows are added.

In the lower part of the plate is shown the application of these various double water-gourd designs to girdles; these are easily recognisable.

In the ribbon at the top of the page the double water-gourd design is very distinct. It should also be noted that the crossing zigzag lines form a god's eye, like a frame for each design. Placing the girdle in a perpendicular position, one will also readily perceive how a second double water-gourd, more conventionalised, has been reproduced on the outside of the frame, enclosing the first one.

The Huichol comb also furnishes a motive for designs, though not very common. It looks like a small whisk-broom and is made from fibre of the century-plant, *lechuguilla*, which is brought from the hikuli country. The twine around the handle has been tied so as to form a butterfly design. The unevenness on the top of the comb, the natural result of the tying of the fibres, has in the design been utilised at both ends.

Huichol Comb of Fibre. Length, 12 ctm.

The steel for striking fire, though of comparatively recent introduction, is closely associated with the religious conceptions of the tribe, because the fire is their

Part of Huichol Ribbon with Alternate Designs of the Comb and the Double Water-gourd.

greatest god, and the steel represents him. Since all sacred things are symbols to primitive man, the Huichols have adopted the implement among their decorative designs. On page 225 is seen the steel as sold by the Mexicans and the three designs evolved from it.

This design is generally applied in rows, being especially utilised as borders to girdles and pouches as seen in its application on the next page. In the two small pouches seen on the upper portion of the page are found other combinations of the steel design : in the one to the

Part of Huichol Ribbon, with the Design of the Steel for Striking Fire.

left two entire designs being represented, in the one to the right halves and quarters. Other designs here are : on the girdle to the left the double-headed serpent, and on the pouch following, two leaves and a flower of the banana placed lengthwise ; on the girdle to the right, which is a beautiful imitation of a serpent's back, a series of god's eyes.

The notched lines and the zigzag lines seen as borders of pouches and ribbons, both here and in other cases, signify generally, the first one, notched deer-bones ; the second, either lightning or squash-vines.

The royal eagle is a favourite design on pouches. The young female eagle, which is believed to hold the world in its talons, guards specially the corn ; hence the

The Design of the Steel for Striking Fire and its Application. A Reproduction of the Steel Itself is Seen in the Upper Left-hand Corner.

flower toto, the symbol of corn, is pictured on the breasts of these eagle designs.   As before explained, the designs

Pouch, with Design of the Royal Eagle.
Width, 13 ctm.

have absolutely no connection with the double-eagle heraldic devices of Europe, but about the heads of the design

Pouch, with Designs of the Royal Eagle.
Width, 22 ctm.

on the first pouch may be observed crowns which are due to contact with civilisation.   The guardian young mother-eagle above is to the Huichol synonymous with the Virgin Mary, whose image they have seen provided with a crown, which here is reproduced. Of more interest, because showing no contamination with the white man's ideas, is the beautiful and effective design of eagles in the second pouch. The plumes on the heads are executed in daring and impressive curves, and the combination of the two eagles into one is highly artistic and

Pouch with Designs Showing Insect Borings on Trees ; also the Flower Toto.   Width, about 11 ctm.

may be favourably compared with the best heraldic designs of mediæval times. The right and left border is composed of the toto flower, parts of which are also seen to fill out the space between the heads in a tasteful manner. The main design in the upper border is one very often seen. It is, in the Huichol conception, a conventionalised rendering of the linking of hands as seen from the side.

The pouch with the two large zigzags

Part of Ribbon, with Design of Dogs.

has an interesting design, the zigzags representing the
borings which a certain insect makes under the bark of
trees. The borings are also called the "facial paintings
of the tree." The rest of the designs is almost entirely
the toto flower.

In the Huichol country the little white flower called
tōtó grows during the wet, corn-producing season, and

Woman and Child with the Corollas of the Flower Toto Stuck to the Cheeks.

therefore becomes a prayer as well as a symbol for corn.
The women, especially, are often seen with the corolla
of this flower stuck with saliva to each cheek, thereby
expressing their wishes to the gods. To have the flowers permanently with them the Huichols weave them
into their girdles, and embroider them on their garments. As the thought conveyed by this flower is
ever uppermost in the mind of the people, the design
appears very frequently. I have gathered all the various
forms in which this design is utilised. A slight simi-

larity to oriental designs may suggest some foreign influence; on the other hand, flower designs are by their
nature subject to limitations, so that a certain likeness
between the productions of distant tribes and races must

Evolution of the Toto Design, Based on Explanations Supplied by the
Natives.   All Are Inwoven or Embroidered Except the Last, which is
Bead-work and Represents the Flower in Side View.

always be expected.   A curious discrepancy is here ob-
servable.   The real flower has five petals, but convention-
ally it is represented with four or eight, or sometimes six.

This may be due either to the desire to make the flower conform to the four corners or the six regions of the world, or to lack of skill in making an evenly five-pointed star.

Various forms of this design may be seen on the shirt, which is woven from white wool and embroidered

Man's Woollen Shirt, with Embroidered Designs of the Flower Toto.

in red. The conspicuous toto design in front has eight small totos within it. Within the petals on the shoulders macaos are represented.

In the beautiful pouch on page 233, which has mainly designs of this flower, it may be noticed that each flower is placed within another more conventionalised representation of it (a cross). Even the little rectangular additions above and below are probably extremely conventionalised forms of this design. The oblique lines crossing each

Part of Ribbon, with Designs of the Flower Toto and of Butterflies (the Rows Above and Below of Triangular Figures).

other on the entire side of the pouch produce god's eyes, one for each flower. The several transverse rows of zig-zag lines symbolise squash-vines, the middle row having

Pouch, with Designs of the Flower Toto. Width, 10.5 ctm.

also the squashes expressed by dots.

I have been able to reproduce here but a small portion of Huichol designs, but enough, I hope, to show that barbaric people have more innate artistic sense than they are credited with.

Why is it people of what we call inferior races, or even savages, are artistic in the productions which they make for their daily use, while civilised man requires to be stimulated to an appreciation of art? Compare the markings of even an Australian cannibal, the lowest savage on earth, on his shield or his basketry work, with any ornamental attempts of the common white labourer. The result is not flattering to the white race. I have often pondered this. Sometimes I have thought it was because we lived too far from nature. Is there perhaps something wrong in our boasted civilisation?

I do not mean to say that the backward races have any appreciation whatsoever of our art ; but the astounding fact is that they unconsciously turn out such beautiful conventionalised designs, as for instance may be seen among the Huichols, while in civilisation we have to

Pouch Having as Main Design the Flower Toto.   Width, 38 ctm.

establish societies to encourage people to surround themselves with objects of beauty.   *L'art domine la nature* seems to be true in more than one sense.

From the symbolism of the Huichols it must be inferred that the main consideration of all their prayers is food.   The means of securing good crops is rain ; therefore most of their prayers ask for rain.

Many of the Huichol symbols are ambiguous in their significance.   This is largely due to the fact that, owing to a strong tendency to see analogies, what to us are called heterogeneous phenomena are by them considered as identical. For instance, most of the gods and goddesses are believed to be serpents; so are the pools of water and the springs in which the deities live, and even the staffs of the gods; these last beside being regarded as arrows.

The most striking feature in the world, as the Huichol looks upon it, is the prevalence of serpents. In all ages, and in most religions, serpents have played an important part. The serpent, by shedding its skin, rejuvenates itself, and thus becomes the symbol of health and strength. As it is the only animal that moves on the ground without legs, and swims without fins, it is particularly cunning. Its great skill is further manifested in the beautiful markings on its back. When a Huichol woman wants to weave or embroider anything, her husband catches a large serpent, the neck of which he places in the split of a stick, and the reptile is thus held up while the woman strokes it with one hand down the entire length of its back; then she passes the same hand over her forehead and eyes, that she may gain ability to do beautiful work. As in olden times, so to-day, serpents are considered guardians of treasures, and the Indians leave their fields to be watched by them.

The sea, which to the Huichol mind surrounds the entire world, is, with its serpent-like motions, the largest of all serpents. It is the great, all-devouring one, and has two heads. The sun has to plunge past its open jaws as day sinks into night and all becomes darkness; and with it human beings disappear caught by the serpent. In the sky, in the wind sweeping through the grass, in the moving waves of the sea, in the sinuously flowing rivers, the darting lightning, the descending rain, in fire, smoke, and clouds, in fact in all natural phenomena, even in the trails of man winding over the land, and in the religious processions, the Huichols see serpents. Maize, the plant itself and the ears of corn; the bow with its elastic reaction; the piercing arrow; the tobacco-gourds—all are looked upon as serpents. It may be added that the Huichols see serpents in their own flowing hair, in one organ of the body, in the girdles around their waists, in the ribbons streaming from their heads and pouches, in their wristlets and anklets, and in the ropes and twines they make for all possible uses.

The symbolic sacrifices may often seem mere trifles; but it should be remembered that the Indians are poor indeed, and have not much to give away, and that the making of the symbolic objects requires a considerable expenditure of time and labour. The Mexican Indian never gives or expects to receive anything for nothing; therefore he pays his gods for everything he asks from them, and he gives according to his means, realising that "only a knave gives more than he has." To us his efforts are of intense interest, as they reveal the first faltering steps of the human mind toward expressing thought in visible form, when there dawned the possibilities of that art which has become the most fundamental and powerful—the art of writing.

CHAPTER XII

ANYBODY who has a natural gift for it may become a shaman. Such a gift will be evidenced from his early youth by his being more interested in the ceremonies and paying more attention to the singing than ordinary boys do. The feasts, where they acquire their knowledge of the gods and their doings by listening to the songs of the shaman, are the only school the people attend. I have heard children no older than five or six years sing very well indeed temple songs caught as the street boys in our cities catch popular airs. In addition a young man may, of course, ask an older shaman for information, but there is no regular system of teaching. The imaginative mind of the Huichols and their emotional temperament, as well as their musical genius, lead to an extraordinary preponderance of shamans among them.

A man who wants to become a shaman must be faithful to his wife for five years. If he violates this rule, he is sure to be taken ill, and will lose the power of curing. Not until the stated period of probation is passed may he have love affairs. "But who likes a man then? Surely the girls don't," said a great shaman to me. The shamans, with their long flowing hair, their

tobacco-gourds, and their ability to cure and to sing, are
thought to resemble the gods.   They are able to talk
with the Fire and with the Sun, and when they die they
go to the country where the sun rises and where it is
warm and pleasant.   Ordinary people go to the place

Young Huichol Shaman.

where the sun sets, and where they have only bad water
to drink.   A little south of Ratontita lives a woman who
is recognised as a singing shaman, but she is the only
female shaman I ever heard of.   She is frequently employed at the ranches near by both to sing and to cure.
But she is very chary with her patronage, and though

the people have wanted her to sing in the temple, she has never consented to do so.

All disease comes from the gods, who are thought to come down at night to make people ill. They may have been offended because the people did not sacrifice enough, or did not hunt deer sufficiently, or did not properly conduct the ceremonies at a feast. Or one of the principal gods may have been invoked by a bad shaman to help him in destroying an enemy, for there is the usual conception that disease may be due to sorcery ; in which case it becomes a question of power among the shamans which of them can influence the gods more effectively—the bad one to make ill, or the good one to cure.

Knowledge of witchcraft may come to the shaman as he grows old. Abstinence from salt and separation from his wife are necessary to insure his success in doing harm. At night, through the owl and the goatsucker, he gets a hair from the man whom he wishes to make sick. The birds pull the hair from the head of the unfortunate victim, while their employer dreams that they bring it to him ; and in the morning when he wakes up he finds the hair near his bed. He puts it into a small reed, each end of which he seals carefully with wax ; then he ties it to an arrow of the god to whose wrath he leaves his antagonist. If the god does not help him the shaman cannot work sorcery. A person accused of sorcery may be burned, or hanged, or thrown down a precipice.

The services of a Huichol doctor are much valued, though the fee varies according to the patient's ability to pay. For singing all night and curing in the morning the charge is from ten to fifteen dollars, or its equivalent in *naturalia*, and a travelling shaman may return from a professional tour outside of his country with eight or ten cows as net profit, beside sheep, goats, and donkeys. A good shaman learns the nature of the disease through dreams, and advises the patient what to do to get well again; as, for instance, to make certain ceremonial objects, chairs, beds, etc., or to hunt deer or grey squirrels, or to catch fish, or do something to reconcile the offended god who caused the illness. At the subsequent feast, a part of the animal sacrificed is first offered to the god, and then the people partake of it.

To my knowledge the Huichols make no use of remedies except, perhaps, of hikuli; they prefer to cure even scorpion stings with blowing of the mouth and wafting of the hands. To cure a patient the shaman resorts to the following means:

(1) He wrings his hands several times as if washing them; then quickly stretches his fingers, one after the other, so that the joints crack. This he does in imitation of the crackling of the fire, the greatest of all shamans, in order that his fingers may remain well and strong.

(2) He breathes into his hands.

(3) He holds his hands together, spits into them, and holds them out toward the south, north, west, east, and also toward the ground.

4. He places his mouth on the part of the patient's body which is in pain, makes a kind of gurgling noise, and then sucks out the disease in the shape of a grain of corn, a small stone, or what not, coughing as he does so. The object produced represents the illness, and is either burned, or thrown on the ground that the whirlwind may carry it off.

5. He breathes on the patient's head, or wherever the pain may be, making at the same time passes with his hand as if wafting the illness away. The passes and the blowing may also be made over other parts of the body besides the afflicted one, and are sometimes executed in combination with means No. 2.

It is rather striking to note the names the Huichols give their various maladies, indicating as they do the close relation between the ailment and the god who is supposed to have sent it. This will become clear at a

glance at the list of diseases compiled in accordance with the Indian point of view:

1. Ailment of the foot is called rikúa, the word for certain rattling objects or bells. In this connection it refers to the rattling anklets worn by the dancers, as well as to the familiar noise made by the deer in walking. The disease is attributed to Great-grand-

Shaman Wafting Away Illness.

father Deer-Tail, and is cured by extracting grains of corn from the suffering limb.

2. Pains in the hand are designated matzúwa (wristlet), and are sent by Seliákami, also called Cometámai, a deity connected with the nether world. They are relieved by extracting grains of corn.

3. Pain in the pit of the stomach, or indigestion, is called ōwǽn (chair), because the person afflicted is apt to draw his knees up, as in a sitting posture. The Young Mother Eagle above is thought to cause the malady, which is cured by removing small pieces of charcoal.

4. Colic is called rukúli (gourd-bowl). The stomach, with evident good reason, is considered a food-bowl. The Goddess of the Western Clouds sends the affliction,

which is cured by the removal of small round stones or a little earth.

5. Pain in the chest, pleurisy, is called mūrí (fish), the pain being compared to that caused by the swallowing of a fish-bone. A bone, therefore, has to be removed to alleviate the trouble, which is sent by the Goddess of the Eastern Clouds.

6. Disease of the lungs, consumption, is called ūlú (arrow). The inference is that the flint arrow-point shot by the Setting Sun causes the spitting of blood, and the coldness of the flint brings on the chills. An arrow-point, therefore, has to be removed from the patient's breast before a cure can be effected.

7. Toothache is looked upon as Great-grandmother Nakawe's pipe, because the root of the tooth resembles that of the bamboo-plant, specially sacred to this goddess, whose pipe is a piece of bamboo-reed and who therefore is considered as the one who sent the pain. To cure it, earth or grains of corn have to be sucked from the jaw of the sufferer.

8. Faceache, or fever, is called nealíka itáli (bed in the face), the God of Fire, in such maladies, being conceived of as making his bed in the patient's face. As will be easily understood, the affliction was sent by the God of Fire, the source of all heat, and is cured by the removal of grains of corn.

9. Throat-trouble, bronchitis, is designated as mōyǽli, (plumes). Splinters of deer-antlers, or deer-hair, have to be removed, as they are supposed to cause the tickling in the throat, and the cough indicates to the Indian that the illness is caused by the God of Wind and of Hikuli.

10. Headache is called rútsi (squash), suggested by the similarity between the form and hardness of the head and the squash. The comparison may go even farther, since a severe headache gives one the sensation of having

something loose inside, like seeds in the squash. The pain is ascribed either to the Mother of the Gods or to the Goddess of the Northern Clouds.

1. Insanity, too, is believed to come from the last-named deity, or else from Tamats Kowyumali, the god who put the world into shape and had to fight with the people of the nether world to accomplish the feat. To remedy the trouble, any small object, generally grains of corn, must be drawn out of the skull.

Stomach troubles and also malarial fever may be sent by the God of Wind and of Hikuli. These afflictions are cured by the removal of a water animal called kuli, which somewhat resembles a leech.

Without discussing the merits of this mode of treatment, the fact is that here, as everywhere else, the people finally die.

In the southern part of the country the dead are buried in the middle of the house, in graves a little more than a yard deep. The Huichols do not pull down the house in which a person dies; but when four generations have lived in it, it is abandoned. In the other parts of the country, caves are utilised for burial purposes and the entrances closed with a wall of stone and mud. In any case, the body is placed with the feet toward the east. A dead person immediately receives a gift of water in a hollow reed, and five tortillas. No one in the family eats until after the burial, which takes place at sunrise next morning. The deceased takes away with him all his clothes and the reed of water. Five days after his death a feast is made on the patio outside of the house.

The funeral rites for a young married man were described to me by a shaman from the southeastern part of the country as follows: All the dead man's belongings are gathered in a heap in the middle of the patio, and all kinds of food are placed on top of them. During the night the shaman sings to all the quarters of the world. At daybreak he stops, and, standing up, stretches out his plumes toward the east. This he does because the dead always go first to the hikuli country, though afterward they settle in the west. As the shaman stands facing the east, the soul of the dead comes flying through the air like a white fly, or a small bird, and seats itself among the plumes. The shaman takes it into his hands; but the little bird begins to weep as it salutes all its forefathers and mothers, who in the beginning put the world in shape. The father and mother of the dead now step forward. They, too, weep, and bring the food of which their son in his life has been specially fond. The little apparition flaps its wings to receive the dainties, and the shaman says: "Give him all the food that he used to like best!" Then the little bird makes a courtesy and flies away, first toward the south, and from there to the west—away from his father and his mother and from his brothers, and loses himself in the darkness of the early morn. As the sun rises a gourd filled with flowers is offered to the dead man, and the shaman spreads out all his property. Then the father says to his widowed daughter-in-law: "My son is dead, my daughter, but do not weep over him! All the things that he left belong to you now. Do not fear that I will take anything my children make for themselves. All is left in your care and goes to my grandchildren." The widow then divides the heirlooms among the children and stores everything away.

No liquor is used at burial feasts. Instead a cross, made from a kind of *salvia*, is hung up in the house for some time to prevent the deceased from re-entering the premises; and to keep him from getting into the distilleries and spoiling the wine. Branches of the

zapote-trees are put upon the paths leading to the place
and the jars containing tesvino are covered. When a
Huichol on any occasion takes his first gourd of liquor
—whether of tesvino, or his native brandy, or mescal—
he first dips his finger into the bowl and sprinkles a few
drops of the contents to either side of him as a sacrifice
to the dead, "who crowd around him like children."
Should he omit this, the drink would make his body
swell up. This sacrifice is always immediately followed
by one to the six regions of the world, and is performed
in the same way as the preceding offering.

On the western side of the Chapalagana the dead are
chased off with branches of zapote-trees, as among the
Coras.

CHAPTER XIII

THE government in the Huichol villages remains
as it was when instituted by the missionaries, a
mixture of the rule of State and
Church. Though this condition of
affairs is contrary to the laws of
the republic, it is still in full force
among the tribes not yet Mexicanised. The number of civil and
ecclesiastical authorities annually
elected by the people makes their
village government quite a formidable apparatus. The civil functionaries are : The alcalde, the gobernador, the captain (or sheriff), and
four messengers (batopiles). It is
not necessary to go further into
detail about them. Suffice it to say
that the three higher officers are
called judges, and must obtain the
sanction of the nearest Mexican
government official before they can
assume office. In ancient times
tradition says, women held these
high offices.

Court Messenger with his
Staff.

245

The ecclesiastical authorities are headed by the ma-
jor-domos, each the custodian of a saint. Their number therefore varies in accordance with the number of
images belonging to the different churches; in Santa
Catarina, for instance, there are four. Their principal
duty is the care of the money belonging to the respective
pictures. Other functionaries of that body are the *algua-
ciles*, a kind of constables, and the four *priostes*, or church
messengers, whose entire duty is to remove the "saints"
as occasion requires. They are always married.

Eight women office-holders should also be mentioned.
They are selected from among the unmarried ones, and
are called tenanchas. They sweep the church, place
flowers before the saints, make tortillas at the feasts, etc.
Five of these women are appointed to live each in the
house of a principal church officer, whose wife she has to
assist in her household duties; in fact, they are only a
kind of servant. Each of the three principal civil authorities has also a tenancha, but the duties of these girls
are exclusively domestic. The servant institution is entirely foreign to the Indian mind, which considers all
persons equals. It only contributes toward making the
Indians immoral, as the young girl often becomes the
mistress of the Indian in whose house she lives.

Aside from this double series of authorities, the
Huichols have their pagan officials—in Santa Catarina, for instance, more than twenty. It will thus be
seen that few men in the tribe can escape from public
service in one capacity or another. Luckily for the
community, all the positions are honorary, and there are
no taxes levied on the people on account of salaries to
be paid.

On the other hand, if it were not for the boundary
disputes with neighbouring districts these judges would
have very little to decide upon. Disagreements about

real estate within a district do not occur, because the land is held in common. Thefts do not engage much of the attention of the judges, as a Huichol never steals corn, believing that grain illegitimately acquired will not grow when sown, or would not last anyway. The misdemeanour of appropriating some bit of clothing—a girdle, a hair-ribbon, or the like—is settled with an inherited ease and tact, as if the judges here found themselves in their own sphere. In case an Indian steals sheep or cattle, which, as recent introductions, are not yet allowed for in their code, the punishment meted out is imprisonment for five days without food or drink, and twenty-five, or, as the Indians say, "an *arroba*," of lashes. An arroba used to be the Mexican standard weight, equal to twenty-five pounds. By the common people the term is yet loosely used as a synonym for twenty-five. In the same way, half an *arroba* means twelve.

As homicide is very rare, and according to the law of the land has to be tried in the Mexican courts, there remains practically nothing for the judges to do but to celebrate marriages and to punish elopements; and to these duties they devote themselves with an astonishing zest and vim, in spite of the fact that in their own hearts they do not see any wrong in the breaking of the seventh commandment, unless a man is preparing to be a shaman, or wants to gain some special boon from the gods. Often, indeed, an Indian is punished for doing something the harm of which he cannot see any more clearly than the judges who inflict the punishment.

The judges come naturally to consider themselves the supreme arbiters in cupid's court, though not always without their difficulties. There was a sly old fellow living in a cave near Santa Catarina, Pancho by name, a widower with several small children, but with no one

to grind corn and make tortillas for him.   He went **to**
the judges and asked them to provide him with a wife,
having his eye particularly on a good-looking young
girl, who had been appointed tenancha, but did not attend
over-zealously to her duties.   Pancho had some influence

Pancho.

with the judges, as he spoke Spanish tolerably well and
could help them in their dealings with the Mexicans.   So
they ordered the girl to appear before them, and informed
her that she was to become Pancho's wife.   She wept
and protested, as she had many younger admirers whom
she would have preferred to the old beau.   But the hard-

hearted officials insisted, and a messenger with a staff in his girdle was deputed to escort the unhappy bride to her new home.

Arriving at the place, she began to make nixtamal— that is, she put corn to boil with lime water to remove the hulls preparatory to the grinding. The officer, seeing her at work, thought her safe and went away. But when Pancho came home, expecting to find his tortillas ready and a pretty wife to greet him, he was sadly disappointed, for the girl had seized the first opportunity to run off. The sight of the white kernels ready for grinding must have been extremely tantalising to Pancho. If he wanted tortillas he had to make them himself.

Of course he immediately complained to the judges, who were very angry, and promised to punish the recalcitrant maiden and force her to return to him. But no trace of her could be found, not even at her father's house, whither court messengers were sent to arrest her. However, after several days, her father and mother of their own accord brought her to Santa Catarina, where all three were promptly put in the stocks until the following day, when the case was brought up for trial. The old man pleaded that he himself needed his daughter, because his wife's eyesight was failing so that she was no longer able to make tortillas. Perhaps assisted by some other considerations the judges rendered a verdict in favour of the father, and Pancho lost his last chance to secure a young wife.

Affairs of this kind do not always, however, end so happily, and it is evident that the changes made by the white man in the native governmental system have been productive of much harm. The Huichol is naturally fond of increasing his possessions ; money and cattle are to him temptations not to be resisted, and they are powerful agents in influencing a judge's goodwill for or against a party on trial. Some judges impose fines for trivial or absurd offences, and divide the spoils among themselves. The victimised Indian never dares to resist his authorities and the power of the staff, for which he has a superstitious reverence descended from ancient times.

The governmental system instituted by the missionaries is artificial, and, well-meant as no doubt it was, apparently proves itself entirely beyond the grasp of the primitive mind, and so is mischievous. Has not the Indian's condition of life been improved by the cattle, the iron implements, etc., which the white man brought to him? It is certainly undeniable that his life has at least been affected by these commodities, which we consider the first essentials for comfort in life. Formerly nothing was owned individually except the house, some dogs, and the corn gathered at the harvest, besides the clothing and whatever a man made for himself in the way of bows and arrows, household utensils, and the like.

But now that the Huichol has become the owner of cattle, mules and horses, sheep and hens, and a number of iron implements, what benefit has he derived from the new order of things? Benefits that are only slight, it seems to me.

It must be understood that the country is by no means overrun with domestic animals. Perhaps half of the people have none. The well-to-do have a few cows, two or three mules, half a dozen sheep, and several hens. Only three or four men in the whole country own herds of cattle of, say, two hundred heads, and several dozens of other animals. Oxen are used for ploughing, where ploughing is possible. Enabling their owner to improve his agriculture and obtain better crops they would, no doubt, be a great advantage if the physical condition of

the country did not so often prevent an advanced style
of tilling from being extensively adopted.

Milk is never drunk. In the course of the year
three or four mule-loads of cheese are taken to the market as the country's entire output of dairy products.
Beef varies the diet of deer-meat on which the people
formerly depended, but, being by no means essential to
the Indians, is generally dispensed with except when
sacrifices are made to the gods. Aside from sacrificial
occasions, oxen serve as food only in case they die a
natural death. Hides are utilised as beds to sleep on,
or are cut into straps or used for making sandals. To
make his footwear out of such material is, of course, less
troublesome for the Huichol than to plait it out of strips
of palm leaves, though the old style is not only better
looking, but also less slippery and therefore more serviceable.

Mules and horses are bought from the Mexicans,
but are not very common. They are seldom used for
riding. The mules are the more valued because they
carry burdens which the Indian in former times had to
take upon himself. They also bring the corn from the
field in the barrancas to the houses, or take the cheese
to the Mexican towns. I should not omit to mention
a new industry which has sprung up in consequence
of the acquisition of mules, namely, the sale of resinous pine-wood, mule-loads of which are taken to the
nearest Mexican village, Mezquitic. Considering, however, that the journey is one of several days' duration,
and that an insignificant price, counted only in centavos,
is paid for a load, this way of earning money is absurd,
even in the eyes of the Indians, whose time has no value.
What the Huichols consider the greatest gain they de-
rive from their beast of burden is its enabling them to
bring great quantities of the sacred hikuli from the far

East. To their eyes the advantages that accrue from the possession of mules and horses have a pious rather than a practical or economic aspect.

Sheep, which are not numerous, are kept for the sake of the wool, which the women spin into yarn. From this they weave girdles, ribbons, pouches, and shirts, and sometimes tunics and skirts. It was undeniably a benefit for these people to be able to substitute wool for the vegetable fibres which formerly were their only textile material. Of late years, however, coarse cotton cloth (manta) bought from the Mexicans has almost entirely taken the place of the homespun woollen clothing, for it is easier to sell a sheep to a " neighbour " for cotton cloth than to laboriously spin and weave yarn. The consequence is that the women are becoming indifferent toward practising an important domestic art, which is thus in danger of being lost. With this comes the doom of the beautiful symbolic figures which form such an attraction in the Huichol textile work.

The Huichols have also received from the white man iron implements, the steel for striking fire, axes, hoes, machetes, and knives, as well as needles, the value of all of which the native readily grasps, though it is clear that none of these acquisitions is of absolute necessity to his existence.

Anything the Huichol may possess, outside of his house and land, he will generally consent to sell, after due deliberation, for money, of which, in contrast with other tribes I know, he is very fond. At times the Mexicans make tours through the entire Huichol country and buy up what cattle, mules, or sheep the Indian may get permission from his gods to dispose of. Since they have acquired a taste for riches a few now exert themselves sufficiently to plant more corn than they actually need, and what surplus of corn and beans a household may

Part of Ribbon, Representing Humming-birds on Pochote Flowers.

have is also, if opportunity occur, offered for barter. In this way some Huichols get a few silver dollars every year; but the wealth thus gained is buried in great secrecy, often not even a man's wife knowing the hiding-place. The only commodities for which money is ever expended are cotton cloth and red flannel, thirty yards of the former, and a yard of the latter being extravagant purchases. Glass beads are considered good invest-ments, as diamonds are among Americans. Money, too, enables the Huichol to get more beautifully drunk on the white man's brandy, which is so much stronger than his native liquor. With Indians intoxicating drinks of their own manufacture, including that made from hikuli, are intimately connected with their religion and are not indulged in outside of feasts and ceremonies. That is one reason why the white man's brandy is so demoralising.

Taking it all in all, the advantages the Indian derives from the advent of the white man are doubtful. The Huichol's standard of life has not on the whole been raised. The few who are well off and could afford better things live no better than the others; they eat their tortillas and beans and sleep on the floor, as they always did, and know no better. On the other hand, the dis-advantages are very manifest. Since the acquisition of domestic animals, the people have begun to realise that there are rich and poor in this world, and those who own little are filled with envy of their more opulent relations. In order to attend to a number of animals, it is necessary to employ helpers, and thus the foundations are laid for social distinctions which not so long ago were entirely unknown among them. Their lesson in modern sociology will be taught them still more severely when once their land is divided up. Yet thus far they have strenuously resisted all attempts of the Mexican Government in this direction. To have everybody plant corn and graze his cattle where he pleases is happiness to them and in accord with their condition of life, which asks for nothing more than sufficient food and shelter for all.

With new possessions come also new anxieties. Some of the cattle may fall ill, or a sheep may break a leg, or cattle or sheep may be hurt by wild beasts. Such contingencies must be avoided at any cost. Therefore the duties toward the gods increase, and to the observances and sacrifices necessary to make the crops grow are added others to preserve and multiply the cattle. Even where only a few hens are owned profits must be shared with the gods.

Added to this is the possibility that the money may be stolen, as in the case of a rich Huichol who lived near Santa Catarina. He was reputed to keep underneath the floor of his hut several pots with silver pesos, and a certain Mexican persuaded a civilised Indian to help him in securing this money. One dark night the unsuspecting nabob was suddenly seized, and tightly bound and thrashed until he disclosed the place where he kept his treasure, which was carried off, a sum amounting, it is said, to five hundred pesos.

Unless it is held that universal happiness is not the aim of civilisation, it appears that the Huichols were better off before than after the white man's arrival, when there was not much to steal, when there was nothing for the judges to "grab," neither cattle nor money, and when there were no police and no prison.

CHAPTER XIV

I HAD about this time an instance of Pablo's agreeable faithfulness to me. I had occasion to send him
to San Andres, and on his return a few days later he told
me that my old friend Carillo had strongly advised him
not to remain with me any longer if he did not wish
surely to fall ill and die. Carillo, it seems, on his return
from Mezquitic had suddenly been taken so ill that he
could not even eat tortillas, and had to employ a good
shaman for two nights in order to recover. His son-in-
law, too, who had also been in my service, felt badly,
and dreamed every night that I was falling over him.
But even such strong evidence could not sway Pablo's
faithfulness. " I never get tired of you," he said to me
one day, and he would have remained with me still
longer had it not been for a final love-affair.

At the ranch from which every morning he fetched
milk for my breakfast he had met and made overtures
to a good-looking young girl. Her father wanted him
to postpone his marriage with her until he returned from
his trip with me ; but to this the ardent lover demurred.
With a characteristic change of heart he deserted her
and decided to marry another girl whom the judges in
Santa Catarina had picked out for a tenancha. For this
girl's sake he accepted a position as prioste. The judges

told the couple to live together—in other words, married them, *pro tem.*, as most of their acquaintances thought, because both of them were true Huichols and fickle—and this, of course, put an end to his connection with me.

Pablo was, no doubt, sometimes provoking. He had no system at all in taking care of my baggage, etc., and toward the end he lost his head completely, and was absent-minded because the women paid so much attention to him. They would even follow him into my tent, and whenever they could get an opportunity speak to him in a low voice and with their eyes cast to the ground. However, he had been very valuable to me. He made me his confidential friend, and his truthfulness and honesty, so unusual in an Indian, are the redeeming features of the picture I keep of him in my memory.

The weather had been cold, cloudy, and rainy, but on the day of my departure from Santa Catarina it turned out at its best. It was a delightfully sunny day in the middle of January on which we climbed the hills above the village, and the pleasant weather continued until the middle of the following month.

In order to reach the village of San Sebastian, on the other side of the deep valley south of Santa Catarina, one has to make a circuit of a day and a half up toward the east. About half-way around, at a place called Tierra Azul, we passed a temple and its adjoining small god-houses, all in complete ruins. The people of the district had emigrated to a locality in the southwest called Nogal, which too had once belonged to the Huichols, but was now under the control of the "neighbours," by whom the original owners have been graciously permitted to settle again. However, no temple has been erected in this their new home, as the people

seem to have reasons of their own for taking their ceremonial arrows and votive bowls to the temple of Santa
Catarina. On the second day we passed the ranch of a
very old woman, probably over a hundred years of age,
at any rate so old that the people believe her when she
says that she has seen the Mother of the Gods.

San Sebastian is not well situated at the bottom of
a cold and windy arroyo. Indians would never have
selected such a place, and the remnants of native houses
and of the old pagan temple are outside of the village
proper in more cheerful surroundings. Many people
were gathered at the time of my arrival, attracted by the
Feast of Changing Authorities, which had been going
on for several days. As I was making for a little plain
that looked suitable for a camping-place, on the other
side of the creek, many men and women started out to
see me. One man fell on his knees in front of my
mule, and as I approached rose and kissed my hand, as
the people are taught by the padres to salute them.
Several of the others showed their respect in a less
devout though equally expressive manner. The population here is still unsophisticated, and a white man is
rarely seen. In this respect they are very different from
the inhabitants of Santa Catarina. It was easy for me
here to get provisions, that is, hens and corn ; and a
sheep, too, was fetched from a ranch half a day's journey distant.

Next day the authorities had sobered down sufficiently to have a meeting with me. I was given permission to excavate underneath the fireplace of the old
temple, where, according to Huichol custom, there is
always a cavity, in which probably a statue of the God of
Fire is kept. But I found nothing except a flat, circular
stone that had never been worked upon, lying at the
bottom of a cylindrical hole, half a yard deep. The

temple, some thirty years ago, was completely burned down, and, as the principal shaman had soon afterward died, had never been rebuilt. At present some of the people worship their native gods in the temples of the vicinity; but with a great many families the church has in a measure replaced the original cult, and a rather curious religion has sprung up. This is the only locality where I found the old and the new belief actually blended; everywhere else the two existed side by side. Here the guardians of the saints, and there are over a dozen, have instituted a cult for them exactly like that of the heathen gods. Each major-domo takes care that votive bowls and ceremonial arrows and shields are duly presented to his particular ward. They have even transferred the names and qualities of the heathen gods to the saints. San Sebastian, represented in a very large oil painting, is Grandfather Fire. The Crucifix is named Elder Brother, God of Wind and of Hikuli; and the Virgin Mary is called Young Mother Eagle Above.

The people were friendly and obliging, and the judges sent me two tenanchas to make tortillas for the road. They also appointed an elderly woman to act as my interpreter while I was in the vicinity. She spoke Spanish remarkably well, and told me proudly that her mother had been a "neighbour," from the village of Soledad. She showed no traces of white blood: but any Indian who speaks and behaves like a Mexican is called a "neighbour." While the Indians in their natural surroundings hate the intruders, those who have grown up among the whites pride themselves on resembling them.

I next wended my way toward the temple of Ocota (Huichol: Okótsali, "Where there is resinous pine-wood"). It is a small aggregation of ranches situated on a beautiful sloping mesa, which came into view as

soon as we passed the pine-clad ridge. The country
from here southward presented a different aspect from
the high sierra, being more undulating. At this time of
the year water is scarce hereabouts, and can only be
found in the deep arroyos. Standing wide apart were
three enormous fig-trees (salate), whose intense green
contrasted pleasingly with the dry fields all about.
This kind of fig-tree is looked upon with reverence, as
its wood is the particular food of the God of Fire.
Closer to the houses there were some aguacate trees,
fine specimens, but less majestic than the other forest
kings. The temple at the extreme right of the plain
looked, with its many adjoining god-houses, like a ranch
by itself. I noticed both here and in San Sebastian
that the dogs were particularly well fed.

Having pitched my tent near one of the ranches,
I went over to the temple and found a few men still
lingering there after the hikuli feast just finished.
Being too late for this occasion, I wanted to make
sure not to miss the one at the next temple, that of
Ratontita, and as no one seemed to know just when
this would be held, I prevailed upon the men to send
someone to find out about it. Huichol messengers
always go on a run, and the man who had been despatched to Ratontita returned in an incredibly short
time. He had made a bee-line over the mesa, down the
steep arroyo, and up again on the other side. The distance, going and coming, could not have been less than
twenty miles, and more than half the way through very
rough country. He brought the information that the
feast would not come off for nearly a week; so I resolved to remain here for a few days.

The authorities advised the custodian of the God of
Fire, the principal man of Ocota, to come and meet me.
In the evening, after I had retired, I was astonished to

hear somebody walking outside of my tent and exclaiming : *"Buenas noches !"* (Good evening!) The visitor,
who spoke excellent Spanish, turned out to be the man
who had been sent for.   He wanted to know who I was
and what was the object of my visit.   I briefly explained this to him and added that as I had retired I
would rather see him in the morning. To this he acceded, telling me, how-
ever, that he, with all
the other men, was go-
ing to cut grass for the
new roof of the temple,
and would be very busy
during the next few
days. I had indeed no-
ticed that the roof of
the temple was in a
very dilapidated condi-
tion.

It was quite an un-
usual proceeding for
an Indian to rouse a
stranger so late at night;
it showed that this man
was very courageous.
Next day I had a very
satisfactory interview
with him, and found

My Ocota Friend and his Wife.

him the most intelligent Indian I ever met. He told
me that his father was a Tepecano, his mother an Aztec,
and he was born in Alquestan ; in his boyhood he had
been adopted by the Huichols and had followed the
hikuli-seekers on many journeys. Being interested in
the significance of what he saw, be easily gained great
knowledge of the religious rites and customs, and grad-

ually became the most influential man of the neighbourhood. His word was law, and his advice was asked and
followed not only in religious but in secular affairs. In
his many travels he had become familiar with the ways
of the Mexicans, and was thus enabled to protect the
land of his brethren against the intruders. White men
are looked upon with suspicion, and are never allowed
to stay long.

This man had a great faculty of explaining things,
and seldom used the wrong expression for his purpose.
His Spanish was remarkable. He used many words that
I had never heard in conversation with even better-class
Mexicans, a gift the more astonishing in view of the
fact that he could neither read nor write. He dictated
to me long traditions which I took down verbatim. Several times he insisted upon my writing more than was
necessary, because, as he said, he wanted me to have my
information complete. Among other things he told me
that it was fifty years since any nahuales had lived here.
These were singing shamans who would eat *yerba de lobo*
five times in order to make themselves into wolves; in
that shape they would hunt deer, but on the sixth day
they became men again.

As may be imagined, I was disposed to make the
most of this man, and during my stay at Ocota I interviewed him every day as much as he could stand. Like
all natives when called upon to exert their brains, he
was easily tired, and when tired he became sullen and
short of words, and after a while impossible to deal
with.

One day an emissary arrived from Ratontita to learn
all about me and the purpose of my proposed visit to
that place. My new friend reassured him in regard to
me, and I then received a formal invitation to visit
Ratontita. I also urged my influential intercessor to

accompany me on the trip, which he consented to do for a consideration of one peso a day and his rations.

The trail we had to follow passed a deep arroyo and was at some places dangerous for loaded mules, but we reached our destination without mishap. On the second day we came to a ranch which from a distance looked like a small hacienda. I found the son of the owner busy at a distillery in an arroyo close by, making toach to sell at the approaching feast. This is the only instance where I saw a Huichol redistilling the native brandy, for the sake of making it stronger. This kind of liquor is sold at thirty-seven centavos per quart bottle. In this, the southern, part of the Huichol country I frequently noticed tame macaos at the ranches. It was a common thing to see a pair of these birds sitting in a tree next to the house.

Ratontita, as we approached it, looked even more picturesque than Ocota. It is a cluster of ranches grouped around the temple and its adjoining god-houses. As to the people, experience has taught them to be wary of strangers, and they appeared reticent and inhospitable. Inside of the temple hung a stuffed mouse, from which the Indians would not part at any price. It was, no doubt, the hero-god of the locality, and the Mexicans had it in mind when they named the place Ratontita (*raton*=mouse). The Huichols, however, have a very different name for the precinct namely, Taquitzata, which means " The silk of the corn is falling."

Next morning before daybreak my companion was called to a consultation concerning me with the principal men. After he had fully posted them they made up their minds that I could help them in their land difficulties, and sent for their escribano (secretary), who lived a couple of days' journey distant in the mining town of Bolaños. They wanted me to write a letter to the Presi-

dent of the Republic asking him not to have their land
parcelled out to them individually. The secretary was
to see that I did it right, but happily he did not turn up
while I was at Ratontita. In the meantime my guide,
who was also to have a hand in the letter, got very drunk
and remained in this blissful condition all the time the
feast was going on. Thus I was saved from the delicate
position in which they might have placed me.

The Huichol whom I had brought with me from
Santa Catarina came to me one day very excitedly, com-
plaining that the people here had loudly expressed their
dislike of him, although he had not done them any harm.
They did not even know him, but the fact that he was
from Santa Catarina was sufficient reason for their objecting to him. Feeling runs high on account of the
incessant land disputes between the different districts.
When the missionaries established the pueblos they also
decided upon the extent of territory that was to belong
to each. In other words, they divided the land into districts ; but their boundaries, which were not marked out
with precision, have been a bone of contention between
the villagers ever since. The trouble is aggravated by
the natural jealousy between the different sections of the
tribe. The longer I was with the Indians the more I
saw how little solidarity there was within the tribe. Every district is interested only in its own individual affairs ;
the fate of the neighbouring natives is a matter of indifference to them. It is not too much to say that no
one district would care much if the " neighbours " were
to gobble up all the rest of the tribe's domain so long as
its own particular territory remained intact. Still less
does one tribe concern itself with what is going on beyond its borders. This, the usual condition of primitive
society, no doubt explains why it was comparatively easy
for the Spaniards to conquer the Indians of Mexico.

Not only do the various tribes neglect to unite against a common foe, but even in the same tribe there are always dissensions.

Meanwhile preparations for putting new roofs on two of the god-houses had been coming on apace, and I had a chance to witness this performance. To the average white man putting a roof on a house or a church is a plain and practical matter; but with the Huichols it is a solemn, religious rite, full of symbolism in every detail. On my arrival I had noticed in front of the god-houses heaps of the peculiar coarse grass used in thatching. Long sticks of bamboo, each reed split in two, were lying ready for use in holding the grass in place on the roof, and near by were stacks of palm leaves to be torn into strips for tying together the woodwork of the roof. In close proximity to this material, last but not least, lay the ceremonial objects which for the time being had been taken out of the god-houses.

The ceremony began when the principal shaman selected four big bunches of grass and solemnly laid eight long bamboo-sticks over them. He conducted himself with as much dignity and as great an air of superiority as if nothing in the wide world were at that moment of such supreme importance as the thatching of those god-houses. He was powerfully built, with large, coarse features, but a kind and child-like expression on his face shining out under a halo of long, unkempt hair. It was unusually coarse and abundant, was this hair, and very black, except for a pronounced sprinkling of flaxen-coloured strands in irregular, longitudinal stripes. There seemed to be no white blood in him, because his body was as dark as that of the ordinary Huichol, although his face was somewhat lighter.

He and his assistant next sat down in chairs near by and began in an off-hand way to make eight straw ani-

mals, four for each god-house.   They were representations of opossums, necessary adjuncts to the god-
houses as to the temples.   A thin roll of grass formed
the body, and two long straws were tied to the upper and
lower end so as to protrude far beyond it.   The bunch
was then adorned with feathers of the parrot and the
macao, the former symbolising prayers for rain, the latter expressive of adoration of the fire and the sun.   The
two men repeatedly spat on these straw animals and
placed their hands over them prayerfully.

A bunch of leaves from a tree called tempiske was
also prepared to be hung up under the roof to drive off
any evil approaching the house.

When everything was in readiness four young men
climbed up on the roof with the straw opossums.   After
having made the inevitable ceremonial circuit on the
skeleton roof, a somewhat difficult feat, they tied the
four bunches underneath the upper portions of the rafters, one opposite another, bodies down, tails up and
protruding above the ridge of the roof.   This done, they
quickly descended.

Now the thatching of the roof could begin.   The
shaman, holding two laths of bamboo in his hand, rose,
presenting them to the six regions of the world, and
carried them toward the house, followed by four men,
each carrying one of the four bundles of straw in his
arms.   They made the ceremonial circuit around the
building and then stopped to put on the lowest row of
thatch, first on the right side of the roof, then on the
left—two bundles on each side.   A bamboo lath was
placed across the upper end of the straw and tied securely to the rafters and crosspieces with strips of palm
leaves.   It was all done accurately and quickly, everybody knowing his duty, and fulfilling it.   After they had
finished the row of thatch the men remained standing in

their places and raised their voices in prayer. They offered the house to the gods, and in return asked for health. The next layer was put on with the same ceremonies, repeated until the entire job was finished. In spite of the considerable time consumed in prayers and

Praying while Putting a New Roof on a God-house in Ratontita.

ceremonial rounds, the roofing was completed in about an hour. The new roof looked neat and tidy, and above the four opossum-tails stuck out deftly.

Four men now entered the house. One of them jumped up on the altar, and all diligently gathered up any stray bit of grass that had fallen down during the roofing. As they did this they began to shout as though they were calling the dogs in hunting deer, and when they came out each of them had a handful of straws. They now seated themselves on the ground, each one by himself, and examined their collections, discarding all small pieces and whatever remnants of earth might still be among the grass, and keeping only the long stalks, which were carried back into the temple and burned. Their search was for deer-hairs. This may seem to the reader like looking for a needle in a haystack, but the Huichols assured me that occasionally some hairs were really found. This, after all, is not impossible, as deer are plentiful and some hair may cling to the grass as it is brought in. The finding of hairs foretells success in the deer-hunting of the coming year; in other words, they are an omen of prosperity. The lucky finder hands his treasure to the shaman, who spits on it and returns it to him.

The ceremonial objects were then put back in their places in the god-house, and all the builders entered the edifice and prayed for awhile; then all was over. Temple roofs are put on in the same manner.

CHAPTER XV

THE preliminaries incidental to the great hikuli feast
seemed at last to be nearing an end. The deer
chase over, the second requirement was being complied
with—namely, the clearing of the temple fields preparatory to the planting of the corn next June. This work
must be done by the hikuli-seekers, whom I had for several days seen go out in the morning and return in the
early afternoon. In due season the officers of the temple attend to the cultivation of the land.

Every private ranch, so much does Huichol agriculture depend on the deer-hunt and the procuring of
hikuli, is subject to the same law as obtains with the temple lands. To the Huichol so closely are corn, deer, and
hikuli associated that by consuming the broth of the deer-
meat and the hikuli they think the same effect is produced—namely, making the corn grow. Therefore, when
clearing the fields they eat hikuli before starting the day's
work. Every man takes up a field wherever he likes,
and uses the same piece of land for five years, adding
every year a new field, so that in all he has five to cultivate.

On a fine old tree in front of the temple of Ratontita
were hanging large bundles of deer-meat threaded on
strings, as well as large coils of fresh hikuli. Everything

Preparing for the Hikuli Feast at Ratontita.

seemed ready for the feast, when I unexpectedly discovered that the Rancho Hediondo, three miles away,
would have its celebration first.   Some two or three
years ago the population of that locality had quarrelled
with Ratontita, and withdrawn from worshipping here.
They were preparing a temple of their own, and they
had even gone separately for hikuli.   When I received
word that the women there had put corn to boil preparatory to making tesvino (which is always done in the
morning, the liquor being ready the next evening) I
knew that their feast was to come off the following day,
and I lost no time, therefore, in going over to the Rancho
Hediondo to witness the proceedings.

The new temple had not yet been built, and a corral
of brushwood had been put up to serve in its stead.   Inside of this inclosure everything had been arranged exactly as it would have been in the temple.   There was
also the usual open space in front surrounded by god-
houses.   All of these had a new appearance, being
freshly plastered with a whitish earth common in that
region.   The spot was a charming one, and afforded a
fine view of the country round about.

Just as I arrived, soon after sunset on a rather chilly
day at the end of January, the hikuli-seekers and their
wives were returning from their bath, the first they had
had since the start upon the hikuli journey four months
before.   Their hair was still wet, and their clothes, which
they had washed on the previous day, were nice and
clean.

The observances began at dusk.   In pouches slung
over their shoulders the men carried tamales, which, after
due ceremonial circuits round the fire, were deposited on
a blanket spread out in front of the altar, a mat raised
on four forked sticks.   Then the tamales were distributed among the people present, and immediately

afterward everyone, even the children, drank a little of the water brought from the hikuli country.

My friend from Ocota contemptuously remarked to me that things were not properly managed here. "They ought to have given tamales first of all to the fire," he said; "this is nothing but a ranch!" Later, however, I was informed that this ceremony of "feeding the fire" had been properly performed on the preceding day. The different districts very naturally have slight diversities of customs; even in the same temple there may be variations in regard to the religious rites, according to the orders of the shaman.

All the hikuli dances are performed in the open air, on the patio, and here all the preparations were made, the most important being the grinding of the hikuli, to which two women conscientiously attended, while at the southern end of the dancing-place no less than twenty large jars with tesvino were kept boiling.

Three fires were made, one inside of the corral and another near the extreme eastern limit of the patio, where the shaman was to sing. The purpose of this was to give light to the people while dancing, or, in Indian conception, to guard them. The third fire was lighted at the northern end of the patio for the people of the underworld, that they too might look at the feast. All the fires were made in the following way: A procession of five men appeared on the scene, each with an armful of firewood. They were led by a shaman carrying in his open palms a piece of green wood scarcely half a yard long. This was the pillow (molitáli) of Grandfather Fire, and had to be carried as carefully as a baby. On arriving at the fireplace of the temple, the bearer lifted the pillow toward the five regions of the world, and, lastly, offered it to the sixth by placing it on the ground. His companions then built a fire over it, arranging the pieces so as to point east and west. The other fires were built in a similar way and quickly.

The shaman and the hikuli-seekers now disappeared into the god-house of the Sun, where I could hear them praying aloud. They were giving an account of themselves and of their long journey which they had undertaken in compliance with an ancient custom established by the gods themselves. In return for it they asked for life, and that no evil may happen to them during the night.

Meanwhile two important participants in the feast, the grey squirrel and the small striped skunk, were placed in the northwestern part of the patio. Both were fairly well stuffed, the squirrel in a squatting position. They were tied to sticks stuck firmly into the ground to keep them upright. These animals play a conspicuous part in the cult. The squirrel, which sees better than ordinary people and guards against evil, is supposed to guide the hikuli-seekers on their way. It was dressed in a curious fashion ; around part of its body was wrapped a weather-stained old piece of newspaper, tied up with

The Squirrel at the Feast.

twine, which also kept the tail in position. There were feathers stuck under the twine, and round the neck were suspended two shining dark-green wing-covers of a beetle, and two small coloured birds of clay bought in Mexican stores. The most extraordinary ornament, however, was a large metal crucifix that hung from its neck down over its stomach. A small fire was built in front of the animals and two jars were placed beside them, one containing tesvino, the other water from the

hikuli country, of which the people had just been drinking. The vessel was still half-filled, and the stick with
which the shaman had first sacrificed the water to the
six regions of the world remained in it until the end of
the feast.

About midnight the hikuli-seekers were still praying
in the god-house, and nobody seemed to know when the
dance would commence. It always lasts twenty-four
hours, however, and next morning I awoke reasonably
sure to find the people dancing. Never had I seen
the Huichols so profusely ornamented as on this occasion.

There was, of course, the usual array of pouches for
the men ; but to-day not only the men but the women
also excelled in a lavish display of feathers. The men
had stuck them under their hair-ribbons, or some of
them had their hats liberally decked with macao and
hawk feathers, while the women wore strings of red and
yellow plumes across their backs.

The shaman sat in front of the fire, facing east, thus
turning his back to the dancing-place. On either side
of him sat an assistant who now and then took turns in
helping him with the singing. There is no drum used
at this feast, and the shaman sings without any accompaniment. At the feet of the singers was placed a
jar with hikuli liquor, and the usual complement of ceremonial arrows, plumes, tamales, etc.

Both men and women take part in the dancing, which
consists in a quick, jumping walk with frequent jerky
turns of the body, differing little from the hikuli dance
of the Tarahumares. They dance against the apparent
course of the sun, moving around the shamans and their
fire in a circle, which, however, soon becomes an ellipse
on account of the tendency of the dancers to draw
nearer to the stuffed animals. Most of the dancing is

The Hikuli Dance near Ratontita.

thus performed behind the backs of the shamans. No special place is assigned to the women.

A prominent feature of the dance is the carrying by both men and women, held in their hands and resting against the shoulders, of bamboo sticks carved to represent serpents ; the men besides hold in their hands deertails mounted on short sticks. With these they constantly gesticulate, thrusting them into the air in all directions as they dance. These movements recall the animal itself, because the tail of the deer is raised in running and is a conspicuous object to the hunter. It was in the shape of a gigantic deer that the hikuli first appeared to the forefathers of the Huichol, and in his tracks were growing small plants of the same kind. From the girdles of the dancers hang new combs in the usual Indian shape of small whisk-brooms, the material of which is brought yearly from the land of the hikuli.

The dancing is not continuous. Every now and then it stops, and the starting and finishing points are always at the right-hand side of the shamans. Two men and their wives are the leaders. They are better dressed than the rest and make many turns round and round during the dancing. This is the most interesting dance I saw among the Huichols, and I was not tired watching their queer movements in spite of the violent wind which wrapped the dancers in clouds of dust and made things in general unpleasant. Sometimes it seemed as if the shaman's voice would be choked with the mass of earthy particles that filled the air and powdered the faces of the three men. But they sat motionless as statues, except the singer, who from time to time spat out the dust, drank a little hikuli water, and started afresh.

About noon the people sat down to paint each other's faces with the curious designs in yellow. Strangely enough, this very important feature had not been attended to at the beginning of the dance.

The third and last day of the feast was one of great rejoicing, because now at last the long period of abstinence was over. Out of respect for Father Sun all the

HUICHOL SONG AT THE HIKULI DANCE

HUICHOL SONGS AT THE HIKULI DANCE

Transcribed from graphophone.

These songs are repeated several times, and sometimes the notes marked × are omitted, but the time is preserved by a rest.

tesvino was consumed, and then native brandy was offered for sale. Of course all present got drunk, and it was impossible to do anything with them. To make matters worse, the " neighbours," who always know when such feasts come off, did not miss the opportunity. Some of them arrived from Bolaños with a barrel of sotol brandy and did a rushing business. It is a pity that this liquor traffic cannot be suppressed. The Indians' own stimulating drinks apparently do them no harm; but an hour or two after a Mexican brandy-vendor has arrived unconscious men and women are fairly strewn about the dancing-place; and they are miserable for some time afterward. On this occasion, as usual, the white man's brandy knocked them out so quickly that they could not even finish the feast properly. The final ceremony toward which the feast tends is the toasting of corn, which gives its name indeed to the entire festival Rarikira from raki (toasted corn). Whereas it should have been performed at sunrise, it had this time to be delayed until mid-day.

Enthusiastic Hikuli Dancer.

At that hour the shaman fastened a plume with a hair-ribbon to the head of the woman who had been appointed to do the toasting, and gave her a bunch of coarse straw with which to stir the corn. She now made ready her comal, on which the corn was to be toasted, placing it on three stones over the fire, and then she waited for the men to bring the corn. The hikuli-seekers appeared, carrying in their pouches extra large ears of corn of different colours. After having made the usual ceremonial rounds, they placed the ears in a heap on the ground, and sat down to shell the corn. Five grains were sacrificed to the fire, and the rest were given to the women to toast, which does not require much time. The esquite, as the dish is called, was then offered to all present, together with meat and broth of the deer.

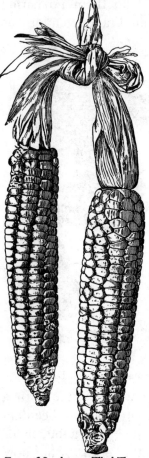

Ears of Seed-corn Tied Together to be Hung for Winter Keeping.

The Huichol regards all his staple food as a distinct gift from the gods, and ceremonies are periodically performed in connection with it. It never occurs to the Indian that he has to eat in accordance with natural laws in order to sustain life. He will not partake of his new crop of corn or beans or squashes until a feast has been made and a part of the harvest offered to the gods. Even the various forms in which he eats corn, such as tamales, toasted corn, etc., have to be sacrificed to the deities before he may enjoy the new dishes. The same rules are observed in regard to his intoxicating drinks, and in certain cases also with water. The Indian respects his food and drink, and eats with care, with his thoughts on the gods who are pleased to grant it to him.

Corn, the principal cereal, is naturally looked upon with special reverence. The Huichol carefully avoids stepping on a grain of it, for to do so would crush out its life. Maize is a little girl whom one sometimes can hear weeping in the fields; she is afraid of the wild beasts, the coyote and others, that eat corn. There is a different name for each stage of the growth of corn—the seed grain, the first shoot, the plant with two or three leaves, the plant with stalk, in flower, with green corn, with the ears ready for harvesting, and finally the corn in the store-house ready for consumption. There are five kinds of corn, each of a different colour—red, yellow, white, black, and that with mottled ears—all belonging to different gods. So far do the Indians go in personifying this cereal that they keep five ears of corn in the sacred bowl of the house "to wait for the corn's sons," the crop of the new year, even though for some months they may not have enough themselves for their daily needs.

The locality of the Rancho Hediondo proved interesting, and I obtained everything I could get there, including the stuffed animals that had witnessed the feast. I was now anxious to continue my journey ; yet, though a guide had been promised me for the road, in the general drunkenness all agreements were forgotten. Only after much coaxing and bargaining could I secure a man, and him only for one day. At last, however, we started late in the afternoon and descended into a deep arroyo, where we made camp.

To add to my annoyance at having to deal with drunken people, with no guide to get away from them, I suddenly became aware that I had lost my bunch of keys. After a fruitless search I gave them up, contenting myself with the reflection that some future traveller would find them decorating the neck of the grey squirrel in the temple. But after a while one of my men stumbled over them and returned them to me. By another stroke of good luck a young Indian going home from the feast passed our camp and was pressed into service as a guide. His ranch was only half a day's journey off, but I persuaded him to continue with us for two days. Travelling westward through the lonely forest we found the track comparatively good and the country fairly level. We passed one fan palm, about twelve feet high, growing among pine and oak trees.

At another point, on high land, we came upon a large heap of stones intermixed with bunches of grass. I had seen many similar heaps while travelling in the Sierra Madre. With the Tarahumares and Tepehuanes they are composed mainly of stones and sticks; but here as there they are always encountered on high points, where the track leads over a ridge between two or more valleys, or what the Mexicans call a *puerta* (gateway). Although three, four, or even five feet high, the mounds are formed without any attempt at plan or order. Every Indian who passes such a pile adds a stone or a stick to it in order to gain strength for his journey. Among the Tarahumares only the old men observe this custom. Whenever the Tepehuanes carry a corpse, they rest it for some fifteen minutes on such a heap by the way-side that the deceased may not be fatigued, but strong enough to finish his long journey to the land of the dead.

One of my Huichol companions stopped on reaching this pile, pulled up some grass from the ground and picked up a stone as big as his fist. Holding both to-gether he spat on the grass and on the stone and then rubbed them quickly over his knees. He also made a couple of passes with them over his chest and shoulders, exclaiming "Kenestíquai!" (May I not get tired!) and then put the grass on the heap and the stone on top of the grass. This particular pile was called Nutíquayë (He who knows how to cure). Some such agglomera-tions have no proper names, but all are under the do-minion of the Goddess of the Southern Clouds. The Mexicans call such heaps *mojoneras*.

Our guide here insisted on returning to his home to take part in a hikuli feast there. I had to let him go, and be thankful that he had served us thus far. Happily we soon ran across another Indian who showed us the track leading from the highland down into the broad barranca, on the other side of which, half-way up the slope, lies the pueblo of Guadalupe Ocotan. The de-

Huichol Family from Guadalupe Ocotan.

scent was so circuitous that, although we travelled near-ly the whole day, we covered only fourteen miles, a distance in a straight line of not more than six. The following day we arrived at the village. The place looked abandoned, and tall, dry grass was growing every-where, even close to the church. I made my camp under some shady trees, first cutting away the grass sufficiently to avoid danger from fire.

Guadalupe Ocotan, the most southern of the Huichol villages, is of recent origin, having been formed only in 1853. Before that the district belonged to San Andres, and, while situated on the eastern side of the river, is by customs and affinities yet allied to the western part of the land. Inside of the small church here I found some novel decorations: the official gazettes of the Government of the State, carefully hung up in long files as clothes-lines. The State Government sends this source of information to all courts within its jurisdiction, white or Indian. Some day, when the judges are able to read, they may find these messages of service.

From the dilapidated condition of the pagan temple I inferred that the native religion was neglected, but it seems the ancient dances and ceremonies are faithfully kept up. The women are shy, and many of the people do not speak Spanish. Altogether they appear little affected by civilisation except that the men cut their hair rather short. This peculiarity is due, of course, to the influence of the "neighbours," who have appropriated the land a few miles to the south, and established the village of Huajimi. Otherwise this part of the country, taking in the southern end of the Sierra Madre, is very secluded and has little communication with the outer world.

The native authorities, as well as the people themselves, were very nice to me and all contributed toward making my stay among them profitable. As this was my last opportunity to secure ethnological specimens from the tribe, I was anxious to complete my collections. The women here excel in making shirts and tunics, which they richly embroider with ancient designs. Through the kindness of the alcalde I obtained several of these valuable garments, with which the people themselves were loath to part. It was he who sold me the elaborately worked shirt that is illustrated on page 231. He also helped me out in another matter. While at Ocota I bought a drum which the seller agreed to deliver to me here. Fourteen days had elapsed, but the drum had not arrived. To save me time and trouble in hunting it up the generous alcalde offered to let me have his own drum, payment for which he proposed to collect from the man in Ocota.

Being desirous of securing here some skulls from an ancient burial-place in a distant valley, but unable to make the trip myself, I persuaded the Indians to go alone to fetch them for me. They brought the precious load back safely in two bags which I had lent to them. This was remarkable in proving that the Huichols are not afraid of dead who passed out of life long enough ago.

CHAPTER XVI

LEAVING THE HUICHOL COUNTRY FOR THE COAST—DRESS-REFORM AS A MEANS OF SPREADING CIVILISATION—A QUESTION OF DRAWERS—ARRIVAL AT THE CITY OF TEPIC—AGRICULTURAL PROSPECTS OF THE TERRITORY — PERNICIOUS MALARIA — SPLENDID ANTIQUITIES DUG UP IN A GARDEN—CERAMICS.

WELL satisfied with what I had gained at this place, I started on February 11th toward the coast, bound for the City of Tepic. My company now consisted of the four Mexicans who had been with me since my visit to Mezquitic, five Huichols, and one civilised Indian from Huajimi. We had first to climb once more to the cold and windy sierra, which we followed for about eighteen miles to the south. The view from this ridge toward the sea was magnificent. The mighty extinct volcano Sanganguey, which hides the basin of Tepic, rose in a blue mist some sixty miles to the south-west above a wave of low ridges extending from north to south, between us and the peak. Right below us was the tract of land designated as Nogal, its extensive slopes and rugged crests covered with dense pine-forests as with a carpet. In the midst of this green expanse there was a quiet lagoon, like an eye, in the solitary landscape. The Mexicans believe that this lake is connected with the sea, and that cattle are frequently seen ascending from it. The locality is almost uninhabited. The few Huichols and Mexicans who exist here must be regarded as colonists.

Our track presently struck the camino real from Huajimi to Tepic, and we now descended from what was once Huichol country, and is still called Sierra de los Huicholes or Sierra de Alica. Our road from here on, in a westerly direction, was quite good, or at least appeared so to one accustomed to mountain travel in Mexico. Having passed the pine region we reached the oak forests. The country continued very lonely until about a day's journey from Tepic. It seemed used only for grazing purposes, strangely enough, since it was well-watered and apparently fertile. This entire region is also well known as the ultimate retreat of General Lozada of revolutionary fame, who was here captured by the Government troops. He had begun his career as a brigand, or ladron, but when he came into power he prosecuted robbers himself. Though a fanatical Catholic, if he had anything against a padre it is said that he would not hesitate to " kill the man whose hand he kissed."

We passed two cattle ranches, which, however, being occupied only during the wet season, were now deserted. At a third, we could discern some inhabitants in the distance. As we descended toward the coast the grass continued as far as the eye could reach over endless hills. Along the creeks there was always a verdant shrub growing densely. Presently we crossed the Rio Alica, a river having its origin in the Laguna de Chapala near Guadalajara. Called by different names in different parts of its course, it falls into the sea under the name of Rio de Santiago and at the point where we crossed it the stream was quite wide. My Huichol attendants were excellent swimmers and it was mainly due to them that I safely landed all my mules on the other side. The water reached to their aparejos.

A few minutes later we came to the first civilised settlement, the hacienda Agua y Pan, where a good deal of mining is carried on. Here I bought some oranges, which though sour refreshed me very much. Is there any fruit like an orange to the weary traveller? Its beautiful form, rich colour, delicious fragrance, and incomparable taste carry with them the suggestion of a better world. I also secured at this remote place some French sardines, each box costing twelve cents in American money, but the contents were delicious.

I suppose my long abstinence from civilised food had something to do with my appreciation. For three months I had been living mainly on the monotonous diet of the thin corn gruel called atole blanco, boiled hens, and eggs. The Indians give no corn to their fowl, so that the birds are lean and the eggs taste like soap. The gruel, of course, is tasty enough, especially when flavoured with a little honey; but being merely a drink it does not satisfy. Such a diet without variation soon palled. I find in my note-book a characteristic jotting: " I have gradually accustomed myself not to eat anything in the middle of the day while on the road, because it is not expedient to keep the mules waiting with their loads on while only some miserable tortillas are heated for me. In the evening I am often too tired to bother about the cooking, and in the morning there is nothing to eat that I care for." After all these years I was not yet sufficiently Indianised to content myself with tortillas and water. No wonder I grew thin and weak, an easy prey to malarial fever when I reached the coast.

It was quite a long journey for pack-mules from the hacienda Agua y Pan to the City of Tepic, and we did not reach our final destination that day, camping instead at the sugar plantation of Puga. Hearing from a muleteer that a couple of nights before he had had to fire at two robbers to protect his animals, I ordered my men to take turns in watching that night. Nothing

happened to us, however, and next day we continued
our journey.

The aspect of the country was now entirely changed,
and so was the temperature of the air, at that season
warm and pleasant. Green fields of sugar-cane and of
barley delighted the eye. The climate is so damp and
the ground so moist that the latter crop is sown and har-
vested in winter time without either precipitation or
irrigation.

The many ox wagons we met on the dusty road
reminded us that we were approaching civilisation, and
early in the afternoon we arrived at Tepic after a journey of six days and a half. My men, both Mexicans
and Indians, had been much worried about their entry
into the city, because the law of the Territory forbids
anyone to appear in the streets of the towns without
pantalones (trousers). This law, in operation in one or
two of the States of Mexico, is intended to promote culture by improving the appearance of the natives. It is
argued that the loose white cotton drawers (*calzones*)
worn by the working classes and the civilised Indians
are not decent enough. Happily the enlightened com-
mander of the Territory has modified the law in favour
of the Indians, allowing them to wear cotton drawers.
An Indian in tight trousers is a comical sight to
behold.

I entered unmolested, however, with my naked-
legged Huichols and drawered Mexicans, for the Mexican laws are enforced with common-sense consideration,
and visitors not up to date are given an opportunity of
buying trousers after they get into town. But woe to
the one who should linger too long about the streets
without the prescribed attire ! He would be promptly
arrested and condemned to pay a fine amounting to more
than the cost of the garment.

To be sure, trousers may be bought very cheap, or may even be hired for the day. There are here in Tepic some enterprising speculators who rent them to their Mexican country cousins as well as to the Huichols. One of my Mexicans obtained a pair so tight that he could not sit down all the time he was in Tepic; but as he was going to remain only one day, he could easily "stand" it. Muleteers visiting towns periodically generally carry this requisite property of civilisa-

The City of Tepic.

tion with them and array themselves duly before entering.

My opinion and that of other foreigners whom I met in Mexico is that the white drawers are in every way preferable to trousers. The latter, according to the custom of the country, are worn very tight and are really the less modest looking of the two. The drawers are more becoming, more healthful in the tropical climate, easily kept clean, and, being also much cheaper, are less onerous an expense for the poor country people. It would be well if the authorities would reconsider the matter.

There is a tolerably good hotel in Tepic; but, coming as I did with so many Indians and mules and with my large collections, I had perforce to put up at one of the numerous *mesones*, a small, dirty, noisy place, although the best there was. I should advise anyone to go to the hotel, which has the advantage of a second story, where if you get a room the air is far better than nearer to the ground.

After having unburdened the mules and got my things safely stored, I went at once, although it was already late in the day, to see the commanding chief of the Territory, General Don Leopoldo Romano, who knew of me already through correspondence. A man of much force of character and unusual administrative ability, he proved charming and obliging to anyone who had the good fortune to meet him. Mexicans as well as Indians, high or low, all were sure to get a hearing with him in any just case. His death since my visit has been generally mourned.

I had only one Mexican dollar left, but secured enough money to pay off my men next day. The general considered me very unfortunately located in the meson, and through his kindness I was enabled to take my things to a private house, where I remained during my stay in Tepic. He also put me in prompt communication with persons who he thought would be of service to me.

The meaning of the word Tepic has not yet been definitely settled. Perhaps it is Nahuatl : Tetl=stone; and pic=hard—hard stone. The city, at an elevation of 3,069 feet, is beautifully situated on a large plain almost at the foot of the picturesque extinct volcano Sanganguey. A small river passes the town in a northerly direction and empties into the Rio de Santiago, having its origin in a spring near the village of Jalisco (Nahuatl : " Where the land is sandy "), hardly four leagues off. The population (14,000) consists largely of descendants of colonists from Guadalajara and is refined and sympathetic. The city has a fine plaza, and besides the principal hotel there is quite a good restaurant, where I took my meals. My visit was in Lent, and every Friday magnificent oysters were brought up from the port of San Blas to the market.

The Territory of Tepic contains some excellent land for tropical agriculture. Sugar-cane, rice, and coffee are raised so successfully that the cultivation of these products is sure to assume even greater importance in the near future. The climate of the coast region is, however, bad, and malaria often proves fatal not only to new-comers but even to natives. I heard that some haciendas had to be deserted during certain seasons of the year on this account. The fever often assumes a most pernicious character, and death may follow within a few hours. The priest of Iztlan told me that, out of nine young men who simultaneously with himself had left the college to take up their work as priests on the western coast, all had died excepting himself, who had never been ill.

In the City of Tepic itself the climate is damp and exceedingly changeable, the temperature varying greatly in the course of the day. The unhealthfulness of the place is undoubtedly increased in recent years owing to the fact that a large lagoon close to the city has been drained off in order to gain the land.

There are, to my knowledge, no architectural ruins of any importance within the Territory of Tepic, although mounds abound in certain parts, and splendid little figures of burnt clay, painted and polished, are frequently turned up by the plough. As the finders are generally ignorant of the value of these *monos* (literally, monkeys, the popular name for ancient idols and figures) they give them to the children to play with. Some may be sufficiently interested to keep them as curios; others, believing that they bring health and luck, and that by selling them they would make themselves poor, absolutely refuse to part with them. The so-called civilised Indians even grow angry when asked whether they have monos. One man indignantly replied: " I am not a sorcerer. There is only one God and that is the One Above." Some, on the contrary, when I expressed a desire to buy monos, wonderingly said: "How much money that man must have! He does not know what to do with it all." Still others suspected that I was protestante and wanted to kill people with the monos.

Yellow Clay Figure, Polished, Probably Representing an Acrobat. Compostela, Tepic. Height, 14.2 ctm.

A reliable friend of mine told me some interesting facts of a cave near Ayutlan, which he had visited. Noticing that the floor was artificial, made of hardened volcanic ash, he suspected that there was something underneath, and started to excavate. After digging for two days he found many earthenware jars and bowls rather poorly made. He soon got tired of this, and left. Other treasure-seekers came and continued the digging, who also finding nothing but earthenware vessels and a few figures, grew tired and desisted. In this way many came, dug for a while, and went away. My informant estimates that at least two thousand jars, bowls, and figures were taken out and thrown down into the arroyo. Finally a lucky fellow reached the bottom, some thirty yards deep, and there he found an idol of gold, twelve inches high, which he melted down and sold as bullion.

There are many gardens all over the City of Tepic, and the soil, on which orange and coffee trees grow, is black to a depth of two yards. Below this is a layer of yellow earth, half a yard deep, and beneath this again a layer of volcanic ashes. One man had been making systematic excavations in his garden in search of antiquities, of which he was a great admirer, although he had no knowledge whatever of archæology. He kept a man constantly at work digging, and in the course of five years he had gone over one quarter of his plot, sixty yards in length by twenty-five in width. It lay alongside of, and partly on, a very low ridge, running north and south for about three hundred yards, and to a width of twenty-five, its northerly end being about sixty yards from the river of Tepic.

Clay Figure, Painted Red and Black. Jalisco near Tepic. Height, 15.3 ctm.

The curiosity of the owner of the garden was first aroused by the edges of some stones which he discovered among his trees in a position indicating that they had been put down by man. The tops of the stones scarcely showed above the surface, but on the earth's being removed a circular arrangement was laid bare. Below this, a wall running north and south was built upon the layer of ashes. Here a number of poorly preserved skeletons were found, lying with the heads

toward the wall and the feet toward the west.   In other
words, he had struck an ancient burial-place, perhaps of
some Nahuatl people, and as the excavations proceeded
he constantly found more skeletons.   Thus far he had
unearthed eleven.

The owner of the garden told me that they were
stretched directly on the ashes, except in a few instances,
where they rested on thin flat stones.   All were covered
as well as flanked with such slabs, the space within the
inclosures being filled in with clay ; there was no fixed
distance between the skeletons.   With them many interesting objects were brought to light.   Earthenware jars
filled with ashes were frequently found standing near the
dead, sometimes also jars of carbonate of lime.   With
persons who in my wise friend's opinion had been poor
in life he had found only a single earthen jar near the
head, and they had no beads around their necks.   The
excavations were not carried farther than the layer of
ashes.

As luck would have it, while I was staying in Tepic
this man disinterred the most valuable objects he had
yet found in the course of his digging.   They were
come upon near two skeletons around whose necks were
altogether twenty-six small bells of solid gold, besides
some turquoises.   On the breast of one of the dead was
a large plate of solid hammered gold which had been
used as an ornament.   A number of similar breast-plates
were found in the famous excavation in the city of
Mexico in 1900.   Near the feet stood a much-corroded
jar of carbonate of lime, in the shape of a sitting man ;
also a magnificent terra-cotta jar designed and decorated in imitation of a turkey; a black earthenware bowl
stood between the two.   This turkey jar (Plate VII.),
which is more than six and a half inches high, is most
interesting from many points of view.   It is excellently

made of fine-grain material, slate-coloured, that, though
thin, is of remarkable resistance, as evidenced by the

fact that the man who dug it up
brought his pick down on it with
full force, but made only a hole
at the point of contact. The
head and neck of the bird, which
are hollow, were evidently made
separately and put on after the
body was finished.

Gold Bell from the Tepic
Find. Front and Side
View. Length, 2.2 ctm.

The brilliant surface of the
jar, resembling a glaze, is a light
olive-brown running into slate,
mottled in places with spots of a brick-red colour. The
head and neck of the turkey-handle are painted bright
red, and the wattles, all clearly indicated, are each orna-

mented with a thin
little leaf of gold.
The same bright
red outlines the
whitish band round
the neck of the jar
as well as the tur-
key's feet and up-
per part of wings on
the body of the ves-
sel. This colour,
which is the same
commonly found
in the funeral relics
of the ancient Az-
tecs, Zapotecs and

Breast Ornament of Hammered Gold from the
Tepic Find. Diameter, 16.5 ctm.

Mayas, probably serves to indicate the purpose of the jar.

Around the neck of the jar is a broad band of a whitish coating, which material also marks the main part of

PLATE VII

the wings, legs, and feet. The band as well as the middle part of the wings, the legs, and the feet were once covered with thin gold-foil; on the middle part of the wings remains of a cross-band of gold leaves may still

The Jar Seen from the Front ; the Design Extended.

be seen. There are indications that the upper part of the wings was painted greenish-blue. The lower part of the wings as well as the tail are represented by fluting. Ornamentation with gold-foil has been found on ancient beads and potsherds of the Tarasco country ; but to my knowledge never before on a vessel as complete as this one.

Not many specimens of such ware are to be seen in the museums of the world, and in some respects none of them is comparable with the one here described, which was found farther north than the rest. All of them seem to have come from one common source, and are distinguished by what at first sight appears to be glazing. Professor Morris Loeb, of New York University, who has had the kindness to analyse a fragment from the lower part of the body of the jar, found, however, that the smooth, glistening surface was not a glaze. The fragment consisted of a greyish mass covered on both sides with a cream-white coating somewhat less than a millimetre thick.

Both the interior and the coated outside slightly adhered to the tongue. The coating, after being removed with a steel file, was passed over a magnet. It may be remarked, in this connection, that it was much easier to file the outer coating than the inner. The former was analysed separately from the latter, but according to the same method.

This analysis did not convince Professor Loeb that the "glaze" and the body are of widely different material; nor that the glaze is more fusible than the body—rather the reverse. The body, although grey, contains very little carbon, whereas the glaze contains a large amount of it. The outside white layer he declared to be an unburnt coating of a fat clay, merely sun-baked, and remaining white because the organic matter had never been charred.

As regards the yellowish-white coating that partly served as a cement for the gold-foil, it is not, as at first sight appears, pulverised shell. According to the experiments of Dr. E. O. Hovey, of the American Museum of Natural History, this substance is not acted upon by cold hydrochloric acid. On the other hand, the fact that it is greatly affected by caustic potash indicates that it contains much alumina and is some form of clay. That part which is underneath the gold-foil apparently contains a larger percentage of clay.

The bird which the jar represents is rendered so well that even the species of turkey is unmistakable. The red, wart-like wattles, as well as the erectile process on the head, are those of the so-called Yucatan or ocellated turkey (*Meleagris ocellata*). The elegant ribbon of golden bronze across the middle part of the wing is as conspicuous in the original as in the jar. The turquoise green-blue, that once represented the wing covers of the bird, as well as the profusion of gold and the high polish of the jar, combine to give an impression of the iridescent gold and green colours of the brilliant turkey itself.

The noble shape and fine workmanship of this jar make it one of the most remarkable specimens of ancient American ceramics. There is reason to believe that a factory or factories of this kind of ware existed at some place in the Tierra Caliente of Guatemala, or southernmost Mexico, and that through commerce it reached the more northern tribes. So far, however, the locality has not been discovered.

CHAPTER XVII

A S soon as I had recovered from a severe attack of malarial fever sufficiently to be able to travel I started out again. People on the coast are lazy and generally unfamiliar with the handling of mules, but with the help of the authorities I engaged the best drivers that could be found. Even with these, however, I experienced, as usual, occasional losses and delays due to the men's carelessness in allowing the backs of the animals to become sore.

Terra-cotta Figure from Iztlan, Tepic. Painted with White and Yellow. Height, 17.5 ctm.

Among the fellows I secured was Angel, a civilised but purebred Indian, whose family had originally lived in the vicinity of Zacatecas but was now settled in Tequila, whence he had come to Tepic with a party of prospectors who had left him to work his way home. He could speak only Spanish, but my first impression of him was favourable, and from that time on he remained with me in all for over a year, and I always found him intelligent and straightforward, and of exceptional value as a body-servant.

It was toward the end of March that we travelled over the lowlands of Compostela, south of Tepic, and then east, passing San Pedro La-gunillas, where many antiquities had been found. The people received me hospitably, and from here I reached the camino real that connects Tepic with Guadalajara.

Clay Figure, Blackish and Polished, from Iztlan, Tepic. Height, 15 ctm.

Once, as I approached a miserable little borough on the road, I was suddenly startled by the gay chatter and odd appearance of a party of men with long, flowing hair, bathing some big horses in a deep pool of the river. They were gypsies, part of an encampment resting in the hamlet. As soon as the women espied me, they came over to beg, and to offer to tell our fortunes. I understand that these palmists do quite a good business in Mexico. They demand only one real for an examination, but this gives them a chance to excite the curiosity of the customer, who is induced to spend many another real to gratify it. The chief source of income with the men is the making and mending of copper vessels, for which they manage to extort exorbitant prices. They also do considerable trading in horses, but they never steal here. The Mexicans, on the other hand, seize every opportunity to abduct the gypsies' horses, especially at night, although the authorities protect the strangers as best they can. At Ahuacatlan (Nahuatl : " Where there are aguacates ") we saw some mischievous boys throwing stones at them, but they were promptly taken into custody by the police.

The gypsies apparently lived well and had plenty of money. Their favourite food seemed to be pork. They quarrelled much among themselves and there was a

great jabbering around their fire which kept me awake until far into the night. There were many Bosnians and a sprinkling of Turks and Greeks among the troupe, the latter having bears and monkeys with them ; but as most of these people come from Hungary they all are called Hungaros throughout Mexico. Some spoke excellent French and English, and one of them told me that his father, also a member of the party, knew my country.

Terra-cotta Figure in Shirt, Iztlan, Tepic.   Height, 18.5 ctm.

Next morning the Hungaros started ahead of us, but we soon overtook some of them sleeping in the heat of the day with their bears. For a couple of hours I separated from my own train to travel with a family of these rovers, who were much pleased when I told them their tribal name. They said that there were one hundred and seventy of their race at the time wandering about in Mexico in separate groups. All of them had landed together in Vera Cruz and then travelled all over the land as far as Mazatlan. Now they were on their way to Acapulco, and they expected to return to Europe in the following year. They assured me that gypsies now travel over all the Americas, both north and south, and I noticed that some of the women had twisted in their braids silver dollars from Chile and other South American countries.

Passing on the road the slumbering volcano Ceboruco (Nahuatl: "Many Stones"; height, 5,004 feet) I arrived in the dreary town of Ahuacatlan (elevation, 3,350 feet), where I had difficulty in finding quarters for the night. I almost envied the gypsies who had just put up their tents on the plaza near the river. One of their women had her child baptised that afternoon in the church, and there was great hilarity among her compatriots, which found vent in such exclamations as: "Viva the padre!" "Viva the church bells!" I heard one gypsy woman greet a Mexican: "Viva Dios! Where is the brandy, friend?"

Tripod Clay Vessel with Two Animal Heads. Mespan, near Iztlan, Tepic. Height, 14.8 ctm.

At Ahuacatlan I was told of an ancient tunnel recently discovered in the vicinity, and give this information concerning it for what it is worth. It runs horizontally, though its mouth goes almost perpendicularly downward, and a hacienda not far from the place was said to have kept twenty men at work day and night for three weeks to clear out the earth with which the tunnel was filled. It had many ramifications, and the workmen advanced over a hundred yards without finding anything but a few earthenware figures.

The dust on the road was dreadful, enough to choke one, and I was glad to get to the town of Iztlan de Buenos Aires ("Delightful Breezes"). Iztlan is a Nahuatl name meaning "Where there is obsidian" (itztli). The vicinity is of great archæological interest, for the bottom of the valley, some twenty-five miles in extent and comparatively level, abounds in mounds. There are at least a thousand of them, according to the estimate of the priest of Iztlan, who takes an active interest in archæology. During the ten years in which he has had charge of this parish he has made excavations almost every year, and has taken out a great number of terra-cotta figures peculiar to the district. People from far and near hear of his finds, and passengers on the stage that runs between Tepic and Guadalajara often stop here to induce the Cura to sell them some of his relics. But so good-natured is he that he had already given them all away, except one, which he now presented to me.

He took me to a large mound which with twelve men he had spent four months in excavating. He had cut a section clear across from south to north and had also made smaller sections from the east. Though most of the mound was still intact his excavations were sufficient to give an idea of what it contained. There was a circular building inside, seventy-seven and one-half feet in diameter, and consisting mainly of a double wall of stone and clay. The stones were flat and showed marks of cutting. Stairways of cut stones led up to the top of the wall in the south and north, and two other flights of stairs descended from the landings into the centre of the mound. These inner stairs were of the same material as the outer one, and had stone banisters on either side. Where they met at the bottom were five, or possibly six, crypts all around, each three yards long, built of stone and clay. Underneath the staircase junction, and apparently underneath the entire central part of the building, were found large, round stones in a layer about one yard deep. The space between the inner stair-

cases had been filled up with stones and earth to a height
of about four yards, and here, on top of all, had been
placed slabs of stones as a cover. Over and around
these was an accumulation of stone and earth two yards
deep, which rounded off the mound.

This is the only mound in which nothing but walls
and staircases had been found. Possibly this structure
had been used for religious purposes. In all the other
mounds which the priest had excavated he had unearthed
skeletons with their belongings, but nowhere else had
he come upon walls. Many mounds could be seen from
here. Close by was a square one; but all the others
were round.

We also visited some petroglyphs two leagues south
of Iztlan. No doubt it was accidental, but one face
picked on the rock was strikingly Egyptian. There
were also two small deer, with an arrow-point above
each, and a large coiled serpent. The weather was very
warm for such excursions, but the country was interesting, and my congenial companion always had a well-
stocked lunch-basket ready to refresh us after our exertions.

The Cura also told me of some tall mounds near
Mespan (a Nahuatl name, Metzpan, which means
" Place of the moon " *i.e.*, metztli). He even accompanied me to the place and got men to dig, a task
which might have proved too difficult for me. We
ascended a mesa literally covered with mounds, most
of them round. The first one we came upon looked
promising, and we at once began excavating it. The
men worked eagerly, expecting to turn up a treasure, while
the priest and I watched the progress seated under
a guisachi tree over which one of the men had thrown a
blanket for shade. While we were thus occupied an old
treasure-seeker arrived and offered us his services. He

had seen a white flame near his home—the sure sign of buried treasure. Like all Mexicans he was eager after buried money, which, as they express it, does no good to either God or the Devil. A flame might have signified the dead, too, it seems, but their flame is a green one.

The mound we excavated was sixteen feet high and forty-eight feet in diameter. From its top twenty-four other mounds could be seen to the west and north. In the very beginning of our digging we found near the top, toward the east, about an inch below the surface, several fine lance-points of obsidian; but strangely enough, in spite of our excavating the entire mound, no other object was brought to light; nor were

Pottery Vessel of Unusual Shape. Mespan, near Iztlan, Tepic. Height, 18 ctm.

there any skeletons. The mound merely inclosed four chambers of equal size, grouped together in a square, with walls of stone and clay, eight feet high and four feet thick. These chambers were filled with large stones resting on a layer of soft earth about nine inches deep. Underneath this was spread a layer of pulverised charcoal and ashes five inches in depth, and then again a bed of soft earth half a yard or less through.

The very intelligent Cura in Santa Magdalena told me later that in an arroyo behind Mespan, in the river bank, he had been shown stone walls about five yards below the surface.   A piece of fossilised wood and fossil teeth had also been found in that locality.   Near Tambura, a short distance to the south of Iztlan, he declared he had found hieroglyphs of Nahua origin.

Certain it is that the opportunities for archæological research in the vicinity of Iztlan are great.   Even before my arrival at the place I had heard of the wonderful monos that were in possession of the druggist of that town.   They had been discovered at a little ranch nestled among the hills at an elevation a little higher than Iztlan and about three miles south of the town. The resident had observed some small stones in one of the fields arranged in regular order ; and thinking that there might be a treasure underneath he began one evening, with a couple of assistants, to dig.   In the morning they came upon a subterranean vault divided into two sections, and in the vault they perceived twenty-seven figures, together with many beautifully made vessels. According to my informant the larger figures were all in one room, and the smaller ones in the other ; and both chambers were partly immersed in water, a rather strange assertion, as the vault was on comparatively high ground.

Unfortunately the discoverers were ignorant of the scientific value of their finds, which, being sent into the town on donkeys, were presently scattered among the people as curios.   Some of the largest were deliberately broken, because the purchasers hoped to find them filled with gold.   The figures proved of the highest interest, and this time, as well as in 1898, I succeeded in rescuing for science what was left of this important find.   A number of other terra-cotta figures from the neighbourhood of Iztlan were also secured.

The most valuable of these figures are those from the subterranean chamber mentioned above, which I

visited.   The opening which had been excavated down
to it had filled up, but appeared to have been five or six
yards deep.   The name of the ranch was given to me as
Rancho del Veladero.   I collected altogether nineteen
pieces from this locality, three of them being tiny,
roughly made red figurines, from three to four inches
high.   From Jomulco, a village in the vicinity, I
secured ten, and from Jala,
also near Iztlan, three terra-
cotta figures.

The terra-cotta figures
from Iztlan and its neighbourhood, reproduced in
Plates I.–V., are superior to
those found throughout the
States of Jalisco and Colima
and the Territory of Tepic.
The latter are characterised
by flattened heads curving
upward and backward, are
generally red, yellow, or
whitish in colour, and are
polished.   An example of
this kind of ceramics is seen
in the accompanying illustration.

Typical Terra-cotta Figure from
  Amatitan near Tequila, Jalisco.
  Painted Red, e x c e p t Face.
  Height, 30.8 ctm.

In the figures of the Iztlan locality we find, to be
sure, a certain likeness to the usual kind of ancient
pottery from that part of Mexico; for instance, the fingers, with few exceptions, are of equal length, and so
are the toes.   But the specimens from Rancho del Veladero, the highest type of the locality, are for America
unusually well moulded, though in quality and conception they do not compare with those produced by the
ancient Zapotecs and certain Nahuatl people.   The fig-

ures are rather grotesque in appearance, yet they are fairly well proportioned. The realistic attempt of their maker suggests either that he was a great master or that they were the product of a somewhat different people.

The figures of the Iztlan locality are mainly interesting as showing the dress and ornaments of certain ancient people of Mexico, their mode ot wearing the hair and of painting the body, their occupations, weapons, and implements, and the mode of sitting of both sexes. Necklaces of beads, mostly of the small discoidal kind, are represented by painting or applied clay, as are also wristlets, armlets, and other ornaments.

The ware of these figures is a coarse grain and of a terra-cotta red, more or less murky in appearance because of age. They are not polished, but quite extensively painted on body and face with black or white. Sometimes the dress and head-gear show yellow, but to the rest of the figures, not excepting the nose, ear, and arm ornaments, no colour but black or white is applied. Where red appears it is always the colour of the ware itself. The body and head are hollow, as are also, in some cases, the limbs. There is nearly always a hole in the upper back part of the head. The figures are generally made with teeth.

Plate I.

From Rancho del Veladero, Iztlan.
Heights : *a*, 37.3 ctm. ; *b*, 37.3 ctm. ; *c*, 31.7 ctm. ; *d*, 40 ctm.

These figures, as well as those on Plates II., III. and IV., *a*, all from Rancho del Veladero, Iztlan, are of a type of ware hitherto unknown. All of this group are represented nude, except for a breech-cloth for the male figures and a short skirt for the female. The breech-cloths are white, but the skirts are adorned with various designs. The large, crooked noses, the remarkable ways of wearing the hair, the nose and ear ornaments are all very striking. They represent evidently a chorus of priests and priestesses.

Figures *a* and *b* show front and side views of a musician beating a turtle-shell with an antler of a deer, as many southern tribes of Mexico were wont to do. The facial decoration may represent a cray-fish. A small shell is fastened to the right armlet. The hair has been formed into a queue that begins in the front of the head, is wound around the head, and kept in place by having the end adjusted under the queue in front. Around the queue is wound a ribbon, the end of which lies backward along the top of the head.

In several of the rest of the figures of this group (Plate II., *c*, and Plate III., *b, c,* and *d*) similar queues are found. But the queue is here made from the back of the head, and there are no indications of hair on the rest of the head, as in Plate I., *a* and *d*, where a profusion of hair is indicated. Perhaps we may take this latter as the most perfect type, and, disregarding the others, deduce that the hair was shaved *à la chinoise*.

In Plate I., *c* and *d*, and Plate III., *a*, and Plate IV., *a*, the head evidently is adorned with a ribbon, which in Plate I., *c*, has transverse sections alternately white and red; in Plate I., *d*, the ribbon is white.

c represents a musician playing in the same manner. The body and face are white; the arms and the paintings are black.

d has a white skirt with vertical yellow stripes.

PLATE II.

From Rancho del Veladero.

Heights: *a*, 45.7 ctm.; *b*, 45.7 ctm.; *c*, 55 ctm.; *d*, 43.5 ctm.

a and *b*, front and side views, show another way of wearing the hair. The arms are of a deep black colour. A serpent is coiled over each of the shoulders, the head facing the man's neck. He appears engaged in making a tortilla.

c is the largest figure of the Iztlan collection. The body has a scanty coating of black, so that the red shows through it very plainly. The pattern of the shirt consists of square and diagonal designs made by white or yellow lines, the triangles being yellow or red.

d is distinguished by its head-dress, which is held in place by a ribbon that passes under the chin. At the back three pendants hang down from it. The legs are painted white; there is also a white band around the arms below the elbows. One peculiarity is that the white part of the left leg and the left arm has been painted over with black.

PLATE III.

From Rancho del Veladero.
Heights: *a*, 41 ctm. ; *b*, 41.3 ctm. ; *c*, 42 ctm. ; *d*, 42 ctm.

a. One end of the skirt is plainly to be observed on the right side and shows the usual ancient way of wearing the skirt by simply enveloping the hips with a piece of cloth. The custom still survives among the natives of the remote parts of Mexico.

b. The legs below the knee are white. On the left arm is painted a black band. The designs on the skirt are black with the exception of the lower row of patterns, where white and yellow also appear.

c and *d* are different views of the same figure. The body is white, but sprinkled with small black spots, as is the case also with some of the other figures.

PLATE IV.

a and *b* from Rancho del Veladero ; *c* from Mezpan, near Iztlan ; and *d* from Jomulco.
Heights: *a*, 34 ctm.; *b*, 26.5 ctm.; *c*, 23.1 ctm.; *d*, 35.9 ctm.

a. The decoration of the skirt is very indistinct, but of a pattern similar to that found on the rest of the skirts.

b. The figure is one of lesser size and is inferior in make, resembling somewhat the tiny figures of the group mentioned above. It is black, but a little white too is noticeable, especially on the face and neck. In its right hand it holds a kind of pointed weapon.

c is light red in colour, with white and some yellow decorations.

d evidently represents a soldier holding a club. The statue is made to stand upright by two attached supports behind. Its colour is a dark red, like that of all the figures on Plate V., which are from the same locality, Jomulco. This group is distinguished by much painting and somewhat elaborate ornamentation of the dress.

PLATE V.

From Jomulco.

Heights: *a*, 50 ctm.; *b*, 29 ctm.; *c*, 18.8 ctm.; *d*, 43.5 ctm.

a appears to hold a throwing stick and may represent a soldier. The lower part of the arm is white. The colour of the dress is that of the terra-cotta, with black and white longitudinal stripes and white concentric circles. The head-dress is black and white and a prominent decoration is a lightning design. Note also a lightning design painted on the chin.

b. To judge from the head-gear, this grotesque figure also represents a soldier. He leans on an attached support at the back. He is without arms, but has some peculiar sort of attachment in front. The colour of the helmet is white, with longitudinal black or red stripes.

c is a musician engaged in rubbing or rasping on a notched stick which he holds in his left hand. The right arm with the exception of the hand is missing. The lower part of the legs is whitish.

d has a white band around the lower part of the right and the left arm. The colours of the dress are black, white, and yellow, and in the scroll-like decorations that of the terra-cotta. The head-band has white and black zigzag lines on the red terra-cotta background.

PLATE I

Terra-cotta Figures from the Neighbourhood of Iztlan.

a   *b*   *c*   *d*

PLATE II

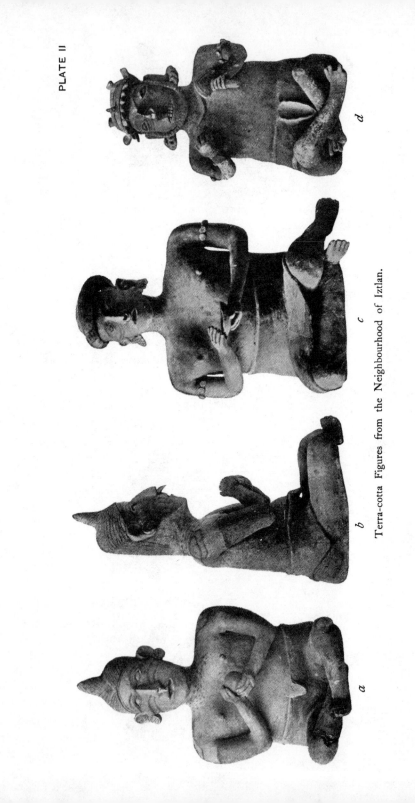

Terra-cotta Figures from the Neighbourhood of Iztlan.

PLATE III

Terra-cotta Figures from the Neighbourhood of Iztlan.

a

b

c

d

PLATE IV

a   *b*   *c*   *d*

Terra-cotta Figures from the Neighbourhood of Iztlan.

PLATE V

a   *b*   *c*   *d*

Terra-cotta Figures from the Neighbourhood of Iztlan.

It is difficult to decide what people produced these terra-cotta figures, especially those of Rancho del Veladero. Were they Nahuatl people or their predecessors or perhaps Tarascos? Against the first assumption speaks the fact that no similar objects have been found elsewhere in Nahuatl territory, which else might have been expected. The Tarascos of Michoacan in early times extended their dominion over the neighbouring States of Guanajuato, Queretaro, Colima, Jalisco, and the Territory of Tepic, but the boundaries of this once powerful nation are ill defined and little known, especially toward the west.

As far as our present knowledge goes, we may call the ancient culture of the States of Jalisco and Colima and of the Territory of Tepic Tarascan, though the Nahuas (Aztecs) have exercised much influence here. The region around Lake Chapala belongs decidedly to the ancient Tarasco country, and pottery ware of the same character as here has been found as far north as Nostic and Colotlan in Jalisco. The State of Colima was almost certainly Tarascan, for the ceramics excavated here are identical with those excavated in the present Tarasco country. But as regards the ceramics I received in the Territory of Tepic and the southwestern part of the State of Jalisco I was unable to find any strong similarity to those of the Tarasco country proper.

Whosoever the manufacturers of the terra-cotta figures of Rancho del Veladero were, certain it is that a Tarascan influence is recognisable here. The peculiarly pointed coiffure seen in Plate II., *a* and *b*, is a case in point, for I once secured from the mountains near Cheran in the Tarasco country a stone head, part of a statue, the hair of which was similarly dressed (page 402). In regard to this fashion of wearing the hair I was informed at Zacapu, that the Tarascos around Tirandaro, northeast of Zacapu, were called Wangáseus, "those who wear pine cones" (wangás), which may have been used in building up the hair in this style of top-knot.

In continuing our trip from Iztlan we came to a barranca, by no means formidable in itself, but nevertheless presenting the only topographical obstacle against the construction of a railway along this path. At a miserable little village the people were just making preparations for a series of cock-fights that were to last nine days. Laguna de Santa Magdalena, another point of interest, is a body of water about ten miles in extent, orginally much larger, but diminished by recent volcanic action. One can see it from quite a distance over the large plain before arriving at the village at its northern end. Here I found a meson and a little restaurant (fonda) which supplied very greasy food to travellers. But the hostess was nice, and everything, comparatively speaking, clean.

The cura of Santa Magdalena, who was much interested in science, told me that he had found fossilised sea-shells in perfect condition in Cacalutan, a small pueblo four leagues to the northeast, and in his estimate at least a hundred yards lower than Iztlan, which is 3,510 feet above sea-level. He said that one idol of obsidian and another of nephrite had been found two years ago on a ranch two leagues east of Santa Magdalena. He declared that every year, during the wet season, there were water-spouts on the lake near Santa Magdalena, and once two and three-quarters inches of rain had fallen in one hour. The water of the lagoon, he thought, contains carbonate of lime and magnesia, and benefits dyspeptics.

It was a very pleasant journey along the edge of the lake to the village of San Juanito at its farther extremity. On the road we passed a hill over the surface of which small lumps of obsidian were thickly strewn ; indeed, it seemed as if the elevation consisted, in great part, of this mineral. I was well received in the house of the padre in San Juanito, from where I made a trip to an island at this end of the lake with several artificial caves about level with the shore. One small cavity was entirely taken up by a square dug-out about two yards on a side. Clearing this out I found it to be one and a half yards deep, but containing nothing except the bones of an armadillo at the bottom. Aside from the smoke that coloured the walls I could find no traces of human habitation in these caves. To mark the general effect of

Head of Ancient Terracotta Figure from the Island of Laguna de Magdalena.

isolation and desertion, while we were busy digging we were startled by a jaguar, that lives on the ground squirrels of the island.

CHAPTER XVIII

AT the best fonda at Ahualulco (Nahuatl, "Surrounded by hills") I treated myself and Angel to a
table d'hôte lunch consisting of the following courses :

First : Consommé en tasse, with herbs, rice, and garbanzo
(big yellow peas).
Second : Boiled meat.
Third : Beans.

The meal, though light, was satisfying, and the
charge for the two of us together was ten cents, Mexican
currency.

When I reached Tixipan I learned that the padre
there was temporarily absent. This I regretted the more
as he was reputed to be constantly digging for relics, so
much so that his parishioners had made a complaint
about it. When they came to have a child baptised, or
on some other business, the padre, as often as not, would
be away in the hills digging.

The country from Laguna de Santa Magdalena to
the town of Zacualco consists of extensive fertile plains
with low ridges to the east and west. The name of the
latter place means "Inclosed," or "Besieged," referring to some fight in this part of the country. Just before arriving at Zacualco we passed a shallow, stagnant

lagoon, the miasma from which made the surrounding country very unhealthful. In the evening I fell ill with a kind of fever and nausea ; but after a good dose of quinine and heavy perspiration throughout the night, was able to travel on next morning. Early in the afternoon

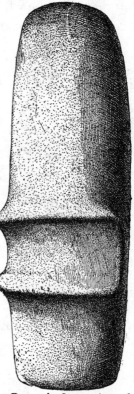

we arrived at the edge of La Playa, as the people designate a certain sagging of the country, about twenty-five miles in length and nine miles at its greatest breadth. It is the dry bottom of a saline lagoon, the water of which, at least in places, still reappears after continued heavy rains. We stopped over night in the warehouse of a man who owns one of the several small salt-works established at this end of La Playa.

At the time of my arrival La Playa was enveloped in a thick yellow mist, but a refreshing wind was blowing. The mornings were clear, with mirages later, as in a desert. The town of Sayula (Nahuatl, "Where there are sayolin": flies), on the southwest border, is noted for the dryness of its climate, but in

Grooved Stone Axe from Atoyac, Jalisco. Length, 20.4 ctm.

May, 1896, a cloud-burst fell on Cerro de Tepic, near by, demolishing houses and killing eight persons.

I deputed Angel to go along the west side of La Playa to buy any antiquities which the people might have in their houses. In the meantime, with the mules, I crossed to Atoyac (Nahuatl, "Where there is an arroyo "). As we passed across the brown, level soil of La Playa one of my dogs yelped with thirst, but managed to get on, nevertheless. Atoyac is a healthful place and has excellent water brought from some distance in lead pipes. From here I went to see some mounds, several miles to the north, and near the hacienda San José de Gracia. The locality is called Cerro Colorado, after

Ancient Tripod Vase of Brownish Black Ware, Highly Polished. The Feet are Rattles. Atoyac, Jalisco. Height, 13.7 ctm.

the largest of the mounds, which is really several mounds connected together. The whole is about ten yards high, one hundred and eighty-five paces long and of approximately the same breadth. Excavations have at some time been made on it, and layers of broken pottery, two yards thick, and some house walls had been laid bare. From the surface I picked up some red, white, and brown sherds which were very well decorated, and some pieces of obsidian. The smaller mounds appeared to be simply layers of potsherds sometimes two yards high.

Among the men who accompanied me on this excursion was an Indian who could handle scorpions with a remarkable degree of immunity. He used to play with a small light-brown one, making it run up his sleeves, or teasing it by twisting it between his thumb and forefinger. The animal died at last, "from anger," the man said. Sometimes, he told me, the scorpions would sting him; for instance when he mistreated them, as he was apt to do when he was drunk; but then he would simply open the little creature and apply it to the wound. I understand that this antidote is commonly

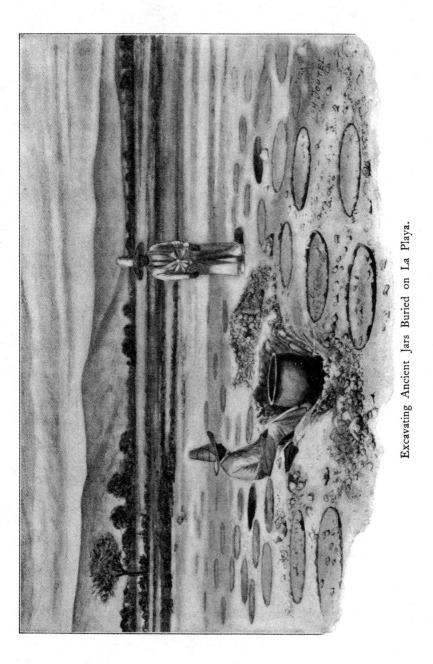

Excavating Ancient Jars Buried on La Playa.

used along the west coast. Some people eat plenty of sweet potatoes to protect themselves against the evil effects of scorpion stings.

La Playa was in ancient times, according to tradition, a bone of contention between the Tarascos and the Aztecs* on account of its salt. The influence of the latter tribe apparently preponderated, for most of the local names along my route southward continued to be Nahuatl, and I soon came across natives who still retain ancient customs and beliefs, though they have lost their language. Even in the Tarasco country proper one comes upon localities the Nahuatl names of which are still used along with the Tarasco ones, although the Aztecs never really conquered the Tarascos.

At the southern end of La Playa, near Reparo, I was shown a number of ancient earthenware vessels buried up to their wide, circular rims. At one place I counted forty of these jars, which were sunk in rows with some regularity, about fifteen inches apart. I excavated four, all made of burnt clay, of a somewhat coarse red grain. They were more or less shallow, the lowest one being seven inches in depth. Although I succeeded in unearthing one entire, it was too fragile to be carried away. It measured eighteen inches in height and nearly twenty-one inches in diameter. The wall was about three-quarters of an inch thick, but decreased in the body toward the bottom. Whether these jars had ever been used in connection with the salt-works no one was able to say. In 1880 a man found in this part of La Playa a silver idol, weighing thirteen ounces. It was discovered inside of a jar that had been covered with a slab and buried in the ground just below the surface. The

* The word Aztec, as being the most familiar, is throughout the book used to indicate the people who speak the Nahuatl language and are more properly called Nahuas; their main territory was and is the valley of Mexico and they are the real Mexicans.

lucky finder sold the relic at Sayula at eighty-two cents
an ounce.

On ascending the plateau across which runs the road
to Zapotlan (Nahuatl, " Where there are zapote-trees ")
one gets a fine view of La Playa behind. The two lofty
volcanoes of Colima, lying close together, one emitting
smoke, the other (elevation, 14,225 feet) extinct and snow-
capped, look more imposing when seen from the south
and east than from Zapotlan. The summits also appear to advantage when viewed from the southern end
of La Playa. The inhabitants of the villages in the
neighbourhood owe the luxury of ice-cream to El Ne-
vado (the snow-clad volcano), from which they gather
the ice with which they freeze their dainty.

The town of Zapotlan, called el grande, consists
mainly of low Indian adobe huts in long narrow streets.
The plaza is large, but it looks bare and naked now that
its magnificent ash-trees are cut down to make room for
a garden which the scarcity of water will never permit
to amount to anything. Altogether the town is not
very attractive, the hotel is grandiose enough but badly
kept. The number of professional beggars is astonishing, many young and well-dressed persons attacking
you on the street and in the meson. Even small boys
practise this industry. It was the first time I had encountered beggars on my route.

In former times the country north and south of Zapotlan was infested with robbers, now, however, said to
be a thing of the past. Not so many years ago the
stage-coach between here and Guadalajara used to be
held up regularly, sometimes at several places on one
trip. The highwaymen who came last would take from
the passengers even their underwear, though with inborn
chivalry they allowed the ladies to keep their crinolines.
The unfortunate travellers would arrive at Zapotlan

gowned in newspapers and the curtains of the coach. Whenever the curtains were seen not to be in their proper places it was at once understood in the town what had happened. On one occasion the soldiers guarding the road succeeded in catching the captain of a gang of brigands. They placed their prisoner on a donkey and took him to the nearest village to deliver him to the local magistrate. But when they inquired for the judge, the people replied: "There you have him on the donkey!"

When one thinks of the insecurity of life and property that prevailed in Mexico until far into the second half of the century, the present administration can never have too much credit for bringing the republic, in this as in so many other respects, up to the standard of civilised lands. Formerly the safest way for anyone who wished to keep what money he had was to bury it. Many a time moneyed men died without divulging the secret of their hidden treasure, or gave the information orally, usually either too vaguely to be of practical use, or delivered in times which made the recipient of the confidence decide to wait for days more secure before venturing to profit by it. Occasionally the directions were written down, but such documents had to be as carefully hidden as the treasure itself. The knowledge of reading being far less general than it is now, some of these papers were kept unopened for generations, till the landmarks indicated in them had disappeared and the statements of the deponent could no longer be verified.

This latter condition seems to be true of a curious document in the possession of a prospector who was full of schemes for the recovery of such buried wealth. It gives a flashlight view of the social conditions of the time from which it dates, and I reproduce it here in

English as far as the illiterate original will yield itself to translation :

ACCOUNT OF MONEY BURIED BY A BAND OF HIGH-
WAYMEN ON THE CAMINO REAL

Signs for the location of treasure hidden by Captain Santa Cruz Santos. For more than seven years his occupation was that of a captain over more than forty men, who enjoyed his distinguished confidence.

It is thus, my brethren, that we have agreed, in the name of the Most Holy Trinity and the Most Holy Virgin Mary, to hide these riches, which were gained by working upon our neighbours who travel on the road. A pack-train was on its way to the coast with money to be shipped to the other side, when we attacked it in Corcobado, on the Gabilan mountain, at the coal-pit of Las Navajas. At that point the cañon is terrible, and thus convenient to our purpose. Our muleteers here surrounded the enemy, and as soon as the attack was made our opponents, filled with fear, threw down their arms and surrendered. They placed at our disposition the loads of money which they were conveying at their own risk. We made them prisoners and took them to Cerro de San Miguel, where we had a ranch, on which we hid our booty.

We kept seven muleteers of the enemy as criminals. In the meantime our Captain Santa Cruz Santos co-operated with the rest of us in disposing of the money. We were forced to hide it on account of a violent persecution which the sub-delegate of Jala started against us over the mountains. Then one of our men, Guerra, said that Captain Santa Cruz Santos had better decide where the treasure should be hidden securely deep down in the ground, under some outward mark. Thus it is, my Brethren :—

Near the first stone fence, the oldest and most out of the way, on the right-hand side of the road from Cocula, just where there are some big stones, two loads of money were taken off the mules.   As a further sign : in the fence is a big stone which projects from it and is half-buried in the ground.   From this stone you measure twelve yards toward sunset, from the junction of the stone and the wall.   Then turn toward the front and measure six yards.   Then turn toward sunset, four yards : there the hole was made.   A grave, two yards at the top was dug, pretty deep, and here the two loads of money were buried, besides three demijohns with money, which we had previously secured on the road to Tepic. I had seven men to help me.   Into the hole we lowered the chest, which we covered with slabs.   I then ordered Casiano Murillo to jump down, and by my order he was chastised with the penalty of death.   He was given two bullets, and he frantically rolled over in his blood with frightful screams.   But he soon grew stiff and cold, and remained there to watch the treasure.   This punishment was inflicted on him because on his account some men of our band had had to enter the prison of the Court and perish on the gallows.   It was to put a stop to such harm that he was executed.   The grave was filled and a few stones were placed over it.

We went away and assembled again in the Cerro de San Miguel, and then we took the muleteers of the enemy to the woods of Santa Ana de los Negros, in the suburbs of Guadalajara, where we left them blindfolded. Our band divided, and some of us rode to Cerro de Tequila, and others to the Cerro de Coyutlan, where another mine of money is buried.   Upon the person who finds this money rest the same conditions as are attached to the other lot, to wit :

I hereby order that the person who lifts the money,

whosoever he may be, has to pay as due to the sinners :

One mass sung with vigils, to the Lord of Penitence ;

Three masses recited to the Lord of Penitence ;

Three masses to the Lord of the Water of the Cathedral ;

Three masses for the Lost Souls in Purgatory ;

Three masses to the Lord of Pardons ; and

Nine masses more to Our Lady of the Rose of the Cathedral.

The wealth left, after all this is paid for, shall belong to the person who found it, be he of this community or from any other land. Likewise he has the obligation to bury in consecrated ground the remains of the man who was left to guard the money.

Such is the information which I give this day, month, and year, 1794, by means of which the place of the treasure can be located. Also on the Cerro de Coyutlan, toward the north, at one side of a big stone, there is buried a box full of precious jewels, next to a stone from which issues a vein of water.

As Captain of this troop I sign this.

SANTA CRUZ SANTOS.

I made an interesting excursion up toward the foothills of the volcano, and in the vicinity of a ranch I was shown a number of stone heaps, perhaps the remains of a fortress, in part covered with earth. Here I picked up several large stones, with crude carvings of the rain-god Tlaloc. On the ridges near by I perceived similar ruins.

As regards the Indians, their customs are now entirely lost and hardly any of them remember anything of their native language, which was a dialect of Nahuatl.* Yet, in

* I gathered here the following few words : Man = tequíli. Wife = Chivápin. Boy = piltónti. Girl = siwápin. Head = motontécko. Mouth = molang-cótchi. Hand = móma. Water = al. Beans = éshol. Maize = xlayule.

The Two Volcanoes of Colima, Seen from Zapotiltic, Jalisco.

spite of all this Mexicanisation, the gods of their forefathers still rule the minds of the descendants. For instance, San Isidro, they think, directs the clouds and the
rains and makes the seed grow. Santiago is a good deal
of a liar and has made himself rich at the expense of the
Indians. Though the people do not like him he always
has his way because he frightens them. San Mateo
makes wind and frost.

For the rest the entire time of the poor mortals is
consumed in earning money by labouring for the whites
and spending it in making feasts for the saints. For the
inauguration of a patron saint of a house, whose picture
is bought for one cent, the Indians of Zapotlan will, as
one of their padres told me, spend such sums as the following :

Glass and frame for the picture.........$ 0.10
Blessing of the padre.................. 0.25
Two musicians........................ 12.00
Food and mescal brandy............... 50.00
Three or four dozen rockets........... 2.00
Total.........................$64.35

Never does the ancient idea of the importance of a
feast become eradicated. To the Indian health and luck
are assured by taking part in it ; hence the impossibility
of getting even a civilised Indian to work when a feast
is coming on. Once such a man was offered twenty-
five cents for watching the house of a Mexican for one
day, but declined the job because he was going to a feast.
"One tamal of a feast is worth more than twenty-five
cents," he said. When separating after a feast these
Indians never bid one another good-bye, but simply turn
the saddles on their mules or horses and start off.

Between Zapotlan and the foot of the peak some
four hundred Indians work for the whites on the fertile
llanos, and it is a curious sight every evening to see

these labourers come running as fast as their legs can carry them from all directions over the plain toward their homes, ten miles away or more, in the town. At sunrise they must again be at their work ; hence they have to make a daily run of twenty-odd miles in addition to their regular twelve hours of labour. For what? To extract, in the shape of twenty-five cents, their daily wages, a livelihood from the soil their forefathers owned. What white man could stand such a life ? The regard the Indians have for their Mexican masters is shown in the name by which they refer to them—coyotes.

While detained in Zapotlan hunting for men with whom to resume my wanderings I one morning missed Angel, and later in the day received the following communication from him, evidently pencilled, at his dictation, by some friend in need :

CARCEL NACIONAL (National Prison).

SR. D. CARLOS,
    Respected Sir :
        The object of the present is to salute you, and to tell you that I find myself a prisoner here, because they did not know who I was, and I want you to do me the favour and give information about me, that I am your servant. Last night I went out to buy cigarettes, and a policeman met me and took me to the prison. I rely on your protection.
                Without more, I am,
                    Your servant,
                    ANGEL CASTAÑEDA.

It cost me, of course, only a visit to the prefect to have him at once liberated.

CHAPTER XIX

IN Zapotlan I saw for the first time some rain-cloaks of primitive invention which are more or less common in the country. They are called chinos, shirgos, or capotes, and are neatly made of strips of palm leaves, with the rough side out. The garment is tied around the neck and worn like a cape over the shoulders, reaching below the hips. It is used throughout the Tierra Caliente of the West by the Indians as well as by the Mexicans of the working classes, giving the wearer a curious oriental look. Recent investigations favour the idea that these rain-cloaks came originally from China. For more than two hundred years and up to the time of

The Author in Mexican Rain-cloak.

Mexican independence there existed a lively commerce between Acapulco and Manila. Mr. W. Hough draws attention to the fact that in this way the cocoanut tree, the banana, the mango, and other useful plants have been introduced in America from the Philippine Islands, and that, on the other hand, these islands owe to Mexico the century plant, the prickly pear, and the pineapple, which furnishes the fibre for the piña cloth for which the Philippines are famous.

It struck me that by wearing three such cloaks, one over the shoulders and one over each leg, a rider might effectually protect himself in the rainy season, and I carried out my idea with great success. I wore my chinos in spite of the laughter of the high-class Mexicans, who would never dream of wearing them. A mackintosh heats one too much, and woollen clothing grows heavy with the wet ; but my chinos were light and cool. Even the heaviest and most persistent rain ran off from it as from a thatched roof. The chinos are the best rain protectors ever devised.

The town of Tuxpan (Nahuatl, Tuchtlan, " Place of rabbits ") boasts of two mesones, and at the better one they put at my disposal a very large, dusty, and forlorn-looking room with plenty of saints' pictures on the walls. This was the parlour and only room of the house ; and the patrons of the establishment generally stayed with their animals in the corridors. I slept splendidly in spite of the bedbugs and the strong smell from the yard with its crowd of animals and pools of stagnant, fetid water. Yet, although the three daughters of the landlord were nice and did all they could to make me comfortable, my sojourn in this hostelry was not exactly pleasant. The son of the house had epileptic fits every day, and was fast growing idiotic. The weather was damp and sultry and I felt feverish. The nauseating smell from the yard filled the house all the time.   To add to my depression, when I went out on the street timid women furtively closed the doors of their houses.

In the afternoon the female population of the town appear on the streets.   They look, however, more like some order of nuns than Aztec women, because some padre has taught them that God does not like women with uncovered heads and has induced them to hide themselves under an absurd extra tunic which makes them as unattractive as possible. The only redeeming trait in the make-up of these poor females is their cleanliness, con-

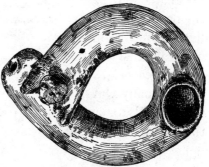

Pottery Vessel, Probably Representing a Squirrel. Zapotiltic, Jalisco. Greatest width across, 28.7 ctm.

spicuous even with the poorest.   Never is a spot seen on the white colotones, or tunics, and at least once a week, but often as many as three times, every woman washes herself and all her wearing apparel, including the heavy skirt of black woollen cloth.   This is all the more admirable, as water is scarce, and has to be taken up from wells sixty yards deep.

The Aztecs here are of medium height, though I photographed one man who measured five feet seven inches.   They are also more homely than I had expected, and all the eight girls whom the padre selected as the best looking for me to photograph had large hands and feet.   There must be some mixture of another tribe ; they at least do not resemble much the inhabitants of the valley of Mexico.   The teacher of the school here told me that the Indian children are more intelligent than the other scholars, and that when an Indian boy has done anything wrong he takes his chastisement like a little man, never denying his guilt. A peculiarity of the Indian pupils, however, is that when learning Spanish they always make masculine words feminine, and vice versa.

Monkey's Head of Volcanic Rock. Tuxpan, Jalisco. Height, 11.5 ctm.

Gradually the fear the Indians felt about me abated as they saw me associating with the padre and a Mexican gentleman who lived here. Both of these friends helped me much with the natives, and I am indebted especially to Don Trinidad Cardenas in many ways. By-and-by the women would even make bold to come to my room to sell antiquities and their own handiwork, and in this way I got a good collection of the beautiful girdles and ribbons in various designs which still are made here.

Ancient Clay Vessel, with Hollow Handle and Spout. Tuxpan, Jalisco. Height, 23 ctm.

Among the antiquities secured here was an ancient piece of pottery, a polished vessel of rare shape, and provided with a large hollow handle and spout. It is painted red with white designs, the chief of which is on top and consists of a cross section of a conch. A similar vessel was later secured in Uruapan, Michoacan.

The ancient club-heads pictured here are also of much interest as being almost identical with those yet in use in certain parts of British New Guinea. The knobbed club-head is quite frequently met with in the neighbourhood of La Playa, where I also secured a clay vessel made in the same shape.

The Indians always asked very high prices, which they gradually lowered to induce me to buy. If I still

Flanged, Knobbed Club-head of Volcanic Rock. La Playa, Jalisco. Height, about 5 ctm.

did not care to make a purchase I must at least express admiration of the things offered, and find some plausible excuse for not buying, for they were really offended if I declined to trade. At first they seemed to me possessed of an unpleasantly intense desire to get money, but as my stay extended over four weeks I had the satisfaction of seeing them in a somewhat better light. The women told me how difficult it was for them to make both ends meet, and how the incessant feasts were ruining them when their husbands earned only twenty-five cents a day to suffice for the necessities of the whole family. To make matters still worse, the men often spent all their earnings in mescal on Sunday.

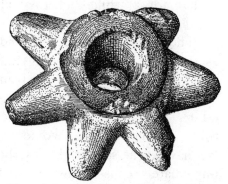

Flanged Star Club-head of Volcanic Rock. Tuxpan, Jalisco. Width, 8 ctm.

Some are so fond of drink that their wives have to provide the wherewithal to feed and clothe the little ones, and even to buy clothes for their husbands. Indeed, the

Indian men at Tuxpan seemed a careless set. The
women besides attending to their domestic duties worked
in the field, cut wood, etc., and altogether toiled harder
than the men, though neither sex is lazy. They go out
to work even when ill with intermittent fever and pneumonia. The rate of mortality among the Indians here is
higher than among the Mexicans. I observed one albino
boy in the town.

Passing through the gate of a house in Tuxpan, one
is always pleasantly surprised to find one's self in a large
court-yard planted with maize and fruit-trees and often
beautified with flowers. Here is the well, and here too
may frequently be seen a distillery for the manufacture
of mescal; this is really the principal product of the
community. Every Thursday as many as three hundred persons go over to Zapotlan to market their brandy
and garden-truck. They like trading, and may travel
with their donkeys as far as Colima, Sayula, and Guadalajara, but seldom far inland, bringing back dried fish,
salt, and pottery. People frequently go to the sea-shore
to live for a while, but they always return home at
Easter.

The houses in which the Indians dwell last as long
as their owners live, or longer. After a householder's
death his property is divided among his children, and
there are always disputes about the settlement of the
estate. Most of the sons rebel against giving anything to their sisters, women according to Mexican
law having the same rights as the men. The daughters
immediately consult lawyers to fight the brothers, and
quite often the two sides spend the entire inheritance in
law-suits. The people, all of them, are remarkably fond
of legal discussions; two parties may squander a hundred dollars to have the lawyers settle a question of ten
dollars' worth of property.

There are not many Mexicans living in Tuxpan. The alcalde, a pure-bred Indian, is the richest man in the town, and worth about $10,000, yet he goes in his calzones and without sandals to the market with his load of mescal and baked squashes, corn, and beans. His son likes to ride a horse, and wears a good coat. The alcalde is very kind-hearted, and lends money without interest to both Indians and Mexicans, taking security in land.

There are, of course, other well-to-do Indians living here. The ladies of one civilised family had gold necklaces and bracelets, wore patent leather shoes, and had a house nicely furnished with carpets and rocking - chairs, though they never made use of these. Indians are quickly tired of sitting in a chair, and after a quarter of an hour squat on the floor to rest themselves.

Among the Aztecs here are many talented sculptors, who make very good images of saints. The men take espe-

Ancient Stone Idol with Base. Neighbourhood of Tuxpan, Jalisco. Height, nearly 45 ctm.

cially to carpenter work, an ability which I think common among Indian tribes, as it is, for instance, with the Tarahumares. The more remarkable is it that Mexicans of mixed breed or even of pure Indian blood are generally so clumsy at carpentry. Their faculties have too long been employed in other directions. This is specially the case with muleteers. Nevertheless, it is a fact that I never met a Mexican, unless he were a carpenter, who could nail my boxes. They do not hit the nails straight and they put the boards together unevenly.

The Indians here are more clever in building houses than as cobblers or blacksmiths. They also excel in making rockets, buying the sulphur for the powder, and

Ancient Stone Idols. Neighbourhood of Tuxpan, Jalisco.
Height of the highest, 45.5 ctm.

finding the charcoal and the saltpetre themselves. Day and night these rockets are fired off in honour of some saint, or at any other provocation. The padre of the place estimated the cost of rockets to exceed a thousand dollars a year. As I could hardly endure the incessant cannonade I ventured a protest, pleading that the Virgin did not like all that noise; but my argument was of no avail; they knew her better.

The members of a family are fond of one another; but it is a utilitarian kind of affection. Father and mother, when they grow too old and feeble to work,

have to go out begging for alms from the " Kistianos" (Christians). I photographed a woman who was
over a hundred years old and had two daughters and
many grandchildren, but who for the last twenty years
had had to support herself by begging.

Unmarried women wear a bracelet on the right arm
and a big silver ring on the middle finger of the right
hand, while married women have a bracelet on each arm

Ancient Stone Idols.   Neighbourhood of Tuxpan, Jalisco.
Height of the highest, 50 ctm.

and a ring on each middle finger. The young men in
Tuxpan carry stuffed humming-birds in their girdles in
order to have luck in love affairs. Many Mexicans believe in the potentiality of this charm, and I have seen
similar birds offered for sale in the markets of Guadalajara.

Another love-charm which the Mexicans of Durango
and Jalisco have adopted from the Indians is that of
keeping about one's person the fang of a rattlesnake.
The Cora Indians wrap such a fang in a leaf from the
big-leaved oak-tree and stick it under the girdle. Among

the half-breeds in the states mentioned the poison of the rattlesnake is used as an aphrodisiac, and secretly given to a woman to gain her love.

I noticed that the Indians who came to visit me, even repeatedly, would never accept eatables from me, invariably finding an excuse to decline. I could only conjecture that this reluctance was due to a fear of being poisoned. It was intimated to me that a woman angry with her husband or paramour would sometimes put poison in his food or wine.

Both sexes are to a certain extent lascivious, and men as well as women have paramours. They are very jealous, nevertheless, of their marital rights, and a suspicious man may beat his wife oftener than not. To this, strange to say, the women do not object. They rather take it as a proof of love, and a wife, if occasion requires, may say to her spouse : " You do not beat me any more. Perhaps you have ceased to care for me !" This peculiarity may also be observed among the working-people in the City of Mexico who are of the same race. A gentleman once reproached his porter for beating his wife, when the latter turned upon her would-be defender and hotly informed him that her husband had a perfect right to beat her. There are legions of stories to the same purport among the Aztecs and the Tarascos.

When a man marries, he has to stay for one year with his father-in-law to help him. As a wedding present it is customary for the bridegroom to give the bride twenty-five dollars to invest as best she can, buying cotton to do textile work ; or corn to make tortillas ; or vegetables, flowers, etc., and selling her stock in the plaza. The groom, on the other hand, receives from her a shirt or a girdle that she has made for him.

A woman who is going to be confined has first to take a bath. In other ways the advent of the child does not seem much to incommode the Aztec mother. A *naturala*, as an Indian woman is called, once went down to the river about a mile and a half from Tuxpan and a good distance down in the barranca, to do a day's washing. In the midst of it her child was born ; but she finished her work, and late in the afternoon walked home with the little one in her arms and on her head the heap of wet clothes, which must have weighed at least thirty-five pounds.

The Aztecs of Tuxpan are rather prone to steal and then strenuously deny the charge. Nothing can ever make an Indian here admit a theft, not even the threat of death. This strange fortitude is inspired by the fact that the people have not forgotten that the country was once theirs, and from this point of view everything belongs, or, rather, should belong, to them. Especially at night they do not scruple to steal even cows and corn from the " Kistianos," whom they do not like any way. Even Indian boys at school want nothing to do with the white boys, though the latter have no objection to associating with the young " Indios." Mexicans are never welcome guests at Indian feasts. If, when the Indians are fighting among themselves, some Mexicans feel called upon to help one side or the other, the Indians spontaneously combine against their would-be umpires.

But with all their faults I still look upon these Aztecs as superior to the Mexicans of the labouring classes found among them. Most of them still retain the indescribable charm of nature's own ways. Artificiality has not yet taken real hold of them. Both men and women are far better workers than their white companions and therefore much in demand at the haciendas. They are also more musical. There are two Indian orchestras in Tuxpan.

The Indians are never liberal givers, and for favours they extend they expect something in return ; nor are they at all obliging ; it is difficult to induce them to render any service even for payment, though in this connection it should be remembered how much they have been cheated by the whites. The Aztecs of the Tierra Caliente have made excellent soldiers whenever occasion has required, and there is a saying that they do not suffer from hunger, thirst, or fear. This, however, is the case with all Indians. Though pressed into service, they will go hungry and in rags without complaint, sing while fighting, and die like Stoics, without asking quarter.

The Indians here have manifested their religious devotion in the many inscriptions which one sees painted on the walls and corners, such as " Viva the Lord of Pardons ! " (Jesus), "Viva the Purity of Maria ! " " Viva Santa Cecilia ! " (the patron saint of the place), etc. Yet with all this piety, their ideas remain pagan. As elsewhere the saints of the different wards are simply the old idols modernised.

If saint or idol does not answer the prayers of the people they sometimes give him a whipping. Once when rain was badly needed they took out of the church the very heavy picture of Jesus, and carried it over the fields for at least eight miles' distance, presumably to convince him that they had good reasons for the urgency with which they demanded rain. Still no rain came. Then they carried the picture of the Virgin Mary around, and this time they were rewarded with copious downpours. Therefore they made a feast, serenaded her picture, and did her all possible honour ; beautiful offerings were hung around her, and the principal men expressed their thanks and satisfaction to her. But Jesus was considered " no good." On the gables of a few houses I noticed small images of animals made of burnt clay ; no doubt a remnant of the former religious system.

On All Souls' Day (November 2) they set aside some extra nice food for the departed to come and eat of, leaving it standing from three o'clock in the after-noon until noon next day, when the family eat it them-selves.

There is, of course, the usual belief in the evil eye. The victim has to induce the miscreant owner of a

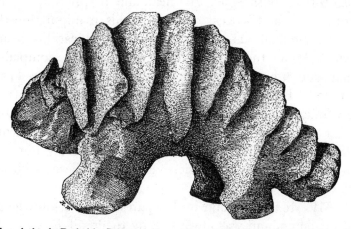

Clay Animal, Probably Representing an Armadillo, Kept on the Gable of a House in Tuxpan, Jalisco. Length, 17 ctm.

wicked vision to remove the spell and cure him, as no one else has the power to do this. If he fails to win the goodwill of his enemy he has to die. Many people keep their faces well covered to escape the effect of baneful glances, and for the same purpose a kind of cat-erpillar in its cocoon is hung around the neck of a baby.

Gentle as the people are to any of their kin who are ill and suffering, they consider it a kindness toward the patient when the ailment lasts for any length of time— say from three weeks to four months—to end his mis-ery. They resort to what is called in Spanish *sobar*,

which may be translated as squeezing out the patient's
life.   The family decides upon this step, saying : " It is
time for him to die ; we will not let him suffer any
longer.   Pity does not do him any good."   The patient
gives his consent, and big jars of corn and beans are
put over the fire, preparatory to the feast that is to follow his demise.   Then the relatives, together with the
compadres and commadres, place him on a mat on the
floor; some hold his head, others his feet, and others
begin from both sides to knead and to press upon him
with hands and knees.   Through this manipulation the
air in the body is supposed to rise and eat his heart.
All the time they ejaculate : " What a pity, compadre,
that you are going to die from your disease.   Holy
Credo !   How bad this is !" while the agonised patient
naturally enough prays to all the saints he knows, and
soon afterward dies.   The Indians then proceed with
the feast, eat a hearty meal, and next day carry him out
to the cemetery with music.   Everybody here is buried
with music.

My Mexican friend in Tuxpan had some knowledge
of medicine, and was always ready to do all he could in
behalf of the ill of the place.   He had considerable influence with the Indians and told me several stories from
his experience to illustrate this strange custom of squeezing out life.   An Indian about fifty years old was taken
seriously ill with fever and erysipelas in one leg.   Upon
Don Trinidad's giving him some remedy the fever subsided, his appetite grew stronger, and altogether his leg
was in a fair way to get better, when one day a woman
asked permission for the family to use another kind of
treatment.   The gentleman, of course, told her that they
might do as they liked about it.   Next day he went to
the house and found it full of people, the patient lying on the mat trying to catch his breath.   " What

happened to you?" he asked, very much astonished. "They did *sobar* to me," the sufferer replied between gasps, and that was the end of him.

On another occasion Don Trinidad was treating a woman, also about fifty years old. Her husband came to him every day to get medicine for her. Though she improved, her convalescence was protracted over four months, and one day the man told his benefactor that they were going to do *sobar* to her. He and the commadres and the woman herself had agreed to this course; but Don Trinidad forbade it and threatened to have them all arrested if they carried out their plan. The man replied: "I came here to ask your permission. If you do not allow it of course we will not do it." The woman, though at the time very thin and too weak to do her housework, by-and-by recovered, and to-day is strong and healthy.

Peculiar Ceremonial Object of Stone. Tuxpan, Jalisco. Length, 17.6 ctm.

According to the same gentleman, couvade exists among the Aztecs northwest of the city of Colima; at the birtl of a child the husband goes to bed instead of the wife and mother.

In Tuxpan I heard of and later made the acquaintance of two interesting Aztec brothers. They lived by themselves, and were known to read books and keep a skull in their house, and from all this the inference was drawn that they were protestantes, or free-masons, or something equally bad. When I went to see them I found only one of the brothers at home, a small man, about forty years old, with a hectic flush on his cheeks but a kindly expression in his eyes. He proved to be intelligent, and obligingly showed me his books, which were all about saints, and adorned with mediæval illustrations. "How is it that you are a protestante?" I asked. "I am not," he replied, "but I like to read in books."

"The gentleman wants to see the head," volunteered the Mexican who was with me. The Indian immediately fetched from the other room a small box, from which he took a skull. "This I wash every year," he said; "it is very clean"—and he fondly smoothed it with his hand as he passed it on to me. "Why do you keep this?" I inquired. "Señor," he answered, "I feel much better in the company of the dead. When I am downhearted I take out this skull, which is my father's. I feel as if I were again in his company, and my sadness leaves me." "Why, have you no wife?" I asked him. "No, Señor," he said, "not yet, because I always feel ill; perhaps some day I may be all right." "Perhaps I can cure you," I suggested; "what is the trouble?"

The hysterical-looking man opened his small black eyes in joyous surprise and explained that he was suffering from hæmorrhoids. I told him that I had a remedy that might relieve and cure him, and that I would send it to him that evening. Having thus opened his heart I told him that I should like to have that skull; would he not sell it to me? As he seemed to hesitate I told him that the skull would be well taken care of and put in a large house behind glass; and that whatever became of the bones did not matter to a man's soul, which lives for ever; it would make no difference to his father, I said, whether his skull was on the other side of the big water or here. I succeeded so well in overcoming his religious scruples that he offered to let me have the head for one dollar and a half and the remedy.   He had to ask for that much money, he explained, as he must have another head and would have to pay someone to go to the grave-yard to dig up his mother or some other relative.

That very evening I sent him a bottle with extract of hamamelis, and when I went over on the following day to tell him how to use it he gave me the skull.   A few days afterward I heard that he was on the road to recovery.

As a curiosity I will give here a prescription for the cure of hydrophobia which I also owe to Don Trinidad, who had inherited it from his father, who in turn had got it from an uncle with the understanding that no one should charge anything for curing with this remedy. It came from Almoloyan, a village in the state of Colima.

Half a pint of juice of rue.   (Ruta v. Galego officinalis.)
Half a pint of olive-oil.
Half a pint of deer-rennet.
Half a pint of grape-vinegar.
Half a pint of lemon-juice.

Stir all together and divide into three drinks.   Take one on three consecutive mornings, before breakfast.   The remedy should be taken at once, after a person has been bitten, to avoid his giving the disease to others.   Those whom he bites after having taken the remedy are not harmed.

I made an excursion to the neighbouring Cerro de la India, and on this side of the mountain, about four hundred feet above the plain, I found numerous fossil marine shells lying, as far as the surface indications went, in two or three sections, one above the other.   My an-eroid was no longer to be depended upon, and I could not get the exact altitude of the site, but it seemed to me that it could not be much lower than Zapotlan,

4,906 feet above sea-level, which could be seen from here. I collected three varieties of shells.

In regard to antiquities I heard of an ancient cemetery where skeletons had been found in a sitting position. There were also mounds to the southward, on the other side of the river ; but as the latter at the time had overflowed its banks I could not visit them. I was told that some time ago a jar full of yellow dust had been discovered in one of the mounds. The people, ignorant of its value, threw the contents into the river ; but one man out of curiosity picked up some, melted it, and found that it was gold.

CHAPTER XX

MY next aim was to reach the country of the Tarascos, and I made an attempt to get there by way of the notoriously unhealthy town of Tamazula. Heavy rains, however, forced me to turn back and take the other way, through Jilotlan de los Dolores, by a road running across a low sierra, and hard on the mules, but not quite so bad as rumour had reported. A couple of days' journey west of Pihuamo, a fever-haunted town nearer the sea than my route, there is a mound which is said to be composed

Mexican Rain-cloak, from Behind.

entirely of metates. My informant estimated that there must be as many as 2,000 of them. The place is called

349

Loma de los Metates, and the ground on which the mound is located belongs to the hacienda Hihuitlan.

At Jilotlan I put up in the house of the postmaster, a pure-bred Aztec, who was the most popular man in the place. It was difficult to get anything to eat but tortillas and beans, but the people were nice and I had a comparatively pleasant stay. The little village of Jilotlan (Nahuatl, " Where there are young ears of corn ") is situated in a kettle-shaped valley on a small mesa, and the surrounding hills and valleys, decked with a variety of trees and shrubs, were all clothed in luxuriant green. An arroyo ran swiftly through the smiling landscape, which invited to excursions. The climate is hot and dry and therefore not so unhealthy as is usual on the coast. Four days' observations (April 27th to 30th) showed a maximum temperature in the middle of the day of 36° C., and a minimum at 8 P.M. of 27° C.

The people here had much to say about a venomous wasp which the Mexicans call *borachadora*—that is, one who makes drunk. The effect of its sting shows itself in a veiling of the vision and swelling of the throat which may become so serious that the sufferer chokes to death. To counteract the effect he has to throw himself as quickly as possible into water. The poison acts very quickly and delay may prove fatal. If he is out of reach of water when stung he washes with urine, and beats two stones together in front of his nose, smelling at them.

I also give for what it is worth a story I heard of a kind of poisonous honey. The bee which makes it is black and frequents a shrub whose flowers are called *causiri*. Where the tree is rare honey can always be eaten with impunity. In taste and appearance the poisonous honey cannot be distinguished from the other, but there is a belief that you may test it by bringing a hair into contact with it ; the hair curls up if the honey is injurious. The poison affects the skin and the hair, sometimes causing baldness and in extreme cases death.

Only about thirty pure-bred Indians live here, and these are so far civilised as to wish no longer to be considered naturales. Here I also met for the first time the so-called Pintos, or coloured persons, who are found in comparatively narrow areas in the coast-lands of southern Mexico and Central America. Their bodies are covered more or less completely with numerous red, black, bluish, and whitish spots, which give them quite a repulsive appearance. Even the Mexicans do not like to eat food prepared by women thus marked. The Pintos live only in the Tierra Caliente and are exceedingly sensitive to cold weather. The discolourations of the skin are considered by some as a syphilitic affection ; by others they are attributed to the water of the localities. They occur mainly among Mestizos, whose children, however, are often born quite healthy. It is not supposed that the affection is contagious. Goitre is another affliction prevalent among the inhabitants of certain parts of the Tierra Caliente of Michoacan.

The mothers in Jilotlan pull their babies' noses for two or three months after birth to prevent the children from being pug-nosed. The mother of the postmaster, in whose house I stayed, used to tell her son how he owed his long nose to her pulling it for him.

I gathered here the following superstitious beliefs, a mixture of Spanish and Indian notions:

When the cat washes herself visitors are coming. Another sign that guests are to be expected is the crackling of the fire and sputtering of embers ; the people then drop some water on the flame.

When a hen crows like a cock she must be killed and thrown away, as the devil is inside of her.

A girl should never allow the people to eat out of the pot in which the food is cooked if she does not wish it to rain hard on her wedding-day.

If a woman leaves the sweeping of the room behind the door the devil will go there.

When something has been lost in the house it is well to light a candle at the wrong end and leave it burning.

When someone has cast the spell of the evil eye on a child the hair of the little one must be tied up in a top-knot.

If one steps on the saliva of a twin he will get a boil in the groin region.

If a person shows symptoms of leprosy, or syphilis, a powder is made from the dried meat of a rattlesnake and given him to eat.

I take this opportunity of mentioning also a few Mexican superstitions: In Eastern Sonora the people believe that a harmless kind of serpent comes at night and suckles at a woman's breast, putting its tail into the mouth of her child. Some of these serpents are quite large and black, others are thin, long, and red. Another notion of the same locality is that some bad people make candles of coyote fat which when lighted and thrown into a room where people are dancing cause constipation and flatulence. A custom universal among Mexican working-men, amounting almost to a superstition, is to avoid contact with water when warm from their labour. I could never induce them to wash their hands under such circumstances, as they were afraid of catching cold, or getting influenza or pneumonia.

From my servant Angel I gathered the following beliefs from Tequila, in the central part of Jalisco:

When a man has been away for a long time, for instance, in prison, and his wife longs for his return, she ties a string around the feet of a saint; or she brings earth from the prison and throws it into the doorway of the house as a means of bringing him back.

When a woman intends to *tromper son mari*, she gives him a soup made of a donkey's ear; or she holds the little finger of her left hand in the water she gives him to drink.

A soup of a donkey's ear is also given to a bullying husband, to make him more tractable.

A virgin points with the left foot; other women with the right one.

Of the efficiency of sorcery Angel was firmly convinced. "The Indians that you know," he said to me, "the Coras and the Huichols, are smarter to make ill and to cure because they have another religion. They know right away after the first treatment whether the patient will get well or not."

In Tequila, he told me, there are many sorcerers and witches. Their eyes are very deep set and red. At night they appear as owls or turkeys, and they talk to people. He had seen them. The owl seats itself on the roof of a house, blows up its feathers, and gulps uncannily. His father used to shoot at these birds of evil omen, but was never able to hit one. His mother, however, muttered a prayer like this: "Tecolote (owl), that bad bird! Sing, if you have to sing! The Virgin is pure, without original sin!" If it was a bad owl, it flew away; but if it was a good one it kept on hooting.

In order to do harm to an enemy people may engage a sorcerer, who puts something into the victim's cigar or food or water. When a person is bewitched he has to find a healer who is more powerful than the sorcerer that made him ill. The two doctors then make an agreement and divide the fee. As soon as the healer succeeds in arranging matters with the sorcerer, the latter makes

himself invisible, goes to the patient, and smears saliva
under his arm, which affords instant relief.   In the
middle of next day, when there are no people outside, a
woman comes and brings food.   Those in the house see
her, but cannot recognise who she is.   The patient, after
eating this food, which consists of his favourite dishes,
begins to improve.

It does not require especial skill to bewitch a person.
The harm can be done in most any way.   Nor is it difficult to cure, because the saliva applied to the patient's
armpit is a sure cure.   The only difficulty is in settling
matters with the party who did the bewitching.   The
healer comes either on Thursday or Friday or Tuesday,
because on other days he does not hear the sorcerers and
witches.   He arrives at eight o'clock, just about the
time when the owls begin to fly about.   He may find
the witch on the first night and make arrangements with
her at once ; or he may have to work hard hunting her
most of the night, or even every night for a month or
longer.   With some people six months are required for
a restoration.   The healer places the ill man's sandals
soles up, reverses his shirt and drawers, and recites
the credo backward in order that the owl may come
down for him to catch her.   Then he gathers a great
heap of old rags, to which he adds some mariguana, a
plant which many persons carry with them in their
girdles as a protection against sorcery.   When the pile
is ready he sets fire to it and the house is filled with
smoke.   All the inmates have to leave it, except the ill
one, who no longer knows whether he is ill or well.
The fee for such a cure is, in Tequila, ten dollars, and
the patient has also to provide the material to produce
the smoke.   Even if he does not recover, he has always
given the healer something for his trouble, as a rule,
three or five dollars.

In short, belief in sorcery seems to cling to the Indian, however civilised he may have become. An Indian was reproached for believing in sorcerers. "It is a sin to believe in them," he was told, and he replied : "That may be true, but that they exist is certain ; it is the great effort of our life to fight against them."

After leaving Jilotlan I stopped for the first night at a ranch, in accordance with the custom of that part of the country ; for travellers in the Tierra Caliente are always allowed to sleep wherever they choose, on the ranches, under some shed, on the veranda, or even in the house, without being charged for lodging. Our host offered to put up a bedstead for my use, so that I could sleep high above the floor and its centipedes, turicata, scorpions, and other vermin. I gladly accepted his offer, and we moved the contrivance inside of the house, where plenty of fresh air entered through the open door. Angel lit a candle, and perceiving a jar in a box close to the bed tried to use it as a candlestick. Fortunately his efforts to stick the taper in the mouth of the jar were unsuccessful, for our host presently stepped forward, remarking quietly : " It is better to put the candle somewhere else, because this is dynamite." He had bought a quantity of explosives from some American miners with the intention of retailing it to prospectors that came along. He readily acceded to my request to have the box placed at a safe distance from the house over night.

August is a month in which the gnats make life uncomfortable for man and beast, but luckily they rest at night and avoid darkness. In the morning they are dreadful. In order to get even a few moments' respite for breakfast, I had to shut myself up in the house, which, as usual, had no windows.

On our way to Tepalcatepec (Nahuatl: "Where

there are tapalcatl," potsherds) we passed extensive tropical forests, and it grew late before we arrived at the village. Its large meson was temporarily deserted, as few travellers stop here, but with the help of the presidente, a barber by profession, I procured the key, and we made ourselves at home. The village is situated on a high bank, surrounded by sloping hills, which invite one to walk among their many beautiful trees and shrubs, at their best at this time of the year. Toward sunset, when the air cooled off a little, whole families came out for recreation after the day's work in a charming, natural park close to their very doors. It was especially noteworthy and pleasant to see no empty tin cans, no old newspapers or refuse of any kind strewn about; nor were there any advertising signs, or warnings to keep off the grass. Evidently Mexicans are not even yet up-to-date.

Ancient Stone Sculpture. Man on Pedestal. Tepalcatepec, Michoacan. Height, 32.6 ctm.

The neighbourhood is noted for its invariably fat cattle. When there is no grass they feed on shrubs of all kinds. Dried beef, as well as cheese from this place, is famous as the best in the State of Michoacan.

At Tepalcatepec I procured an exceedingly well-carved stone idol, which had been found together with a number of larger ones in a mound some fifty miles west. There is no doubt that in all this coast country once owned by the Aztecs there are yet many antiquities to be secured. The country is full of remains of ancient houses, broken pottery, and mounds, the latter designated here by the same word as among the Tarasco Indians—

yacatas. Large snail-shells from the sea, used as trumpets by the ancient Aztecs, are frequently found inside of these structures.

The river San Francisco, which later joins the Rio de las Balsas, ran here large and muddy, and the crossing was not effected without risk, the mules having to be led one by one along a submerged ridge known to our guide. Gradually we ascended from the hot and dry

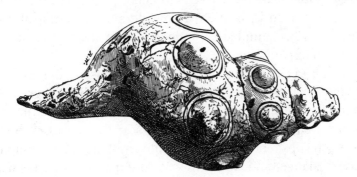

Snail-shell Used as Trumpet by the Ancient Aztecs. Neighbourhood of Lake Chapala. Length, 31 ctm.

Plan de la Tierra Caliente, which at the point where we crossed was about nine miles broad.

I must not leave the hot country without mentioning two very characteristic trees, of which I have not yet been able to ascertain the scientific names. The first one, called variously matixeran, quetchalalate, and pacueco, has been found to contain a new alkaloid. The people apply the sap that spurts out of the incised bark for curing old wounds; and as an internal remedy, to purify the blood and allay fever, they drink the water in which a piece of the bark or the wood has been soaked. From my own experience I can testify to the beneficial effect of such an infusion in convalescence from malaria.

The other tree, which with its red stem and pinnate leaves, is quite beautiful, is noted for its very poisonous qualities, which seem to affect people in about the same way as poison ivy, only more severely. Certain individuals are apparently immune, but to most persons it is really a serious matter to come in contact with its leaves, especially when they are wet. Even sitting under the tree without actual contact with it is said to have disastrous effects on sensitive subjects. One manifestation of the poison is, in men, a considerable swelling of the testes; a fact alluded to, indeed, in the derivation of the trees of Spanish name.

The tax collector in one of the Tarasco villages had twice been poisoned by it, and gave me his experience. The day after he had been infected he suffered much from itching in his face and gradually his entire body swelled up. His face lost all semblance to a human countenance, and his scalp was so expanded that his hair stood up. He could not move, but lay an unrecognisable mass, suffering terribly from the itching. He suffered from fever and loss of appetite, and could only with difficulty swallow atole, as his tongue too was much swollen. Relief was obtained by applications of cold atole over the entire body; as soon as it dried fresh quantities were put on, and after a fortnight he was entirely restored. Another remedy recommended is lukewarm water with brandy and the white of an egg, applied in the same manner as the atole. People who neglect to cure themselves are for months afflicted with nasty sores and may ultimately die. The swelling of the body is, of course, more painful in hot weather; cool air is grateful and alleviating.

The popular belief is that the male tree strikes only women and the female tree only men. If the information given me can be relied upon, the poisonous tree does not affect drunken people, just as the sting of the scorpion and the bite of the turicata are said to do no harm to persons under the influence of alcohol. Even temperance has its drawbacks!

CHAPTER XXI

ON August 11th I arrived at Periban (a corruption of Pirian, "Lightning"), the first town I came to in the Tarasco country. It is of quite considerable size, but I found the Indians living here all civilised and busy, for the bishop of Zamora was paying the place one of his periodical visits. I did get, however, a glimpse of some Tarascos from the interior, a band of musicians journeying to the Tierra Caliente "to see what providence might give them there," as they expressed it. They were

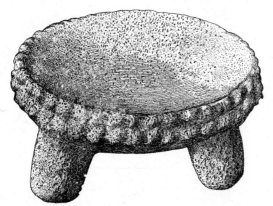

Ancient Tripod Stone Mortar. Periban, Michoacan. Diameter, 31 ctm.

dressed in the ordinary garb of the working-class of Mexico, and were small of stature but very agile and quick in their movements. I noticed that all of them had moustaches and some beard around the chin. For a little while they camped on the plaza, and then in spite of the heavy rain started off the same afternoon, simply covering themselves with their chinos of palm-leaves, called in Tarasco tchiréki, or tchirépara.

The road from Periban ascended gradually over long, fertile slopes, and brought us before long among the pines, where a chilly wind blew. Just north of the majestic peak of Tancitaro (tancita=sign; hence,

Parangaricutiro, Seen from the North.

"Where there is a landmark") lies the pueblo of Parangaricutiro amidst pine-clad hills, romantically located upon a plateau overlooking a broad valley; hence its name, "Situated upon a high mesa." Literally, Parángari means "carrying something high upon the hands;" cutíro is "situated." Its Spanish name, San Juan de las Colchas, it owes to the extensive manufacture of counterpanes (*colchas*) carried on by the villagers. Two kinds are woven by the women on their primitive looms. One, consisting entirely of cotton, would pass as a perfect imitation of the bedspreads used wherever white housewives have their tidy homes, were it not for the grotesque designs of animals and birds which none but Indian fancy could devise or Indian hands execute. The other and more common kind has a cotton warp heavily interwoven with woollen yarn of many brillant colours in a variety of conventionalised patterns. It is extensively used throughout the State by the Indians and Mexicans of the working-class as a serape or blanket; or else a slit is cut through the middle for the head to pass through, and it serves as a poncho.

We were now in the Sierra de los Tarascos, a designation applying to a stretch of hilly country reaching to the north of Cheran and broader than it is long. It includes the lofty peak of Tancitaro (elevation, 13,669 feet) at its southern extremity, and Pico the Quintzeo (elevation, 10,908 feet); but the general character of the landscape is more pleasing and idyllic than imposing or magnificent. Sometimes it seemed as if the mountains, fields, and trees had been arranged by some artistic landscape gardener for the express purpose of delighting the eye. But one thing is missing to make its charm perfect: there are no rivers. In former times there used to be wolves in the Sierra; but since 1870 they have disappeared.

Within this region pure-bred Tarascos are the dominant class. In some of the communities, as for instance in the one in which I found myself now, the best lands have gone into the hands of half-castes, who, while few in number, outdo the naturales in shrewdness. But in such places as Capacuaro (Tarasco: Cápacuri = " Between two mountains ") or the still larger Cheran, and some others, the population is pure Indian ; and as within this sierra lies the last piece of territory left to the tribe they are suspicious of all strangers and strenuously resist the intrusion of the Mexicans. Like all people who love their own customs and are conservative toward new ones, the Tarascos of the Sierra are inclined to be fanatical, and when they are aroused it is difficult if not impossible to reason with them. They are not to be trifled with, and so valiant are they, moreover, that the Government has deemed it wise to put telegraph and telephone lines through their mountains. Those which we saw were therefore not be taken as evidence of the commercial development of the populace, but rather the reverse.

On the plaza of the village grew some stately ash-trees, and at the left-hand side as we came up I noticed two small wooden buildings the heavy grated doors of which indicated their use as prisons, unmistakable sign of the onward march of civilisation. Judged, however, from their abandoned appearance, the inhabitants could not yet have had much use for these modern improvements. As a rule, such *carceles* or jails, which have no other ventilators than the grated doors, exhibit throngs of human heads eagerly looking out and begging for centavos from passers-by.

Like the prisons, the town itself looked deserted. As I knocked at the door of the wooden meson it was opened by a rapacious-looking old Mexican hag, who at a glance took in the unexpected prospect of profit and eagerly led me to her best room, a dark den which probably had not been scoured in the last hundred years. I thought of my own country, where the peasants every week scrub their wooden abodes with soap and water from ceiling to floor. Here the furniture consisted of a large, dirt-laden table in one corner, and an old door resting on two boxes—in other words, a bedstead—in another. These two pieces occupied about

half of the floor space. As I contemplated stopping in
the village for some time I first resolved to ask the presidente if there were were no better accommodations to
be had. To my sorrow I soon learned that this was the
best available. True, there was another meson, but it
had no lodging-room ; it was merely an inclosure within
which a traveller might keep his animals and things.
In out-of-the-way places this style of meson, where a
man may spend the night close to his belongings, is

The Meson at Parangaricutiro.

sometimes preferred to more pretentious hostelries. I
accordingly contented myself with what I could get and
made myself at home in the old woman's house. Next
day I discharged my muleteers and remained alone with
my faithful Indian servant Angel.

During the wet season in this region, from June till
November, it rains regularly every day, commencing
about noon. Sometimes violent winds rage at the same
time, and here and there tear off a house-roof. Snow
often lies for some two months on the top of Tancitaro,

but elsewhere in the Sierra is rare, although the cold makes itself felt even outside of the winter season. Water has been known to freeze on the 10th of June not only in Cheran but also in Zacapu, which lies much lower and outside of the Sierra. One year the maize froze in the Sierra during the month of October. Having been for six months in Tierra Caliente, and not having entirely recovered from malarial fever, I was intensely affected by the cold weather, which sent chills through my very bones until I felt as if I must freeze to death. Gradually, however, I became accustomed to it, and then felt the benefit of the elevation and the fresh air.

The pueblo is merely an aggregation of low dirty trojas, or square houses built of heavy pine planks well fitted together and topped with a four-pitched, shingle-covered roof projecting far enough beyond the walls to take in spacious porches on all sides. They reminded one a little of the dwellings of the Japanese. Of course such houses can be built only near the pine-forests, and are therefore seen chiefly in the higher altitudes of the country. Each stands about a foot or more above the ground, consists of only one room, and has only one door, and no windows, though many in the village as well as along the road have in the front wall near the door a square aperture that can be closed with a shutter. Through this opening is carried on a small business in cigarettes and brandy. It costs a man only four cents, Mexican currency, to get drunk in this way.

All the Indians here have their little patches of corn and beans, which, however, do not yield enough to carry their owners through the year. In order to eke out an existence the women, who are very industrious, do a great deal of textile work and besides sell fruit, eggs, milk, tamales, tortillas, and flowers. Many of the men allow their wives to support them, but there are also many who pursue some trade. They will, for instance, go out into the forest of Tancitaro, camping there for weeks and making wooden troughs and spoons, and especially shingles with which their houses are roofed.

The village groups itself mainly around the plaza and along one narrow street grandiloquently named Calle Real—Royal Street. Formerly it boasted of two street-lamps, suspended by wires in the middle of the main thoroughfare, to give until about ten o'clock light to be-lated wayfarers. But the innovation proved too great a temptation to mischievous boys, who promptly made one of the lamps a target for their stone-throwing prac-tice. The other, owing to the fact that it hung in front of the presidente's dwelling, had thus far escaped total destruction by the young hopefuls of the community.

The peace of the village was guarded by a single policeman, a native of the place, the son of a priest and an Indian woman. He had very little to do except to arrest now and then someone for drunkenness, a weak-ness with which he himself was afflicted. The presi-dente scarcely gave him money enough to buy his food, for fear that he might turn it into drink. He was not arrayed in a gaudy uniform with which to impress his authority upon the multitude; on the contrary, his ap-pearance was more like that of a bandit, wrapped to his ears in a ragged blanket that also concealed the only emblem of his distinction, an old sabre, of which the wearer seemed to be ashamed. A dilapidated straw hat left nothing to be seen of the dark face but a pair of staring eyes peeping out from underneath the broken rim. He walked about with rapid strides, as if just in hot pur-suit of some dangerous villain who was to feel the strong arm of law and justice. As he had no home, he used to sleep in front of the gaol door.

One day this unique specimen of constabulary al-

lowed me to photograph him; but a few days later I
was pained to see four stalwart Indians carry him toward
the gaol in a sadly irresponsible condition. He bellowed
like a bull, and resisted with all his might such high-
handed interference with his prerogative. Often enough

had he been in a similar plight; but
this time matters were aggravated
by the fact that he had lost the key
to the prison. Thus the village was,
for a series of hours, deprived not
only of its police force, but of the
prison as well. Fortunately it survived, and when the Indians found
the key and promptly delivered it
to the proper authority the guardian
of public safety was lodged behind
the bars, and his career as a public
official came to an abrupt and ig-
nominious end.

On Sunday the Indians from all
around flock into town to sell
fruit, pottery, and the like; and
the plaza then becomes as animated as it is dull and devoid of
life on other days. In addition
to the goods brought in from the
neighbouring villages there are

The Policeman.

some from considerable distances offered for sale by
Tarasco peddlers, the so-called *huacaleros* (crate-carriers).
These men travel all over the country, carrying on their
backs enormous crates (*huacales*) made of bamboo-
sticks, resembling those used for loading mules, only
very much larger and rectangular in shape. Into this
light receptacle the merchant packs his wares, whatever
they may be, chiefly pottery, and closes it with a netting

of ixtle. Often he ties to the outside the baskets which he also has for sale, and on top of all he fastens his chino.

These itinerant merchants forcibly demonstrate the commercial instinct of the Tarasco tribe. The peddlers, generally natives of the Sierra, travel on foot as far as to the city of Mexico in the east, to Guadalajara in the west, and to the coast towns of Acapulco, Colima, and Tepic. I have met a Tarasco as far north as Las Cinco Llagas, a village of the Northern Tepehuanes, where he had settled and married. In former times Tarasco merchants used to make their way as far north as the present Territory of New Mexico, and south into Guatemala and Yucatan. A journey from Paracho to Mexico city, going and coming, consumes one month, the distance in a straight line being two hundred and fifty miles. The goods the men carry on these trips are home-made articles, guitars, wooden spoons, chocolate-stirrers (*molinillos*), blankets, rope made from maguey-fibre, and cages filled with song-birds ; and they return laden with cotton cloth and violin and guitar strings, which, by the way, are made in Querétaro out of the intestines of goats. For the trip to Acapulco they allow themselves one month going and another for returning, taking down pottery and bringing back cotton cloth, wine, and machetes. This trip is the most profitable of all, for the pottery, which they buy for one real (twelve centavos) a piece, retails at the other end at four reales (fifty centavos), and the goods they purchase on the coast sell well in the Sierra.

Incredible as it sounds, a peddler may, on such a trip, realise as much as a dollar, Mexican currency, for every day of his journey. This, however, is accomplished only by living on a most scanty fare, and by walking twice as far each day as a loaded mule can go—

that is to say, thirty or forty miles. The huacaleros march from daybreak until late in the afternoon, resting only for a little while in the middle of the day to eat. Their gait is not the common half trot of the Indian carrying a burden, but an even pace at a moderate speed, and they always carry a long, iron-pointed walking-stick, to help them to rise from their resting-places with their burden or get over difficult places in the road. Some- times, in going over slippery ground, as they often have to do in the Sierra, they may fall, but they seldom break more than one or two pieces of their cumbersome load.

To guard against being robbed they usually travel in companies of two or three; even as many as twenty- five may be seen marching together. But as soon as they get out of the Sierra they feel safe to go alone, for the people in the Tierra Caliente are not thieves.

Two such wan- derers arrived one

Tarasco Peddler.

day at my meson with pottery from Patamban ("Where there are patámo," bamboo sticks). Small of stature and wet through and through with the rain, they seemed all the smaller for their towering loads. The larger of these crates weighed 139¾ pounds (sixty-three kilos). Accordding to its carrier's statement and that of all present this was a light load. Once he had carried 190⅘ pounds (eighty-six kilos) from Colima to Morelia in the incredibly short time of six days. The men themselves never seem to realise how heavily they are laden, but the size of a pack attracts attention and arouses curiosity, and when they pass haciendas where there is a pair of scales they are sometimes asked to have their crates weighed. At first my man positively refused to submit himself to this operation. Only after considering the matter for a day and a night did he think better of the compensation offered and consent to subject himself to the humiliating ordeal. He tipped the scales at 155⅖ pounds (seventy kilos), or only about sixteen pounds (seven kilos) more than his burden. This man was short-necked and muscular, particularly in the legs. He told me that the last time the cholera was raging in the country, in 1850, he was fifteen years old; so that he must now have been, in 1895, sixty years of age. He had been a huacalero for thirty-five years, and supported his family entirely by his trade, never doing agricultural work. Now he was on his way to Rio Grande, on the coast, to dispose of two dollars' worth of pottery, and to bring back the rich cheese made there, which is eagerly bought in the Sierra. The trip would last twenty-six days and net him twelve dollars, Mexican money.

CHAPTER XXII

Here, as in other pueblos of the Sierra de los Tarascos, the Indians still attach much importance to ancient
idols, which they call Tares (the plural of Taré, a vener-
able person of old). From an artistic point of view,
they are much inferior to those found in the Tierra
Caliente. Nevertheless, every Tarasco has an idol buried
in his fields. Idols are also kept in the houses, and
more especially in the granaries, because the images are
considered the guardians of the maize. It forebodes ill-
luck to show them to anyone, and I found it difficult to
induce any to part with these Lares and Penates.
When it became known that I desired to buy monos the
people hid them and denied their existence. Some of
the most courageous and mercenary promised to bring
me some, but except in one instance never did ; probably, after all, their consciences forbade the impiety.

One day a man rather stealthily approached my
domicile, looking furtively behind him now and then to
make sure no one observed him. When he at last entered he disclosed to me a mono hidden under his
blanket, saying that a woman in the neighbouring village of Paricuti (" On the other side of the valley ") had
commissioned him to sell it. It was an exceedingly

poor stone image, made in the rudest manner, and not
worth more than six centavos.   But when I offered
him three times that price, he exclaimed : " No, no,
no!   The woman told me to ask fourteen pesos for it."
He then quickly hid it again under his blanket, and without further parley walked off rapidly, evidently much
relieved that the deal had come to nothing.

Having learned that there were a great many yacatas
or mounds in the neighbourhood, I resolved to spend a
few days exploring them, but the Indians complained
to their authorities that their sacred mounds were being
interfered with, and forbade my going on.   They knew
from dear experience the result of anyone's disturbing
the hallowed piles.   Only a short time before some
boys, from curiosity, had dug into a mound and taken
out monos ; whereupon terrible hail-storms, five in one
day, had swept the corn-fields.   The figures were quickly
buried again, and the mere thought that another calamity might befall them through a desecration of the yacatas agitated them immensely.   They were firmly resolved to resist all further attempts in that direction.

I, on the other hand, was just as determined to
carry out my investigations.   My object was not so
much to obtain relics as to see how these mounds were
constructed.   Going over to the little village of Paricuti, where most of the complaints came from, I soon
found a great many Indians assembling around me,
among them the alcalde who owned the territory where
my excavations had been started.   " It is certain that
some evil will befall us !" he cried, and all the others
showed by the expression of their faces how keenly
alive they were to the seriousness of the situation.   One
man voiced their thoughts by exclaiming defiantly :
" If we do not want any excavations made no authority
can force us."   Not even the argument of my Mexican

companion that "God is in heaven, and not buried in the earth," could bring about a change in the attitude of the earnest-looking assemblage.

As I wished to photograph the mound at all events I suggested quietly that we all go up and see it, and thirty or more Indians went with me, some on horseback. As we ascended the hills my attention was called to the sad condition of the maize-fields, with the plants all split into tatters by the hail-storms, and I could not wonder that the poor fellows were troubled, although their supposition as to the cause of their misfortune was so vexatious to me. Knowing them as I did, however, I desisted from any attempt to make them see the real relation between cause and effect. The only way to accomplish my purpose was to reach their hearts. If the Indians like you they may give you permission to do things

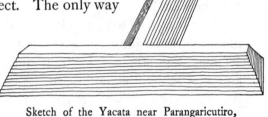

Sketch of the Yacata near Parangaricutiro, Restored.

for which they would otherwise kill you. After an hour's ride through fine pine-forests which cover the shoulders of the peak of Tancitaro we arrived on a partly open plateau under the summit. Immediately on entering it we passed three small yacatas lying in a row from east to west; and a few minutes later a large stone mound showed itself, presenting quite a remarkable sight in the solitary wilderness. Sheltered all about by stately pines and guarded by the majestic mountain above, its original features had been so far undisturbed by the hand of time as to make recognition of its original shape easy.

The mound is built of stones, without mortar, in the shape of a " T," each arm about fifty feet long and thirty-two feet high. The western arm terminates in a circular construction, a kind of knob. The sides all rise in regular steps from the ground, and the level surface on top of the arms is only six feet wide, while the base is twenty feet broad. These encircling steps make the monument singularly symmetrical and graceful.

The Indians as well as the Mexicans assured me that there were no such stones as those of which the yacata was made in its immediate vicinity. All must have been taken from the naked top of Tancitaro, about two leagues and a half off, the same distance as lies between the mound and Parangaricutiro. From the top of the mound one gets a fine view of the broad valley below and the hills beyond.

I quite agreed with the Indians that this grand monument of times long gone by should not be destroyed. At least a month would be required to investigate it, and besides it was almost sure to contain nothing but stones. My companions seeing this began to lose their fear of me, and allowed me to photograph them and their yacata. Then, distributing among them some wafers I happened to have with me, and gradually moulding them into good-humour, I easily obtained permission to excavate one of the smaller mounds, with the proviso that the owner should receive half the value of whatever might be found in it. As we returned to the village they showed me another large mound, presenting the appearance of a huge pile of earth.

The yacata I was allowed to excavate lay the farthest to the north on the plateau and yielded but insignificant results. It differed from other yacatas in being only a low accumulation of stones on the surface. Digging into the earth below the stones we came, at the depth of nearly a yard, upon a heavy stone a foot and a half long, nine inches broad, and six inches thick. On one side of it two shallow circular basins had been scooped out. A yard and a quarter below this stone we found a gourd placed upside down against a stone, and also a well-made clay vessel, undoubtedly of recent origin. With it we unearthed a skeleton or corpse with a distinct odour of decomposition about it, proving that the ancient mode of burying in that kind of yacata must have been observed until quite recently.

In brief this pile was just a grave, and I am convinced that the purpose of all yacatas of this shape, as well as of the small earth mounds without stone covers, was to shelter the dead, while the large T-shaped mounds probably owed their existence to the religious cult. Dr. N. Leon concludes from ancient pictures that the Tarascos had temples on the yacatas, their houses being round and of two stories. Dr. Eduardo Ruiz, on the other hand, thinks that they were tombs, and that the conquerors in their greed for treasure destroyed many of them. Five such T-shaped mounds lie in a row near the ancient capital of Tzintzuntzan. In the neighbourhood of Zacapu I saw a number of yacatas of still another kind, made of lava blocks.

I resolved to remain in Parangaricutiro to behold the great religious feast of the Miraculous Christ on September 14th, because it would give me an opportunity of seeing the crowds of Indians that gather here from all parts of Michoacan. No less than fourteen thousand people, mostly Indians, congregate every year on that and the following days to do homage to an image of Christ Crucified. I had still further inducement to remain here in the fact that along with the crowds of worshippers come many rascals, even from as far as Guadalajara, to ply their trade and make the roads unsafe.

Preparations began about the 1st of September. The Mexicans also took an active interest in them, the authorities measuring out spaces on the plaza for the booths and sheds of the merchants, gamblers, liquor-dealers, etc., who would come here from distant parts to attend the fair, for the festival presents the usual combination of religious and commercial interests. The erstwhile desolate-looking plaza was soon transformed into a small city of board shanties, among which a large gambling tent rose conspicuously.

The feast is of recent origin, having been inaugurated during the last thirty or forty years by a Cura of the place. A crucifix of medium size, said to have come originally from Frontera, had been kept for a long time in a private house in Parangaricutiro when someone discovered that it was possessed of miraculous powers. It was accordingly raised from its obscurity to the prominent place it now occupies in the church. The people, of course, maintain that one day it appeared among them mysteriously. To my irreverent eyes it seemed, at any rate, that whoever made it could not have possessed the slightest artistic taste or anatomical knowledge, for it was badly executed, the limbs in particular grossly out of proportion. Though Christian in character, the feast, as celebrated by extraordinary dancing, is decidedly Indian, notwithstanding the fact that it has been taken up among the great Mexican feasts.

The village filled up with people streaming into it from far and near. Every room that had a key was rented at fifteen and twenty times the usual rate. My "hotel" became crowded to its utmost capacity; people slept everywhere, inside and outside. Even the loft above my quarters had been let to fifteen men, who found there a safe store-room for their stock of rebozos.

Everywhere were throngs of noisy, bustling people.

Prices of the necessities of life were four times as high
as before, to the great delight of the natives. Women
who were the happy possessors of cows combined to
make a corner in milk and manipulated the market with
the cleverness of experienced stockbrokers. A troop of
soldiers arrived to guard public safety, for fights and
homicides must be expected, and a good deal of thieving
and swindling was going on all the time.

Following the general trend, I went from the teem-
ing plaza toward the church, through the spacious cemetery that looks rather like a beautiful park. The size
of the sacred edifice is very much out of proportion to
the lowly huts of the village, which apparently was intended by the early missionaries to become a place of
importance. As I hurried onward I heard a subdued
rhythmic noise, emanating, as I conjectured, from the
church.

The entrance was filled with the candle-venders, who
dispose of their wares to pious souls come to pay reverence to the image. As I passed into the vestibule I
encountered another swarm of peddlers offering photographs of the wonder-working image, rosaries, and other
mementos of the sanctuary. Had any of them ever
heard the story of Jesus driving from the Temple the
venders and usurers? The inside of the church I was not
a little surprised to find chockful of people dancing la
danza up and down, with lighted tapers. I could only
dimly perceive them in the dense cloud of dust in which
they were enveloped, and the hundreds and hundreds of
flickering lights seemed to be so many will-o'-the-wisps.
There must have been upward of a thousand persons
in that church, endeavouring to reach the image on the
high altar, and then retreating, dancing backward. To
complete the tour took about an hour, on account of the
denseness of the crowd, but nevertheless there were

many whose religious zeal prompted them to repeat the ceremony several times.

Gradually I made my way up along one side of the church, where many people knelt in silent prayer, and finally reached the railing that separated the choir from the nave. Here a number of church officials were kept busy receiving the remainders of the candles that were not consumed in the dancing, now presented to the church as a thank-offering. Some of the well-to-do Mexicans sacrifice large and expensive wax candles, but the tributes of the poor, who often go without food in order to save six centavos for a taper, are of very moderate dimensions. Whether large or small, the candles are seldom allowed to be entirely consumed in the dancing ; more frequently the larger portion is handed over to the church servants, who give in return a small stump of burned candle as a memento of the occasion. Quantities of wax are thus donated to the church, to be at once remelted and again sold at the church-door. I was assured that the church derives an income of several thousand dollars each year from the sale of candles and relics.

I was much impressed with the sincerity of the devotion of the people ; but the enormous throng, the dust, the heat, and the smell soon drove me out again into the open air, where I seated myself on a chair which one of the candle-venders rented to me for a while. The stream of people going in and coming out of the church flowed on incessantly. Endless files of humanity came moving on their knees along the main path of the cemetery to fulfil their vows to the image. Some may have walked in this way for nearly three miles, and I noticed that most of the women walked on their bare knees, lifting up their dresses, the only ones they possessed. Some have been known to faint from exhaustion before reaching the church, where they rise to dance. Many persons on each side of the road endeavour to ameliorate the suffering of the pious pilgrims by spreading their blankets and rebozos out on the road before them, not so much from mercy and charity as on account of the indulgence granted to all who assist the procession, as my Indian ervant explained to me; in this way both parties are benefited by the act. A rich man, on the other hand, is wont to come to church accompanied by a band of musicians, who are kept playing outside while he makes his devotions inside.

Indians from all the Tarasco villages arrived in groups, entering the cemetery by the gates at the right and the left, and then turning into the main road leading up to the church. They were dressed in their finest attire, and adorned with flowers, ribbons, pieces of variegated cloth, etc. Some had bells fastened to their clothing, others wore crowns of gilded pasteboard on their heads, in other words, the festive garb of the matachines of previous generations. Some even wore masks, relics of ancient times, the significance of which has long been lost.

Every Indian procession approached the church to the tune of a march-like hymn sung in two voices. Although coming from places as far apart as Patzcuaro and Periban all sang the same hymn. At the head of each group was carried the patron saint of its respective community incased in a wooden box with a glass front, through which the image could be seen decorated with flowers, ribbons, and beads. As the procession passed, hundreds of people kissed the saints' boxes, and the faces of the Indians reflected the pride and pleasure of their hearts at the homage paid to their patron.

Before entering the church each procession came to a halt, and the men danced " matachines " for a while.

Violins and flutes furnished the music, and the gaudy make-up of the dancers was much admired by the crowd. Many of the women were weeping from excitement, moved by the singing, the dancing, the ceaseless crackling of rockets, and the restlessly surging multitude, all in such overwhelming contrast to their lonesome lives. As I sat there watching the ever-varying spectacle I too felt moved, although in a different way.

Indeed, it makes an ethnologist sad to think how completely the ancient customs have been destroyed in the course of a few centuries by the Spanish friars. They made the pagans forget the profound thoughts their ancient ceremonies at once hid and revealed, by substituting the gorgeous display of the Christian feasts without the inner meaning of Christianity. Nothing but a senseless jumble remains of the learning and splendour of the olden times. Then every movement, every bit of adornment, even the clothing itself, had its special object and meaning. Now the intelligence of the race has become blunted and the Indian himself degraded and poor. His religious devotion alone remains undiminished. He dances to-day before the Miraculous Christ with the same zeal as his ancestors did before their own gods, and for the same purpose— to acquire health and material benefits.

Rousing from such reflections finally I noticed some miserably executed pictures hung up on the walls of the vestibule. They represented scenes in which persons had been cured from disease, or rescued from danger, or benefited in some other way, by the image, whose virtues were further extolled by tract-venders outside of the church, their shrill voices rising above the buzz of the restless multitude and the music of the Indians. The little pamphlets recounted stories of the miracles wrought by the image, as well as moral tales for children. In order to make a sale a vender would read the entire tract at the top of his voice, the task requiring fully ten minutes, and close the supreme effort of patience and lung-power with the statement : " It costs only two centavos !" A few copies might then be sold to bystanders, but to gain more customers he had immediately to start afresh from beginning to end.

Three professional beggars, Mexicans, also appeared on the scene. Two of them, presumably blind, were led by the third to a convenient spot in the crowd, then placed face to face at a distance of about ten yards apart, whereupon they commenced a vociferous discourse on the Christian doctrine. I listened to a catechisation on the ten commandments, the questions and answers following in rapid succession, and each commandment gone through in a singularly thorough manner. When the lesson was over the beggars fell upon their knees in fervent prayer for alms. Some of those whose minds have been enlightened usually show their appreciation by giving a few centavos. On this particular occasion the efforts of the three mendicants were not very substantially rewarded ; but I was assured that in other instances they had made thirty dollars in one day. There are many professional beggars who earn a good living in this way, travelling from feast to feast all the year round, often dragging themselves about on their naked knees to excite pity, and raising their voices everywhere in appeals to the charitably inclined. A good many pretend to be afflicted with physical ailments, and I saw one such impostor, who professed to have some infirmity of the leg, walk perfectly straight when he thought himself unobserved.

One thing in this vast throng was admirable, namely, its orderliness. There needed no policeman to tell you :

"Move on, move on! Don't block the road!" etc.
The pickpockets, on the other hand, reaped a harvest,
especially inside of the church, where the minds of the
people were so completely engrossed with devotion that
earthly goods were forgotten. Not less than forty persons were caught rifling other people's pockets in the
church at the height of the feast. The wise ones carry
their money in their shoes, which is the reason, as a
candle-vender told me, why the money of the poor is so
dirty.

As I left the cemetery and went back to the plaza, I
entered upon an entirely different scene, namely, the
fair. It was almost impossible to get through the tremendous mass of bustling people engaged in buying and
selling. The most attractive of all the wares displayed
were beautiful rebozos hung up on strings as on clothes-
lines. In the stalls were sold sweets from Colima, pottery, wax candles, dry-goods, etc. Some of the women
offered food for sale. The best business, however, is
usually done by the gamblers, the liquor-dealers running
them a close second. About half of the stalls are
"saloons," with customers swarming in front of them as
bees around honey. Singing and twanging of guitars
sounds from most of the booths, while in front of the
more opulent ones professional male and female dancers,
engaged as special attractions, execute the national dance,
jarave, with admirable agility.

The visitors, venders, dancers, gamblers, liquor-dealers, and all invariably go to the church to dance to the
image before they start their business on the plaza.
Even the numerous hetærae, who are the first to come
and the last to go, never neglect the chance to save their
souls by dancing before the Señor de los Milagros.
The townspeople themselves, however, never pay their
respects to the Miraculous Christ until the crowd of

visitors have gone away, as their time is fully occupied in watching their own property or that confided to their care by the strangers.

Interesting as it was to observe this feverishly pulsating life, I soon grew tired of the drunken brawl, which continued for several days and nights without intermission and from which there was no way of escape. Even in my room I found no relief, for the badly made ceiling protected me but little from the drunken rebozo-sellers in the attic, and made my couch anything but a bed of roses.

I learned afterward that several priests, as well as the bishops of the diocese, have tried to stop the extraordinary worship, but encountered the most resolute and determined resistance from the people, who would under no circumstances worship the image in any other way. " He wants to see the dancing," they declare, and this peculiar Indian notion has been adopted even by apparently intelligent Mexicans whom one would consider incapable of such absurdity. Hundreds of them dancing like the Indians in the church prove what an influence a conquered race may wield over the conquerors.

The story goes that one padre made up his mind to put an end to this pagan mode of worship, and the people coming to his church found its doors locked. Before daybreak, nevertheless, the priest was awakened by his sacristan with news that the dancing was going on in spite of him, The two repaired to the church, where to their consternation they perceived hundreds of little lights dancing. The dust was there too and they heard the noise of the shuffling feet, but they could see no people. At this the padre became frightened and ordered the church-doors to be thrown open. And since then no padre has been able to stop the dancing, nor will there ever be one who can do it, the people declare.

CHAPTER XXIII

PARACHO—THE MUSICAL TALENT OF THE TARASCO—A TARASCO LEGEND — CHERAN — MEXICAN INFLUENCE KEPT OUT — THE PRESIDENTE—WHAT I WANTED AND WHAT I GOT—A BRAVE CURA—A VISIT TO A YACATA—EXCAVATIONS—APPROACHING THE DANGER-LINE—A FRIEND IN NEED—THE INSIDE OF A YACATA—BULL-RIDING—A DETOUR TO ZACAPU.

ON September 18th I bade good-bye to the kindly disposed inhabitants of Parangaricutiro, and arrived the same day at Paracho. This name, formed from the Tarasco word paráni (to envelop), means breech-cloth, and derives itself possibly from the outlandish garb of the founders of the town. In the beginning of our journey we had considerable difficulty in getting over the slippery ground. The soil since we left El Plan de la Tierra Caliente consisted of sand and clay, which after heavy rains becomes dangerously slippery, though the surface dries up again in a few hours.

Paracho is in the heart of the Tarasco country, but its population is very much mixed with "neighbours," and consequently much more civilised than in Parangaricutiro, and the ancient customs are almost entirely lost. There is some commerce here, enough for the place to have been called the capital of the Sierra, although it does not impress the visitor by its exterior. Its site upon a plain exposed to the raw winds from the mountains is unfavourable, but its surroundings are delightful, as everywhere in the Sierra. It lies almost at the foot of the high Pico de Quintzeo, called in Tarasco

Paracho. The Peak of Tarestzuruan in the Background.

Tarestzuruan, "Peak of the Ancient People (tares),"
and there are other pine-clad heights framing the landscape, the names of which recall the ancient history of
the Tarascos.

The Indians of Paracho are said to have come
originally from Zamora, whence they had been driven
during the conquest of Michoacan by Nuño de Guz-
man. They were called Tecos, which my informant in-
terpreted as finger-nails (tǽki), in allusion to the fact that
their finger-nails were blue from indigo-dyeing, their
chief industry. If my informant was correct, one barrio,
or ward, in Zamora is still called Teco, and to this day
the people there have blue finger-nails owing to their
occupation as indigo-dyers.

The immigrants were first allowed to settle in the Mal
Pais ("Bad Lands," the name alluding to lava blocks),
three leagues from Paracho, but afterward established
themselves in the present village. Paracho is gloomy
and its streets are dead. The people go about listlessly,
talking in low voices and without energy enough to raise
an opposition to anything. It seems as if the stamp of
the "Uitlander" had imposed itself upon them for all
time. Yet they are intelligent and industrious, like all
Tarascos. The particular product of this place is a kind
of beautiful blue rebozo with a silken border into which
bird and animal designs are woven. Such a garment
may cost as much as sixteen dollars. The town is also
famous for its artistic girdles, as well as for its guitars,
among them attractive little toy guitars, only a few
inches in length. Everybody here is musical and has
his guitar, as in Italy. Indeed, as musicians the Indians
of Paracho have no equals in the State of Michoacan.
The orchestra leader, a pure-blooded, dark-skinned Tarasco, is a composer of no mean ability. He plays,
to use the padre's expression, any instrument you may

give him. Even in the smallest of the Tarasco villages one will find at least two bands, one composed of wind, the other of stringed instruments, and they both play well. At all feasts, weddings, and funerals it is the custom to engage all the musicians available. The dominant character of the Tarasco music is sad and

The Director of Music in Paracho.

plaintive. Jolly tunes are impossible; to a scherzo or a rondo these people would re-ain absolutely indifferent. Don Eduardo Ruiz informed me that the old women com-pose both the religious and the erotic pieces of the tribe.

It often struck me that throughout the Republic of Mexico there did not seem to be anyone, aborigine, Spanish, or of mixed breed, in whom musical perception was lacking. Anywhere, on Sundays and even once or twice during the week, one can see the entire populace, the well-dressed rubbing shoulders with the ragged, gathered at the plaza, absorbed in the enjoy-ment of the art of Orpheus. This devotion to music imparts to the general character of the masses in Mexico a gentleness and refinement of manner that distinguishes them favourably from the plebeian of the big cities of the north. Many an Indian here is capable of compos-ing music that would delight civilised audiences; and the number of musical compositions yearly produced by Mexicans is far greater than one would imagine. Who among the visitors to the Chicago Fair does not remem-ber with pleasure the playing of the Mexican band on the grounds?

Water is scarce and often brackish in the Sierra.

According to tradition, the women of Paracho had formerly to walk six miles to fetch their supply. Then, as now, the Rebeccas used to go in parties, and shorten the way by chatting in their sonorous language. But nowadays they have a well nearer their town, and the padre told me this poetic legend concerning it :

Among the girls was one, called Tzitzic (Flower), who was a priestess of the Sun. She was very handsome, and much admired by the young fellows. Sometimes she went alone with her jar; then her lover would meet her and they would dally in each other's company so that her father and mother would scold her for being late. Nevertheless, the lovers continued to meet, and on one occasion they again forgot all about the time until it grew too late for the girl to reach the spring and fetch the water. In her trouble she turned to Father Sun and invoked him to give her water near by that she might get home without incurring the anger of her parents. While thus praying she perceived a little bird rise out of the grass and flap its wings, as if it had just had a bath and was shaking the water out of its feathers. Immediately she understood that Father Sun had granted her prayer, that there was a spring close at hand ; and with a happy heart she stopped and filled her lirímaqua, and hastened home.

Her parents were surprised to see her return so early and supposed that her sweetheart had helped her to carry the jar. " No," she said, and then told them that on the very road along which the women had been going for water all these many years she had encountered a spring. All the principal men gathered to hear the marvellous tale, and went out to see the new spring. There they dug a well, twelve yards deep, from which to this day the town draws its main water-supply. It is situated to the east of Paracho, less than a mile from its central part, and the inhabitants call it Queritziaro (quer=big; ítzi= water; aro=where there is); in other words, "The big well."

If the Tarasco girl had known the story of Joshua, she, too, might have asked the sun to stop. Yet, of the two who invoked divine help, which had the nobler

Street in Cheran.

purpose, the warrior, who craved to wreak vengeance on an enemy, or the maiden, who wanted to bring her womanly love into accord with her filial duty?

The town of Cheran (chéri = sandy soil), with its quaint wooden houses, is picturesquely situated on a high, sunny slope among the mountains. Though the climate is much less damp and more genial than in the lower

lying Paracho, even here intermittent fever may develop
if a person does not promptly attend to a cold.   The
distance between Cheran and Paracho is not great, but
the difference between the two places is in every respect
as marked as if they were separated by hundreds of
miles.   Among the 8,000 inhabitants of Cheran there
are only some forty Mexicans, who have learned the
language of the Indians in order to get on.   On the
streets one does not hear Spanish spoken.   A Mexican
who once visited the town said that he might as well
have arrived in an English city, for all that he understood of the speech.

The women still wear the national dress, the skirt of
which weighs twenty-five or thirty pounds, consisting of
a long strip of black cloth pleated all around and held up
at the waist with an artistically woven girdle.   The favourite material for necklaces is here, as with all Tarascos,
red coral.   The fair sex is very shy, and if a maiden on
the street catches sight of a stranger she quickly retires
into her house.

The people, especially the women, are hard workers.
Beggars there are none.   Everybody has enough to eat
and time to spare, because all have managed to keep
their lands undisputed.   Some of them plant much corn
and accumulate money; but they do not fancy the
commodities of civilised life.   They have absolutely no
ambition to be anything but Indios.   At the time of
my visit the richest man in town was a full-blooded
Indian, worth probably $100,000.   He raised corn to the
value of $2,000 every year, while his living expenses
could hardly exceed $150 or $200 in a twelvemonth.
He was the alcalde, yet illiterate; his half-dozen children
had been to school and helped him in his business.

As in all communities in which the people cling to
their ancient customs, foreigners are disliked.   I brought

a letter of introduction to the presidente, and hoped that he would ask me to stay in his modern and quite pretentious house, since the meson in Cheran was miserable; but he had no room for me, as he was making alterations in the building. He offered me the use of a troja which he also owned and which was called after him Meson de Don Sebastian. There being nothing better I accepted this offer and duly installed myself in a typical Tarasco wooden house, with no light except what entered through the door. In the loft above the room some of the presidente's employees were shelling corn, and the kernels that constantly dropped down were eagerly claimed by mice that overran the floor. In one corner of the room the new secretario of the landlord was lodged, and in the troja opposite lived an old woman who was to cook my food.

Next morning, while Don Sebastian was paying me a friendly visit, a party of Indians called on urgent business. I could easily see that they were excited about something, and Don Sebastian explained to me that last night a man had fallen asleep on a high watch-tower, from which the Tarascos are wont to guard their crops. At the primer gallo: "the first cock's crow," as the Mexicans call the small hours of the morning, he had fallen down and killed himself. Now his brother and his widow came to ask the presidente for permission to bury him.

I had been travelling in Mexico all these years looking for just such a chance as now, at last, seemed to present itself. Some of my scientific friends in the United States had urged upon me to procure for them the body of an Indian, one of them even providing me with the proper means of preserving it thoroughly, since the scientific examination of such material would no doubt bring to light interesting facts regarding the structure of the human body. Although I knew that one accomplishes but little with the Indians by being in a hurry, I deemed this a case in which there was no time to lose, and I therefore entreated Don Sebastian to induce the family to let me have the corpse, for which I would compensate them well. But they scorned the very idea of it, especially the widow, who very firmly exclaimed: " Nombe, nombe ! " (No, no !)

Seeing that nothing could be done directly, I hurried over to the Cura, and presented my introductory letters to him. He was a broad-minded and very intelligent man, and when I laid the matter before him he could see no wrong in my purpose, and promised to do his best to make the people yield. I felt as if I had already won my case, and returning to the meson persuaded the presidente to have his horse saddled and accompany me to the house of the mourners. On the way, however, I perceived that he had forgotten to take his courage along, and as we dismounted in front of the house he said in Spanish to one of the Indians outside : "This man wants to buy your brother's body, but I suppose you will not sell it ? " thereby betraying his unfavourable attitude toward my project. If the presidente had been as enlightened and valiant as the Cura much might have been gained for science that day.

I had not given up hope yet, and, making my way through the great crowd of stolid and self-possessed Indians that had already gathered, entered the house to see the dead man. I found the body extended in the middle of the room, surrounded, in Catholic fashion, by lighted candles. He was a splendid specimen of his race. But neither money nor any other argument was of any avail. Chagrined by their obstinacy I thought for a moment of telephoning to the authorities for a peremptory order to compel the surrender of the body, but after all it was perhaps as well that I did not press the matter further, for, though I did not know it at the time, the Tarascos of the Sierra when thoroughly aroused would have been fully capable of making a corpse of me or any other objectionable stranger. Even as it was, this incident so prejudiced the people against me that during the entire time of my stay among them I had to contend with constant opposition and at last was threatened with bodily harm. Still, I was as determined as

Ancient Terra-cotta Bowl. Cheran. Main colours, red and white.
Diameter, 21.5 ctm.

they were, and having been disappointed in the matter of the corpse I at least wanted to obtain some skulls of the present day. Accordingly a few days later I got permission from the presidente and the Cura to excavate in the cemetery. The latter even offered me the services of his peon in disinterring a man who had died about nine years ago at the age of one hundred years. He had been a typical Tarasco, a member of one of the old families and a man of such physical strength that, as the priest himself had noted, he was getting a new growth

of hair in his old age, and was but little bald in front
and only slightly grey.

While the Cura started excavations and promised to
take care of any skull that might be dug up during the
day, I, with my mind at ease, went in company with
Don Sebastian and his wife to see a well-known yacata
in the neighbourhood, taking with me four men to dig.

Ancient Terra-cotta Bowl.   Cheran.   Colours mainly red and white.
Diameter, 17.3 ctm.

This yacata was situated on the slope near the foot of
the peak of Cheran, and was built of stones and covered
with earth.   About a hundred yards southward was a
corn-field laid out over the site of the ancient village of
Cheran, the spring of which, according to tradition, had
been covered up by the ancients.   A few steps from
the yacata, higher up on the slope, we came to one and
then another little terrace, both overgrown with pines,
and to a square area, about twenty yards on a side.   On

this four small mounds could be seen, one in each corner, and from it a double stone wall ran up the slope fifty yards. This arrangement evidently had some connection with the yacata. When, some time before, a way had been cut to the summit of the mountain a skeleton had been exhumed thirty yards south of the little terraces, and on digging there I secured two beautifully painted tripod terra-cotta bowls.

In the evening I returned, well content with the result of the day's work, and hoping that the Cura had been equally successful. But I soon learned that his helpfulness toward me had got the good man into hot water, and that I was the cause of the greatest scandal of the age in Cheran. Some men hostile to the priest, together with the son of the deceased who was to be dug up, had threatened to have the Cura arrested if the excavations were not stopped at once. In spite, therefore, of the latter's noble and generous offer to me to continue the digging with the possible protection of *rurales*, or Mexican federal police, I now deemed discretion the better part of valour, and desisted.

Through all this I became only a deeper puzzle to the natives. Never before had they known a white man to behave like this. Soon a general fear of me developed in town, and the rumour spread that I was killing people, especially women, to get their heads. Every time I showed myself on the street the women threw angry glances at me, hiding their faces and making their escape as best they could. Once one of them who carried a water jar dropped it in her haste and broke it. The men took it more calmly ; they congregated in little groups, resolved if anything should happen to the women to put a bullet through me.

Yet there was much for me to accomplish here before I could give the natives the pleasure of seeing me

leave town. I wanted to excavate the yacata I had
seen on the mountain-side and to secure some of the
stone idols that abounded on the hilltops, and so I remained
for nearly a fortnight longer in spite of all the enmity I
had aroused by being for once in a hurry with Indians.
I was considered the cause of every fatality that happened—hail-storms, unusually heavy rains, miscarriages
in women, etc. The chief of police in a neighbouring
village declared to Don Sebastian : " Antichrist is now
in Cheran. We cannot sell him anything, and we
carefully guard the door of the church, for fear that
he may slip in." A few weeks before my arrival some
imaginative individual had seen a man with only one
eye cutting off the heads of Indians; and it was now
thought that I was that personage. Mothers stopped
their babies from crying by mentioning my name, and a
drunken man secured his wife's forgiveness by threatening to give himself up to me. Some wiseacres even
asked the Cura if it was not for the sake of taking
away their whole pueblo that I wanted to buy so many
things.

To be photographed meant sure death ; not even the
Cura could make anyone pose for me, except his Tarasco servants, whose pictures were secured inside of the
Curato. Yet from a window in his house I did succeed
in taking snapshots at the women when they went to
the spring, and he accompanied me on a trip up a cor-
don where I could photograph Cheran and the beautiful
view down the valley. An even greater service this
charming man rendered me by dictating to me the ety-
mology of the pueblo names of the Tarasco country.
He spoke the Tarasco language as perfectly as any full-
blooded Indian, and was altogether a person of fine
attainments. We became great friends, so much so that
one day he expressed his regret that I was not a member

of his church. " You ought to be one of us," he said,
" because our church gives the best guarantees of any."

For years, in compliance with his office, he had
been fighting against the continuance of certain native
customs that survived among the population, and had
succeeded in abolishing some of them, such as the noto-
rious feasts to the saints which prove the ruin of all
Indians on the verge of civilisation. Pimentel rightly
says that under the pretext of adoring an image of the
Catholic Church the Indians in reality do reverence to
one of their ancient idols. There were annually over
twenty such feasts, each lasting eight days and longer,
and they had to be paid for by the saints' guardians,
many of whom not only bankrupted themselves, but
robbed and stole from others to fulfil the requirement of
their positions. One well-to-do man who had had
charge of San Francisco for one year had to sell his
house and a hundred sheep, all he owned, in order to
serve God, as he said. He was now destitute. With
the feasts was connected a great deal of drunkenness,
because without brandy the Indians say the feast is no
good, and they cannot comply with the demands of God
unless they are drunk. To put a stop to this nuisance
the Cura had to resort to such radical means as the abolishing of the office of guardian to the saints, or even to
take the saints themselves away, and "imprison them,"
as he expressed it to the Indians, so that the people
should not have anyone to make the feasts for.

He also forbade the custom of stealing a girl away to
marry her, and suppressed the feast of green corn, as well
as the custom of dancing for a whole night at the wake
of an "angel" or baby. Finally he abolished the ceremonies connected with the periodical re-roofing of the
church and the sojourn of the men in charge of the edifice in the forest for weeks at a time with their families

and relatives making shingles, together with the per-
fervid praying in the morning and the music and dancing at night.

The Cura's active interest in me and my work benefited me not only directly but also indirectly. Don
Sebastian, not to be outdone by my clerical friend, invited several of his most faithful followers to his house
that I might take their photographs. One old dame,
who had to be solemnly assured that her head was not to
be cut off, still protested violently and grew very angry
when I took her by the arm to put her in the right position. The rich alcalde also grew better disposed toward
me. He had once gone to Mexico "to see how it
looked," and he had visited other distant places, and his
travels had broadened his views. Besides, his beautiful
daughter, the belle of the town, had fallen in love with
Angel, who was a constant visitor to their little store.
No doubt he had talked about me, and the family began
to look upon me with favour. It was through them
finally that I secured the men I needed for making excavations.

When I at last opened the yacata I found the inside
a mass of cobble-stones, the base of which was kept confined by a wall of slabs about a foot and a half thick.
This I cut through; but to make a section through the
middle of the heap would have involved too great an
expense, and therefore after six days' work I gave up
the task. Only two very rude stone images had been
found, simply natural, oblong stones, on which the features of a human face had been picked in a crude way.
The stones were very large, with thin necks and small
heads; and only by a stretch of imagination could they
be made to assume human shape. I hardly think there
was more to be found in this stone heap; but the Indians
believe that they hear bells ringing inside of this as well

as of other yacatas higher up in the silent pine-forest that covers the slopes of the peak.

On the day of San Francisco there was a fair in Cheran, when loads of vegetables, mostly chile, were brought in from the villages roundabout, chiefly from Patzcuaro, and the population indulged in the favourite local sport, bull-riding. A corral is made and high

Lower Side of Ancient Terra-cotta Bowl, Extended.   Colours, black, red, and white.   Cheran.   Diameter, 25 ctm.

benches placed all around for the public.   When the ox comes in he is lassoed and thrown down, and while he lies someone has the courage to mount him.   The rider has nothing to hold on to except a strap tied securely around the chest of the half-wild animal.   As the bull rises he begins to buck and try to throw off his rider, who requires an enormous amount of strength and nerve. The sport is amusing to watch, and far more humane than a bull-fight, yet sufficiently dangerous to make it

exciting It might well take the place of the other
spectacle.

Angel, who had accompanied me to the arena, grew
very much excited at it and suddenly cried out that he
too must try it. His offer was taken up, and everybody
laughed to think how soon this stranger would be igno-
miniously thrown. Yet he mounted undauntedly, got
hold of the strap, and held on. In spite of all the jumps
and sharp turns of the enraged ox he kept his seat, to
the surprise of the scoffers and the intense gratification
of his lady-love and her family. The girl was deeply
enamoured of the good-looking fellow; but when he
considered how rich she was, and how great a distance
lay between Cheran and his own home, which he would
not leave for her, he finally made up his mind not to
marry her. I noticed hardly any Mexicans at this fair.

Of the several excursions which I made into the
neighbouring country, the last one was toward the north,
to the highest point of the ridge, from where I got a fine
view of Tangancicuaro. This name is derived from
Tangacecua, a pole; the locality is swampy, and the inhabitants have tried to improve matters by driving poles
into the soil. Even the lagoon of Chapala can be seen
from this ridge. Just as I was packing my camera the
blacksmith of Cheran, a Mexican with whom I had become acquainted, came along wrapped in his chino and
armed with a pistol, a welcome arrival, for I had only
Angel and two other Indians with me, and the people
we had met on the road did not look very friendly toward me.

It had begun to rain heavily, and while we were standing under a tree to protect ourselves as best we could
against the downpour, the blacksmith told me of Zacapu,
a much better place, he said, for me to go. There I could
see the palace of King Caltzontzin, and "lots of dead."

Many curious things had been excavated there. He grew quite eloquent as he pictured to me the history of the place, how the ancient monarch ate food in Zacapu, prepared for him in Tzintzuntzan, thirty or forty miles off, and brought to him every day by runners in an underground passage.

On my return to Cheran I consulted the priest about the archæological features of Zacapu, and he assured me that the black-smith's account, as far as the present state of affairs was concerned, was true. Zacapu was only a day's journey to the northeast of Cheran, so I decided to go there, although it took me in a direction opposite to the one I had intended to follow. As the blacksmith enjoyed friendly relations with the Indians, I engaged him at a dollar a day to go with me. Angel urged me not to start from Cheran without an escort; he had gone out much among the people, he pleaded, and had heard the men talk very threateningly about me; one night a fellow had even followed me with the intention of assaulting me, thinking, as many of them did, that I was endangering the lives of their women. I knew, however, that the population would be so glad to see the hated white man take his departure that there would be little danger of anyone following me, and I decided to start off as usual.

Head of a Stone Statue. Cheran. Height, 24.3 ctm.

As my expedition wound its way through the crooked streets of the town I met with the unusual sight of smiling faces everywhere; everybody seemed to draw a sigh of relief.

The feeling soon communicated itself to me as

I travelled through the lovely landscape of waving corn-fields and pine-clad hills. I was glad of any change from the miserable shed of Don Sebastian, and from the weeks of sulky distrust and ill-feeling in which the whole-souled friendship of the noble Cura had been the only redeeming circumstance.

CHAPTER XXIV

TARASCO Indians never call themselves **Tarasco**,
but Purépecha, the meaning of which word is un-
certain ; nor is the origin of the word " Tarasco," " Son-
in-law," clear, though several traditions refer to it.

In colour these people resemble much the other
Indian tribes I visited ; but I take this opportunity of
stating that here as elsewhere I was surprised to note
that families who for generations had mixed with other
tribes and the whites often become darker than they
were originally. Many of the so-called *mixtos*, or
mixed breed Indians, are several shades darker than
the pure-bred. This was especially noticeable at the
congregating of the people at the feast of the Miraculous Christ.

While many of the Tarascos have bad and irregular
teeth, the greater number possess magnificent sets,
small and pearly. The canine teeth are like the inci-
sors in appearance, and the two middle front teeth of the
upper row are set as with the Huichols. According to
Dr. N. Leon, the babies begin to get their teeth when
from six to nine months old. Children walk at a year
and a half, and talk at two. The letter L does not
occur in the Tarasco language.

Ancient Pottery Collected Along my Route between Iztlan and Arantepacua. The six pieces to the left are from the Tarasco country proper. Height of highest jar, 27 ctm.

The resting position for the women is squatting on one haunch, for the men crouching. The men move more slowly than the women, who walk always with quick, short steps, often with the toes turned in. The women are more cleanly than the men, who bathe only once a year, while the women take a bath at least once every other week. Both sexes every morning at sunrise wash their faces and feet, and in Uruapan a wooden trough is kept in the house for the purpose. In some places, as for instance in Arantepacua, only the women observe this custom, which no doubt is of religious origin.

The diet of the Tarascos, even when they are well off, is as frugal as that of other Indians. Outside of the Sierra poverty makes the struggle for life a hard one. Most of the beans raised by the people are sold, and as they seldom get any meat their main food is corn, served now and then with a side-dish of cooked herbs or fungi. The common beverage of the people is supplied by a bush called nurite, which grows in altitudes higher than the Tierra Caliente. From its leaves is extracted a tea which in flavour resembles Chinese teas, and is more wholesome in effect. It aids digestion and soothes the nerves, and is also prized as an emmenagogue. It is taken with the morning meal, and as the leaves do not lose their good qualities when dry they can be used all the year round.

The Tarascos, like all other Indian tribes, are thoroughly healthy. Many individuals go through life without ever learning how it feels to be ill, and die finally of old age. On the other hand, in many the climate of the Sierra induces coughs, pneumonia, and pleurisy, though curiously enough the most prevalent disease is jaundice (in Spanish *ictericia*), particularly in Paracho. Both young and old are attacked and may suffer from it for years, until it finally proves fatal. In many cases this disease is traceable to fits of anger ; but other causes are responsible for the majority of them—perhaps the absence of running water. There is also much typhoid fever among the Tarascos, which, although not very malignant, nearly always proves fatal, because the people do not know how to cure it.

Any kind of illness is called " Tata (Father) Illness," and is talked to with devout respect. When there is an epidemic, for instance of small-pox, the people start out from their houses with burning incense in order that the disease may arrive in a family in good-humour. If, after all, it should prove fatal, the family of the victim are very angry at the illness, do not call it Tata any more, and beat about with sticks in the corners of the house to drive it out quickly.

When a person has been ailing very long and does not improve, the Tarascos resort to a proceeding somewhat similar to that used by the Aztecs in Tuxpan. It is presumed that the patient's body is twisted because he took upon himself a very heavy burden when young, and bunches of ten or twelve cords of different colours are brought in, each bunch held together by pieces of reed wound around it in different places. The feet of the patient are held down by sticks fastened to the floor, and those present stroke him with the bundles of cord from head to foot. In former times there were women specially appointed to " disentangle " dying persons.

Nevertheless the Tarascos have some knowledge of herb remedies and of surgery. The women of Parangaricutiro claim to know a cure for barrenness, as well as a decoction that brings about abortion. The Indians also understand how to let blood, and how to replace dislocated joints. They cure fractures perfectly well by applying dry grass and corn-stalks as bandages and splints.

Throughout the Tarasco country syphilis is cured through excessive perspiration induced by certain herbs, in combination with a low diet of milk, rice, hens, potatoes, and atole blanco.   Such a sweat cure lasts for nine days, but the diet is continued for forty days longer.

Tarascos from Cheran.

There are women who take patients for such treatment and charge a moderate fee for their services.   It is difficult to say whether this treatment is aboriginal, but it appears to be so.

In ordinary cases a family does not go to any expense to procure medical aid or remedies for a member's health ; but when he succumbs they spend, comparatively

speaking, large sums on the funeral.   As much as four
fanegas of corn may be ground ; a barrel of brandy is
provided, and an ox killed.   The feast lasts for about
three days, during which time the Indians dance all
night and part of the day along-side of the corpse, on its
candle-lit bier.   Violins and guitars are played and songs
intoned in honour of the dead.   The family continues to
live in the same room in which the dead is laid out, and

Ancient Tarasco Copper Ornament.   Santa Fée de la Laguna.
Length, 5.5 ctm.

Ancient Tarasco Bronze Tweez-
ers.   Santa Fée de la Laguna.
Length, 7.8 ctm.

everybody gets gloriously drunk.   Not until the last mor-
sel of the food is consumed is the feast considered over.
On such occasions the people show what their stomachs
can   endure ; all   their   immoderate   eating   does   not
seem to impair their constitutions so much as drinking
the white man's brandy does.

In their original state the Tarascos are upright and
courageous, and when Mexican robbers plied their voca-
tion in the Sierra they were mercilessly killed as soon as
caught.   Even the women fight, using the rubbing-stone
of the metate as a weapon.   On the other hand, the
" civilised " Tarascos quickly adopt the bad traits of the
white man's character, and outside of the Sierra up to a
few years ago many Indian robber bands were found.
At the pueblo of Azaco, fifteen miles east of Cheran.
the people were such robbers that, as the saying goes,
only Santiago, the patron saint, did not steal, though
even he would lend his horse to the plunderers.   When

cattle were stolen the hearts were brought to the saint and hung on his neck.   In Cocucho (cocucho-earthenware jar), another robber nest about fifteen miles west of Cheran, the people until recently adored the Devil. He was represented by an armadillo tricked out with horns and claws, and his worshippers sacrificed part of

Tarascos from Patzcuaro.

their booty to the "Cocucho Saint," el Santo Cocucho, as the image was called.   So strong was the belief in its potency that once during a revolution the Mexicans abducted it in order to use it against their enemies.   It was kept in a secret place, and once a year carried around at night in a torch-light procession, until finally it fell into the hands of a priest, who burned it and thus ended its worship.

To the casual observer the Tarascos seem to be as
calm and stoical as most other Indians; but they are in
reality of a much more choleric temperament, easily
offended and quick in anger.   Grown people, of course,
show their irritation less than children, who more than
once astonished me with their sudden outbreaks of pas-
sion, becoming actually unmanageable in their fury.
The mother may also fly into a rage, talking violently at
the top of her voice, but she never beats her children,
and in a few minutes the fracas is over.   The men fight
only when drunk, sometimes using oaken sticks such as
they carry with them as canes on their travels.   Suicide
is unknown.   Children show affection for their parents,
and toward each other the people are as kind and hospitable as they are reserved and suspicious with outsiders.

With strangers the Tarasco is polite and always lifts
his hat; but he is never servile.   On the contrary, in
public office he is self-conscious and adopts a haughty
mien.   As soldiers the Tarascos command higher compensation than other tribes.   Many men distinguished
as lawyers, writers, and priests were pure-bred Tarascos.
The tribe possesses naturally the gift of oratory, the
women even more than the men; in court the women
know their business better and make more valid arguments than the men.   The following anecdotes illustrate
their reasoning power:

At a confession a priest asked an Indian : " Do you
believe that our Lord Christ will come back to judge
the world?"   The Indian replied: " Yes, I believe it,
padrecito, but you will see he never comes."   Surprised,
the confessor asked: " But why, my son?"   The
answer was: " Because he did not fare well when he
was here the first time."   On another occasion the confessor said: "Everything God made is perfect," to
which an Indian said: " Not the water gourds."   He

had in mind the fact that the gourds have to be cut in half to be prepared for use as drinking vessels.

According to Beaumont, the old chronicler of Michoacan the Tarascos were the finest looking of all Indian races. They were not only warlike and experts at shooting with bow and arrow, but also very industrious and in handicraft had no superiors. They utilised obsidian for making a multitude of objects, and manu-

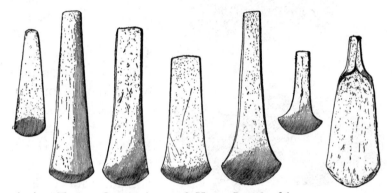

Ancient Tarasco Copper Axes and Hoe. Length of longest, 23.7 ctm.; of shortest, 10.7 ctm.

factured flutes which could imitate the song of birds, the roar of the tiger, or the hissing of the serpent.

The old Tarascos made paper from the bast of the fig-tree called ciranda. In tanning, as well as in weaving with many colours and in " feather mosaic " work, they were even more skilful than the Aztecs, though, taking it all in all, they were less advanced in general culture. The pigments they used in dyeing textile fabrics were fast. They excelled in the founding of metals, and they made axes, hoes, awls, pincers, and many kinds of ornaments out of copper. In Jilotlan I secured my first ancient copper axes, and before I left the land of the Tarascos I came upon a considerable number of copper implements which had been either found accidentally or excavated together with skeletons. The most interesting things of this sort were three bells of remarkable workmanship, in the shape of turtles, each with a little ball inside. They were in filigree work of soldered wire, and the most remarkable bells found in Mexico— quite works of art. They were made, as American Indian pottery often is, on the principle of coiling a rope of clay. The late Frank Hamilton Cushing told me that he had found bells of terra-cotta made by this method. These turtle-bells, or rattles, are provided with a loop on the underside, by which they were attached to the person, probably to the leg.

I was told that the Tarascos near Santa Clara still know the ancient method of tempering copper to make it as hard as steel. The process is said to depend on the application of an herb, a rumour which probably has no more

Upper Side.

Side View.

Lower Side.

Ancient Rattle in the Shape of a Turtle with Young on Its Back. Naranja, near Zacapu. Length, 9.4 ctm.

foundation than the hints that an herb is used in the working of pure gold. The father of my informant once offered to an Indian four cows if he would tell him his method of tempering copper; but the Indian said that his grandfather had taught him the art on condition that he would never reveal the secret to an outsider, for if he did God would punish him. This happened in 1860, and the Indian was then eighty years old. At any rate the Tarascos are still clever coppersmiths, though the art as differentiated from the mechanical trade appears to be now lost, like the ceramic art and many other ancient acquirements. Ancient Tarasco pottery seems to possess a slight resemblance to Peruvian ware.

The characteristic tendency toward handicraft still survives in the various industries practised by the tribe to-day. A notable feature is the monopoly of certain lines of manufactures by the different communities, a circumstance probably due in a measure to the celebrated Bishop Vasco de Quiroga, who is credited with many practical innovations in his efforts to Christianise the Tarascos. Parangaricutiro, for instance, is the place for counterpanes, as Paracho is the headquarters for rebozos and guitars. In Uruapan, likewise, there is a business absolutely characteristic of the town—namely, the production of lacquer-ware. The distribution of labour even goes so far as to make the manufacture of plates and plaques on which the lacquer work is done the specialty of another place. One town occupies itself with the digging out of the canoes used on the large lake of Patzcuaro, while another supplies the paddles with which the crafts are propelled. The Tarasco women are so much taken up with housework and home industries that they do not engage in agriculture.

Traces of the ancient form of government are hard

to discover, but I have heard of certain villages that have yet council houses, where guardians called petápes are stationed to watch that no one enters who does not know the watchword. Should a stranger present himself he may be allowed to step in, but the assembly is warned of his presence and no important business is transacted until he takes his departure. A fiscal or major-domo is said to preside at the meetings, one of whose duties it is to offer brandy to all present. As to the present régime, the natives do not love the Mexicans any too well, saying that "what was bad in former times cannot be good nowadays." The Tarascos firmly believe that some day they will again be masters of their land.

Ancient Copper Bell, Patzcuaro. Length, 4.7 ctm.

The Tarascos marry early in life. If a man is bearded, though he may be only twenty, and not yet married, he generally has to content himself with a widow, for the girls are suspicious lest something prevented him from marrying when it was time for him to do so. The women on becoming mothers soon lose their girlish appearance. They never have very many children, rarely more than five or six. The infants are carried on their mothers' backs held up by the rebozo.

Courtship is carried on at the spring whence the girls fetch water, or on the way to and fro, and in Cheran I observed scores of boys going early in the afternoons to meet their sweethearts on their aquatic expeditions. He asks her for water, and she hands him her dipper to drink from. He may make himself agreeable by gallantly filling her jar, but more frequently he contents himself with stopping her on the road, and here and there along the path one may see couples standing, she half turned away from him, bashful and embarrassed, breaking off the leaves of a plant with one hand, while with the other she balances the heavy water jar on her shoulder.   Day after day a young man may thus meet the queen of his heart, but it may be a year or two before they arrive at the question of matrimony.   Since the advent of the white man, to be sure, matters are often brought to a crisis in a much shorter time, and some couples marry after a very brief woo-ing.   A notable fact is that the men never fight among them-selves for any one woman.   A bashful young swain may carry around with him a love-charm in the shape of a dead person's little finger, care-fully dried, in order to "open the door"—that

Tarasco Courtship.

is to say, the heart—of his lady-love.   But here, too, advancing civilisation is making inroads, and a young man whom I asked whether the Tarascos used any love-powder sneeringly replied: "The best love-charm is ready cash" (*plata en el mano*).

In Ihuátzio (Ilihuátzi=coyote), a village situated on the shore of the lake opposite the town of Patzcuaro, there is said to be in vogue among the young people

the following custom : When a boy has been courting
a girl for some time, and believes that his affection is
returned, he will one day, at the spring, take hold of her
rebozo and not let it go until she says "yes." Then,
with an oaken stick which he has kept concealed under
his blanket, he smashes her jar so that the water falls
over her. Her companions, hastening to the scene,
take off all her clothes, even to her necklace and ear-
rings, and lend her another dress and a new jar in which
she can carry water home. Thus she returns in strange
attire and with a strange water vessel, while her beau
appropriates her wet dress. In order to regain it her
father has to pay him one medio (six centavos) for each
piece. On the following day he takes a load of wood
to her house, leaves it outside of the door, and goes
away. Not until after three days does he return, and
if he finds that the wood has been accepted he knows
that his sweetheart consents to follow him to his home,
where he gives back to her the coins, and presents her
with some beautiful flowers, among which yellow ones
are specially conspicuous.

A man from the neighbourhood of Zirahuen (zirani=
to feel cold: a cold place) and Santa Clara told me that
in that locality it is customary to test the good qualities
of a bride by opening a bee's nest in front of her face.
If she shrinks back she is no good ; but if she can stand
it all quietly and without defending herself she proves
that she possesses the fortitude required to bear all the
trials of matrimony.

The people at present are married by the priest, but
the wedding is afterward celebrated in the house of the
bridegroom, and an additional ceremony may be performed in which the bridal couple and their parents
drink together, and a good deal of speechmaking is
indulged in.

In Angagua (Angóni = a stone set up in the centre), a village about two miles from Parangaricutiro, the ancient marriage ceremony of the Tarascos is still in actual practice. In all essential points it is like the one I observed among the Aztecs in Tuxpan and other places from there on along my route on the coast.

An elderly woman, generally an aunt of the bridegroom, is selected as madrina, or guardian of the bridal couple. In the evening she spreads a white sheet over the petate or straw mat that is to serve as the nuptial couch, and then discreetly retires. In the morning she enters upon the execution of her delicate mission, which even among the Indians themselves is considered an onerous duty. The continuation of the feast and the happiness of the bride for years to come depend upon her verdict. In case her inspection reveals the unmistakable proof for which she is looking, she joyfully goes forth to the assembled guests, and, holding the sheet triumphantly aloft, exclaims: "Watstáli!" (She was a virgin!) Every heart is filled with joy, and every lip repeats the glad tidings: "A wats (virgin) was she? Now let the music go on!" shouts the bridegroom, and rockets are fired off. The sheet is carried round on a tray and everybody expresses his reverence of virtue by kissing it as he would the image of a saint. The bride is shown all manner of attention; chocolate and the best of everything are placed before her. All is merriment, and the people revel in dancing, eating, and drinking.

On the second day they perform what is called the canára, to the accompaniment of a special tune. The women dance with spinning-whorls, the loom, or even the metate, and the men with agricultural implements. One of the women makes a rag doll, dances with it, and then gives it to the bridegroom and to the bride, who puts it to her breast as if it were a baby, The father and the mother of the bridal couple dancing with bread and chocolate in their hands, hold the food before the mouth of the girl, but when she opens her lips to receive it, quickly turn round and eat it themselves.

Should the inspection of the sheet not result in favour of the bride, the madrina breaks the woeful news first to the parents-in-law, saying: "We shall all be lost! We do not even deserve water! There will be no more feast!" The fire is extinguished and all the guests set out for their homes very sad, first, however, showing their disapproval by spoiling all the bride's wedding-gifts, which always consist entirely of pottery. To make her ashamed of herself and to punish her, they pierce and perforate the vessels, which can now only be made serviceable by laborious and troublesome mending by the unlucky bride. Repairing is done with a dough in which the milky juice of certain trees, or even cow's milk, is mixed with lime, cotton, mashed beans, and the white of an egg. The pottery has to be fired again, but even then it looks patched. A still more serious consequence is that from now on the hapless young woman, who lives with her mother-in-law, is disliked by everybody. No consideration is shown her; she has to work hard, and not until she is about to become a mother is her burden lightened.

It may be said, however, that the lot of a young Tarasco woman at its best is not a pleasant one. It is a widely spread custom in the Sierra for the sisters of a husband, and still more his mother, to ill-treat the bride as much as they know how. A woman in Paracho told me that her sister died after ten years of married life from such ill-treatment and the incessant torment of her mother-in-law. In the more remote districts this custom still flourishes, though it is dying out among the more advanced Indians.

Indeed, all ancient customs are rapidly disappearing, though, whatever influence may be brought to bear upon the actions of the people, their ancient beliefs still hold sway over their minds, and much valuable folk-lore may yet be gathered. To this day the Tarascos never mention the sun, except as Our Father Sun. At daytime they swear by Our Father Sun, and at night-time by Our Mother Moon, and they say to each other: " Do not tell a lie, because our Father Sun hears you ! " No business is transacted after dark. They never shell corn after the sun has set, nor will they take it down from the loft after nightfall, for then the corn sleeps and must not be disturbed. The Tarascos used to worship the Southern Cross, "the four stars" as they called the constellation.

At the time of an eclipse the Indians show much emotion, thinking that the two celestial bodies are devouring one another. Harelips are attributed to the influence of eclipses. According to Mrs. Z. Nuttall the same notion prevailed among the Aztecs, who saw the figure of a rabbit in the moon. If a pregnant woman looked at the moon in eclipse her child was likely to be marked, a belief which survives among the Mexicans of to-day. A curious parallel to this idea of the pernicious effect of a rabbit is still in vogue in Norway, where hunters cut off the snouts of hares that no pregnant woman may see them.

Nowadays there is found in every house at least one picture of a saint, who, as the people express it, inhabits the best room, while they themselves sleep in the kitchen to avoid offending him. Only strangers are ever allowed to occupy his room. All the saints collectively, as well as any one of them, are called Tata

Dios, Father God. At noon the wife or her husband places a potsherd with smoking copal before the household deity for his food. A visitor entering the house kisses the picture before he states his business. As with other tribes, San Mateo is made responsible for the weather and the crops. If it freezes, his image is taken from the church early in the morning and dumped into cold water as a punishment; but if the crops are successful the people carry him in procession, make a big feast, and treat him to an abundance of brandy and tamales. Every year some old Indian is nominated to represent San Mateo. At All Souls' Day the Tarascos leave flowers, notably yellow ones, in the doorways of their houses to invite the souls of their friends to come in, and they pay a sheep for every paternoster that is said on that day for the dead. For their private feasts they send out oral invitations, the messenger at the same time handing a flower to each invited guest. At the arrival of the visitors at the house these flowers are again collected.

When a man falls and hurts himself his friends, especially the younger ones, go to the place where the accident occurred, and call for the spirits to come. Then they return, sweeping the road and strewing flowers, all the time keeping up a great howling.

When a woman with a baby on her back crosses a river she is much afraid of mischievous water-sprites, and constantly calls the child by name, saying: "Come on, come on, do not linger behind." These water-sprites are called chaníquivry.

A woman who expects to become a mother must not carry salt, chile, or lime, or the child will become deaf and blind.

When two ears of corn grow together they are looked upon with reverence and are preserved.

It is bad to pass a man who is lying down.

When selling milk, the Tarascos always want the purchaser to drink it on the spot; they too have the same superstition that the Mexicans and the Huichols have about milk boiling over into the fire.

The Tarascos do not like strangers to caress their little ones, for fear of the evil eye. The mother anxiously begs the visitor rather to molest and irritate her child that it may remain in good health. Any illness that may befall it afterward is traced to the evil eye; there is no other cause for children's diseases. To avoid its baneful effects many people tie red threads about the wrists and ankles of their babies, and stick the red feather of a woodpecker into their hair, thinking that the red blurs the sorcerer's sight.

When an Indian threatens his adversary in anger he says: "I will make you die in four or five mats!" meaning within the time it takes to use up so many sleeping-mats. Persons who believe that they have been bewitched place spines of nopal in the corners of their houses and on the outsides. To learn the art of bewitching people, some Indians go to remote villages, to Characuaro or Cirandaro. The first of these names alludes to the locality of the village, which to the traveller seems to rise suddenly out of the lagoon (shararani =appear); the other name is derived from ciranda= paper, and also the fig-tree from which it was made.

I noted the methods of a female fortune-teller, who was consulted in many cases of robberies and losses of property. She placed a tallow candle in a large jar, and divined the direction in which to look for the lost article from the movements of the flame; from the way in which the tallow melted she predicted whether it would be found in forest or valley.

The owl is in disfavour, and whenever the people see

one they curse it and threaten it with the machete. If an owl flies over the house the owner takes it for an omen that he will soon die and he prays to God.

Rattlesnakes must never be touched, much less killed.

CHAPTER XXV

ZACAPU—THE "PALACE" OF KING CALTZONTZIN—AN ANCIENT
BURIAL-PLACE—FILED TEETH—A SEPULCHRAL URN—MARKED
HUMAN BONES—"HERE COMES THE MAN WHO EATS PEOPLE!"
—FICTION AND TRUTH—PHOTOGRAPHY A CAPITAL CRIME—THE
TARASCOS UP IN ARMS AGAINST ME—THEY SUBMIT TO
REASON.

NOT far from Cheran one enters into magnificent
virgin pine-forests which close the hillsides to the
northwest of the town of Nahuatzen (Tarasco: Yahuatzen,
" Where it freezes "). The track used to be unsafe on
account of robbers, bands of twenty and more Indians
from Chilchota and other villages frequently extending
their operations into this region ; and my blacksmith
friend pointed out to me the spot where only three years
ago, the town-clerk of Nahuatzen had been held up and
robbed even of his clothes. The name Chilchota is Aztec, the Tarasco name of the place being Tzirápo (tziri
=maiz ; xapo=ashes : " Place where nixtamal is made
with ashes [instead of lime]).

We soon left the easy zigzag road of the Sierra behind, passing now and then some splendid oak-trees.
Once in a while a view opened out over the country
around Zacapu far below like a large swamp full of lagoons. Zacapu itself (" Place of stones," alluding to the
great, ancient lava flow near by) is a charming, sunny
town, blessed with a fine spring, the source of a short
but crystal clear river that passes slowly into a pond on
which many varieties of water-fowl disport themselves as

fearlessly as in a park. The town used to be one of the
important places in the Tarasco country, but now the
Mexicans have manifestly the upper hand. Although
there is still a large number—at least half the population
of 3,000—of pure-bred Indians, they are so much civilised that they no longer speak their own tongue and
retain but few of their ancient customs. Until recently
the place had a bad name as an abode of robbers.

We directed our steps toward the uninviting looking
meson, and found the court-yard full of muleteers with
their cargoes and aparejos, all in an almost Egyptian

Filed Teeth.

darkness. The principal men and the presidente cour-
teously helped me next day to engage men to go with
me and excavate at the interesting ruins known locally
as El Palacio.

Pausing a moment as we crossed the little bridge
that spans the river, I enjoyed an extremely picturesque
view ; what with the calm, clear water, the women
washing, the men swimming about or watering horses,
the children playing, and in the background the majestic, pine-clad peak of Tecolote watching over all, it was
an idyllic scene. Close by, toward the west of Zacapu,
rose a ridge of mal pais, perhaps five hundred feet high,
and at its top could be vaguely traced the outlines of
the palacio of King Caltzontzin. Everybody whom we
met was polite, and the entire environment presented a

most pleasing and benign contrast to the prejudice and inhospitality at Cheran.

Our guide led us through little corn-fields up the ridge, and was soon able to indicate a spot where "muertos" could be found. At his suggestion I selected for my excavations a level spot about twenty-five yards square, among eruptive rocks just at the foot and to the northeast of the palacio. Almost immediately we came upon several skeletons, and for five days I continued digging, so that before my departure I had thoroughly exhausted the place. The skeletons were found huddled together without any order whatever, lying two and three deep, those uppermost covered with scarcely three feet of earth. I secured more than a hundred skulls, most of them of Tarascos, but there were at least two other types intermixed with them. Among the latter were

Sepulchral Urn. Height, 91 ctm.; circumference, 2 metres, 25 ctm.

several artificially flattened so that the sides and the back bulged out to an extraordinary degree. Four of these flattened heads were those of females. On a few of the Tarasco skulls the teeth were filed, incisions that made them look like swallow-tails having been made in the front teeth.

There were remarkably few objects with the dead, only about a dozen small copper bells and a few beads. We were lucky enough, however, to come upon a burial jar standing upright among the skeletons toward the eastern part of the cemetery. This earthenware jar, which I took possession of, is quite graceful in shape and has a curved, slightly flaring rim. It is of very good

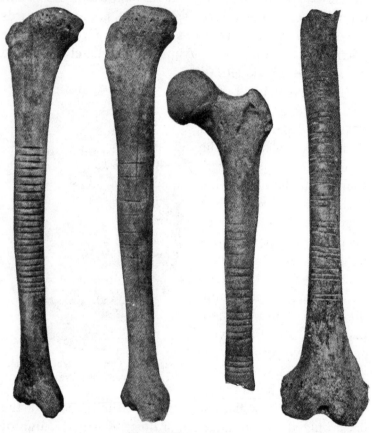

Marked Human Bones.

quality, with thin walls and smooth surface. The cover is of inferior material. Inside of the vessel was nothing but the charred remains of a skeleton. Such burial jars are not altogether rare in the Tarasco country, although it is only by accident that one comes across them. Looking for one expressly may prove a laborious and

thankless task.   We also found a small earthenware
bowl filled with ashes and containing besides a detached
skull and a fetish of lava.

The most curious and interesting objects, however,
which excited the astonishment not only of the Mexicans, but also of my Indian workmen, were human
bones with certain transverse marks carved on them.
Twenty - six such marked bones were
picked up among the skeletons, most of
them femurs and tibias.

My theory, advanced elsewhere, was
that these bones were taken from enemies
killed in battle and worn as charms to give
the victor the strength of the vanquished
foe and thereby luck in fighting. It seemed,
however, to be the consensus of opinion
that the bones were musical instruments,
an opinion which has been corroborated
by my discovery in 1898 of notched deer-
bones in use among the present Huichol
Indians (see page 155).   Any further
doubt in this matter is removed by an
interesting find made in the course of the
excavations behind the Cathedral of Mex-

Ancient Notched
Bone, of Burnt
Clay. City of
M e x i c o .
Length, 16.5
ctm.

ico in the autumn of 1900.   Mr. M. H. Saville, who
was present there, informs me that representations in
clay of notched human bones (femurs) were found,
with similar representations of Aztec musical instruments—the horizontal wooden drum, the rattle, the
turtle-shell, the flageolet (chirimia). There was one
in the shape of the hieroglyph for stone, the original
of which probably gave a metallic sound.   They were
all, including the bowl, made of red earthenware, and
were of more or less uniform size.   There were several
specimens of each instrument, and the whole collection

comprised about a hundred objects. Thus the purpose
of the notched human bone is clearly shown, and even
the instrument with which it was rubbed is reproduced
in relief along one side.

Yet granted that marked human bones were used
as musical instruments, the fact that the arrangement
of the transverse marks differs so much on the vari-

Bottom and Lower Sides of Earthenware Bowl, Extended. Light grey,
with black and red decorations, the principal being the Syastika. Zacapu. Diameter, 26.5 ctm.

ous bones in my collection still remains to be explained; furthermore that the markings on some are
too slight to produce a sound different from that of an
unmarked bone. Last but not least out of a total of
twenty-six bones only three show signs of any considerable handling. May not this indicate that many of the
bones were conventionalised forms of the musical instrument proper, or in other words charms with their
purpose symbolically expressed? From the meaning

the Huichols associate with their rubbing of notched deer-bones one is justified in inferring that the notched human bones were sounded to obtain luck in killing enemies. This interpretation does not conflict with Dr. Eduard Seler's plausible explanation that the bones found by me were used at a burial feast in honor of a dead chief by slaves (or captives), who were then, according to custom, killed, the chief's body being burnt. The burial jar mentioned above would therefore contain the remains of the cremated chief, and the skeletons found would be those of the slaves.

In this part of the country every monument of antiquity is attributed to King Caltzontzin of Tzintzuntzan, just as, north of the State of Michoacan, such monuments are ascribed to Montezuma. The palacio, or fortress, is an esplanade formed by extending the top of a hill to a length of one hundred and thirty yards, with a width of half that number. The masonry consists of chunks of lava put together without mortar. In some places it is a hundred feet high, but where the fortress approaches the highest points of the natural elevation and accordingly would be easy of access a low wall had been raised, traces of which can yet be found. The level space that was thus gained, which is now covered with grass and patches of brushwood, could accommodate from five hundred to six hundred persons. In the vicinity, especially on the western side of the slope of this hill, were numerous square or rectangular yacatas, built of lava blocks without earth.

The old lava flow, on which are the palacio and the yacatas, runs at its eastern edge to a height of about two hundred yards. I once followed this edge from Zacapu northward for sixteen miles, and observed many other fortifications as well as yacatas of the same material and shape as those just mentioned. There were

also some ancient houses, which seemed to be constructed of lava blocks and plastered with mud; but on
account of the roughness of the country I could not get
close to them.   Similar monuments of antiquity may be
encountered for a stretch of some thirty miles to the
north of Zacapu, as far as San Antonio Corupo (" Burnt
on the surface ").   For the large burial jar I had a

Terra-cotta Plate.   Decorated in black and red.   **Zacapu.**
Diameter, 18.3 ctm

box made, and in this it was carried by four men to the
lake of Patzcuaro, placed in a native canoe, and conveyed
to the town of Patzcuaro, thence to be sent to the
United States.   Some of the native canoes on this lake,
those used for hunting, have room for only one man;
but the travelling canoes are large enough to accommodate eight or even more persons, and are safe so long
as the boatmen do not get drunk.

After having packed my osseous treasures and stored
them in the house of the priest I returned to the Sierra,

and in the neighbourhood of Nahuatzen incidentally secured an iron axe which was interesting on account of the way in which the head was fitted to the handle. I soon found that the foolish rumours about me had spread from Cheran, and that the people were afraid of me. When I arrived at Arantepacua ("Where there is a plain"), early in the afternoon, the meson would not receive me, only my animals. But I knew that there was a priest here and I went at once to see him. He was kind enough to offer me a troja about a hundred yards from his curato, where I could stay. He told me that my arrival at the place had been heralded by a woman, who had run up to him in great excitement and announced in frantic tones: "Here comes the man who eats people!"

Nobody wanted to sell me anything, and the children cried with fear when they caught sight of Turis, as they called me— a name the Tarascos apply to white travellers, meaning a man with a black soul, a bad Tarasco. The priest assured the people that I meant them no harm, but he was a recent arrival among them and had no influence; when he told them to come and be photographed no one came. To

Mode of Fastening Iron Axe to the Handle. Sebina. Length of axe, 18.5 ctm.

add to these difficulties, when I began digging at the site of the ancient pueblo in the neighbourhood, I found nothing, and had to content myself with photographs of the landscape.

I was just packing up my camera when two women came running up with expressions of fear and anger on their faces, and cried out to me to quit digging. At the same moment arrived the owner of the ground, whom

I had sent for, but who also desired me to stop my excavations.   I told my men to fill up the holes we had
made, and we were about to start, when another man,
apparently with no authority whatever, came upon the
scene and angrily asked me what I was doing.   I learned
afterward that he was the "boss" of the village, and
that he had advised his "constituents" to run me off with
sticks.   The priest did not think that they would attempt
any acts of violence, though he admitted that the Indians when gathered in a crowd might be so inaccessible
to reason as to be dangerous.   I felt somewhat uneasy
about my note-books and negatives in the event of a
mob attacking the house in which I slept.   If they had
set fire to it at night the well-seasoned old shanty would
have burned lustily, and I should have lost irredeemably
the results of my labours of the last couple of years.   As
for myself, the priest generously offered me a refuge in
his curato in case anything should happen during the
night ; but neither on this nor the following two nights
I spent here was there any disturbance.

About six weeks before, while at Paracho, I had
heard of a mystical colebra (water serpent) of stone,
which had been first seen on top of a mountain near
Quitzeo (quitz=*tecomate*, a round gourd, flat at top and
bottom) by an Indian, whose horse had taken fright at
the sight of the monster.   It was described as having
the shape of a serpent with the beak of a bird and a tail
raised like a scorpion's.   Sometimes it would assume the
shape of a pig, and then again it would change into
a drum, or into a ball.   It was blue in colour, and had
many paintings on it that looked like a Mexican jacket.
I sent Angel and another trustworthy Indian to try and
fetch it, but they returned empty-handed, for the people
of Quitzeo feared that some disaster would follow the
removal of the monster ; there might be hail-storms,

or no rain next year, or something equally direful. Neither the Jefe de la Policia, nor the principal men would assume the terrible responsibility; it was something that concerned the entire community, and the inhabitants were to be called to a meeting that evening to decide whether I was to get the colebra, and at what price, or whether it should be moved at all. In the morning I was to be advised of the result of their deliberations.

To expedite this news I despatched my Indian from Nahuatzen before daybreak, instructing him to bring the "animal" back with him if I was to have it, so that I might continue my journey that day. He soon returned without the serpent, but with the surprising report that the colebra was to be given me *gratis*, though, of course, I was prepared to ward off any possible evil consequences that might be attributed to its removal with some *douceur* to the authorities who had brought about this solution. In the meantime I had heard so many conflicting stories about the monster that I knew there could not be much truth connected with it. Yet I was curious to see out of what the awesome rumours had been manufactured. I despatched Angel with five other men to fetch it, sending with them axes to cut down trees suitable for a carrier and plenty of ropes to tie the serpent fast that it might not get injured on the way. Toward sunset they returned, staggering under a burden which was long and round and wrapped in cloths and bags. It was simply a great, heavy stone, in shape somewhat like an exaggerated eel, which the fervent pantheism of the Indians had made so much of. Its arrival only increased the animosity of the people against me, for they saw in it a dark design on my part to do them harm.

Next day I started for Uruapan. The track passes

the village of Capacuaro (cápacuri=located between two mountains), which, as far as the inhabitants are concerned, resembles Cheran. A Mexican who appeared to be on good terms with the naturales offered to show me some ruins close to the road, and I had taken him on, thinking he might become useful also as an interpreter, since he spoke Tarasco very well. When we arrived at a plain not far from the village, which, however, could not be seen from that point, we came upon several men ploughing. To avoid suspicion, the guide deemed it wise to tell them what we were about to do ; otherwise, he said, they might run to the village, ring the big bell to bring all the people together, and make it unpleasant for us. As it was, the boy I engaged for three reales (thirty-seven centavos) to carry the camera boxes and show us the best track up the hill to the ruins, took fright when arriving at the top, saying that he was afraid his father might see him, and abandoned me in a hurry.

To my disappointment the ruins turned out to be only the four walls of a chapel standing close to what seemed to be an old cemetery. Having gone to the trouble of ascending, I photographed it, as well as the imposing peak of Quitzeo, which rose directly above us to a great height. The place was lovely. We were surrounded by glorious pine-forests, which covered most of the mountain-side ; only around the top had wind and weather left some straggling, gnarled, and twisted veterans scattered here and there. I spent barely half an hour here, and then rapidly descended, to lose no time in reaching Uruapan that evening.

Just as we were emerging from the forest and reached the plain, a dozen Indians from the village came marching toward us. The two leaders were armed with muzzle-loaders, the others with machetes and stones. "What are you doing here?" they demanded angrily. "Who gave you permission to come here?"

I told them that there was no law against photographing, and that I could not see any harm in it. They calmed down somewhat, yet could not understand why I had not asked for permission to take pictures. "That is what I should have done," I said, "if I had had the time, and now I am willing to go with you and explain everything." "The mischief is already done," they retorted, "and who knows but that you will come back and take possession of our lands!"

I assured them that I had no such intentions, and we went together tow-

The Peak of Quintzeo, Seen from the East.

ard the mule which was carrying the camera and which I had left near by. Their anger rose again as they caught sight of the boy who had shown us the path up hill.

The men lifted the hammers of their guns full cock, put
caps on, and pointed the muzzles disagreeably close to
the boy's face, scolding him severely all the time, while
the youngster vigorously and valiantly pleaded his case.
My interpreter grew pale.   "I know these people," he
said ; "they are devils, and I am going now."   "Don't
you think you had better stay and help me explain
matters ?" I asked him.   "You know I do not speak
Tarasco, and surely you are not afraid of the Indians ?"

He would not be persuaded, but maintained that it
was getting late and that he wanted to return home.
With a parting injunction, " Don't forget to speak to
the prefect about these people!" he was off. He had
hardly courage enough to take the money due him, leaving me to settle the matter as best I could with the
fanatical crowd that was gathering in the village.

While the twelve emissaries wended their way back,
Angel and I packed the camera on the mule and joined
the rest of my party, consisting of two Indians, who had
been watching the other mules on the plain farther on.
" Anyway," laughed Angel, whose stout heart never
failed him, "they have only one shot each." He evidently had full confidence in my modern rifle and re-
volver. As for himself, he carried only a small knife on
the road, objecting to large knives, which he considered
good only for "the big balls," where there usually is
fighting. My other followers were also unarmed, though
I had entrusted one with a pistol just for the respect it
commands when dangling from a man's belt ; inasmuch
as he could not shoot I had deemed it safer to leave it
unloaded.

The expedition now set itself in motion, and in a
quarter of an hour we reached a thicket where the road
was narrow. Here I found over thirty Indians waiting
for me, sitting sullenly on each side of the path. None

of them looked up while the mules passed between them.
I ordered my men to wait for me a little farther on, and
asked for the jefe. In silent dignity a man with an
intelligent and quite sympathetic face arose. I drew
from my pocket the letter from President Diaz and
another from the Governor of the State of Michoacan,
and asked my taciturn official whether he could read.
To my surprise he said he could, and then he took the
documents and read them slowly aloud. This finished,
I addressed the assemblage in Spanish :

" I am glad to see that you are able to defend your-
selves so well against the whites; but as regards me, you
are mistaken. You are opposed to me because the
people in Cheran have told you that I kill and eat
people. That is a lie! I am a friend of you Indians,
and that is why I have come from a distant country to
see how you are. I have travelled for nearly five years
among tribes just like you, and none of them has ever
done me harm; why should you? You have many
friends in Mexico and in the countries on the other side
of the big sea, and they want to know how you look and
how you are, and to hear about your old customs and
your ancient history. That is why I have taken pictures
of the people and of the country. Some of you think
that I am seeking treasures; but I am not looking for
money or silver. I have plenty to eat at home, and
need not come here to get tortillas and beans."

The Indians held a little council among themselves,
and soon gave in. They even invited me to stop in
their village, since it was getting late. But when we
arrived the women would not consent to this, and there
was nothing for us to do but provide ourselves with fat
pine-wood and continue the journey by torch-light
through the pitch-dark night.

Thus ended my last day among the Tarascos of the
Sierra. Having been away from civilisation very long

and my time being more than up, I had attempted to get through with this tribe as soon as possible, claiming their confidence before they had become properly acquainted with me. The result was that for the entire four months I stayed among them I had to overcome the antagonism not only of the tribe as a whole, but of every district and every hamlet. Without patience and tact an ethnologist can do nothing with primitive people. I feel confident that if I had had, say, six months more, I should have conquered them all and made them my friends. The same jefe afterward twice took the trouble to visit me in Uruapan, and bring me antiquities for sale. The Indians have been so imposed upon that one should not wonder when valiant tribes like the Tarascos defend with all their might the last piece of land left to them. Even if they had killed me no one could have blamed them for doing as they have been done by for centuries past.

CHAPTER XXVI

WE arrived at ten o'clock at night at Uruapan where I was not a little astonished to find the streets lighted by electricity. It was a great contrast to the domain of the wild mountaineers I had just left; and the disparity became still more glaring next day when I took a walk through the town.

Uruapan is a Spanish corruption of Urupan, "Where flowers are blooming"—that is, where there is constant spring. In popular opinion Uruapan is the "Paradise of Michoacan," a name it deserves on account of its charming locality no less than its delightful people and superb climate. The temperature is pleasantly warm in the day and at night a cool breeze springs up to sweep away all microbes. Near the town is a magnificent spring, in which rises a river whose abundance of crystal-clear water adds variety to the singularly picturesque beauty of the landscape. The water is used for irrigating orchards of banana and coffee trees, and the coffee raised here is famous as the best in Mexico. In the Tierra Caliente below rice is cultivated. The river also furnishes the motor power for the electric plant, and the town boasts also two cotton-mills and a cigar factory.

Uruapan may be called the capital of the Tierra Caliente, of Michoacan, and enjoys a great deal of commerce. Especially on Sundays its streets present a most animated appearance, when the Indians from far and near come to dispose of their products. In the evening a well-trained band discourses beautiful music on the Plaza de los Martiros, which is thronged with quite elegantly dressed people. In the so-called casino

The Spring at Uruapan.

I was surprised to find a table equal to the best in Mexico, with a charge of three reales (thirty-seven centavos) a meal. I thought at first I had ventured by mistake into some private club, but luckily for me it was really the fonda. What a relief, after all the privations and discomforts and fights against prejudice and fanaticism, to find myself at last safe in this haven! To add to my comfort, the photographer of the town, awake to the rare purity of the water, kept a bathing establishment, and I hugely enjoyed the baths, the first since my illness in Tepic.   Think of it!   Here were Old World culture, the comfort of well-prepared food, with Spanish wines, courteous, liberal people who never thought of asking you whether you were protestante or freemason, and only three leagues away barbarians who wanted to kill you for photographing a landscape, who would not allow you to stop over night in their village, and among whom you had either to die of hunger or be thankful for their condescension in selling you miserable tortillas and beans! With all due appreciation for the Indian's many admirable qualities and an honest sympathy for the wrongs he has suffered, what is bred in the bone of civilised man cannot be eradicated at will.   The only sphere in which he

Lacquer-ware Makers, Uruapan.

really feels at home is the one which offers him the benefits of civilisation.

The Tarascos of Uruapan long ago became Mexicanised; that is, they are now without land, spend all the money they earn by their labour in feasts for the saints, and have acquired quite a taste for the white man's brandy   The women, however, are still very industrious.   A nice, hard-working girl of thirty told me that among her compatriots there was no one whom she could marry, for she did not like drunken people. Among the Indians in the population there is much goitre, and accordingly many who are deaf and dumb or imbecile.

I did not lose much time in visiting the barrio—that is, "the ward of the Indians"—to make myself acquainted with the manufacture of the beautiful lacquer-ware for which Uruapan is famous. The work is done on table-tops, gourds, or principally on trays, the latter mostly round in shape, and in all sizes, from the delicate miniature pieces of barely an inch and a half to large waiters two feet in diameter or even bigger. The wooden shapes are bought from Indians of another place, whose habit it is, while engaged in the making of this ware, to camp at certain seasons in the woods of the peak of Tancitaro.

Gourd-bowl, Lacquer-ware, with Decorations Suggesting Ancient Designs. Uruapan. Height, 14 ctm.

The vessel to be lacquered is first covered with a coating of lithomarge (a clay). On this the men trace the designs, which are then cut out with a knife, and the women fill in the incisions with various colours, smoothing them over with their thumbs. Sometimes the same person both draws the design and executes it. Details are added by means of a finely pointed instrument. Then the varnish is put on, and the beautiful polish produced by patiently rubbing the surface with a bit of cotton. The lacquer thereby becomes so hard that it will even resist for a time the action of water. Gourds are lacquered only on the outside. The varnish is produced from a plant louse called in Spanish *aje*, which is gathered during the wet season by the Indians of Huetamo, six days' journey southeast of Uruapan. The name Huetamo is composed of huué=come and tamo=four. "Where four came together," in allusion possibly to four chiefs who united here to fight the Aztecs.

The designs nearly always represent flowers, which the artists draw from models before them. The work is

Manufacture of Lacquer-ware.   Uruapan.

admirable, but there is a monotony of ideas. No doubt it could be developed into an art if the painters were properly educated and had a wider scope. A French merchant of the place once supplied a man with a French flag, and I saw it reproduced on a table-top, the design being enhanced by a new flower motive evolved from directions given by the same gentleman. The best pintadora was eighty-seven years old. One finds also a good deal of rubbish in the market, manufactured mainly by Mexican women, whose product is inferior to that of the Indians.

A private gentleman in Uruapan had a few good antiquities which he permitted me to photograph. The sitting stone idol reproduced here is from this collection. It has a hole opened through its side, in which probably food was offered.

Being now almost at my journey's end, I began to sell off my mules. Some of them had been with me ever since I had started on my expeditions six years

Side View. Front View.

Tarasco Idol from Corupo.

before, among them El Chino, the big white mule that had so many narrow escapes in the Sierra and always landed right side up. I did not enjoy parting from these old friends, who had shared all my adventures and had many of their own besides.

As the road to Patzcuaro (a name meaning, according to Dr. N. Leon, "Temple Seat") had of late been infested with robbers, I for the first time in my experience in Mexico considered it best to get an escort, and started at the end of November in company with a sergeant and two cavalrymen. The road leads over much mal pais, which of course is of great advantage to the robbers, and to judge from the sixteen crosses I saw cut into the bark of one tree, *fusilados* (shot ones—that is, robbers who had been executed) must have been plentiful. In travelling along toward Tingambato ("Where it is warm") I noticed many very large custard-apple trees, called in Mexico chiremoya.

Half-caste Tarascos.   Uruapan.

The lodging-house here was utterly uninhabitable for a civilised being, so I stretched myself out for the night in a sheltered place outside of the kitchen, expecting this to be my last uncomfortable night in Mexico.

From here to Patzcuaro the road was patrolled by rurales, on account of a robbery that had been committed the week before. At dusk we arrived at Patzcuaro, at an elevation of 7,000 feet, which had been described to me as a dull place, "where there are plenty of masses and the people sleep late in the morning." The town is old and quaint, and has eleven churches and a great many priests—more than I had seen in any other place of similar size. The eight thousand inhabitants came originally, for the most part, from Biscaya, and are nice and obliging. From the neighbourhood one gets a fine view over the lake with its dirty, greyish-green water, in which thrives the

The Lake of Patzcuaro, from the South.

famous salamander, the axolotl, frequently offered for sale in the plaza of the town. It is eaten, and from its skin an extract is made which is used as a remedy for asthma.

The shores and islands of the lake are thickly populated with Tarasco Indians. There are more than twenty towns and villages on its banks. An interesting pre-Columbian instrument is still in use among the natives here, namely, a throwing-stick, with which they hurl their long reed spears at aquatic birds. The spear nowadays is provided with a triple-pointed iron tip, and the throwing-stick, tsipahki, has two holes for the fingers, and a groove in which the spear shaft lies.

At certain fixed seasons of the year, and especially prior to the feast of the tutelary saint, it is customary to arrange a chase of all kinds of fowl, principally ducks, geese, widgeons, and sandpipers. The sport is original and picturesque, and Dr. N. Leon, who himself has witnessed such a hunting expedition, described it to me as follows:

A fleet of from eighty to a hundred small canoes meet, each of the dug-outs manned by three or four individuals, two of whom propel and steer the little craft while the others are left free for the chase. They start from the shore in orderly array, proceeding toward a pre-arranged locality known to harbour an abundance of water-birds. On the approach to this spot they form in a half-moon, and the game is concentrated in a place which is clear and at the same time not very distant from the shore. Then each hunter gets on his feet, holding in his right hand the throwing-stick and the long spear. He bends his body slightly backward, lifts his right arm high up, and hurls his light and sharp-pointed weapon into the multitude of birds. He is pretty sure to harpoon one or two of them. If a bird is hit the spear remains in a nearly vertical position, with an oscillating motion; but if it should have missed, the spear floats on the surface gently rocked by the move-

Tarasco Throw-ing-stick.

Tarasco Spear.

ment of the water. While the hunt is on the canoes maintain the semi-lunar formation, as anyone pushing ahead would run the risk of being wounded by flying spears; besides, only by remaining together can they keep the birds confined. Such hunting expeditions may last for several days and nights, and altogether a considerable number of birds is bagged. As each spear bears the mark of its owner, there are no disputes about the game. Before pulling the spear out of the body they kill the bird and throw it into the bottom of the canoe. The rich meat of these birds forms an indispensable part of the savoury tama-

The Yacata Cleared on One Side.
Tzintzuntzan.

les served at the public banquet with which the feast of the patron saint is celebrated.

I visited the ancient capital of the Tarascos, Tzin-tzuntzan, which the Aztecs called Huitzizilan, either name meaning "Where there are humming-birds." The town lies near the lake and can easily be reached on horse-back. It is now insignificant, but according to Beau-

mont it was once six miles long. The inhabitants are
civilised and speak Spanish only. An attraction which
occasionally brings tourists to the place
is a large oil painting, supposed to be
a Titian, representing the descent from
the cross. The Indians zealously guard
it, and it is said that neither the desire
of the Church nor an offer of twenty-
five thousand dollars from an American has induced them to part with it.

The most notable archæological
feature here is a row of five yacatas
running from east to west on top of a
low ridge close to the town. The
space occupied by these huge mounds
measures altogether 466 paces in length
and 95 in width. The fourth mound
from the east is the largest, and here
the débris has been cleared away sufficiently to show that in
construction as well as in
shape it is exactly like

Human Lion, with
Coyote's Head, of
Volcanic Rock.
Patzcuaro. Height,
41.3 ctm.

Figure of Volcanic Rock.   Jhuatzio.
Height, 27.5 ctm.

the large mound of Parangaricutiro. The
stem of the "T" is
eleven paces across.

In Patzcuaro I
bought from a padre
a mirror of ob-
sidian, velvety
black with veins
of pale green,
probably the lar-
gest in existence.

He had found it in the curato of the village of Ci-
rahuen. Later I secured two statues of hard volcanic

rock, both unmistakably representing the same figure which Dr. Le Plonchon found in Yucatan and called Chac-mool. One of these was brought to light in the village of Ihuátzio.

For the sake of comparison I also give an illustration of an animal figure made of the same material, which was discovered in the pueblo of San Andres, south of Guadalajara, State of Jalisco, during the digging of a well. With it was unearthed a stone axe. The animal has its head turned to one side in the same way as the Chac-mool, and may have been intended to represent the original animal god (a coyote?) which appears in the statues.

Figure of Volcanic Rock. San Andres, near Guadalajara.
Height, 42.5 ctm.

CHAPTER XXVII

THE railway which connects Patzcuaro with the City of Mexico runs in its western half through fertile open country which once belonged to the Tarascos. Near Morelia remnants of the Pirinda tribe may yet be found, but they no longer speak their native language and are wholly Mexicanised. The country along the route is by no means level or monotonous; near Toluca,

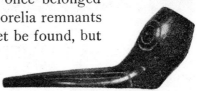

Black, Polished Clay Pipe, in the Shape of a Conventionalised Duck's Head. Valley of Mexico.

fifty miles this side of Mexico City, the grade rising to some 8,500 feet.

There had been great changes in Mexico City since I was here three years ago. The principal streets now were lighted by electricity and looked straight and clean. The people moved about busily, as in the great capitals of Europe, and law and order prevailed everywhere. Happily the picturesqueness of the city has not been effaced, and everywhere one is reminded that this is a historical place full of archæological and even ethnological interest. Otomi women bring in live ducks from the lakes in the same way as of old, or a young Indian drives a large flock of turkeys through the Ala-

453

meda with a whip, or water-carriers go about peddling their ware. The flower market near the great cathedral continues another custom of ancient times. In the garden of my hotel the trees were green in December, and the birds were singing.

In the wards of the poor and in the suburbs pure-

The Extinct Volcanos Popocatepetl (Smoking Mountain) and Iztaccihuatl (White Woman) Seen from the Southeast.

bred Atzecs are yet numerous, leading a hand-to-mouth existence as best they can. Some of them are skilful makers of idols and gain a living by an industry for which their ancestors were killed. Others are enterprising enough to make trips into remote Aztec villages

Engraved Breast Ornament of Shell. Valley of Mexico. Length, 12 ctm.

to buy up genuine relics accidentally found in the fields. Such curios sell well in the capital, but the profits are not easily earned. One dealer told me how hard his work was. The naturales are very distrustful of all strangers, even of those belonging to their own tribe.

In order to do business with them he had to take along someone who possessed their friendship and confidence or they were unapproachable. Before entering a house he had to defy two or three big dogs; and when, all outer obstacles overcome, he at last broached the subject of muñecas (puppets), another name for antiquities, the people would exclaim : "Ave Maria Purissima ! You must be Antichrist !" Yet by-and-by he might succeed in persuading them to sell what they had of that sort.

The wife of this dealer was also a pure-bred Aztec. She had four children, one in arms, the others running about on the street. The oldest boy, aged ten, was in business for himself, trying to foist fraudulent idols on unsuspecting foreigners, to whom he told the wildest stories about his wares. He was altogether a terrible little liar, and doubtless will some day land in Belem (the prison of Mexico), though the prospect seemed to have no terror for him. His mother one day astonished me with the statement that she had ten children more in heaven. Two had died of pneumonia, the others of whooping-cough or of intermittent fever. Most of these diseases come among the Indians with the other blessings of civilisation. In the villages the naturales drink great quantities of pulque and brandy on Sundays and are prone to fighting a good deal with knives.

Copper Awl, with Handle of a Turkey's T i b i a. Valley of Mexico. Length, 18.9 ctm.

The Aztecs, though of only medium height, are strong and full of endurance. An American acquaintance in Mexico told me that he had seen an Aztec cargador carry on his back a barrel of claret weighing four hundred pounds. In a sense the Aztecs were the Romans of the New World. Theirs was the great language that was revered by many tribes. If you ask one of their descendants in his own tongue for anything you want to buy he may make you a present of it.

A German-Mexican gentleman, whose sporting proclivities take him far out into the country, on one occasion dislocated his arm, upon which an Aztec friend of his set the injured limb with gentle manipulations without causing him much pain. Aztec surgical skill he considers so great that if another accident of this kind should happen to him, he says, he would rather go to his dusky friends for treatment than to a white doctor. Some Aztec families have excellent remedies, the prescriptions for which are handed down as heirlooms from father to son, and the secret is never revealed to outsiders.

Spinning Whorl of Clay, with Incised Design of a Monkey. Valley of Mexico. Actual size.

The same gentleman is authority for the statement that these Indians kill their wives for infidelity, a crime they never condone. He spoke of eight cases of this kind known to him. There is not much filial affection, but parents are fond of their children, and it is hard to take one away from them. The mothers pet and indulge their youngsters as all Indians do, and the trait has impressed itself on Mexican mothers of to-day even to the detriment of a boy's career.

Much may yet be learned in regard to the ancient

habits and customs of the tribes in the more remote villages, where the people still speak their own language,
as, for instance, on the slopes of Iztaccihuatl ("White
Woman"), the extinct volcano. Father Hunt Cortes,
who has spent many years among these Indians, informed
me that they still sacrifice children to the rain-god
Tlaloc, throwing them into the lagoon of Texcoco, and
that the same custom is observed in Xochimilco ("Flow-
er-beds") and Chalco. The children are usually only two
or three years old, but even older ones, up to ten years of
age, may be drowned in this way. Some of the children
so sacrificed are of poor, others of well-to-do parentage.

In the afternoon of December 13th I had an audience with President Porfirio Diaz, my third meeting with
him. His hair and moustache had turned grey since I
saw him last, but he still looked as vigorous as a man in
the fifties. I told him of what important service I had
found the letter which he had been kind enough to give
me, and how even where the Indians could not read they
had convinced themselves of its genuineness and of my
safe character by feeling the paper and looking at the
seal. Of course they had never fully grasped the object
of my visit, but the purpose of the document had been
attained by the word *importante*, which occurred in one
of the sentences; it always attracted their attention and
paved the way for me to their confidence.

When I mentioned that the President's name was
known among the remote tribes I had explored, he
smiled and said : "The Indians are good people, if one
explains matters to them, but they have been so cheated
and imposed upon that they have become distrustful.
During the French intervention nearly all the soldiers of
the Liberal Party were Indians, and they have been of
the greatest service in saving the country."

I did not forget the message with which the Coras

and the Huichols had charged me—namely, that Don Porfirio should issue an order that their land should never be given to the whites. To my surprise he asked:

Schlactman Hermanos.
President Porfirio Diaz. From a photograph taken in 1901.

"Are there any among them who can write?" I told him that there were and offered to give him names. "Then I will write to them," he said. I hope that letter reached the Indians. The President himself could hardly realise of what service it would be to them. They would treasure it as a powerful talisman against the "neighbours" for ages to come.

General Diaz has a strain of Mixtec blood in his veins, a fact suggested in his physique and physiognomy, which shows also great force of character, strong will-power, and at the same time benevolence and kindness of heart. In bearing he is dignified, and in manner courteous and urbane, and his great personal magnetism fascinates everybody with whom he comes in contact. He knows his country and its needs better than any other Mexican living, and for nearly a quarter of a century he has governed it judiciously and with rare sagacity. How he has reconstructed the republic, built up a state, and developed a nation is a matter of history. General Diaz is not only a great man on this continent, but one of the great men of our time.

Ancient Terra-cotta Figure.

Guadalajara, the capital of the State of Jalisco, and the second largest city of the Republic, is easily reached by rail. Pleasingly situated in a pretty valley, at an elevation of nearly 5,000 feet, its climate is much warmer than that of the federal capital. The city is nice and clean and its inhabitants contented and pleasant to deal with ; and, as good hotels are to be found here, this is one of the most desirable places to visit in Mexico. It is famous for its pottery, which though largely based on the ancient ceramic art, is now losing its national character. I reproduce here a figure, found near Guadalajara, representing a woman *enceinte*.

Jalisco is rich in ancient remains. Burial-places are constantly discovered, though the material unearthed falls, at least to a great extent, into the hands of shrewd dealers, who sell it to tourists and thus scatter it over the earth. In 1898 I secured here an exceedingly interesting collection of ceramics which some working-men had unearthed on the hacienda Estan-

Ancient Jar from Estanzuela.
Height, 12.2 ctm.

zuela, between Guadalajara and Ameca. They reported that they had come across a great many dead, some in a sitting position, others standing or lying down, and with them a number of jars. I secured a hundred and twelve pieces,

Ancient Jar from Estanzuela.
Height, 12.6 ctm.

thirty-five of them being decorated with encaustic painting and several in a very well preserved state. When I

PLATE XIII.

PLATE XIV.

heard of the find the best jar had already been taken away by a dealer, but luckily I got it back from him. It is represented on preceding page, while the decorative design extended is shown in Plate XIII. Two more jars of this find are shown on page 460 and this page, and their complete patterns in Plates XIV. and XV. Dr. Hrdlicka, my companion, curiously enough excavated about the same time or a little before, near Nostic, farther north in Jalisco, near Mezquitic, one plate of the same kind of pottery. In 1902 he succeeded in unearthing at the same place several pieces of the same ware.

As far as my knowledge goes, this was the first ware of this kind that had been met with in Mexico. The method of decoration was the same as that employed in making lacquer-ware among the present Tarasco Indians. The accessible surface of each piece

Ancient Jar from Estanzuela.
Height, 16.7 ctm.

was evidently first covered with a thick bluish-grey coating of a kind of clay, into which the patterns were cut, the incisions being filled with the different colours, and the piece then was fired. The designs represent mostly human figures, though there are some so-called geometric designs.

The ware is thick, moderately fine grain, and of a brick-red colour. The largest decorated jar is eight inches high. Those that are not decorated are smaller, from two to four inches high, and are largely cup-shaped.

Several of the decorated pieces show distinct evidence of having been made in two sections of about equal size, horizontally, and these were afterward fastened together. While the greater number are symmetrical in outline, many of the decorated pieces seem to have lost some of their gracefulness in the process of manufacture.

In the Aztec village of San Pedro, easily reached from Guadalajara by tramway, lives Timoteo Panduro, a pure-bred Aztec sculptor, self-taught, but of no mean

Ceremonial Hatchet, Used at Sacred Rites. Neighbourhood of Chapala. Length, 9 ctm.

Ceremonial Hatchet, Used at Sacred Rites. Neighbourhood of Chapala. Length, 10.6 ctm.

ability. Tourists to Guadalajara invite him to come to their hotels, and during a few hours' sitting he then and there models their busts in clay. His charge of sixteen dollars, Mexican money, is out of proportion to the merit of his work.

I made also an excursion to the beautiful lake of Chapala, the largest sheet of fresh water in Mexico, fifty miles long and from fifteen to eighteen broad. Its name is Nahuatl, which should really be Chapalal, in onomatopoetic imitation of the sound of the waves playing on the beach. The stage runs to a small village of the same name, lying on the shore, where some pretty country houses have been built.

In this lake, especially at its western end, are found great quantities of ancient, roughly made, diminutive jars, and a number of other objects. Near the village of Axixic (Nahuatl, "Where water [atl] pours forth) the people make a business of diving for them, threading them on strings, and selling them to visitors to the village of Chapala. I gathered several hundreds of them, and the supply seemed inexhaustible. No one knows when or why they were thrown into the lake. Most likely they were votive offerings to the deity of this water, to secure luck and health and other material benefits.

In Guadalajara I had a call one day from Angel's father and mother, both pure-bred Indians. The old lady had been worried about her son, from whom she had not heard for a long time, and being intelligent and able to read and write, she had poured out her heart in a letter to me, which she addressed in the following laconic way :

Don Carlos
Noruega (Norway).

Even modern postal facilities had not been equal to the task she had set them.

Well, she got him back! Here I finally parted with my faithful and devoted valet, who returned to his home doubtless a wiser if not a better creature for his

Angel.

year's outing. As a specimen of a civilised Indian who had never known his native language he was an object

of interest.   He was absolutely honest and reliable, and
though I had many a time sent him out on trips of several days' duration to collect relics on the ranches he
had never misappropriated a cent.   He looked after my
interests and property as if they were his own.   What he
did not know he was quick to learn, and if only he had

Church at Santa Cruz de las Flores, One of the Oldest Buildings in Jalisco.

been able to read and write he could have filled important business positions.   I did my best to induce him
to master the "three R's," and I got him to promise
that he would make an attempt; but I am afraid that
the tricks from which he had run away as a puppy
could never be taught to the old dog.   " Solomon left
his books over there in your country," he said, " and

that is why you know more than we, not because you can read and write."

Angel was a sincere Catholic, but had a vein of frivolity in his make-up and was not over-zealous in attending mass. One woman reproached him for this, saying that "good Christians do not miss mass, least of all during Lent," to which he dryly replied : " Why do you want so many Christians, anyway ? " One day he remarked to me : "I have been thinking of asking you what religion the people have in the land you come from ? Do they believe in God on the other side of the great water ? I have noticed that you spend much money when we stop in places ; you buy many things and you do not sell anything, nor do you make use of the articles. That's what is bad."

Portal in Church of Santa Cruz de las Flores.

In spite of the keenness of his mind he adhered to many superstitions, and being illiterate retained his queer notions about the things of this world. Of railways, for instance, he had a poor opinion. The matter-of-fact and unceremonious way in which they are run and managed shocked his sense of reverence. The trains, to the Indians, are manifestations of the devil, and in former times had to stop, they believed, when a padre stepped on board. It is only recently that it has become at all safe to travel by trains, since the people have succeeded in conjuring them.

"Mexico," he opined, "is now giving away altogether, since the railways came and the foreigners began to do as they pleased. The railway has done a good deal of

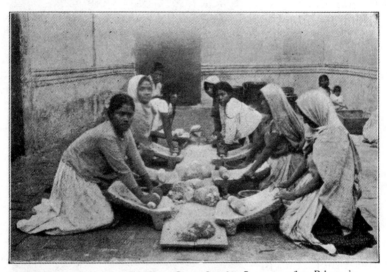

Women Criminals Grinding Corn for the Inmates of a Prison in Queretaro.

harm, because now there is no work for the poor people, with pack animals." "But look at all the money they are making in working for the railway," I suggested. "Well," he replied, "that money does not do them any good. On Saturdays they spend it all, and they even have to borrow sometimes to live through the week. I think," he continued, "that even the money I earn now from you is bad for me and my family, because I do not see how you make it. Who knows what you are going to do afterward? Some day I suppose you

will with the help of all that you carry off take possession of the villages and of large tracts of our country.
You have made notes of everything, if you please."

Before I revisited the Sierra Madre in 1898, I wrote
to Angel from New York, asking him to meet me on a
certain day in Colotlan, State of Jalisco, nearly a week's
journey on foot from
his home. When I
arrived at the place
he had already been
waiting for me two
days. Yet he told me
that on the day on
which my letter
reached him he was
just about to get mar-
ried. His people had
killed an ox, and had
prepared a big feast;
but he left every-
thing, including his
bride, to meet me.
"Are you not afraid
of losing her?" I
asked. "As if there
were no other girls!"
he replied. As a

Mexican Family on the Road.

matter of fact, he had been wavering between two
charmers, and now he had made up his mind that he
would on his return home take the one who had been
the more concerned about his absence.

About two days' railroad journey brings one from
Guadalajara to El Paso, Texas. After three years'
absence from the United States, the Americans at the
border-land impressed me as just the opposite of what

the Mexican calls *simpatico*. Everybody seemed so
stern, so "strictly business," as if there were no room
for the enjoyment of life. Even eating seemed a routine to be gone through with on schedule time. At the
hotel, clumsy waiters brought one ice-water, raw beef,
hot bread, and pork and beans. While laying the cover
they obligingly polished the apparently clean table implements with the inevitable dish-towel, with which also
they occasionally wiped their faces or curled their moustaches. Involuntarily I thought of the delightful hotel
at Guadalajara, with its well-prepared dinner served on
an airy, roomy piazza surrounded by a fresh and fra-
grant garden. All these comforts were mine for the
modest sum of two dollars a day, Mexican money. On
this side of the Rio Grande everything, from the small
bottle of beer to the berth in the Pullman car, cost
twice as much as on the other side.

I was glad to be back among the many warm friends,
however, whom it has been my good fortune to make in
the great republic. I am even more fond of civilised
than of primitive man, yet much as I depend upon the
comforts and pleasures of life they cannot altogether
efface the impressions I stored up during my wanderings
in unknown Mexico. The delight of being in close
touch with nature can be appreciated by those only who
have enjoyed keenly this relation. They will understand
the fascination of that region not yet reached by man's
aggressive spirit. I suffered a good deal in Mexico; malaria has a peculiar power of making one feel the misery
of life; but the pleasant memories by far outrank the
disagreeable. More often I recall some beautiful morning down there when everything seemed peaceful and
harmonious in the bright sunshine after the rainy night,
with the birds singing and nothing to disturb one, than
the inevitable hardships. As for the dusky friends I left

behind me in their rugged mountains and sunny valleys, I had never felt lonely among them. So much is constantly happening in that little world of theirs that one could not help feeling interested and stimulated to observe and study them. Sharing their joys and sorrows, entering into their thoughts and learning to understand their lore and symbolism, I felt myself carried back thousands of years into the early stages of human history. Primitive people as they are they taught me a new philosophy of life, for their ignorance is nearer to truth than our prejudice.

CONCLUSION

A T the beginning of my expeditions, when I still employed Americans as well as Mexicans as muleteers, I had constantly to shield the latter against the arrogance of the former. Later, among the Indians, I often saw the Mexicans treat the natives as they had themselves been treated by the Americans and again had to interfere for the oppressed. Finally, one day in the barranca, my Tarahumare carriers were quite offended when I gave my dog the heart, lungs, liver, etc., of a sheep we had killed. " Is the dog better than we that he should have all this ? " they pouted : the dog would have starved for all the Indians would give him. Thus I had, in turn, to protect the dog from the Indians, the Indians from the Mexicans, the Mexicans from the Americans.

As a well-bred dog or horse may show finer and no-bler qualities than many a man, so it seems to me, after my long experience with the Mexican Indians, that in their natural state they are in certain points superior, not only to the average Mexican half-caste, but to the com-mon run of whites. We are brought up to look upon primitive people as synonyms of all that is crude, evil, and vicious. Nothing could be more erroneous. I could cite a heathen tribe in India who consider a lie the blackest dishonour, and a tribe on the islands of Ber-ing Sea who when discovered by Russian missionaries were leading a life so nearly in accord with the Gospel of Christ that the teachers confessed they had better let them alone. No more is needed, however, than a comparison of the natives of Mexico as they were of old with the same people as they appear now in the light of modern civilisation.

The Aztecs, who were only one of several tribes in Mexico who had attained a degree of civilisation, were at the time of the conquest, to use Mr. Bandelier's expression, not subject to a despotic power, but organised after a barbarous, but free, military democracy. Their administration was admirable. Conquest was never followed by partition of land. Laws were obeyed and rulers respected, which is a great deal more than can be said of the Europe of that time. The erudite Spanish missionary, the monk Diego Duran, sixty years after the conquest, wrote a book on Mexico which is of interest on this head. Referring to the false opinion the Spaniards entertained in regard to the savage and uncivilised state of the Indian race, this otherwise fanatical missionary says : " There was never a nation in the wc ld where harmony, order, and politeness reigned so supreme as in this infidel nation. In what country of the world were there ever so many laws and regulations of the state at once so just and so well appointed ? Where have kings ever been so feared and obeyed, their laws and orders so well observed as in this land ? . . . In regard indeed to their laws and ancient mode of living all is much changed or wholly lost. Nothing but a shadow remains now of that good order. . . . Our admiration is compelled by the strict account and census which they kept of all persons in town or country, who were by this means to be called upon for help in anything they might be ordered to do. They had their presidents and chiefs and lesser authorities to look after the old, or the married, or the young about to be married. with such system and order that not even the newly born escaped their notice. So thorough was their superintendence of public works, that the man who laboured one week was not allowed to present himself for toil the next, everybody taking his turn with much harmony and order to the end that nobody might feel aggrieved."

In all kinds of handicraft, for instance, in carving on stone, wood, and so forth, the ancient people of Mexico have no equal to-day for accuracy of execution and beauty of outline. The ancient gold-workers of the Zapotec-Mixtecs are considered by so excellent an authority as Dr. N. Leon inimitable in their filigree work. The Aztec calendar system, which is about as old as the Christian, according to Mrs. Z. Nuttall, who has specially studied it, was based on accurate observations of the sun, the moon, and Venus, and still excites the admiration of the scientific world. It was simpler than that of the Europeans at the time, but if anything more nearly correct. A blot on their civilisation was the sacrifice of human beings; but it must be remembered that this was a religious compliance, the accounts of which, moreover, have been exaggerated. The sufferings of the victims, first made unconscious by drugs, were incomparably less inhuman than the fires and the tortures which the Inquisition applied to human beings at the altar of a God of peace and mercy. The instinct for human sacrifices was once innate in all races and nations; even the highest, the Jews, the Greeks, the Romans, the Teutons, and the Aztecs, were no exceptions. Only as mankind develops does it become capable of comprehending the nobler views of religion.

It is a very common mistake to look upon a barbarian as a third-rate white man. The Indian's physique is better developed and his senses are better trained than the white man's : his intellect and clearnness of thought average higher than the common people's of Europe and America. I cannot but recall the reply a North American Indian once made on an occasion connected, as so many occasions are, with a scheme of the whites to drive the tribe from its native heath. The representative white man tried to cajole the Indians with their own style of rhetoric : " My brothers," he said, " the Great Father [the President of the United States] has heard how you have been wronged, and he said : ' I will send my red children an honest man to talk to them ; ' and he looked to the north, to the east, to the south, and to the west, and he said, ' Here is an honest man ; ' and he sent me. So, my brothers, look at me : The winds of fifty-five years have blown over my head and silvered it over with grey, and during that time I have never done any wrong to any man. I am your friend, my red brothers, and as your friend I ask you to sign this treaty." When he had finished one of the chiefs rose and said : " My friend, look at me. The winds of more than fifty winters have blown over my head and silvered it over with grey ; but they have not blown my brains away." Then he sat down, and the council was ended.

The mental gifts of many Indians would entitle them to fill responsible positions ; but unfortunately they prefer to remain among themselves, and to live in accordance with their own customs and in their own ways. Primitive man is as modest in his ambition as he is in his demands upon nature ; he asks for no more than he needs, hence the smallness of his field. But as civilisation depends so largely upon the accumulation of property, his very abstemiousness becomes an obstacle to his progress.

The innate artistic sense of the natives of Mexico shows itself in the beautiful, ever-varying patterns of their textile and other decorated work, evolved from the simple motives of their daily life. Though they do not cultivate flowers merely for the sake of their beauty, they never fail to pay attention to their colours, and, beyond comparison, both men and women know the flora of their country better than even the cultivated classes among ourselves. They have much sharper and quicker eyes to distinguish the slightest variation in the forms of the leaves, etc., especially in plants of economic value.

Among Mexican natives monogamy is the recognised foundation of the family, and the social standing of the woman is that of a junior partner. Each sex has its own sphere. In their behaviour toward one another these Indians never become beastly, as low-class whites will; what we call their vices are due not to depravity, but to their religious practices. Personal modesty is innate in the race.

Justice with them is inexorable. Mitigating circumstances are never considered, and every misdeed has to be expiated according to the law of an eye for an eye and a tooth for a tooth. Before he becomes civilised the Mexican Indian is never servile. In his behaviour toward his tribesmen, as well as toward strangers, he is ceremonious and strictly observes the laws of etiquette. Though dressed in rags, he is a born gentleman, and as polite and considerate of other persons' feelings as anyone adorned in purple and fine linen. A well-known English archæologist, who in recent years has travelled extensively in Mexico, tells me: "I find that I have to behave toward the natives as circumspectly as if I were among well-bred people in Europe."

Many foreigners look down upon the Mexican natives because they eat with their fingers. I fail to see why this, *per se*, should be a sign of barbarity, especially when it is done so daintily and gracefully as it is by the small hands of the Indians. It is unnecessary to remind the reader that even in Europe forks are a comparatively recent innovation. In England Queen Elizabeth was the first person to own them, and later an English divine in one of his sermons denounced their use as an insult to the Providence that had given us fingers to eat with.

Immortality of the soul is universally recognised by Indians. In their religious fervour the aborigines of Mexico have no equals, certainly not among Christians. Their entire life is one continuous worship of their gods that they may gain happiness. Every act in their lives, every work undertaken is guided by religious thoughts. All that we should call ornament on their clothing and implements owes its very existence to the prayerful thoughts it expresses. Of all that man has the gods get their share ; no crop is so scanty but that some of it is ungrudgingly sacrificed to the deity who gave it. When I saw them perform their religious dances indefatigably for days and nights, and when I heard them in their humble temples invoke divine help with tears, I felt in my heart that their pitiful appeals would be as readily answered as the most eloquent oration of the high priest at the most elaborate altar Christianity ever raised to the greater glory of God. In drifting into the new condition of life the native may lose his worldly possessions, but he still retains the wealth of his religiosity, and is as eager to comply with the new code as he was with the worship of his ancestral idols. " The Indians have too much religion," a padre once said to me ; "and they want more than is good for them."

When the chief of the Zuñis, whom Mr. Cushing had taken to Boston, was asked what had impressed him and his companions mostly in the great city of the whites, he replied : "That the people are not religious! Great crowds are constantly hurrying hither and thither, but no one is praying. I had thought that they would be very religious, because they send missionaries to us; but I find they are not."

Another story of these Zuñi visitors is characteristic of Indian thought and philosophy of life. While receiving them at her country seat, noble Mrs. Hemenway, who did so much for the scientific investigation of the aboriginal American, requested a minister to explain his religion to her visitors without interfering in any way with their religion. In order to make an impression upon his strange congregation, the good divine took pains to beautify the room with draperies and flowers, placing the Bible in the centre and surrounding it with candelabra in which candles were burning. Then he preached a sermon in which he referred to the ancestors of the Americans as having lived in darkness, as having been bad men and robbers, whereas the present people were Christians and very good and happy. The Indians listened attentively, making now and then comments to each other; and when the clergyman had finished, one of them rose and took up his discourse thus: " Father, those ancestors of yours were *men!* It is through them that you have railways and banks, and all the other good things. Everything, even men and gods, came from the darkness, even as the grain of corn begins its growth in darkness. While in the dark the grain grows crooked, but in the sunlight the plant rises erect. Man in the dark stumbles hither and thither; but in the daylight he walks straight forward. Besides, Father, you cannot look over a hill until you have climbed it!"

To be sure, all Mexican Indians are distrustful. They say: "We can see a man's face, but we cannot see his heart!" It is an open question, however, whether this feeling was as pronounced before their acquaintance with the whites. Among travellers it is well known that primitive races are not dangerous to approach until they have been cheated by strangers.

On the other hand, great friend of the Indians as I am, I have to own that even in their native state they have two great faults. They do not tell the truth unless it suits them, and they do steal, though they never stole from me. Still, with the Tarahumares cheating at bargains is unknown until the Mexicans teach them that lesson.

The fact is, primitive people are so different from us in their reasoning and behaviour that it is impossible for us to understand them until long-continued contact makes them familiar. It has therefore become a habit to look upon them as low, deceptive, and unintelligent. But it is not among primitive races that we have to search for the lowest types of humanity. The most depraved and degenerate individuals are found in the slums of the great cities. People who live in close touch with nature are in fact not capable of being as perverted as civilised criminals are in mind and body. The work of missionaries is often needed much more among the conquering soldiers, and the prospectors, "carpet-baggers," brandy traders, and adventurers that follow in their wake, than among the unsophisticated barbarians. Doubtless there are no natives on the earth so wicked as those who profess Christianity, says James Russell Lowell.

Mexican Indians readily accept the white man's teachings. In their opinion, the more religion the better, for then they think themselves the more sure of getting what they ask for, food and health. But as long as they keep their lands their ancient religious ideas cannot be eradicated, and God, Christ, and the Virgin Mary are only so many new gods whom they gladly receive among their old ones. Their lands once lost, the old religion is soon forgotten and with it their language, their traditions, their moral standard, their self-respect, their content in life—everything that makes the true Indian what he is. Most of them became labourers, working for the usurpers, and form the poor class, as may be seen in the suburbs of the City of Mexico, where the once proud Aztecs are now the proletarians.

I cannot help thinking, however, that as long as Mexico was to be made subject to European powers it was well for her to fall among members of a Latin race rather than those of Germanic or Teutonic descent. For the Spanish character and temperament resemble in a degree those of the Indians. The Spaniards are more "easy-going," and better accustomed to the warmer climate and the habits of life it creates. True, in their bigotry and greed for gold they destroyed the ancient civilisations; but, cruel and inhuman as they were, they were little worse than other conquerors even in recent times. War is hell now as it was four hundred years ago. Modern civilisation is even more intolerant in contact with people of lower culture than were the Spanish conquerors of Mexico and Peru, and now as then the civilisers are as eager to take charge of the poor pagans' property as to save their souls. Under modern conditions the sanctity of commerce covers almost any kind of crime.

On the other hand, the Spanish, after subduing a people, did not crush out their virility. Laws were enacted for their protection. The Catholic religion was easily comprehended by the natives, and there was no great difficulty in introducing at least its exterior forms. Nor should it be overlooked that their missionaries always tried to improve also the material condition of their charges, by giving them cattle, sheep, a new kind of clothing, fruit-trees, etc., though their well-meant efforts proved in the course of centuries only of relative advantage to the Indians.

Furthermore, the Spaniards did not shrink from mixing with the conquered, and in the course of time innumerable grades of crossings created a new type. The Mexican of to-day is very different from his Spanish cousin, even more so than American and British. He has little prejudices against " colour," and if the darker types desire to be looked upon as " whites " it is because it flatters them to be considered members of the dominant class, not because they are despised on account of their darker complexion. Even pure-bred Indians have risen to prominence in Mexico as governors, generals, and clergymen. Honest, lion-hearted Benito Juarez, who guided the republic through its most severe crisis, was a pure-bred Zapotec Indian. Among the authors of aboriginal blood I will only mention that charming littéra-teur and critic, Don Manuel Altamirano.

The Indian's influence upon the Mexican nation and its destiny has been and always will be profound. Mexico undoubtedly benefits by the inoculation of aboriginal strength and thought. The Indian has impregnated the new-comers with his religious fervour and has made them more devout Catholics than the Spaniards are, though he has also taught them many pagan superstitions, especially in regard to sorcery. Into the character of the people have been infused a certain honesty of mind and devotion to duty. The Indian mode of living and cooking is adhered to throughout the land, though the architecture of the dwellings, where not Indian, is Moro-Iberian. To the literature of Spanish America the native mind had brought its peculiar originality and its inclination toward the unsophisticated fact. The Spanish language of Mexico has been enriched by many words of Indian origin.

The Mexicans have become so imbued with the Indian spirit that they are proud to mention Montezuma and Guatemotzin as their ancestors, and to erect statues

Benito Juarez.

to them. As far as I know, the Mexicans are the only nation who celebrate every year a feast in memory of the great aboriginal heroes who vainly sacrificed their lives in defence of their country, notwithstanding that the conquerors are ancestors of the dominant race.

I believe the time will come when conquest by force will be judged barbarous, when the method will be as noble as the end. In fact there are symptoms of an awakening of public conscience to the fact that expansion by force is the wrong method of attaining the right thing. Until nations realise that " supremacy should mean service," the superior nation will never elevate the inferior.

The white, though recognised as the highest of all races, has not, as a rule, elevated the races it subdues, but it probably will in time. Hitherto we have often seen examples of what Mark Twain describes as " lifting them down " to our level. A missionary, secular or ecclesiastic, might do natives much good, if he had the power of sympathy with all men, with all conditions of men, and were at least on a level with the people whom he intends to convert.

The faculties of the races of men differ little. It is mainly energy and motive power that are wanting in the backward races. It is with races as with individuals ; both have to pass through a series of progressive stages, from savagery in infancy, to barbarism throughout youth, up to civilisation in manhood. As the child is the father of the man, so the characteristic qualities of even the highest civilised nations have developed from the virtues and vices of the primitive tribe from which they sprang. One is struck by the fact that the blacks of Central Australia, though considered the lowest human beings on the globe, are governed in their conduct by a moral code, crude though it be.

What we now call primitive people have not yet had time enough to reach their full status ; they are nations in their infancy, in a state that, for instance, the Aryans outgrew many thousands of years ago. Europe and America should therefore not overlook the fact that the backward races also need time to develop their state-craft, the germ of which is found wherever we go. We have no patience with the backward races and expect their civilisation to be a matter of a few months where we have consumed centuries.

Instead of seeing in primitive races the equals of our remotest ancestors, whom it should be our duty and privilege to assist in reaching a higher level, we seem to look upon them as existing only in order that we may sell them cotton cloth, glass beads, brandy, and fire-arms. Notwithstanding this, wherever conquest has not been followed too quickly by the extermination of the original inhabitants, the latter have exercised a strong influence upon the conquerors. The Chinese are said to have in this way reconquered their conquerors; the negroes in America, though transferred to another zone and entirely new conditions of life, have not been without an influence upon their masters. The ordinary American of to-day enjoys a coon song more than any other music, except, perhaps, his patriotic airs.

When we thus consider the reciprocal influence conquerors and conquered exert upon each other—furthermore, the ever-growing expansion of commerce into the farthest corners of the globe—and finally the rapid development of means of communication in a degree that we probably can but faintly realise, we are able to perceive how nations and tribes, whether they want to or not, will be stimulated to gradual progress, on lines and by methods that in the natural evolution of things become general. A certain difference in men will always remain, dependent on environment, but surely the general trend of human destiny is toward unity. Civilised mankind is already beginning to have a social and æsthetic solidarity. The calamity of Martinique, the fall of the Campanile in Venice, affects the whole world.

If the Louvre, with its priceless art treasures, should burn, cultivated people of every nation would feel the loss as if it were their own. Undoubtedly this feeling of unity will grow immensely as the centuries pass by. The backward races have much to learn from us, but we have also much to learn from them—not only new art designs, but certain moral qualities. Hypocrisy will be done away with as civilisation advances, and the world will be the better for it.

It is unnatural to be without a special love of the country of one's birth, just as a man has more affection for his family than for other families. But let our allegiance extend to the whole globe on which we travel through the universe, and let us try to serve mankind rather than our country right or wrong.

APPENDIX

A SHORT VOCABULARY FROM THE LANGUAGES OF THE MOST IMPORTANT TRIBES MENTIONED IN "UNKNOWN MEXICO"

The letter *x* is to be given the sound of the Greek χ.

ҁ is pronounced as *th* in *think ;* m̃ has a nasal sound, as in the French *nom.*

English.	Tara-humare.	Northern Tepehuane.	Southern Tepehuane.	Tubar.	Cora.	Huichol.	Tepecano.
man	rehói	cúli	tsháuid	oñvi	tádai	ukki	teáän
woman	múki	óki	uwí	tulí	idai	úkka	ov
boy	tówí	áli gúli or al gúli	alí tsháuid alí	huyír tádai	tádai páluiste	tamáico	arí (lit. little)
girl	tewǽke	áli túxi or ál túxi	alí uwí alí	huyir tulí	idai páluiste	tamáico	arí
infant, child	mútshu-li	áli tzú-ni	alitsh	—	unákai	nonótsi	alíspuc
head	mo-óla	moy	maoú	tafr	mō-ó	mōó	mo
ear	nacála	náxai	nánáca	nacár	nenashǽi	nacá	nác
nose	acabó	dáxai	indác	níkisor	neagulí	tsúli	dác
mouth	rinfla	túni	toní	tinír	netǽni	netáta	tún
tongue	shamáala	nhumú	inóyn	ninír	nenanó-li	není	nún
teeth	ramelá	títamo	tátam	tamár	natamǽ	tamné	tátam
arm	shicála	húkai	katoá	mavolír	namóca	neanoíme [my arm]	innóuv [my arm]
hand	macusuala	nóvi	inauwí	sutír	nashídde	neamamá [my hand]	—
body	—	tócoga	tucó	tamirán	tǽwiti	neyúliapa	
belly	ropála	vócai	inváuk	njolír	náhuga	tánxli	in wóc [my belly]
leg	ronóla	tucáso	incái	moír [leg above knee]	na-úc	kiatá	in tón [my leg]
foot	ronóla	tárai	innausác	njókír	netshapóli	omǽ	combrac
bone	ōtshlá	ohy	aa-o	hotarát	galíti	iyáli	ino-ó [my bone]
heart	shulála	hórai	hurá	aramalír	nasheinúgali	iyáli	inxúr [my heart]
chief	sillami	káj-gi	æscáig	—	tatówa	tatowán	osiácam
house	bititshíki	váki	wáac	{ nerkitá [my house] / catepán [in the house] }	tshi	ki	vaác
bow	atáca	gatóli	gáth	wicolít	tónamo	tōpí	gat
arrow	wáca	oi	o-ó	wacát	uurí	úlú	oó
knife	repiyaca	—	cosír	—	náwo-a	nawára (from Spanish)	nuicár
tobacco	wipáга	vírai	viváí	wihát	yãnã	yã	viv

English.	Tara-humare.	Northern Tepehuane.	Southern Tepehuane.	Tubar.	Cora.	Huichol.	Tepecano.
sun	rayénari	tásai	tanául	tasalít or táta	shigá	táu	tonól
moon	mutsháca	masádai	masán	matsát	mashgilai	metseli	másad
star	saspulí	siávogai	hovág	só-o	tshúlavæ	shulávi	húva
wind	icáca	hívuli	huwîl	honít	æca	æaká	hubúlli
rain	u-kí-ki	dúki	hecáum	horói	háituli	uviyeni	itshvicamduc
fire	nafki	tái	tai	tahamét	taixti or taix	tái	tái
water	bawíki	sódagi	súdai	batá	há or háti	há	sódi
earth, land	bewé-ke	duvúrai	duvúr	kvirát	tshuǽ	kwī	bid
river	vacótshi	akívi	akki	yaván	haíddana	shǽli	gu (large) sódi
mountain	awíki	kavóliki	auiddá	—	xúlí	—	oída
stone, rock	{ ritéke { ritshíki	{ hódai { vapávai	oddái	tetát	de-dǽ	teté	hódai
tree	ushíki	úsi	ūs	—	kú-ya	itáuli	ōs
maize	tatshúki	káibiadu	hōn	ko-ít	yúli	ikú	hōn
flesh, meat	{ tzapáca { bawǽke	bábaidi	vacáz	tikoñvat	wái-ilæ	waí	—
dog	ōcotshí	go-gósi	gagáus	tjutju	ɕik	ɕuk	gogós
grey fox	iyótshi	kashiókai	cashiáu	kahulóvi	alaitshúi	kaura	casió
deer	tshúmalí	svímali	soimál	suhát	moasjá	mára	—
serpent	sinói	koi	gaó	co-ót	kúgoite	oipo	cō
bird	tshuluwí	úrogi	wíg	koló	pínaez	wikí	tshovíte
blue	shiyónami	thudóixami	tjudáug	njo-acar	temoaní	yoáwime	istœdog
yellow	lánami	ōamáxami	isám	kisarakar	tídaome	mutárwi	ishám
light green	shiyónami	thudóixami	momdurmaga	njo-acar	tecó-adi	cílaye	istœdoɼ
cold	rítíco	cúvai	zupíd	—	kemáxela	pohánte	—
warm, hot	—	—	æzóc	—	búxtsha	tiúreka	—

INDEX

A CATALOG OF SELECTED

DOVER BOOKS

IN ALL FIELDS OF INTEREST

A CATALOG OF SELECTED DOVER
BOOKS IN ALL FIELDS OF INTEREST

DRAWINGS OF REMBRANDT, edited by Seymour Slive. Updated Lippmann, Hofstede de Groot edition, with definitive scholarly apparatus. All portraits, biblical sketches, landscapes, nudes. Oriental figures, classical studies, together with selection of work by followers. 550 illustrations. Total of 630pp. 9⅛ × 12¼.
21485-0, 21486-9 Pa., Two-vol. set $25.00

GHOST AND HORROR STORIES OF AMBROSE BIERCE, Ambrose Bierce. 24 tales vividly imagined, strangely prophetic, and decades ahead of their time in technical skill: "The Damned Thing," "An Inhabitant of Carcosa," "The Eyes of the Panther," "Moxon's Master," and 20 more. 199pp. 5⅜ × 8½. 20767-6 Pa. $3.95

ETHICAL WRITINGS OF MAIMONIDES, Maimonides. Most significant ethical works of great medieval sage, newly translated for utmost precision, readability. Laws Concerning Character Traits, Eight Chapters, more. 192pp. 5⅜ × 8½.
24522-5 Pa. $4.50

THE EXPLORATION OF THE COLORADO RIVER AND ITS CANYONS, J. W. Powell. Full text of Powell's 1,000-mile expedition down the fabled Colorado in 1869. Superb account of terrain, geology, vegetation, Indians, famine, mutiny, treacherous rapids, mighty canyons, during exploration of last unknown part of continental U.S. 400pp. 5⅜ × 8½. 20094-9 Pa. $6.95

HISTORY OF PHILOSOPHY, Julián Marías. Clearest one-volume history on the market. Every major philosopher and dozens of others, to Existentialism and later. 505pp. 5⅜ × 8½. 21739-6 Pa. $8.50

ALL ABOUT LIGHTNING, Martin A. Uman. Highly readable non-technical survey of nature and causes of lightning, thunderstorms, ball lightning, St. Elmo's Fire, much more. Illustrated. 192pp. 5⅜ × 8½. 25237-X Pa. $5.95

SAILING ALONE AROUND THE WORLD, Captain Joshua Slocum. First man to sail around the world, alone, in small boat. One of great feats of seamanship told in delightful manner. 67 illustrations. 294pp. 5⅜ × 8½. 20326-3 Pa. $4.50

LETTERS AND NOTES ON THE MANNERS, CUSTOMS AND CONDITIONS OF THE NORTH AMERICAN INDIANS, George Catlin. Classic account of life among Plains Indians: ceremonies, hunt, warfare, etc. 312 plates. 572pp. of text. 6⅛ × 9¼. 22118-0, 22119-9 Pa. Two-vol. set $15.90

ALASKA: The Harriman Expedition, 1899, John Burroughs, John Muir, et al. Informative, engrossing accounts of two-month, 9,000-mile expedition. Native peoples, wildlife, forests, geography, salmon industry, glaciers, more. Profusely illustrated. 240 black-and-white line drawings. 124 black-and-white photographs. 3 maps. Index. 576pp. 5⅜ × 8½. 25109-8 Pa. $11.95

THE BOOK OF BEASTS: Being a Translation from a Latin Bestiary of the Twelfth Century, T. H. White. Wonderful catalog real and fanciful beasts: manticore, griffin, phoenix, amphivius, jaculus, many more. White's witty erudite commentary on scientific, historical aspects. Fascinating glimpse of medieval mind. Illustrated. 296pp. 5⅜ × 8¼. (Available in U.S. only) 24609-4 Pa. $5.95

FRANK LLOYD WRIGHT: ARCHITECTURE AND NATURE With 160 Illustrations, Donald Hoffmann. Profusely illustrated study of influence of nature—especially prairie—on Wright's designs for Fallingwater, Robie House, Guggenheim Museum, other masterpieces. 96pp. 9¼ × 10¾. 25098-9 Pa. $7.95

FRANK LLOYD WRIGHT'S FALLINGWATER, Donald Hoffmann. Wright's famous waterfall house: planning and construction of organic idea. History of site, owners, Wright's personal involvement. Photographs of various stages of building. Preface by Edgar Kaufmann, Jr. 100 illustrations. 112pp. 9¼ × 10. 23671-4 Pa. $7.95

YEARS WITH FRANK LLOYD WRIGHT: Apprentice to Genius, Edgar Tafel. Insightful memoir by a former apprentice presents a revealing portrait of Wright the man, the inspired teacher, the greatest American architect. 372 black-and-white illustrations. Preface. Index. vi + 228pp. 8¼ × 11. 24801-1 Pa. $9.95

THE STORY OF KING ARTHUR AND HIS KNIGHTS, Howard Pyle. Enchanting version of King Arthur fable has delighted generations with imaginative narratives of exciting adventures and unforgettable illustrations by the author. 41 illustrations. xviii + 313pp. 6⅛ × 9¼. 21445-1 Pa. $5.95

THE GODS OF THE EGYPTIANS, E. A. Wallis Budge. Thorough coverage of numerous gods of ancient Egypt by foremost Egyptologist. Information on evolution of cults, rites and gods; the cult of Osiris; the Book of the Dead and its rites; the sacred animals and birds; Heaven and Hell; and more. 956pp. 6⅛ × 9¼. 22055-9, 22056-7 Pa., Two-vol. set $20.00

A THEOLOGICO-POLITICAL TREATISE, Benedict Spinoza. Also contains unfinished *Political Treatise*. Great classic on religious liberty, theory of government on common consent. R. Elwes translation. Total of 421pp. 5⅜ × 8½. 20249-6 Pa. $6.95

INCIDENTS OF TRAVEL IN CENTRAL AMERICA, CHIAPAS, AND YUCATAN, John L. Stephens. Almost single-handed discovery of Maya culture; exploration of ruined cities, monuments, temples; customs of Indians. 115 drawings. 892pp. 5⅜ × 8½. 22404-X, 22405-8 Pa., Two-vol. set $15.90

LOS CAPRICHOS, Francisco Goya. 80 plates of wild, grotesque monsters and caricatures. Prado manuscript included. 183pp. 6⅜ × 9⅝. 22384-1 Pa. $4.95

AUTOBIOGRAPHY: The Story of My Experiments with Truth, Mohandas K. Gandhi. Not hagiography, but Gandhi in his own words. Boyhood, legal studies, purification, the growth of the Satyagraha (nonviolent protest) movement. Critical, inspiring work of the man who freed India. 480pp. 5⅜ × 8½. (Available in U.S. only) 24593-4 Pa. $6.95

ILLUSTRATED DICTIONARY OF HISTORIC ARCHITECTURE, edited by Cyril M. Harris. Extraordinary compendium of clear, concise definitions for over 5,000 important architectural terms complemented by over 2,000 line drawings. Covers full spectrum of architecture from ancient ruins to 20th-century Modernism. Preface. 592pp. 7½ × 9⅝. 24444-X Pa. $14.95

THE NIGHT BEFORE CHRISTMAS, Clement Moore. Full text, and woodcuts from original 1848 book. Also critical, historical material. 19 illustrations. 40pp. 4⅝ × 6. 22797-9 Pa. $2.25

THE LESSON OF JAPANESE ARCHITECTURE: 165 Photographs, Jiro Harada. Memorable gallery of 165 photographs taken in the 1930's of exquisite Japanese homes of the well-to-do and historic buildings. 13 line diagrams. 192pp. 8⅝ × 11¼. 24778-3 Pa. $8.95

THE AUTOBIOGRAPHY OF CHARLES DARWIN AND SELECTED LETTERS, edited by Francis Darwin. The fascinating life of eccentric genius composed of an intimate memoir by Darwin (intended for his children); commentary by his son, Francis; hundreds of fragments from notebooks, journals, papers; and letters to and from Lyell, Hooker, Huxley, Wallace and Henslow. xi + 365pp. 5⅜ × 8. 20479-0 Pa. $5.95

WONDERS OF THE SKY: Observing Rainbows, Comets, Eclipses, the Stars and Other Phenomena, Fred Schaaf. Charming, easy-to-read poetic guide to all manner of celestial events visible to the naked eye. Mock suns, glories, Belt of Venus, more. Illustrated. 299pp. 5¼ × 8¼. 24402-4 Pa. $7.95

BURNHAM'S CELESTIAL HANDBOOK, Robert Burnham, Jr. Thorough guide to the stars beyond our solar system. Exhaustive treatment. Alphabetical by constellation: Andromeda to Cetus in Vol. 1; Chamaeleon to Orion in Vol. 2; and Pavo to Vulpecula in Vol. 3. Hundreds of illustrations. Index in Vol. 3. 2,000pp. 6⅛ × 9¼. 23567-X, 23568-8, 23673-0 Pa., Three-vol. set $36.85

STAR NAMES: Their Lore and Meaning, Richard Hinckley Allen. Fascinating history of names various cultures have given to constellations and literary and folkloristic uses that have been made of stars. Indexes to subjects. Arabic and Greek names. Biblical references. Bibliography. 563pp. 5⅜ × 8½. 21079-0 Pa. $7.95

THIRTY YEARS THAT SHOOK PHYSICS: The Story of Quantum Theory, George Gamow. Lucid, accessible introduction to influential theory of energy and matter. Careful explanations of Dirac's anti-particles, Bohr's model of the atom, much more. 12 plates. Numerous drawings. 240pp. 5⅜ × 8½. 24895-X Pa. $4.95

CHINESE DOMESTIC FURNITURE IN PHOTOGRAPHS AND MEASURED DRAWINGS, Gustav Ecke. A rare volume, now affordably priced for antique collectors, furniture buffs and art historians. Detailed review of styles ranging from early Shang to late Ming. Unabridged republication. 161 black-and-white drawings, photos. Total of 224pp. 8⅜ × 11¼. (Available in U.S. only) 25171-3 Pa. $12.95

VINCENT VAN GOGH: A Biography, Julius Meier-Graefe. Dynamic, penetrating study of artist's life, relationship with brother, Theo, painting techniques, travels, more. Readable, engrossing. 160pp. 5⅜ × 8½. (Available in U.S. only) 25253-1 Pa. $3.95

HOW TO WRITE, Gertrude Stein. Gertrude Stein claimed anyone could understand her unconventional writing—here are clues to help. Fascinating improvisations, language experiments, explanations illuminate Stein's craft and the art of writing. Total of 414pp. 4⅝ × 6⅜. 23144-5 Pa. $5.95

ADVENTURES AT SEA IN THE GREAT AGE OF SAIL: Five Firsthand Narratives, edited by Elliot Snow. Rare true accounts of exploration, whaling, shipwreck, fierce natives, trade, shipboard life, more. 33 illustrations. Introduction. 353pp. 5⅜ × 8½. 25177-2 Pa. $7.95

THE HERBAL OR GENERAL HISTORY OF PLANTS, John Gerard. Classic descriptions of about 2,850 plants—with over 2,700 illustrations—includes Latin and English names, physical descriptions, varieties, time and place of growth, more. 2,706 illustrations. xlv + 1,678pp. 8½ × 12¼. 23147-X Cloth. $75.00

DOROTHY AND THE WIZARD IN OZ, L. Frank Baum. Dorothy and the Wizard visit the center of the Earth, where people are vegetables, glass houses grow and Oz characters reappear. Classic sequel to *Wizard of Oz.* 256pp. 5⅜ × 8. 24714-7 Pa. $4.95

SONGS OF EXPERIENCE: Facsimile Reproduction with 26 Plates in Full Color, William Blake. This facsimile of Blake's original "Illuminated Book" reproduces 26 full-color plates from a rare 1826 edition. Includes "The Tyger," "London," "Holy Thursday," and other immortal poems. 26 color plates. Printed text of poems. 48pp. 5¼ × 7. 24636-1 Pa. $3.50

SONGS OF INNOCENCE, William Blake. The first and most popular of Blake's famous "Illuminated Books," in a facsimile edition reproducing all 31 brightly colored plates. Additional printed text of each poem. 64pp. 5¼ × 7. 22764-2 Pa. $3.50

PRECIOUS STONES, Max Bauer. Classic, thorough study of diamonds, rubies, emeralds, garnets, etc.: physical character, occurrence, properties, use, similar topics. 20 plates, 8 in color. 94 figures. 659pp. 6⅛ × 9¼. 21910-0, 21911-9 Pa., Two-vol. set $14.90

ENCYCLOPEDIA OF VICTORIAN NEEDLEWORK, S. F. A. Caulfeild and Blanche Saward. Full, precise descriptions of stitches, techniques for dozens of needlecrafts—most exhaustive reference of its kind. Over 800 figures. Total of 679pp. 8⅛ × 11. Two volumes. Vol. 1 22800-2 Pa. $10.95 Vol. 2 22801-0 Pa. $10.95

THE MARVELOUS LAND OF OZ, L. Frank Baum. Second Oz book, the Scarecrow and Tin Woodman are back with hero named Tip, Oz magic. 136 illustrations. 287pp. 5⅜ × 8½. 20692-0 Pa. $5.95

WILD FOWL DECOYS, Joel Barber. Basic book on the subject, by foremost authority and collector. Reveals history of decoy making and rigging, place in American culture, different kinds of decoys, how to make them, and how to use them. 140 plates. 156pp. 7⅞ × 10¾. 20011-6 Pa. $7.95

HISTORY OF LACE, Mrs. Bury Palliser. Definitive, profusely illustrated chronicle of lace from earliest times to late 19th century. Laces of Italy, Greece, England, France, Belgium, etc. Landmark of needlework scholarship. 266 illustrations. 672pp. 6⅛ × 9¼. 24742-2 Pa. $14.95

ILLUSTRATED GUIDE TO SHAKER FURNITURE, Robert Meader. All furniture and appurtenances, with much on unknown local styles. 235 photos. 146pp. 9 × 12. 22819-3 Pa. $7.95

WHALE SHIPS AND WHALING: A Pictorial Survey, George Francis Dow. Over 200 vintage engravings, drawings, photographs of barks, brigs, cutters, other vessels. Also harpoons, lances, whaling guns, many other artifacts. Comprehensive text by foremost authority. 207 black-and-white illustrations. 288pp. 6 × 9.
24808-9 Pa. $8.95

THE BERTRAMS, Anthony Trollope. Powerful portrayal of blind self-will and thwarted ambition includes one of Trollope's most heartrending love stories. 497pp. 5⅜ × 8½. 25119-5 Pa. $8.95

ADVENTURES WITH A HAND LENS, Richard Headstrom. Clearly written guide to observing and studying flowers and grasses, fish scales, moth and insect wings, egg cases, buds, feathers, seeds, leaf scars, moss, molds, ferns, common crystals, etc.—all with an ordinary, inexpensive magnifying glass. 209 exact line drawings aid in your discoveries. 220pp. 5⅜ × 8½. 23330-8 Pa. $3.95

RODIN ON ART AND ARTISTS, Auguste Rodin. Great sculptor's candid, wide-ranging comments on meaning of art; great artists; relation of sculpture to poetry, painting, music; philosophy of life, more. 76 superb black-and-white illustrations of Rodin's sculpture, drawings and prints. 119pp. 8⅜ × 11¼. 24487-3 Pa. $6.95

FIFTY CLASSIC FRENCH FILMS, 1912–1982: A Pictorial Record, Anthony Slide. Memorable stills from Grand Illusion, Beauty and the Beast, Hiroshima, Mon Amour, many more. Credits, plot synopses, reviews, etc. 160pp. 8¼ × 11.
25256-6 Pa. $11.95

THE PRINCIPLES OF PSYCHOLOGY, William James. Famous long course complete, unabridged. Stream of thought, time perception, memory, experimental methods; great work decades ahead of its time. 94 figures. 1,391pp. 5⅜ × 8½.
20381-6, 20382-4 Pa., Two-vol. set $19.90

BODIES IN A BOOKSHOP, R. T. Campbell. Challenging mystery of blackmail and murder with ingenious plot and superbly drawn characters. In the best tradition of British suspense fiction. 192pp. 5⅜ × 8½. 24720-1 Pa. $3.95

CALLAS: PORTRAIT OF A PRIMA DONNA, George Jellinek. Renowned commentator on the musical scene chronicles incredible career and life of the most controversial, fascinating, influential operatic personality of our time. 64 black-and-white photographs. 416pp. 5⅜ × 8¼. 25047-4 Pa. $7.95

GEOMETRY, RELATIVITY AND THE FOURTH DIMENSION, Rudolph Rucker. Exposition of fourth dimension, concepts of relativity as Flatland characters continue adventures. Popular, easily followed yet accurate, profound. 141 illustrations. 133pp. 5⅜ × 8½. 23400-2 Pa. $3.50

HOUSEHOLD STORIES BY THE BROTHERS GRIMM, with pictures by Walter Crane. 53 classic stories—Rumpelstiltskin, Rapunzel, Hansel and Gretel, the Fisherman and his Wife, Snow White, Tom Thumb, Sleeping Beauty, Cinderella, and so much more—lavishly illustrated with original 19th century drawings. 114 illustrations. x + 269pp. 5⅜ × 8½. 21080-4 Pa. $4.50

SUNDIALS, Albert Waugh. Far and away the best, most thorough coverage of ideas, mathematics concerned, types, construction, adjusting anywhere. Over 100 illustrations. 230pp. 5⅜ × 8½. 22947-5 Pa. $4.00

PICTURE HISTORY OF THE NORMANDIE: With 190 Illustrations, Frank O. Braynard. Full story of legendary French ocean liner: Art Deco interiors, design innovations, furnishings, celebrities, maiden voyage, tragic fire, much more. Extensive text. 144pp. 8⅞ × 11¼. 25257-4 Pa. $9.95

THE FIRST AMERICAN COOKBOOK: A Facsimile of "American Cookery," 1796, Amelia Simmons. Facsimile of the first American-written cookbook published in the United States contains authentic recipes for colonial favorites—pumpkin pudding, winter squash pudding, spruce beer, Indian slapjacks, and more. Introductory Essay and Glossary of colonial cooking terms. 80pp. 5⅜ × 8½. 24710-4 Pa. $3.50

101 PUZZLES IN THOUGHT AND LOGIC, C. R. Wylie, Jr. Solve murders and robberies, find out which fishermen are liars, how a blind man could possibly identify a color—purely by your own reasoning! 107pp. 5⅜ × 8½. 20367-0 Pa. $2.00

THE BOOK OF WORLD-FAMOUS MUSIC—CLASSICAL, POPULAR AND FOLK, James J. Fuld. Revised and enlarged republication of landmark work in musico-bibliography. Full information about nearly 1,000 songs and compositions including first lines of music and lyrics. New supplement. Index. 800pp. 5⅜ × 8¼. 24857-7 Pa. $14.95

ANTHROPOLOGY AND MODERN LIFE, Franz Boas. Great anthropologist's classic treatise on race and culture. Introduction by Ruth Bunzel. Only inexpensive paperback edition. 255pp. 5⅜ × 8½. 25245-0 Pa. $5.95

THE TALE OF PETER RABBIT, Beatrix Potter. The inimitable Peter's terrifying adventure in Mr. McGregor's garden, with all 27 wonderful, full-color Potter illustrations. 55pp. 4¼ × 5½. (Available in U.S. only) 22827-4 Pa. $1.75

THREE PROPHETIC SCIENCE FICTION NOVELS, H. G. Wells. *When the Sleeper Wakes, A Story of the Days to Come* and *The Time Machine* (full version). 335pp. 5⅜ × 8½. (Available in U.S. only) 20605-X Pa. $5.95

APICIUS COOKERY AND DINING IN IMPERIAL ROME, edited and translated by Joseph Dommers Vehling. Oldest known cookbook in existence offers readers a clear picture of what foods Romans ate, how they prepared them, etc. 49 illustrations. 301pp. 6⅛ × 9¼. 23563-7 Pa. $6.00

SHAKESPEARE LEXICON AND QUOTATION DICTIONARY, Alexander Schmidt. Full definitions, locations, shades of meaning of every word in plays and poems. More than 50,000 exact quotations. 1,485pp. 6½ × 9¼. 22726-X, 22727-8 Pa., Two-vol. set $27.90

THE WORLD'S GREAT SPEECHES, edited by Lewis Copeland and Lawrence W. Lamm. Vast collection of 278 speeches from Greeks to 1970. Powerful and effective models; unique look at history. 842pp. 5⅜ × 8½. 20468-5 Pa. $10.95

THE BLUE FAIRY BOOK, Andrew Lang. The first, most famous collection, with many familiar tales: Little Red Riding Hood, Aladdin and the Wonderful Lamp, Puss in Boots, Sleeping Beauty, Hansel and Gretel, Rumpelstiltskin; 37 in all. 138 illustrations. 390pp. 5⅜ × 8½.   21437-0 Pa. $5.95

THE STORY OF THE CHAMPIONS OF THE ROUND TABLE, Howard Pyle. Sir Launcelot, Sir Tristram and Sir Percival in spirited adventures of love and triumph retold in Pyle's inimitable style. 50 drawings, 31 full-page. xviii + 329pp. 6½ × 9¼.   21883-X Pa. $6.95

AUDUBON AND HIS JOURNALS, Maria Audubon. Unmatched two-volume portrait of the great artist, naturalist and author contains his journals, an excellent biography by his granddaughter, expert annotations by the noted ornithologist, Dr. Elliott Coues, and 37 superb illustrations. Total of 1,200pp. 5⅜ × 8.
Vol. I 25143-8 Pa. $8.95
Vol. II 25144-6 Pa. $8.95

GREAT DINOSAUR HUNTERS AND THEIR DISCOVERIES, Edwin H. Colbert. Fascinating, lavishly illustrated chronicle of dinosaur research, 1820's to 1960. Achievements of Cope, Marsh, Brown, Buckland, Mantell, Huxley, many others. 384pp. 5¼ × 8¼.   24701-5 Pa. $6.95

THE TASTEMAKERS, Russell Lynes. Informal, illustrated social history of American taste 1850's–1950's. First popularized categories Highbrow, Lowbrow, Middlebrow. 129 illustrations. New (1979) afterword. 384pp. 6 × 9.
23993-4 Pa. $6.95

DOUBLE CROSS PURPOSES, Ronald A. Knox. A treasure hunt in the Scottish Highlands, an old map, unidentified corpse, surprise discoveries keep reader guessing in this cleverly intricate tale of financial skullduggery. 2 black-and-white maps. 320pp. 5⅜ × 8½. (Available in U.S. only)   25032-6 Pa. $5.95

AUTHENTIC VICTORIAN DECORATION AND ORNAMENTATION IN FULL COLOR: 46 Plates from "Studies in Design," Christopher Dresser. Superb full-color lithographs reproduced from rare original portfolio of a major Victorian designer. 48pp. 9¼ × 12¼.   25083-0 Pa. $7.95

PRIMITIVE ART, Franz Boas. Remains the best text ever prepared on subject, thoroughly discussing Indian, African, Asian, Australian, and, especially, Northern American primitive art. Over 950 illustrations show ceramics, masks, totem poles, weapons, textiles, paintings, much more. 376pp. 5⅜ × 8. 20025-6 Pa. $6.95

SIDELIGHTS ON RELATIVITY, Albert Einstein. Unabridged republication of two lectures delivered by the great physicist in 1920–21. *Ether and Relativity* and *Geometry and Experience*. Elegant ideas in non-mathematical form, accessible to intelligent layman. vi + 56pp. 5⅜ × 8½.   24511-X Pa. $2.95

THE WIT AND HUMOR OF OSCAR WILDE, edited by Alvin Redman. More than 1,000 ripostes, paradoxes, wisecracks: Work is the curse of the drinking classes, I can resist everything except temptation, etc. 258pp. 5⅜ × 8½.   20602-5 Pa. $3.95

ADVENTURES WITH A MICROSCOPE, Richard Headstrom. 59 adventures with clothing fibers, protozoa, ferns and lichens, roots and leaves, much more. 142 illustrations. 232pp. 5⅜ × 8½.   23471-1 Pa. $3.95

PLANTS OF THE BIBLE, Harold N. Moldenke and Alma L. Moldenke. Standard reference to all 230 plants mentioned in Scriptures. Latin name, biblical reference, uses, modern identity, much more. Unsurpassed encyclopedic resource for scholars, botanists, nature lovers, students of Bible. Bibliography. Indexes. 123 black-and-white illustrations. 384pp. 6 × 9. 25069-5 Pa. $8.95

FAMOUS AMERICAN WOMEN: A Biographical Dictionary from Colonial Times to the Present, Robert McHenry, ed. From Pocahontas to Rosa Parks, 1,035 distinguished American women documented in separate biographical entries. Accurate, up-to-date data, numerous categories, spans 400 years. Indices. 493pp. 6½ × 9¼. 24523-3 Pa. $9.95

THE FABULOUS INTERIORS OF THE GREAT OCEAN LINERS IN HISTORIC PHOTOGRAPHS, William H. Miller, Jr. Some 200 superb photographs capture exquisite interiors of world's great "floating palaces"—1890's to 1980's: *Titanic, Ile de France, Queen Elizabeth, United States, Europa,* more. Approx. 200 black-and-white photographs. Captions. Text. Introduction. 160pp. 8⅞ × 11¾. 24756-2 Pa. $9.95

THE GREAT LUXURY LINERS, 1927–1954: A Photographic Record, William H. Miller, Jr. Nostalgic tribute to heyday of ocean liners. 186 photos of Ile de France, Normandie, Leviathan, Queen Elizabeth, United States, many others. Interior and exterior views. Introduction. Captions. 160pp. 9 × 12. 24056-8 Pa. $9.95

A NATURAL HISTORY OF THE DUCKS, John Charles Phillips. Great landmark of ornithology offers complete detailed coverage of nearly 200 species and subspecies of ducks: gadwall, sheldrake, merganser, pintail, many more. 74 full-color plates, 102 black-and-white. Bibliography. Total of 1,920pp. 8⅝ × 11¼. 25141-1, 25142-X Cloth. Two-vol. set $100.00

THE SEAWEED HANDBOOK: An Illustrated Guide to Seaweeds from North Carolina to Canada, Thomas F. Lee. Concise reference covers 78 species. Scientific and common names, habitat, distribution, more. Finding keys for easy identification. 224pp. 5⅜ × 8½. 25215-9 Pa. $5.95

THE TEN BOOKS OF ARCHITECTURE: The 1755 Leoni Edition, Leon Battista Alberti. Rare classic helped introduce the glories of ancient architecture to the Renaissance. 68 black-and-white plates. 336pp. 8⅜ × 11¼. 25239-6 Pa. $14.95

MISS MACKENZIE, Anthony Trollope. Minor masterpieces by Victorian master unmasks many truths about life in 19th-century England. First inexpensive edition in years. 392pp. 5⅜ × 8½. 25201-9 Pa. $7.95

THE RIME OF THE ANCIENT MARINER, Gustave Doré, Samuel Taylor Coleridge. Dramatic engravings considered by many to be his greatest work. The terrifying space of the open sea, the storms and whirlpools of an unknown ocean, the ice of Antarctica, more—all rendered in a powerful, chilling manner. Full text. 38 plates. 77pp. 9¼ × 12. 22305-1 Pa. $4.95

THE EXPEDITIONS OF ZEBULON MONTGOMERY PIKE, Zebulon Montgomery Pike. Fascinating first-hand accounts (1805–6) of exploration of Mississippi River, Indian wars, capture by Spanish dragoons, much more. 1,088pp. 5⅜ × 8½. 25254-X, 25255-8 Pa. Two-vol. set $23.90

A CONCISE HISTORY OF PHOTOGRAPHY: Third Revised Edition, Helmut Gernsheim. Best one-volume history—camera obscura, photochemistry, daguerreotypes, evolution of cameras, film, more. Also artistic aspects—landscape, portraits, fine art, etc. 281 black-and-white photographs. 26 in color. 176pp. 8⅜ × 11¼. 25128-4 Pa. $12.95

THE DORÉ BIBLE ILLUSTRATIONS, Gustave Doré. 241 detailed plates from the Bible: the Creation scenes, Adam and Eve, Flood, Babylon, battle sequences, life of Jesus, etc. Each plate is accompanied by the verses from the King James version of the Bible. 241pp. 9 × 12. 23004-X Pa. $8.95

HUGGER-MUGGER IN THE LOUVRE, Elliot Paul. Second Homer Evans mystery-comedy. Theft at the Louvre involves sleuth in hilarious, madcap caper. "A knockout."—Books. 336pp. 5⅜ × 8½. 25185-3 Pa. $5.95

FLATLAND, E. A. Abbott. Intriguing and enormously popular science-fiction classic explores the complexities of trying to survive as a two-dimensional being in a three-dimensional world. Amusingly illustrated by the author. 16 illustrations. 103pp. 5⅜ × 8½. 20001-9 Pa. $2.00

THE HISTORY OF THE LEWIS AND CLARK EXPEDITION, Meriwether Lewis and William Clark, edited by Elliott Coues. Classic edition of Lewis and Clark's day-by-day journals that later became the basis for U.S. claims to Oregon and the West. Accurate and invaluable geographical, botanical, biological, meteorological and anthropological material. Total of 1,508pp. 5⅜ × 8½.
21268-8, 21269-6, 21270-X Pa. Three-vol. set $25.50

LANGUAGE, TRUTH AND LOGIC, Alfred J. Ayer. Famous, clear introduction to Vienna, Cambridge schools of Logical Positivism. Role of philosophy, elimination of metaphysics, nature of analysis, etc. 160pp. 5⅜ × 8½. (Available in U.S. and Canada only) 20010-8 Pa. $2.95

MATHEMATICS FOR THE NONMATHEMATICIAN, Morris Kline. Detailed, college-level treatment of mathematics in cultural and historical context, with numerous exercises. For liberal arts students. Preface. Recommended Reading Lists. Tables. Index. Numerous black-and-white figures. xvi + 641pp. 5⅜ × 8½.
24823-2 Pa. $11.95

28 SCIENCE FICTION STORIES, H. G. Wells. Novels, *Star Begotten* and *Men Like Gods,* plus 26 short stories: "Empire of the Ants," "A Story of the Stone Age," "The Stolen Bacillus," "In the Abyss," etc. 915pp. 5⅜ × 8½. (Available in U.S. only)
20265-8 Cloth. $10.95

HANDBOOK OF PICTORIAL SYMBOLS, Rudolph Modley. 3,250 signs and symbols, many systems in full; official or heavy commercial use. Arranged by subject. Most in Pictorial Archive series. 143pp. 8⅛ × 11. 23357-X Pa. $5.95

INCIDENTS OF TRAVEL IN YUCATAN, John L. Stephens. Classic (1843) exploration of jungles of Yucatan, looking for evidences of Maya civilization. Travel adventures, Mexican and Indian culture, etc. Total of 669pp. 5⅜ × 8½.
20926-1, 20927-X Pa., Two-vol. set $9.90

DEGAS: An Intimate Portrait, Ambroise Vollard. Charming, anecdotal memoir by famous art dealer of one of the greatest 19th-century French painters. 14 black-and-white illustrations. Introduction by Harold L. Van Doren. 96pp. 5⅜ × 8½.
25131-4 Pa. $3.95

PERSONAL NARRATIVE OF A PILGRIMAGE TO ALMANDINAH AND MECCAH, Richard Burton. Great travel classic by remarkably colorful personality. Burton, disguised as a Moroccan, visited sacred shrines of Islam, narrowly escaping death. 47 illustrations. 959pp. 5⅜ × 8½. 21217-3, 21218-1 Pa., Two-vol. set $17.90

PHRASE AND WORD ORIGINS, A. H. Holt. Entertaining, reliable, modern study of more than 1,200 colorful words, phrases, origins and histories. Much unexpected information. 254pp. 5⅜ × 8½. 20758-7 Pa. $4.95

THE RED THUMB MARK, R. Austin Freeman. In this first Dr. Thorndyke case, the great scientific detective draws fascinating conclusions from the nature of a single fingerprint. Exciting story, authentic science. 320pp. 5⅜ × 8½. (Available in U.S. only) 25210-8 Pa. $5.95

AN EGYPTIAN HIEROGLYPHIC DICTIONARY, E. A. Wallis Budge. Monumental work containing about 25,000 words or terms that occur in texts ranging from 3000 B.C. to 600 A.D. Each entry consists of a transliteration of the word, the word in hieroglyphs, and the meaning in English. 1,314pp. 6⅝ × 10.
23615-3, 23616-1 Pa., Two-vol. set $27.90

THE COMPLEAT STRATEGYST: Being a Primer on the Theory of Games of Strategy, J. D. Williams. Highly entertaining classic describes, with many illustrated examples, how to select best strategies in conflict situations. Prefaces. Appendices. xvi + 268pp. 5⅜ × 8½. 25101-2 Pa. $5.95

THE ROAD TO OZ, L. Frank Baum. Dorothy meets the Shaggy Man, little Button-Bright and the Rainbow's beautiful daughter in this delightful trip to the magical Land of Oz. 272pp. 5⅜ × 8. 25208-6 Pa. $4.95

POINT AND LINE TO PLANE, Wassily Kandinsky. Seminal exposition of role of point, line, other elements in non-objective painting. Essential to understanding 20th-century art. 127 illustrations. 192pp. 6½ × 9¼. 23808-3 Pa. $4.50

LADY ANNA, Anthony Trollope. Moving chronicle of Countess Lovel's bitter struggle to win for herself and daughter Anna their rightful rank and fortune—perhaps at cost of sanity itself. 384pp. 5⅜ × 8½. 24669-8 Pa. $6.95

EGYPTIAN MAGIC, E. A. Wallis Budge. Sums up all that is known about magic in Ancient Egypt: the role of magic in controlling the gods, powerful amulets that warded off evil spirits, scarabs of immortality, use of wax images, formulas and spells, the secret name, much more. 253pp. 5⅜ × 8½. 22681-6 Pa. $4.00

THE DANCE OF SIVA, Ananda Coomaraswamy. Preeminent authority unfolds the vast metaphysic of India: the revelation of her art, conception of the universe, social organization, etc. 27 reproductions of art masterpieces. 192pp. 5⅜ × 8½.
24817-8 Pa. $5.95

CHRISTMAS CUSTOMS AND TRADITIONS, Clement A. Miles. Origin, evolution, significance of religious, secular practices. Caroling, gifts, yule logs, much more. Full, scholarly yet fascinating; non-sectarian. 400pp. 5⅜ × 8½.
23354-5 Pa. $6.50

THE HUMAN FIGURE IN MOTION, Eadweard Muybridge. More than 4,500 stopped-action photos, in action series, showing undraped men, women, children jumping, lying down, throwing, sitting, wrestling, carrying, etc. 390pp. 7⅞ × 10⅝.
20204-6 Cloth. $19.95

THE MAN WHO WAS THURSDAY, Gilbert Keith Chesterton. Witty, fast-paced novel about a club of anarchists in turn-of-the-century London. Brilliant social, religious, philosophical speculations. 128pp. 5⅜ × 8½.
25121-7 Pa. $3.95

A CEZANNE SKETCHBOOK: Figures, Portraits, Landscapes and Still Lifes, Paul Cezanne. Great artist experiments with tonal effects, light, mass, other qualities in over 100 drawings. A revealing view of developing master painter, precursor of Cubism. 102 black-and-white illustrations. 144pp. 8¾ × 6⅝.
24790-2 Pa. $5.95

AN ENCYCLOPEDIA OF BATTLES: Accounts of Over 1,560 Battles from 1479 B.C. to the Present, David Eggenberger. Presents essential details of every major battle in recorded history, from the first battle of Megiddo in 1479 B.C. to Grenada in 1984. List of Battle Maps. New Appendix covering the years 1967–1984. Index. 99 illustrations. 544pp. 6½ × 9¼.
24913-1 Pa. $14.95

AN ETYMOLOGICAL DICTIONARY OF MODERN ENGLISH, Ernest Weekley. Richest, fullest work, by foremost British lexicographer. Detailed word histories. Inexhaustible. Total of 856pp. 6½ × 9¼.
21873-2, 21874-0 Pa., Two-vol. set $17.00

WEBSTER'S AMERICAN MILITARY BIOGRAPHIES, edited by Robert McHenry. Over 1,000 figures who shaped 3 centuries of American military history. Detailed biographies of Nathan Hale, Douglas MacArthur, Mary Hallaren, others. Chronologies of engagements, more. Introduction. Addenda. 1,033 entries in alphabetical order. xi + 548pp. 6½ × 9¼. (Available in U.S. only)
24758-9 Pa. $11.95

LIFE IN ANCIENT EGYPT, Adolf Erman. Detailed older account, with much not in more recent books: domestic life, religion, magic, medicine, commerce, and whatever else needed for complete picture. Many illustrations. 597pp. 5⅜ × 8½.
22632-8 Pa. $8.50

HISTORIC COSTUME IN PICTURES, Braun & Schneider. Over 1,450 costumed figures shown, covering a wide variety of peoples: kings, emperors, nobles, priests, servants, soldiers, scholars, townsfolk, peasants, merchants, courtiers, cavaliers, and more. 256pp. 8⅜ × 11¼.
23150-X Pa. $7.95

THE NOTEBOOKS OF LEONARDO DA VINCI, edited by J. P. Richter. Extracts from manuscripts reveal great genius; on painting, sculpture, anatomy, sciences, geography, etc. Both Italian and English. 186 ms. pages reproduced, plus 500 additional drawings, including studies for *Last Supper, Sforza* monument, etc. 860pp. 7⅞ × 10¾. (Available in U.S. only) 22572-0, 22573-9 Pa., Two-vol. set $25.90

THE ART NOUVEAU STYLE BOOK OF ALPHONSE MUCHA: All 72 Plates from "Documents Decoratifs" in Original Color, Alphonse Mucha. Rare copyright-free design portfolio by high priest of Art Nouveau. Jewelry, wallpaper, stained glass, furniture, figure studies, plant and animal motifs, etc. Only complete one-volume edition. 80pp. 9⅜ × 12¼. 24044-4 Pa. $8.95

ANIMALS: 1,419 COPYRIGHT-FREE ILLUSTRATIONS OF MAMMALS, BIRDS, FISH, INSECTS, ETC., edited by Jim Harter. Clear wood engravings present, in extremely lifelike poses, over 1,000 species of animals. One of the most extensive pictorial sourcebooks of its kind. Captions. Index. 284pp. 9 × 12. 23766-4 Pa. $9.95

OBELISTS FLY HIGH, C. Daly King. Masterpiece of American detective fiction, long out of print, involves murder on a 1935 transcontinental flight—"a very thrilling story"—NY Times. Unabridged and unaltered republication of the edition published by William Collins Sons & Co. Ltd., London, 1935. 288pp. 5⅜ × 8½. (Available in U.S. only) 25036-9 Pa. $4.95

VICTORIAN AND EDWARDIAN FASHION: A Photographic Survey, Alison Gernsheim. First fashion history completely illustrated by contemporary photographs. Full text plus 235 photos, 1840–1914, in which many celebrities appear. 240pp. 6½ × 9¼. 24205-6 Pa. $6.00

THE ART OF THE FRENCH ILLUSTRATED BOOK, 1700–1914, Gordon N. Ray. Over 630 superb book illustrations by Fragonard, Delacroix, Daumier, Doré, Grandville, Manet, Mucha, Steinlen, Toulouse-Lautrec and many others. Preface. Introduction. 633 halftones. Indices of artists, authors & titles, binders and provenances. Appendices. Bibliography. 608pp. 8⅜ × 11¼. 25086-5 Pa. $24.95

THE WONDERFUL WIZARD OF OZ, L. Frank Baum. Facsimile in full color of America's finest children's classic. 143 illustrations by W. W. Denslow. 267pp. 5⅜ × 8½. 20691-2 Pa. $5.95

FRONTIERS OF MODERN PHYSICS: New Perspectives on Cosmology, Relativity, Black Holes and Extraterrestrial Intelligence, Tony Rothman, et al. For the intelligent layman. Subjects include: cosmological models of the universe; black holes; the neutrino; the search for extraterrestrial intelligence. Introduction. 46 black-and-white illustrations. 192pp. 5⅜ × 8½. 24587-X Pa. $6.95

THE FRIENDLY STARS, Martha Evans Martin & Donald Howard Menzel. Classic text marshalls the stars together in an engaging, non-technical survey, presenting them as sources of beauty in night sky. 23 illustrations. Foreword. 2 star charts. Index. 147pp. 5⅜ × 8½. 21099-5 Pa. $3.50

FADS AND FALLACIES IN THE NAME OF SCIENCE, Martin Gardner. Fair, witty appraisal of cranks, quacks, and quackeries of science and pseudoscience: hollow earth, Velikovsky, orgone energy, Dianetics, flying saucers, Bridey Murphy, food and medical fads, etc. Revised, expanded In the Name of Science. "A very able and even-tempered presentation."—The New Yorker. 363pp. 5⅜ × 8. 20394-8 Pa. $5.95

ANCIENT EGYPT: ITS CULTURE AND HISTORY, J. E Manchip White. From pre-dynastics through Ptolemies: society, history, political structure, religion, daily life, literature, cultural heritage. 48 plates. 217pp. 5⅜ × 8½. 22548-8 Pa. $4.95

SIR HARRY HOTSPUR OF HUMBLETHWAITE, Anthony Trollope. Incisive, unconventional psychological study of a conflict between a wealthy baronet, his idealistic daughter, and their scapegrace cousin. The 1870 novel in its first inexpensive edition in years. 250pp. 5⅜ × 8½. 24953-0 Pa. $4.95

LASERS AND HOLOGRAPHY, Winston E. Kock. Sound introduction to burgeoning field, expanded (1981) for second edition. Wave patterns, coherence, lasers, diffraction, zone plates, properties of holograms, recent advances. 84 illustrations. 160pp. 5⅜ × 8¼. (Except in United Kingdom) 24041-X Pa. $3.50

INTRODUCTION TO ARTIFICIAL INTELLIGENCE: SECOND, EN-LARGED EDITION, Philip C. Jackson, Jr. Comprehensive survey of artificial intelligence—the study of how machines (computers) can be made to act intelligently. Includes introductory and advanced material. Extensive notes updating the main text. 132 black-and-white illustrations. 512pp. 5⅜ × 8½. 24864-X Pa. $8.95

HISTORY OF INDIAN AND INDONESIAN ART, Ananda K. Coomaraswamy. Over 400 illustrations illuminate classic study of Indian art from earliest Harappa finds to early 20th century. Provides philosophical, religious and social insights. 304pp. 6⅜ × 9⅜. 25005-9 Pa. $8.95

THE GOLEM, Gustav Meyrink. Most famous supernatural novel in modern European literature, set in Ghetto of Old Prague around 1890. Compelling story of mystical experiences, strange transformations, profound terror. 13 black-and-white illustrations. 224pp. 5⅜ × 8½. (Available in U.S. only) 25025-3 Pa. $5.95

ARMADALE, Wilkie Collins. Third great mystery novel by the author of *The Woman in White* and *The Moonstone*. Original magazine version with 40 illustrations. 597pp. 5⅜ × 8½. 23429-0 Pa. $7.95

PICTORIAL ENCYCLOPEDIA OF HISTORIC ARCHITECTURAL PLANS, DETAILS AND ELEMENTS: With 1,880 Line Drawings of Arches, Domes, Doorways, Facades, Gables, Windows, etc., John Theodore Haneman. Sourcebook of inspiration for architects, designers, others. Bibliography. Captions. 141pp. 9 × 12. 24605-1 Pa. $6.95

BENCHLEY LOST AND FOUND, Robert Benchley. Finest humor from early 30's, about pet peeves, child psychologists, post office and others. Mostly unavailable elsewhere. 73 illustrations by Peter Arno and others. 183pp. 5⅜ × 8½. 22410-4 Pa. $3.95

ERTÉ GRAPHICS, Erté. Collection of striking color graphics: *Seasons, Alphabet, Numerals, Aces* and *Precious Stones*. 50 plates, including 4 on covers. 48pp. 9⅜ × 12¼. 23580-7 Pa. $6.95

THE JOURNAL OF HENRY D. THOREAU, edited by Bradford Torrey, F. H. Allen. Complete reprinting of 14 volumes, 1837–61, over two million words; the sourcebooks for *Walden*, etc. Definitive. All original sketches, plus 75 photographs. 1,804pp. 8½ × 12¼. 20312-3, 20313-1 Cloth., Two-vol. set $80.00

CASTLES: THEIR CONSTRUCTION AND HISTORY, Sidney Toy. Traces castle development from ancient roots. Nearly 200 photographs and drawings illustrate moats, keeps, baileys, many other features. Caernarvon, Dover Castles, Hadrian's Wall, Tower of London, dozens more. 256pp. 5⅜ × 8¼.

24898-4 Pa. $5.95

CATALOG OF DOVER BOOKS

AMERICAN CLIPPER SHIPS: 1833–1858, Octavius T. Howe & Frederick C. Matthews. Fully-illustrated, encyclopedic review of 352 clipper ships from the period of America's greatest maritime supremacy. Introduction. 109 halftones. 5 black-and-white line illustrations. Index. Total of 928pp. 5⅜ × 8½.
25115-2, 25116-0 Pa., Two-vol. set $17.90

TOWARDS A NEW ARCHITECTURE, Le Corbusier. Pioneering manifesto by great architect, near legendary founder of "International School." Technical and aesthetic theories, views on industry, economics, relation of form to function, "mass-production spirit," much more. Profusely illustrated. Unabridged translation of 13th French edition. Introduction by Frederick Etchells. 320pp. 6⅛ × 9¼. (Available in U.S. only)
25023-7 Pa. $8.95

THE BOOK OF KELLS, edited by Blanche Cirker. Inexpensive collection of 32 full-color, full-page plates from the greatest illuminated manuscript of the Middle Ages, painstakingly reproduced from rare facsimile edition. Publisher's Note. Captions. 32pp. 9⅜ × 12¼.
24345-1 Pa. $4.50

BEST SCIENCE FICTION STORIES OF H. G. WELLS, H. G. Wells. Full novel *The Invisible Man*, plus 17 short stories: "The Crystal Egg," "Aepyornis Island," "The Strange Orchid," etc. 303pp. 5⅜ × 8½. (Available in U.S. only)
21531-8 Pa. $4.95

AMERICAN SAILING SHIPS: Their Plans and History, Charles G. Davis. Photos, construction details of schooners, frigates, clippers, other sailcraft of 18th to early 20th centuries—plus entertaining discourse on design, rigging, nautical lore, much more. 137 black-and-white illustrations. 240pp. 6⅛ × 9¼.
24658-2 Pa. $5.95

ENTERTAINING MATHEMATICAL PUZZLES, Martin Gardner. Selection of author's favorite conundrums involving arithmetic, money, speed, etc., with lively commentary. Complete solutions. 112pp. 5⅜ × 8½. 25211-6 Pa. $2.95

THE WILL TO BELIEVE, HUMAN IMMORTALITY, William James. Two books bound together. Effect of irrational on logical, and arguments for human immortality. 402pp. 5⅜ × 8½. 20291-7 Pa. $7.50

THE HAUNTED MONASTERY and THE CHINESE MAZE MURDERS, Robert Van Gulik. 2 full novels by Van Gulik continue adventures of Judge Dee and his companions. An evil Taoist monastery, seemingly supernatural events; overgrown topiary maze that hides strange crimes. Set in 7th-century China. 27 illustrations. 328pp. 5⅜ × 8½. 23502-5 Pa. $5.00

CELEBRATED CASES OF JUDGE DEE (DEE GOONG AN), translated by Robert Van Gulik. Authentic 18th-century Chinese detective novel; Dee and associates solve three interlocked cases. Led to Van Gulik's own stories with same characters. Extensive introduction. 9 illustrations. 237pp. 5⅜ × 8½.
23337-5 Pa. $4.95

Prices subject to change without notice.
Available at your book dealer or write for free catalog to Dept. GI, Dover Publications, Inc., 31 East 2nd St., Mineola, N.Y. 11501. Dover publishes more than 175 books each year on science, elementary and advanced mathematics, biology, music, art, literary history, social sciences and other areas.